S0-ADO-758

Making Waves

Politics, Propaganda, and the Emergence of
the Imperial Japanese Navy, 1868–1922

Making Waves

Politics, Propaganda, and the Emergence of
the Imperial Japanese Navy, 1868–1922

J. Charles Schencking

STANFORD UNIVERSITY PRESS 2005

Stanford, California

Stanford University Press
Stanford, California
© 2005 by the Board of Trustees of the
Leland Stanford Junior University

Library of Congress Cataloging-in-Publication Data

Schencking , J. Charles.
    Making waves : politics, propaganda, and the emergence of
the Imperial Japanese Navy, 1868–1922 / J. Charles Schencking.
        p. cm.
    Includes bibliographical references and index.
    ISBN 0-8047-4977-9 (cloth : alk. paper)—
    1. Japan. Kaigun—History.   2. Japan. Kaigun—Political
activity.   3. Japan—Politics and government—1868–1912.
4 Japan—Politics and government—1912–1926.   5. Japan—
History, Naval—19th century.   6 Japan—History, Naval—20th
century.   I. Title.
VA653.S38   2005
322'.5'095209034—dc22

                                              2004010793

Printed in the United States of America
Original Printing 2005
Last figure below indicates year of this printing:
14   13   12   11   10   09   08   07   06   05

Typeset at Stanford University Press in 10/13 Galliard

DEDICATED TO:

Stephen S. Large, John J. Stephan, and David W. Ziegler

Acknowledgments

It is a genuine pleasure to be able to thank the many individuals, institutions, and organizations that have provided me with assistance, support, and guidance during the project which has culminated with the publication of this book. A core theme of my study revolves around one institution's attempts to secure funding, so I think it is entirely appropriate that I begin by thanking the many organizations that have provided monetary assistance during the course of my study. Between 1995 and 1998 I was the fortunate recipient of the Yasuda Banking and Trust Scholarship. This scholarship allowed me to pursue studies as a Ph.D. student in the Faculty of Oriental Studies at the University of Cambridge, and without this generous award I would not have been able to undertake postgraduate work at Cambridge. After completing my dissertation in 1998, I received continued support from the Faculty of Oriental Studies as a Yasuda postdoctoral fellow in 1999 and a British Academy Post Doctoral Fellowship in 2000. It was during these years that I began to revise my thesis for publication as a book and charted my next major research project. Support from these two organizations gave me the time and resources to craft *Making Waves* into the book it is at present.

I would also like to take this opportunity to thank a number of other individuals and institutions in Cambridge. First and foremost, the President of Wolfson College, Gordon Johnson, deserves special recognition for all the assistance and guidance he provided throughout my five-year tenure at college. Other fellows and college members who encouraged and supported my work during my residence at Wolfson as a student and then as a fellow include John Seagrave, Timothy Mead, Conrad Guettler, Faith Johnson, and Claire O'Brien. At the Faculty of Oriental Studies in Cambridge, Richard Bowring, Peter Kornicki, Hugh Whittaker, John Swenson-Wright, Noel Pinnington, and Mark Morris proved to be first insightful advisors during my period of study and then supportive colleagues during the years of my postdoctoral research and revision. Chris Bayly, a member of the Department of History at Cambridge, also deserves special recognition for his willingness to share his time and ideas with me from 1998 onwards. As a visiting fellow at Clare Hall, Cambridge, Dick Smethurst also shared his ideas about Japanese military history and provided a number of suggestions that have improved my final manuscript in many ways. Farther afield in the United Kingdom, Ian Nish, Janet Hunter, Anthony Best, Sue Townsend, John Westee, John Chapman, and Hew Strachan were generous with their time and willing to share their ideas concerning the Japanese navy, imperialism, and World War I. Finally, friends in Cambridge who deserve special thanks include Kerstin Large, Roger and Melissa Thompson, Tony Ballentyne, Sally Henderson, Thomas Grant, David Jacques, Joe Hammond, Barry Sweetman, Joviter Katabaro, Robin Naylor, and David Luhrs.

Before attending Cambridge, I completed my M.A. thesis at the University of Hawaii. It was at Manoa that I first began my interest in the Japanese navy. I am extremely grateful for the assistance provided by David Chappell, Idus Newby, Raymond Nunn, Pat Polansky, Robert Valliant, Kakuo Shōji, Masato Matsui, Paul Varley, George Akita, Sharon Minichiello, and Sally Drake. Fellow graduate students who deserve recognition include Sumie Ota, Michiko Itō, Ken Robinson, Betsy Dorn, Craig Parsons, Jeff Dym, and David Atwill. At the University of Hawaii, I made contact with a number of Japan scholars who to this day have given considerable support to me in the United States and Japan. In 1995, I had the great fortune to meet Mark R. Peattie, who was a distinguished visiting fellow for one semester in the Department of History. Mark has been a constant source of encouragement and inspiration in all stages of my revision, and his advice has been absolutely indispensable and invaluable. No other individual apart from my supervisors deserves greater recognition than Mark does. I am also grateful to Henry Frei, Bruce Reynolds, Asada Sadao, Hirama Yōichi, Takahashi Hisashi, Ishizu Tomoyuki, and Igarashi Hirokazu.

Since July 2000, I have been a lecturer at the University of Melbourne, with a joint appointment between the Department of History and the Melbourne Institute of Asian Languages and Societies (MIALS). My final and substantive manuscript revisions took place here, and the following colleagues deserve special recognition for the assistance and encouragement they have provided: Roza Brezac, Bill Coaldrake, Antonia Finnane, Patricia Grimshaw, David Hardy, Robert Horvath, Mary Kidd, John Lack, Elizabeth Malcolm, Kate McGreggor, Peter McPhee, David Philips, Merle Ricklefs, Ron Ridley, Charles Sowerwine, Carolyn Stevens, Steven Welch, Stephen Wheatcroft, and Charles Zika. I would also like to thank Eric van Bemmel for his assistance in preparing the images for this book. In Australia, but not at Melbourne, I have also benefited from comments and suggestions made by Sandra Wilson, Stewart Lone, Elise Tipton, and Ben Tipton. Since my move to Melbourne I have also been introduced to two scholars in Japan, Sakamoto Kazuto and Hashimoto Takehiko, who have been generous with their time in providing comments concerning my work.

I am deeply indebted to Michelle Hall, the Japan Librarian at the University of Melbourne, and to the members of the Inter Library Loan Staff, including Kay Gooding, Deidrie Gregory, Vija Pattison, Diana Schaffer, Bronwyn Thomas, and Vicki West. They have all been a tremendous help in locating and securing resources that have allowed me to complete my manuscript. I have also been assisted by the hard work and thoughtful comments of Hisako Fukusawa, Hideko Nakamura, and Miki Ikeda. Other individuals in Melbourne who have been a constant source of inspiration and encouragement include Janet Borland, Caroline Spencer, Chris Mullis, Teresa Castelvetere, Rachel Saunders, Mike Pottenger, Zoe Saliba, Peter Breadon, Rosalind Hearder, Richard Trembath, and Bart Ziino.

Before I acknowledge my three supervisors, to whom this work is dedicated, there are a few people that deserve special recognition. First, my parents and my late grandfather Arthur supported and encouraged all my educational endeavors. I have benefited immensely from their generosity and love, and the opportunities their sacrifices have created. I would also like to especially thank Zara for the never-ending support and encouragement that she has provided since Hawaii and for making the most of every international opportunity that has presented itself. Next, credit must be given to my Japanese-language instructors, most important among them Michiko Yusa (Western Washington University) and Kakuo Shōji (University of Hawaii). Both of them inspired me to expand my understanding of the Japanese language, and moreover they convinced me early on in my studies that learning the Japanese language would be fundamental to my success as a historian. They were absolutely correct. Historians and other Japanese specialists who provided continuous encouragement in all my academic endeavors include Ulrich Mammitzsch, Edward Kaplan, Ray McInnes, Dal

Symes, Kathleen Tomlonovic, and Patrick Buckley. Last, I would like to thank the editorial team at Stanford University Press, particularly Carmen Borbon-Wu, Muriel Bell, and John Feneron. Their patience has been extraordinary, and they have provided support at every step of the way from reading my first submission to preparing the final draft.

Finally, I would like to thank Stephen S. Large, my Ph.D. supervisor at the University of Cambridge, John J. Stephan, my M.A. supervisor at the University of Hawaii, and David W. Ziegler, my undergraduate supervisor at Western Washington University. This work is dedicated to all three. Without their guidance, assistance, generosity, and friendship this work simply would not have materialized, and I would not have become the historian of Japan that I am today. Each of them instilled in me a love of scholarship and a passion for historical inquiry, critical thinking, and learning. Their generosity was unlimited, their advice was always sound, and their warmth, friendship, and passion for scholarship was always present. In short, they were ideal supervisors.

Contents

Tables and Figures

Tables

Figures

Making Waves

*Politics, Propaganda, and the Emergence of
the Imperial Japanese Navy, 1868–1922*

Introduction

O N A B R I S K autumn day in November 1913, Prime Minister Yamamoto Gonnohyōe looked out to sea and smiled. Assembled before
the admiral–turned–national politician was one of the largest naval flotillas
that would grace Tokyo Bay in Yamamoto's lifetime. The vessels, the pride
and joy of the Imperial Japanese Navy, had gathered for the most impressive Grand Maneuver of the Fleet that had occurred since Japan's victory
celebration, held in October 1905, to commemorate the triumphal return of
Japan's Combined Fleet following the Russo-Japanese War of 1904–5.
Though assembled ostensibly to showcase the prize vessels of the Japanese
navy, including the newly arrived British-built battle cruiser *Kongō*, one of
the largest and most technologically advanced warships afloat in 1913, a pronounced political purpose lay beneath the impressive visual display of
power. Coming exactly one day after Navy Minister Saitō Makoto introduced the navy's proposed five-year expansion program to the full cabinet
in a private session, Yamamoto used this "magnificent spectacle," as one
Tokyo Asahi shinbun reporter described it, to confirm popular speculation
that his government would seek Diet approval for a massive ¥350 million
naval expansion package when parliament opened the following month.[1]
Timing was not a coincidence.

If the event exuded politics and popular pro-navy nationalism, the primary political purpose of this maneuver, selling naval expansion, was perhaps best betrayed by the impressive assemblage of politicians, businessmen, and imperial dignitaries who shared the main reviewing stand with
the prime minister. Moreover, owing to the increasingly important role of

Japan's electorate, Japan's naval leaders opened this event to the public, and in response thousands of citizens gathered at places along the shore to view the navy's vessels. While the collection at sea illustrated the navy's might, technological prowess, and military evolution, the groups gathered on shore, particularly those on the reviewing stand, revealed something just as impressive as the display at sea, if not directly responsible for it: the navy's increased political clout and influence. Yamamoto and others in the navy knew full well that support from groups represented by the navy's invited dignitaries, namely Diet politicians, Seiyūkai leaders, maritime industrialists, members of the press, the new emperor, and citizens, would be instrumental to passage of the navy's highly coveted expansion proposal. This Grand Maneuver of the Fleet illustrated, perhaps better than any other event, the important interplay between power, pageantry, politics, propaganda, and nationalism that contributed to, and reflected, the rise of the modern Japanese navy.

Though this carefully orchestrated event impressed journalists, dignitaries, and citizens alike, the navy did not always enjoy such support or wield such political influence and military power. The navy had, for much of the early to mid-Meiji Period (1868–1900), languished as Japan's junior service. Prior to the 1890s, Japan was not a naval nation. Naval or maritime affairs had been severely restricted during the previous Tokugawa era (1603–1868), and the Meiji government thus inherited neither a spirited naval tradition nor state-of-the-art equipment to serve as the foundation for future naval development. Furthermore, strategic concerns of the new state initially revolved around consolidating control at home and suppressing any possible internal rebellion rather than projecting power overseas. This understandably increased the priority given to the army's spending requests over those of the navy. Finally, factional clan-based politics also constrained naval growth in comparison to that of the army. While leaders of the former Satsuma domain eventually gravitated toward positions of power and influence in the navy during the late 1870s, thus providing this service with greater political representation and influence in the new government, the army's Chōshū ties were pronounced from the beginning of the Meiji Restoration. "Chōshū," in the words of distinguished historian Albert Craig, "was big," and clan connections provided army leaders with greater political access, bureaucratic clout in early Meiji Japan, and their service with appropriations that far exceeded that of the navy's.[2] The navy's annual peacetime budget surpassed the army's only twice from the beginning of the Meiji state to the Russo-Japanese War of 1904–5 and only once between

1905 and 1914. In the realm of national budgetary politics and international naval power, size mattered.

A number of factors accounted for the navy's political emergence and military growth to the world's third largest maritime military force by 1922. Those groups represented at the Grand Fleet Maneuver of 1913 speak volumes. Ironically, the very factors that inhibited naval growth in the early Meiji years compelled navy leaders to seek newly emerging political allies, to immerse themselves in parliamentary politics, to construct real or imagined justifications for fleet expansion, and to create and disseminate innovative naval propaganda that called for larger budgets to fund naval expansion. After gaining ministerial independence from the army in the early 1870s, securing larger budgets became *the* political cause if not overriding preoccupation of Japan's admirals. Fortuitously for the navy's leaders, their pragmatic explorations and political immersion coincided with the development of a more pluralistic and participatory political environment in Japan and an era of imperialism abroad. Both benefited the Japanese navy considerably. This began at home with the opening of parliament in 1890 and became more pronounced as the Seiyūkai political party emerged as the primary force in parliamentary politics after 1905. At home too, an increasingly literate and enfranchised public, more accessible than ever through a burgeoning mass print media, provided farsighted naval leaders with new avenues by which to gain, foster, and channel support for their institution's political objectives at a new and previously untapped level in society. Finally, on a regional or international geopolitical level, imperialism and war afforded the navy with more than one opportunity to enlarge Japan's empire and showcase its military victories within the public sphere. In turn, naval leaders subsequently used such military exploits to justify ever-increasing requests for greater appropriations over the late Meiji and early Taishō eras. Empire begot expansion and military increases.

Fruitful the navy's activities indeed proved. Beginning in earnest and with great calculation and precision after the political ascension of Yamamoto Gonnohyōe—who served as secretariat to the navy minister (1891–96), navy minister (1898–1906), and prime minister (1913–14)—and continuing throughout World War I, the navy evolved as a sophisticated political elite. Under Yamamoto's supervision and leadership, once described by the journalist-cum-historian Uzaki Ryojō as the same care with which a "tiger guards its lair," naval leaders comprehended, adapted to, and manipulated the changing and increasingly pluralistic political environment that developed in late Meiji and Taishō Japan.[3] In short, the navy massaged the newly developing erogenous zones of the Japanese body politic more successfully than almost any other organization in the late Meiji and early Taishō periods. It did so first and foremost to serve its own institutional or parochial ends, but in doing so the navy also strengthened or at least further legitimated parliamentary democracy, demonstrated the potential political effectiveness of mass propaganda and pageantry, fostered nationalism, and enlarged Japan's empire toward the South Seas in perception as well as reality. In doing so as effectively as it did, moreover, it became a significant budgetary and political rival to the army. Heightened interservice rivalry, a by-product of the navy's emergence, shaped politics, empire, and society far more than other historians and scholars of Japan have recognized throughout the years covered by my study, and this important trend continued well up until the end of World War II. The navy's emergence thus, in a phrase, made waves.

New Approaches to Naval History: Institutions, Politics, and Money

While historians have written little on the early Japanese navy, historians of the German, British, and American navies have demonstrated far greater awareness of, and directed far more attention to, the politics which surrounded naval expansion in the late nineteenth and early twentieth century. Eckart Kehr provided the first detailed history of the politics that surrounded the emergence of the Imperial German Navy.[4] In his study *Battleship Building and Party Politics in Germany, 1894–1901*, Kehr explored the German navy's political pursuits to gain appropriations for fleet expansion and the important role that German political parties and parliamentarians in the Reichstag came to play behind the emergence of the German navy as an impressive instrument of state, empire, and ultimately war.[5] In a recent study, Paul Pedisich took a similar theoretical and methodological approach in documenting the critically important role political parties and representatives within the U.S. Congress played in naval expansion in the United States between 1882 and 1916, a role far greater than that played by successive U.S. presidents.[6] Recently too, Mark Shulman and Peter Trubowitz have conducted extensive work on naval politics, at both the regional and the national level, that contributed to the emergence of the American navy.[7] Focusing attention across the Atlantic, John Beeler documented how politics shaped the world's strongest military fleet, Britain's Royal Navy, and its naval policies during the Glandstone-Disraeli era.[8] In Japan too, as my study will document, parliamentarians, particularly those from the Seiyūkai political party, played a similarly vital role behind the navy's political and military emergence. My study will thus add to an emerging body of historical literature that explores the relationships among parliamentary politics, society, and naval development and expansion.

The above-mentioned studies all fall within and considerably strengthen a "new theoretical school" of naval history first expounded by John Sumida, David Rosenberg, and John Hattendorf.[9] Incorporating a methodological approach that privileges the politics, bureaucracy, and economy behind naval development during the late nineteenth and twentieth century, proponents of this new school have convincingly articulated how modern navies evolved into remarkably complex, politically active, and significant organs of state out of simple economic and political necessity. Though often overlooked by military historians interested in battles or military hardware, navies required vast amounts of annual funding to purchase, construct, and maintain warships, land-based infrastructure, naval institutions, and personnel. To fund such programs, admirals in navies around the globe, but particularly those in countries with newly emerging navies that possessed no naval tradition to build upon, found it necessary to implement imaginative and persuasive means to persuade politicians and the public to support the expensive cause of naval development. In doing so, navies significantly altered politics, empire, and society in pursuit of their narrower and more parochial concerns, namely larger budgets. Nowhere was this more evident than in Japan. Moreover, owing to Japan's constitution, nowhere did a military service exhibit a greater ability to shape national politics, society, and empire than in Japan.

The Japanese Navy in a Historiographical Context

Inexplicably, naval historians and scholars of Japan have written very little about the political birth or emergence of the Japanese navy and what this meant for politics and society in pre–World War II Japan. One factor contributing to this omission is that historians have directed far greater interest and inquiry into battle histories, war, and the military and technological emergence of the Japanese navy. On one level this is not surprising. Militarily impressive warships and naval engagements still captivate people's attention today as much as they did a hundred years ago, when in the aftermath of Japan's victory over Russia authors, military observers, and journalists published a plethora of books on Admiral Tōgō's decisive fleet engagement at Tsushima, as well as other victorious exploits of Japan's navy.[10] In the most thoroughly researched and informative study on the Japanese navy to date, *Kaigun: Strategy, Tactics, and Technology in the Imperial Japanese Navy*, David Evans and Mark Peattie likewise directed their attention toward the military and technological development of the Japanese navy. While their study is impressive, the authors admit that the monograph is something "far short of a complete history," as it does not examine in detail such topics as naval budgets, the navy's relation to civilian government, or its involvement in domestic politics. In short, their work provides a narrow discussion of the political and economic factors that lay behind the creation of Japan's modern navy, factors which are the focus of my study.[11]

Though scholars have composed political studies on the Japanese navy, these too are limited in scope. Generally these historical works have focused on one of two topics: either naval disarmament;[12] or the politics behind the navy's formation and execution of a Southern Advance policy in the 1930s.[13] The overall pre-1920s political lacuna associated with the Japanese navy stems in part from the erroneous assumption that the young navy was an apolitical service or one that transcended politics in Meiji-Taishō Japan (1868–1926). The respected military historian Tsunoda Jun went so far as to claim that "the navy rarely engaged in politics" and that "the words navy and politics, when put together, sound odd."[14] The distinguished military and political historian Asada Sadao furthered this position, writing: "Above all, the tradition of the 'silent navy'—non-involvement in politics—lay at the base of its passive attitude toward state affairs in general."[15] While some historians in Japan have recently exhibited greater interest in naval politics in Japan's earlier periods, the interpretation of a nonpolitical navy or a silent service that held itself above politics in the Meiji and Taishō periods persists.[16] This view, as my study will show, simply does not stand up to detailed historical scrutiny. Politics was the lifeblood of the Japanese navy, as it was for the navies of Germany, the United States, and Britain in the same historical period.

Scholars who have looked at the close relationship between the military and politics in pre-1945 Japan have directed far more attention toward the political exploits of the Japanese army. The army, led by politically active and important statesmen such as Yamagata Aritomo, Katsura Tarō, Terauchi Masatake, Hirata Tōsuke, and Tanaka Gi'ichi—or so it has been suggested in many studies—at various times worked with, coerced, and challenged, "constitutional government" to secure its political and budgetary objectives.[17] In his recent biography of General Katsura Tarō, Stewart Lone convincingly argued that army leaders actively engaged in politics to further the political and budgetary aims of their service, concluding that defense budgets were one of the "most powerful engines driving change in Japan's political system."[18] They were. The army, however, held no monopoly on political involvement in Meiji-Taishō and early Shōwa (1926–45) Japan. Using coercion, but far more often pragmatism, the navy also engaged in parliamentary and cabinet-level politics in Meiji-Taishō Japan, and did so with great success. While naval officials did exert their political authority on more than one occasion in an attempt to block the formation of a potential cabinet which they believed would refuse to support the navy's budgetary interests, the navy never sought to "overthrow" constitutional government in Meiji-Taishō Japan. It did not need to do so. Rather, pragmatic naval officials secured their political objectives most successfully by forging alliances and partnerships with other burgeoning political elites: the political parties in the Diet, in particular the Seiyūkai.

Thus, another theoretical fallacy that my study will challenge and dispel within a larger Japanese historiographical context is that the navy was always a retrograde or oppressive force in Japanese politics. Though this view was shared by many prosecutors at the International Military Tribunal for the Far East, also know as the "Tokyo Trials," and is still taken as gospel by some post–World War II historians in Japan, it is flawed. More damaging, however, this misrepresentation exonerates many in the prewar party movement for their involvement in assisting the military services' emergence as strong, well-funded, and politically active elites. The significant emphasis that scholars have placed on the military's "overthrow" of "liberalism," "democracy," and "constitutional government" during the "dark valley" of 1930s Japan has severely obfuscated the sizable role that political parties played in assisting the emergence of the military services, and particularly the navy, as a strong, well-funded, politically active elite in the late Meiji–early Taishō period. Partly this stems from the fact that scholars have mistakenly associated many pre–World War II political parties almost exclusively with "liberalism" and prewar democracy, thus portraying them as victims of Shōwa militarism.[19] These supposed victims, however, were not "principled pacifists" who attempted to rein in the military in Meiji-Taishō Japan only to pay a political price later in the 1930s for their earlier antimilitary attitudes. The leaders of the political parties supported naval expansion for the same reason that compelled their members not to exert more effort to block the growth of military expansion in Meiji-Taishō Japan: the pursuit of power. The political parties of prewar Japan were pragmatic power-seeking organizations led by savvy leaders who actively sought and secured working relationships and political alliances with other elite groups in order to increase their political power and influence. As my study will demonstrate, the newly emerging Japanese navy proved to be an exceedingly attractive alliance partner for the Seiyūkai party in Meiji-Taishō Japan. The military's involvement in politics, including parliamentary and party politics in 1930s Japan, was thus not an aberration or a marker that signified that something had gone terribly wrong in Japan's polity, a disjuncture from the past. Rather, it was a symbol of political continuity, a signpost signaling that both the military's involvement in politics and the parties' support for military expansion that defined politics of the tumultuous 1930s had their precedents well and firmly established in late Meiji–Taishō Japan.

Finally, the navy's emergence as a strong elite in Meiji-Taishō Japan contributed to another phenomenon that manifested itself with increasing regularity in early Shōwa Japan: army-navy rivalry. In pre–World War II Japan, that rivalry expanded well beyond clan-based factionalism and institutional outlook; it encompassed appropriations, research, and development, and it fostered conflicting notions concerning the direction and nature of Japanese imperial expansion. The rivalry grew almost unabated up until the end of 1945. Owing to the unique constitutional and extralegal privileges granted to the military services by Japan's constitution, interservice rivalry and political intervention in the furtherance of each service's institutional aims strongly influenced Japanese politics and society, perhaps more than in any other country. In Meiji-Taishō Japan interservice rivalry and military involvement in politics, whether cooperative and pragmatic or coercive, provided at different times both a dark harbinger and a strong contrast to the politics and society of Japan in the 1930s. The emergence of the Japanese navy indeed made waves and in doing so significantly influenced and thoroughly reflected the rise of modern Japan.

CHAPTER ONE

Maritime Dreams, Meiji Realities,
1868–1878

A force comprised of two hundred ships and twenty-five thousand men, assembled in three stages over twenty-five years is required for Japan.[1]
—Nihon Hyōbushō

The immediate concern of the Military Department is with domestic affairs while external matters are of future significance.[2]
—Yamagata Aritomo

FOR MANY PEOPLE who lived on the Pacific Rim or in East Asia during the waning years of the nineteenth or the first half of the twentieth century, the Imperial Japanese Navy and the emotive Rising Sun flag that flew on each vessel were synonymous with Japan's pre–World War II power, influence, and imperial ambitions. Naval achievements in war and peace brought fortune, international military acclaim, and recognition of Japan as a modern state. When told of the Japanese destruction of the Baltic Fleet at the Battle of Tsushima in May 1905, U.S. President Theodore Roosevelt wrote: "This is the greatest phenomenon the world has ever seen. Even the Battle of Trafalgar could not match this. . . . I believed that this naval battle decided the fate of the Japanese empire."[3] For many ordinary citizens too, particularly those Japanese who relocated to various parts of the Pacific or Asia from the 1880s onward, the navy also served as a powerful symbol, a tangible link, and an impressive reminder of Japan's modern emergence and success. To many, the navy was a symbolic representation of the rise of modern Japan in the Meiji period (1868–1912).

The Japanese navy did not always garner such acclaim or highlight Japan's power. In many ways the young navy symbolized the grandiose dreams that defined the new Meiji era, but it also reflected the hard realities of the young Meiji state far better than any other governmental organization. As did also the leaders of the Freedom and Popular Rights Movement (*Jiyū minken undō*), who sought greater political pluralism and transparency as encapsulated by the Charter Oath of 1868, naval leaders, stirred by the emperor's 1868 proclamation for the establishment of a strong navy and army, sought to create an impressive, awe-inspiring navy on a scale unmatched in East Asia, a modern, two-hundred-ship maritime armada unlike anything Japan had ever possessed. Each group of dreamers, however, faced the hard political, economic, industrial, and military realities associated with state building in late nineteenth-century Japan. Early Meiji Japan was a poor agrarian country with few resources and little industry, populated by a people who possessed only the faintest beginnings of a truly national identity. Moreover, Japan's early naval leaders lacked the political muscle and connections to champion the interests of their service effectively at the elite level. This, coupled with the absence of any naval tradition to draw upon for support, meant that Japan's navy lacked virtually everything that was required to build a strong national fleet: money, material, and men. This fact left a lasting legacy on the navy's leaders and determined in large part how these individuals visualized and approached government, bureaucracy, politics, and finance in future decades. Events of the 1870s compelled naval leaders to serve as political bureaucrats first, admirals second, and forced them to develop their service by the most cost-effective means possible, through people rather than warships. While troubling to those sea hands whose vision looked beyond shore to the sea, the early focus on politics, administration, and finance that Japan's early naval leaders were forced to make eventually paid significant political and military dividends to Japan's navy in the following decades of the Meiji period. Examining the state of the early Meiji navy not only highlights just how impressive its eventual emergence actually was, but goes a long way in demonstrating why Japan's naval officers eagerly and unabashedly ventured into the realm of politics and finance in the following decades. They did so out of necessity, because politics shaped the budgetary process, and because money determined the size, shape, and institutional health of the Japanese navy.

Organization and Composition of the Early Meiji Maritime Forces

Though the Meiji Restoration of 1868 was couched by members of the anti-*bakufu* coalition in conservative-sounding slogans such as "Restore Imperial Rule" and "Revere the Emperor," the restoration was truly a revolutionary event. United against the Tokugawa government from 1867 onward, men from Japan's western domains of Chōshū, Satsuma, Hizen, and Tosa such as Itō Hirobumi, Yamagata Aritomo, Saigō Takamori, Ōkubo Toshimichi, Ōkuma Shigenobu, and Itagaki Taisuke, who orchestrated the restoration together with like-minded court nobles such as Iwakura Tomomi and Kido Koin, fundamentally and irrevocably altered Japan's government and society. Moreover, in the years after 1868 the policies these and other Meiji oligarchs eventually implemented transformed the pace and trajectory of Japan's development as a modern nation-state. Though bound together as a coalition committed to the overthrow of the existing dated and decentralized Tokugawa political order, the restoration leaders did not, however, possess a unified vision or clearly constructed blueprint of how the modern state was to look or function. Nowhere was this more apparent than in the country's young naval forces.

Few among Japan's ruling elite gave much serious thought to the navy. Despite the fact that the Western threat approached Japan from the sea, ground forces held considerably greater significance to both the Tokugawa government and the coalition of *han* (political domains) that had organized and led the Meiji Restoration. To Japan's new leaders, army campaigns shaped politics and the destiny of the restoration movement. During the civil war, in fact, only one significant naval battle erupted, an engagement off Awaji Island in late January 1868. In almost all other situations, naval forces did little except transport ground forces between western Japan and the Kantō area, the area of present-day Tokyo. Maritime concerns were thus an afterthought at best. Accordingly it is unsurprising that the new government did little to separate naval forces from army forces in the organization of the new military after 1868. Naval units existed simply to support ground operations. In February 1868, the government placed the captured forces of the Tokugawa shogunate under the command of the Navy and Army Affairs Section (*Kairikugun jimuka*) of the fledgling Meiji government. Weeks later, government leaders abolished this organization and created the Military Defense Affairs Bureau (*Gunbō jimukyoku*), only to replace the second institution with the Military Affairs Department (*Gunmuken*) less than a month later. Within six months, the government had once again sought better organizational control over the new military forces and created a full-fledged institution, the Military Ministry (*Hyōbushō*).[4] What made this continual reorganization significant for the navy's perspective was that government and military leaders saw no need to make any distinction between army and maritime forces; maritime forces were nothing more than auxiliaries to the new army. As an auxiliary force was how many in Japan's new government saw the navy.[5]

Organizational subservience to army command was only one of the many problems that afflicted Japan's naval forces in the years after 1868. Military decentralization further hindered the establishment of a strong navy, one able to defend Japan's territory from any foreign naval threat. In terms of navy administration, the navy mirrored the national political environment to a remarkable degree. No national, centrally controlled navy truly existed during the first two years of the Meiji state. The new government directly administered only those Tokugawa vessels captured during the War of Restoration of 1867–68. All other naval forces, including some of the most powerful warships, remained under the control of the various political domains that had assembled or purchased military vessels over the preceding fifteen-year *bakumatsu* period (1853–1868). Thus while these domains retained their political and geographic identity apart from the imperial government, so too did they retain their military and naval independence.[6] This was a troubling situation, and no one understood this better than the former Tokugawa naval leader Katsu Kaishū, whom the coalition leaders brought into the new government because of his naval expertise and his ability to control the *bakufu* navy personnel who still retained positions in the new government's maritime force. Soon after taking his position of leadership, Katsu recommended the rapid centralization of all naval forces, imperial as well as domain, under one government agency.[7] Such a move to consolidate control, however, required more military and political force than the new Meiji leaders could exert. The young Meiji government therefore retained a decentralized organizational structure throughout 1869 and into 1870.[8]

If not already apparent to those Meiji leaders apart from Katsu, the weaknesses of a decentralized military and political structure became manifest in 1869. Beginning in late spring and continuing throughout much of the early summer of that year, the former Tokugawa naval leader Enomoto Takeaki led a sizable navy-based revolt against the imperial government. Fleeing Tokyo Bay with many of the former *bakufu*'s best warships, the new ruling coalition faced an embarrassing political and troublesome military situation. The new state simply did not possess enough naval might to quell the rebellion on its own. Faced with this predicament, the Meiji government requested considerable naval assistance from the most powerful domains—Satsuma, Tosa, and Chōshū—to crush the rebellion. As expected, the disparate group of naval warships put together by the government and coalition forces exhibited a considerable lack of coordination and even less military prowess in battle. Though Enomoto eventually surrendered, the government's slow and humiliating response to the rebellion demonstrated to all but the most obtuse the need for a strong, centralized navy.

Enomoto's rebellion notwithstanding, coalition leaders Ōkubo and Kido Kōin had, over the course of 1869, convinced many of their fellow "restorationaries" of the need for and desirability of greater political, military, and economic centralization. The new government, they argued, needed to forge a strong, centrally controlled nation-state if it was to remain intact, let alone prosper. To this end, just prior to Enomoto's rebellion in fact, the domains of Chōshū, Satsuma, Hizen, and Tosa agreed in principle to voluntarily relinquish or "return" their lands and population registers to the emperor. Within six weeks, 118 out of the 276 domain leaders (*daimyō*) followed suit, and by August 1869 all but 17 had surrendered their land to the central government. For the few domain leaders who failed to return their lands voluntarily, the government forced their hands. With enough military and political power behind them after the first act of military centralization, government forces confiscated all remaining land after August 1869. With this act, modern centralized state building had begun. While important, this was not the last act of centralization. Over the next two years the government continued to centralize political and economic power, culminating with the complete abolition of the domains as political entities in the summer of 1871.

Though restoration leaders forged the political entity that became known as Japan in 1869–70, the newly emerging state still lacked a strong, centrally controlled maritime arm. This situation changed in 1870. Mirroring the national pattern of political centralization, and spurred on, no doubt, by Enomoto's rebellion, the government initiated a military centralization campaign in 1870 as well. As with the political centralization, the domains that held the most power in the new regime, Satsuma, Chōshū, Tosa, and Hizen, donated their naval forces to the new government as a symbol of nation building. Though some domains did so only reluctantly, all eventually followed these strongest naval domains, and by 1871 the new government could finally boast a centrally administered naval force, the institutional beginning of the Japanese navy.[9]

The first organization to centrally administer the country's new maritime force was the Military Ministry (*Hyōbushō*), which the Meiji government had earlier established on 8 July 1869 to further coordinate forces seized from the Tokugawa *bakufu*. This institution was a large umbrella organization that administered both army and navy defense matters, with army concerns receiving preference over those voiced by navy officials. This is not entirely surprising, given the fact that Yamagata Aritomo, the Chōshū bureaucrat considered the father of the Japanese army, served as the chief of the *Hyōbushō*. Yamagata's position of authority, however, did not mean that naval affairs were entirely neglected. At the urging of Satsuma military leader Kawamura Sumiyoshi and former *bakufu* naval leader Katsu, restoration leader Ōkubo Toshimichi lobbied for the formation of two administrative organizations within the newly forged Military Ministry, one concerned solely with army affairs and the other with naval maters. Army personnel who possessed little, if any, knowledge of maritime science, Kawamura argued, simply should not be allowed to administer Japan's maritime forces. On 9 February 1870, the *Dajōkan*, the pre-1885 equivalent to the cabinet, established just such a semi-independent maritime administrative structure under the auspices of the military minister Yamagata Aritomo. Underneath Yamagata, Kawamura Sumiyoshi assumed the position of navy section chief, and Saigō Tsugumichi served as army section chief.[10] Thus the navy gained at least some degree of organizational identity, albeit still under an army-dominated institution. Its first leader, Kawamura, would emerge as one of the most important individuals of the early Meiji navy.

While separating naval administrative affairs from the army within the Military Ministry in early 1870 was an important first step toward creating a national navy, the military consolidation of *han* naval forces that ended in 1871 proved more critical to the navy's long-term heath. In February 1871, the government assumed control over ten *han* warships and two transport vessels, including all the officers and enlisted personnel that manned them. This act more than doubled the size of the Military Ministry's naval force. This act had important political as well as military ramifications. Immediately after this enlargement, Kawamura petitioned the government for complete administrative independence.[11] Kawamura's reasoning was sound. First, Kawamura claimed that the large expansion of bureaucratic work associated with the administration of a much larger naval force necessitated an independent service organization. In case such an argument did not convince the Meiji leaders, Kawamura also suggested two other reasons for the creation of an independent navy ministry: international standards and future institutional health.[12] In a document he presented to Ōkubo, Kawamura articulated that all the important navies of Europe and North America possessed independence from army affairs, including England's navy, which had been selected as the model for Japan's by imperial decree in 1870. Kawamura concluded that Japan should be no exception. More important, perhaps, echoing an idea raised earlier by Katsu, Kawamura forcefully argued that naval matters would never be prioritized within a bureaucracy whose ultimate head was an army official.[13] This was a logical assumption. Within months, after careful calculation, Ōkubo agreed with Kawamura, and in June 1871 that Satsuma statesman urged State Councilor Iwakura Tomomi to support calls for the dissolution of the *Hyōbushō* and the creation of two separate service organizations, an army ministry and a navy ministry. Though army leaders in the *Hyōbushō* initially resisted such a separation, the government divided the Military Ministry into two distinct organizations, the *Kaigunshō* (Navy Ministry) and the *Rikugunshō* (Army Ministry), whose respective ministers were directly responsible to the *Dajō Daijin*, Sanjō Sanetomi, the pre-cabinet equivalent of the prime minister.[14] Not surprisingly, in part because of Kawamura's experience in the *Hyōbushō* but more because of his Satsuma connections, Satsuma State Councilors Ōkubo and Ijichi Masaharu recommended him to serve as acting head of the Navy Ministry in 1872. Thus the navy that would gain international acclaim through the destruction of the Russian Far Eastern and Baltic Squadrons in 1904 and 1905, respectively, could trace its bureaucratic lineage back to 1872.

While the creation of the Navy Ministry ushered in an important chapter in the history of the Japanese navy, political and administrative independence alone did not drastically improve the navy's strength at sea. Between 1868 and 1872, the government failed to undertake any naval expansion program, despite proclamations by the emperor that "the establishment of the navy and army [were] matters of utmost urgency."[15] Militarily, the new navy consisted of a motley collection of dated ships, sharing only a lack of significant armament, armor, and size. Heterogeneity was indeed a hallmark of the early Japanese naval forces in both size and strength. This troublesome nonstandardization stemmed in large part from previous Tokugawa *bakufu* policy over the *bakumatsu* period (1853–68). Beginning in the mid- to late 1850s, the Tokugawa government first allowed and then ordered a number of the rich and strategically placed domains, the most important being Satsuma, Chōshū, Hizen, and Tosa, to undertake naval and military development programs in conjunction but not coordination with one another or the *bakufu*. Thus while the *bakufu*, with assistance from the Dutch and French governments, amassed a force of eight warships and thirty-six auxiliaries, Satsuma, with support and guidance from the British,

assembled a force of nine foreign-built steam-powered ships. Other domains followed suit. Chōshū purchased five steam-powered ships from
abroad and built a number of small auxiliary sailing craft. Kaga amassed ten
ships; Tosa accumulated eight, and Chizuken six.[16] While impressive, in
view of Japan's previous isolation and the pre-1850s Tokugawa-era proscriptions on naval construction or development, the vessels afloat in 1868
were hardly the military basis for a strong, centralized national navy in that
year, let alone 1872. Many, in fact, were nothing more than barges suitable
only for transporting ground units, which in fact was the primary role
played by naval forces in the restoration war. Insight into the nature of Japan's naval force of 1868 was perhaps best summarized by the American
shipbuilder Joseph H. Longford, who described Japan as "the recognized
market for the disposal of obsolete and worn-out ships of every degree,
both mercantile and naval."[17] Adding further injury to insult, many of the
best *bakumatsu*-era vessels did not survive beyond the War of Restoration
or Enomoto's abortive rebellion. Thus, the first true national navy of 1872
yielded a force of only fourteen warships with a combined displacement of
12,352 tons, which were manned by 1,593 personnel, including 171 officers.[18]
Though bureaucratically independent and led by a sound naval thinker and
pro-navy enthusiast, the Japanese navy of 1872 was, in the words of future
navy leader Yamamoto Gonnohyōe, nothing more than "a mixed bag of *soldiers* from Satsuma, Chōshū, Tosa, and other fiefs, as well as those from the
shogunate."[19] The Meiji navy of 1872 was anything but an awe-inspiring and
militarily impressive fleet.

The Dreams and Realities of the New Meiji Navy

Japan's early naval leader Kawamura and many of the lesser officials beneath him in the new Navy Ministry did not let the navy's weak military position dampen their respective dreams for a strong Japanese navy. Medioc-
rity, in fact, fostered various schemes, some realistic and others wildly
grandiose, for naval expansion after 1872. In one of his first acts as acting
head of the navy Kawamura let reality dimish his dreams. After only a short
time in his new position, Kawamura proposed a plan to purchase two
1,300-ton warships, one from Britain and the other from Holland. Though
modest in scale, state councilors rejected this proposal on the grounds that
the purchase of even two warships lay beyond the financial means of the
new government. Not deterred by this initial setback, Kawamura reintroduced his plan in August 1872 but like his earlier request, the government

again rejected this plan the following October. Again, finances hindered Kawamura's efforts and limited expansion of the navy.

Owing in part to these initial failures but more to the fact that Kawamura had little maritime experience, his tenure as acting head of the Navy Ministry was short. Believing that a naval expert was needed to run this new organization, the government appointed the former *bakufu* naval official Katsu Kaishū as minister in 1873, while Kawamura assumed the role of vice navy minister, a bureaucratic position in which he excelled.[20] From his position as navy minister, Katsu wasted little time in devising and submitting naval expansion plans that would make Japan's navy the strongest in the Far East. Reality did little to diminish Katsu's dreams. On 19 January 1873, less than forty-eight hours after the government requested that the Navy Ministry submit a detailed expansion plan, Katsu recommended an eighteen-year plan that called for the construction of 104 warships, including 26 steel-hulled vessels, 14 large composite vessels, 32 medium-sized composite vessels, and an assortment of various support and transport ships.[21] This, Katsu suggested, would make Japan the strongest naval power in East Asia. A detailed reading of this plan reveals that it closely resembled many of Katsu's earlier plans devised when he served the Tokugawa *bakufu*, plans that reflected both his unrealistic vision for naval expansion and his unrealistic expectations of Japan's financial and industrial standing. In 1857, for instance, Katsu proposed the formation of a centralized naval force of some 180 ships. Though Tokugawa officials rejected this plan with little discussion, Katsu was not deterred. Five years later, in 1862, the naval enthusiast proposed establishing a 370-ship navy that was to be divided into six centrally administered maritime defense zones. Each district was to contain a naval training center, shipyards, and support facilities for the vessels. Such an impressive fleet, Katsu acknowledged, would require around sixty thousand men, whom he suggested should be selected without regard to lineage or class.[22] Eight years later, when working under the military minister, Katsu called for a smaller yet no less unrealistic two-hundred-ship navy, comprising twenty-five thousand men, to be built or purchased over a twenty-year period. This expansion plan, Katsu estimated, would command roughly an eighth of Japan's national revenue over the lifetime of the plan.[23] Similar to the starry-eyed leader's earlier plans, the 1873 proposal shared the fate of his earlier expansion requests. Specifically, the government rejected Katsu's 1873 plan. The following year, as vice minister, Kawamura reintroduced his previously defeated expansion plan and argued that the deteriorating relationship between China and Japan necessitated naval expansion.[24]

Writing a pointed memorandum to State Councilor Sanjō Sanetomi, Kawamura claimed that a weak navy not only threatened Japan's military position but hindered its diplomatic position: a strong navy, he suggested, would increase Japan's stature in East Asia, as well as with the European powers and the United States.[25] After heated discussions, on 19 October 1874 the *Dajōkan* agreed to fund the purchase of three warships from England.[26] By 1878, the government had provided funds for the purchase and construction of six of the originally proposed 104 warships, a paltry number, but triple what Kawamura had originally requested in 1872.

Many factors, apart from the inheritance of a weak *bakumatsu*-era force and the absence of any naval tradition in Japan, conspired against significant naval expansion in early Meiji years, let alone expansion as envisaged by Katsu. Strategic priorities of the new Meiji state certainly favored army expansion over naval increases. While government leaders initially concerned themselves with western naval expansion in East Asia and the Pacific, domestic rebellions were a far more significant threat to the new Meiji government. Between 1868 and 1872, more than 160 internal revolts or peasant uprisings erupted, requiring the government to use force to quell these acts of violent protest. More significant threats to the new state developed in 1874 and 1877. In 1874, the government was forced to employ more than two thousand soldiers to quell a rebellion in Saga led by Etō Shimpei. Three years later, the government called upon much of the nation's standing army to crush the Satsuma Rebellion, an insurgency led by Saigō Takamori. In each conflict, naval forces contributed little to the overall outcome and when used at all served primarily though not exclusively as transports for ferrying army troops. Appropriations for the suppression of each disturbance reflected the army's preeminent role. During the eight-month-long Satsuma Rebellion of 1877, the Japanese government appropriated over ¥35 million to combat the insurgency. From this total, the army received ¥34,641,055 (98.2%), while the navy, on the other hand, garnered only ¥654,526 (1.8%).[27] Even during the overseas Taiwan expedition of 1874, an expedition launched as a punitive mission against natives who had earlier killed fifty-four Japanese in 1871 and injured four others in 1874, the army's role proved instrumental. In fact, the navy again did little more than serve as transport force.[28] It was not surprising, therefore, what with domestic concerns taking precedence over external or foreign military matters, that ordinary army funding and force levels far surpassed those of the navy throughout the 1870s.

Strategic priorities aside, the sheer complexity associated with developing a modern navy also slowed the growth of Japanese naval power. To amass a powerful navy in the late nineteenth century required a sizable naval infrastructure that included not only shipyards but naval ports as well. Nowhere was Japan's naval weakness more apparent than in the domestic navy yards.[29] Neither the *bakufu* nor the independent *han* had left a legacy of shipbuilding for the new government, and during the 1870s little changed. The facilities at the Nagasaki and Tokyo shipyards were too small and crude to construct anything like what naval leaders such as Katsu sought, either in size of vessel or in number of ships. While the Ishikawa-jima dockyard in Tokyo commenced work on the *Jingei* (1,450 tons) and the *Seiki* (897 tons) in 1873 and completed these vessels in 1875 and 1876, respectively, only five other significant navy ships were built in Japanese yards between 1876 and 1881, all of them wooden and none exceeding 1,600 tons. In fact, the first domestically built Japanese warship not made entirely of wood was not launched until 1887. While the navy began constructing new facilities at Yokosuka during the 1870s, this like the older arsenals would not produce significant warships until the late 1880s. The *bakumatsu*-era reliance on the purchase of warships from abroad was felt throughout the early Meiji period.

Though Japan could not produce a sizable naval force in the early 1870s through domestic construction alone, other opportunities existed to augment the navy. Katsu and Kawamura both suggested the purchase of warships from overseas, but government leaders for the most part rejected these suggestions as well. While the government purchased an ironclad and two steel-framed warships from England in 1875, all three of which were delivered in 1878 (the *Fusō* at 3,717 tons, and the *Kongō* and *Hiei* each at 2,248 tons), purchasing an entire fleet from overseas, even if enough money existed, was a risky proposition in an era of rapidly evolving naval technology. No guarantee existed that the vessels ordered in 1875 would still be state-of-the-art when delivered, often three to five years later. Under such circumstances, the Meiji leadership decided against purchasing a fleet that could be dated before arrival and argued that such a policy was a luxury that Japan simply could not afford. It was.

Indeed, financial considerations restricted naval growth more significantly than almost any other factor in the early 1870s. Japan of the early Meiji period was not a wealthy state. Prior to the introduction of a 3.5-percent tax on the value of land in 1873, Japan's government continued to use an antiquated in-kind payment based on crop yield. This provided the government with no reliable source of income upon which to base multiyear budgetary expansion commitments as required by the navy. Recognizing this problem, Kawamura had, prior to the implementation of the land tax, recommended that a percentage of all tariff revenue secured at Yokohama and other treaty ports be directed toward military expansion, with the navy securing the largest amount.[30] The Meiji leaders rejected this proposal, however, and with it any real hope for even Kawamura's modest expansion requests. Indeed, the young Meiji government rejected Kawamura's three-ship proposal of 1872 strictly on financial considerations, both in May 1872 and again when he resubmitted it in October the same year. Not surprisingly, then, the same state councilors rejected outright Katsu's 104-vessel expansion program of January 1873, claiming that it would be "financially impossible" to implement.[31]

If a lack of money was not bad enough for the new navy, clan-based politics also hindered naval expansion to a degree in the early Meiji years. Men from the former domains of Satsuma, Chōshū, and to a lesser extent Hizen dominated the new government. While Satsuma and Chōshū men held many of the important positions in the new army, former *bakufu* officials, most notable among them Katsu Kaishū, held many of the most influential political positions within the navy. As a leader in the Tokugawa navy who had studied Western naval learning as early as the late 1850s, he held maritime credentials such as few in Japan could match. However, he lacked the political stature and influence that many of his Chōshū and Satsuma counterparts, such as Yamagata and Saigō, possessed in spades. While Katsu delegated much of the navy's administration to his Satsuma-born subordinate Kawamura, a fact that would be critically important to the navy's development in the 1880s, the ex-*bakufu* navy minister was ultimately responsible for representing the navy at the highest level in government. Katsu had, for all intents and purposes, fought on the losing side of the War of Restoration, and this, he believed, influenced the early relations between the government and the navy. Moreover, aside from Enomoto and Katsu, many ex-Tokugawa retainers came to hold many of the lesser positions within the new naval administration.[32] Thus while Satsuma men held a plurality of line-officer appointments, they did not, at least until 1878, hold a plurality of elite-level positions within the navy's new administration. Until Satsuma men came to dominate the navy and view it as their reserve of power within the government, the navy would get far less elite-level support than the army, and with far less elite-level support came far smaller budgets.

On top of strategic concerns that favored the army's expansion over that of the navy, the lack of political clout held by elite-level naval officials, a shortage of finances, and the complexities associated with assembling the human component of a modern navy also hindered rapid naval development throughout the 1870s. Great warships, as envisioned by Katsu and Kawamura in their respective expansion plans, required skilled officers and crews to operate effectively, as events of the Sino-Japanese War of 1894–95 later proved.[33] Owing in part to the absence of any naval tradition, Japan lacked a well-trained cadre of naval officers and sailors in the early Meiji period. Well before Japan's first successful overseas war, though, Katsu and Kawamura recognized the need for selective recruitment of officers and enlisted personnel to serve the country's new navy. Earlier, when he served the Tokugawa navy, Katsu remarked to one official: "If we do not select promising men of talent, casting aside distinctions between high and low, noble and commoner, it will be difficult to realize national defense."[34] Years later, as a Meiji naval official, Katsu reiterated this opinion, claiming: "Officers are the heart of a warship."[35]

Initially, the officers and sailors who manned the new navy mirrored the composition of the government's bureaucracy. Samurai who originated from the victorious coalition of western domains dominated the navy's small officer corps. This Satsuma-Chōshū-Tosa-Hizen stranglehold over the officer corps was in large part a vestige of, and reflected, pre–Meiji era naval strength that had been accumulated by the various anti-Tokugawa domains. When, beginning in 1870, the most powerful *han* with independent naval forces offered them to the state, they did so on the condition that the officers and enlisted personnel who manned their forces should subsequently obtain positions and rank in the new navy.[36] Thus Satsuma, the domain that offered the three largest warships to the new government, also provided more officers and enlisted sailors than any other domain. Japan's important western domains, particularly Satsuma, also dominated the numbers of recruits sent to the government's new Naval Studies School which opened in October 1869.[37] In the initial recruitment of new cadets for the school, also referred to as the Naval Dormitory or the Naval Academy, the Military Ministry drew heavily from *bakumatsu*-era precedents. Similar to the recruitment of cadets at the two Dutch-assisted *bakufu* naval training centers that opened 1855 and 1857, respectively, the *Hyōbushō* continued the "tribute system" to secure cadets in Tokyo.[38] In short, the Military Ministry ordered seventeen *han* of the original anti-*bakufu* coalition that possessed naval units to provide cadets to the academy based on the size of their respective *han*. Within this framework, the larger political domains provided five students, and the smaller ones provided three each.[39] As Chōshū, Satsuma, and

Hizen were three of the most important naval domains, they sent the largest contingents. Moreover, Satsuma officials also sent fourteen full-fee-paying "day students" along with the five "tribute students," giving their *han* the largest single representation at the school.[40]

Quality did not match quantity, however. The first batch of students sent under the tribute system did little to impress either the academy authorities or officials in the *Hyōbushō*. Of the original 114 students who attended the academy in 1870, only two remained for the full course and graduated in 1873.[41] This abysmal performance motivated Katsu and Kawamura to implement changes. Well aware that officers could not be trained overnight, both men set about a reorganization of the naval academy in Japan. Not only did they view this as essential; both realized that this was a cost-effective means of establishing the foundations for a future navy. After the first full year of subjects, therefore, the academy implemented a revised program to secure better recruits. As a first step, Katsu suggested that the government should abolish the feudal recruitment and enrollment program retained by the new government. Not only did such a system provide no quality control over cadets, argued the former *bakufu* leader, but it also led to a furtherance of regional identities among cadets and did little to create the atmosphere of a national navy. As a result of Katsu's suggestions, in 1871 the government implemented a new policy for naval officer recruitment, one that had wide-ranging political, geographical, and social implications for the navy throughout the Meiji and Taishō periods.[42] First, the navy made enrollment contingent upon the successful completion of an entrance examination. Second, in order to attract anyone of outstanding intellectual ability and in an effort to make the navy a national service, the navy opened applications to anyone "who desired a naval career, regardless of their social and geographical origin."[43] Although individuals of samurai background made up the vast majority of cadets in the early Meiji period, accounting for 90 percent of those who began study in 1874, the implementation of an examination-based entrance qualification led to a noticeable increase in officers of commoner background, who had been exposed to little or no previous military training.[44] By 1891 in fact, commoners (*heimin*) accounted for just over 21 percent of the academy's graduates, a figure which would increase to 34 percent in 1901.

Finally, along with altering the social composition of the navy, the navy's new examination system also influenced the geographic makeup of the officer corps. Over time, this system fostered a nationally oriented officer corps drawn predominantly from urban communities. As the government conducted entrance examinations only once per year and only in Tokyo up until 1889, Tokyo began to supply an increasing number of cadets to the naval academy. Though Satsuma officers held a plurality of positions within the officer corps in the early Meiji period, by 1890 cadets from the Tokyo metropolitan area outnumbered cadets from Satsuma, the navy's original geographical power base. Although Satsuma men continued to possess a near monopoly of power at the admiral level, Satsuma men held no commensurate monopoly in the navy's midlevel officer corps. Moreover, after the navy opened examination centers in seventeen other urban locations during the 1890s, the proportion of Satsuma men continually declined, while the urban component of the officer corps increased. By the time of the Sino-Japanese War of 1894–95, the academy received on average over five hundred applications for just forty positions yearly and was training cadets from all but three of Japan's prefectures.[45] In 1906, 2,981 individuals applied for entry at the naval academy for only 181 offered places.[46]

The naval officer corps became a popular choice for young, ambitious, educated Japanese for a variety of reasons. The three-year course, which also included an additional eight-month sea-based training exercise, offered promising Japanese students access to foreign learning. English, mathematics, physics, chemistry, and engineering served as core courses for all students, though they were allowed to specialize in a selected professional stream in their final year.[47] Moreover, naval education, first at Tsukiji and later when the academy moved to Etajima in 1888, offered direct educational contact with foreigners. Throughout the 1870s and into the 1880s, British instructors taught at the academy, and this was important both in attracting students and in encouraging more practical, hands-on learning. Finally, academy education gave the best cadets the opportunity to study overseas. Twenty-seven students studied overseas for at least a year's duration between 1870 and 1884, and all students received overseas seafaring experience in their final year as cadets. True to its recruitment's rhetoric, the navy offered young Japanese an avenue to foreign learning and world experience.

Along with assembling a well-skilled officer corps, similar efforts were undertaken to build a strong cadre of enlisted personnel and noncommissioned officers in the early 1870s. A month after the *Hyōbushō* invited prospective officers to sit entrance examinations for a place at the naval academy, the same ministry called for volunteers between the age of eighteen and twenty-five to enlist in the new navy. Enlistment targets were set by first the *Kaigungakari* of the Military Ministry and then, after 1872, by the navy minister. Once decided, representatives at each of Japan's two main naval centers (expanded to four by 1888) assumed responsibility for filling the set quota.[48] Once accepted into such categories as seamen, signalmen, coalstokers, carpenters, artificers, sick-berth attendants, cooks, and musicians, volunteers served for a period of eight years and received extensive training.[49] As with officers' education, but with more emphasis on applied rather than theoretical learning, enlisted personnel received continual training as advances in naval technology dictated the continual training of personnel. While the navy could, in theory, draw conscripts after passage of the Conscription Law of 1873, it generally accepted conscripts only as a matter of last resort. In the first place, many in the navy felt that the three-year period of service spelled out in the conscription law was too short a time to train and utilize prospective sailors. Furthermore, naval officials, believing that their army counterparts who administered the conscription system kept the best conscripts for their own service branch, often complained that recruits made available to the navy were too weak physically or too inept to serve in the navy. Though an 1889 amendment to the conscription law required that those drafted into the navy serve a four-year term, the navy continued to accept far more volunteers than conscripts well into the Taishō period. It did so primarily because the navy remained a popular service for potential officers as well as enlisted personnel. In 1904, the navy accepted 2,997 enlisted personnel from a total pool of applicants that numbered 18,470.[50] The navy, or so recruitment pamphlets claimed, offered volunteers a chance to further Western learning, see the world, and the very real benefit of receiving better food and higher wages than being drafted into the army.[51] While the early Meiji navy may have lacked the great warships, the impressive squadrons, and the acclaim of Japan's army, its leaders had begun the process of expansion as best they could in a world restricted by a short supply of money and in which the army's needs and political power far outweighed those of the navy. It was a remarkably humble beginning for the service that would become a powerful and emotive symbol of the Japanese state.

Synopsis

Naval development and expansion during the first decade of the new Meiji era was a mixed proposition in Japan. While the navy made great strides in developing the "human side" of their institution, albeit slowly, it was clear to any observer of politics, military affairs, or society that the Japanese navy of the 1870s was the junior service. Despite all the grandiose plans issued by naval leaders, only a minute percentage of the proposed increases in hardware ever materialized during the first decade of the new Meiji state. Only three significant steel-hulled warships were added to Japan's inventory, the British-built *Fusō*, *Kongō*, and *Hiei*, at a cost of just over ¥3 million. Though the navy of 1878 was no longer just the "collection of soldiers" that Yamamoto Gonnohyōe had described in 1872, it was not a force of great military power or influence.

Many factors conspired against naval expansion in the 1870s, and they left an important, lasting legacy on the navy's elite administrators. First and foremost, military expansion required money, and to secure the money necessary for expansion, a service needed to engage in politics or possess an overwhelming and obvious justification for funding. For much of the 1870s, the navy lacked both the political clout and a strategic or even tactical justification for a fleet that even came close to resembling the ones proposed by Katsu or Kawamura. Securing funds was the most pressing challenge faced by those who led the navy. Political power and patronage as well as strategic necessity shaped military policy and appropriations, and these facts were not lost on either of Japan's earliest naval leaders. While the navy lost on both counts in the 1870s, domestic political developments, international naval expansion, and the growing romance of what some viewed as Japan's imperial destiny in the South Seas in the 1880s, would give far greater weight and authority to calls for naval expansion. With its growing number of well-trained officers and sailors—not to mention its increasingly well-connected political elite that emerged from Satsuma—the navy was well placed to make the most of the limited funds available to enlarge the material aspects of its service over the next thirteen years.

CHAPTER TWO

Parochialism and Empire

Satsuma, the South Seas,
and Naval Expansion, 1878–1889

> All I see is a Satsuma navy. . . . Any amateur, so long as he happens to come from Satsuma, can become [navy] minister.[1]
> —Parliamentarian Ozaki Yukio

> The navy is the main factor in our national defense. . . . Expansion of the commercial fleet should also be achieved by promotion of trade and settlement in the South Seas.[2]
> —Economist Taguchi Ukichi

MEIJI RESTORATION leader Iwakura Tomomi approached the 19 August 1882 *Dajōkan* meeting with considerable trepidation. The issue he planned to raise with state councilors that day, naval expansion, had always proven a contentious topic at the elite political level in Japan. When the meeting commenced, Iwakura urged his fellow oligarchs and councilors to support a previously submitted armaments expansion plan written by Navy Minister Kawamura Sumiyoshi. Expecting debate, Iwakura came to the meeting well prepared: he presented a paper entitled "Opinions Regarding Naval Expansion" that Kawamura had drawn up. In submitting this document, Iwakura claimed that a strong navy was essential to maintaining the security of Japan, its citizens, and their assets. Knowing full well that many of his fellow leaders would immediately question both the budgetary aspects and military necessity of Kawamura's plan, the pro-Satsuma councilor argued forcefully that naval affairs must take precedence over army concerns. In presenting this argument, Iwakura suggested that domestic rebellion was no longer Japan's primary military concern and that a strong navy was more important than a sizable army to preserve the Japanese state. Moreover, a large, modern navy, he suggested, had the added potential benefit of imbuing Japan with greater international prestige and recognition: navies were internationally recognized benchmarks of power and status. In terms of finance, the issue that Iwakura assumed would be *the* point of debate concerning the naval expansion question, he suggested that the government could support naval growth by increasing taxes on tobacco, sake, and soy. After lengthy discussions with Finance Minister Matsukata Masayoshi and with the pre-cabinet equivalent of a prime minister, Chief Minister Sanjō Saneyoshi, the former from Satsuma, Iwakura eventually convinced the ruling coalition to support the first multiyear naval expansion plan in Japan's history. In a world where national budgets were decided by state ministers and councilors behind closed doors, access, status, and influence meant everything. Fortunately for the navy, newly forged Satsuma ties provided all the above. In May 1883, the government approved a plan that, when carried to completion, added thirty-two warships over eight years at a cost of just over ¥26 million.[3] This was no small amount. On the contrary, this sum virtually equaled the navy's entire budget for the years between 1873 and 1882. The year 1883 was like no other yet experienced for the Japanese navy, which could attribute such success in large part to clan politics.

Not every budgetary discussion would be as rewarding for the navy. In fact, naval expansion remained a highly contentious issue for the government and the navy throughout much of the 1880s. Advances in overseas naval technology increased the costs of purchasing large components of a modern fleet, and by 1885 cost overruns jeopardized the entire 1883 plan. More important, increased costs abroad, coupled with decreased tax revenues at home, heightened concern and political tension in Japan with regard to funding fleet expansion. These developments demanded that naval leaders more deeply involve themselves in politics, far more than they had in the 1870s. Fortunately for the navy, two developments helped further establish this service as independent and increasingly well endowed: Satsuma clan patronage, and dreams of empire. Throughout the 1880s the navy became a bastion of Satsuma influence and power, a counter to the growing influence that the Chōshū clan exerted over the army. Satsuma leaders looked to bolster their national representation and power within the government, and they did so through patronage of the navy. By building up the navy as a strong, independent institution whose elite-level positions were dominated by Satsuma men, clan leaders believed they could guarantee that their clan's influence would remain strong in the new government. A Satsuma navy, in the minds of Ōkubo, Matsukata, Iwakura, Saigō, and Kawamura, could serve as an effective balance to the increasingly strong position that Chōshū leaders had secured through developing the army as a reserve for their clan's power.

While critically important to the development of the navy as a political elite, Satsuma ties were not the only means by which the navy strengthened its position. The navy, in conjunction with journalists, explorers, economists, and academics, attempted to foster a South Seas consciousness in Japan and used this for their institutional ends. Specifically, the navy helped to create and eventually endeavored to tap into the increased interest in the South Seas in order to develop an independent strategic rationale or justification distinct from the army's, with its growing continental aspirations. As early as the late 1870s, certain naval leaders realized that if Japan acquired South Seas territories or successfully linked Japan's economy in perception or reality to the tropical paradises of the *Nan'yō*, these territories could serve as an important justification for the navy in its political, budgetary, and institutional pursuits. Though naval expansion in the 1880s paled in comparison with expansion in later decades, elite-level patronage, increased political involvement, and a more clearly articulated strategic and economic interest in the South Seas by Japan as well as other foreign powers fostered broader support for naval increases, allowing the navy to expand from a force of twelve small vessels in 1878 to a force which included twenty-one capital warships and numerous torpedo cruisers by 1890.

Satsuma Ascendancy and Elite-Level Political Support

Though the Meiji regime was a national government, its institutions and organization were strongly colored by forces from the former domains of Satsuma and Chōshū. Individuals from these domains had played key roles in the Meiji Restoration and took steps in the following years to guarantee that they would have substantial control over the direction and shape of national affairs. Building ties to a military service that many oligarchs mistakenly believed would always be immune to the dictates of popular politics proved an attractive course of action for Satsuma statesmen. Leaders of Japan's early popular-rights movement such as Itagaki Taisuke (from Tosa), Okuma Shigenobu (Hizen), Gotō Shōjirō (Tosa), and Ozaki Yukio (Kanagawa) claimed that Satsuma-Chōshū influence, often abbreviated as *Satchō*, more closely resembled political domination. In many ways, such critiques were well founded. *Satchō* men such as Ōkubo Toshimichi, Kido Kōin, Itō Hirobumi, Yamagata Aritomo, Kuroda Kiyotaka, Iwakura Tomomi, Ijichi

Masaharu, Shimazu Hisamitsu, Ōyama Iwao, and Matsukata Masayoshi did wield significant, unmatched power and influence within the government. While *Satchō* domination may have indeed frustrated those espousing popular rights and their shared desire for the quick establishment of representative parliamentary government, it unquestionably benefited the Japanese navy. Satsuma men came to dominate elite-level positions within this service and effectively used their ties to other elites in government to advance the navy's political and budgetary agenda in government.

Satsuma leaders, as Chapter 1 illustrated, had played an important role in fostering naval development during the *bakumatsu* era. It was only natural, then, that this domain possessed a certain degree of influence within the new navy. In part, this influence became institutionalized at the line-officer level as a result of the military centralization program of 1870–71. When the Meiji state merged the naval forces of the domains into one national navy, Satsuma contributed more men and officers than any other *han*, thus solidifying their privileged naval position within the new government. Satsuma men comprised nearly 23 percent of the officer corps of the early Meiji navy, an impressive figure which rose to just over 28 percent in 1883. In short, Satsuma men held a plurality of positions at the operational level within the navy.

This did not mean that Satsuma influence emerged at the top of the new Navy Ministry immediately after the formation of a centralized administration in 1872. It was a slow and steady process that initially revolved around one important individual, Kawamura Sumiyoshi. Kawamura was not the most obvious choice to emerge as a naval leader, given the fact that he rose to stature in land forces during the restoration. Satsuma ties, however, more than compensated for this practical fault. Though Kawamura briefly studied naval science in the 1860s, his most important assets were his previous combat exploits and his pedigree. It was of considerable importance that Kawamura was born in the same area of Kagoshima as Satsuma stalwarts Ōkubo Toshimichi and the Saigō brothers, Takamori and Tsugumichi. Moreover, Kawamura had distinguished himself as an army leader commanding Satsuma forces during the War of Restoration. Though Kawamura later added to his credentials by serving as superintendent of the naval academy as well as division chief over naval affairs in the Military Ministry, he was for all intents and purposes an army man who emerged in the navy because of his Satsuma connections.[4] Clan background and personal ties within a tightly controlled oligarchy were far more important than mere rank in securing success in the early Meiji government.

Over two distinct phases, however, Kawamura slowly stamped a Satsuma character on the navy, which eventually gave it greater political weight and influence, and contributed to increased patronage from civilian Satsuma officials in government. The first phase covered the period from 1873 to 1877, when Kawamura served as vice navy minister. During this period, Kawamura worked under Katsu, but the navy minister's style of leadership allowed Kawamura to assert greater bureaucratic influence over naval affairs and appointments than he might otherwise have enjoyed under a minister more singularly focused or control-minded, or both.[5] Moreover, Kawamura had access to and influence within Satsuma circles that Katsu could never obtain. Accordingly, Kawamura played a key role in securing and negotiating the contracts for Japan's first large-scale overseas purchase of warships, the *Fusō*, the *Hiei*, and the *Kongō*, in 1875, an achievement of no small significance in view of the financial limitations of the new state.[6] Moreover, Kawamura played an important role in selecting Kure and Sasebo as the proposed locations for Japan's future naval bases.[7] Kawamura's most significant legacy, however, surrounded the appointment of navy personnel. Kawamura surrounded himself with Satsuma men and championed them within the service above all others, both at sea and on shore. Line officers Itō Sukemaro, Itō Yūkō, Inoue Yoshika, and Sanejima Kazunori, to name only a few, received considerable patronage and support from Kawamura. On shore too, Kawamura supported Satsuma men. The future naval minister Nire Kagenori and Matsumura Junzō both advanced within the navy's administration with Kawamura's backing.[8]

While Kawamura's early appointments laid the foundations for increased Satsuma influence within the navy, nearly complete elite-level Satsuma institutional dominance emerged after the tumultuous events of 1877. In that year, Saigō Takamori, an embittered Satsuma leader of the restoration who previously resigned from the government in 1873 over a dispute with fellow oligarchs, led a six-month-long military rebellion against the Meiji state. This rebellion, significant in its size, intensity, and duration, is often considered the last major rebellion launched against the Meiji government. For the navy, its important ramifications went well beyond the apparent national political level. Prior to 1877, Satsuma energies had been almost equally divided between gaining greater influence and power within both the navy and the army through appointments and patronage. Saigō's rebellion all but ended Satsuma men's ambitions to gain a strong degree of influence, if not control, over the army. Throughout much of 1876, following Saigō's establishment of a private, quasi-military training center, a sizable number of midlevel Satsuma men within the army left this service to join Saigō. Many of these soldiers—some of them starry-eyed idealists hoping to bring about government reform through violence, and others merely disgruntled with the consequences of modernization—lost their lives in the rebellion. No naval officer resigned and joined Saigō's ranks, however, leaving Satsuma influence entirely undiminished in this service.[9] Thus, after government forces crushed the rebellion, such men as Ōkubo, Iwakura, Kuroda, and Ijichi correctly assumed that rebuilding their clan's position in the army via appointments would be much more difficult than expanding on what Kawamura had already established in the navy. Many Satsuma officials therefore agreed that the best course of action would be to focus their energies and efforts on expanding Satsuma influence and power almost exclusively within the navy. They did this with considerable help from Kawamura, who after the rebellion found himself in an even stronger position to further Satsuma interests.

Indeed, the rebellion increased Kawamura's status and thus Satsuma fortunes on a number of tangible levels within the navy. For one, the suppression of the rebellion gave Kawamura his first military combat experience as a naval officer.[10] As a Satsuma man, the government sent Kawamura to Kagoshima in early 1877 to persuade Saigō to surrender before open hostilities commenced. When this failed, the government placed Kawamura in command of the country's naval forces. From Nagasaki, Kawamura administered the seaborne logistics of the campaign and, on more than one occasion, directed naval and military bombardments against rebel-held positions from the warship *Takao*. His military and command experience earned Kawamura considerable praise and led to calls among Japan's ruling coalition to replace Navy Minister Katsu with Kawamura. In May 1878, upon formal review of his previous tenure as vice navy minister and his recent military exploits, the oligarchs bestowed upon Kawamura the title of state councilor (*sangi*) and appointed him navy minister. Kawamura served in that position until 1885, except for the period between February 1880 and April 1881.

As navy minister, Kawamura continued his policy of appointing and promoting Satsuma men to any number of positions within the navy with much greater abandon. Significantly, and no doubt demonstrating his desire to further Satsuma strength in the navy, Kawamura appointed domain men regardless of their naval experience. One of Kawamura's most important appointments, Kabayama Sukenori, was even more of an "army man" than the navy minister.[11] Like Kawamura, Kabayama had been born in

Kagoshima in 1836. In 1871, the year in which Kawamura took a position in the Military Ministry, Kabayama assumed command of the Kyushu army garrison based at Kagoshima. From this position, Kabayama rose rapidly within the army, gaining valuable combat experience in both the Taiwan Expedition of 1874 and the Satsuma Rebellion of 1877. As a result of his performance in the latter, Kabayama became chief of staff of the Imperial Guard in 1878. Three years later, he left the active service and took the prestigious yet demanding post of Tokyo police commissioner.[12] Though he had attained the rank of major general within the army, Kabayama transferred to the navy in 1883 at the urging of Kawamura and other Satsuma leader, Saigō Tsugumichi, and assumed the rank of rear admiral. Adding to his illustrious political portfolio, Kabayama also assumed the position of vice navy minister, a significant feat for someone who had never served on, let alone commanded, a warship or served in any capacity within the navy. A Satsuma pedigree more than made up for any practical or vocational omissions.

Kawamura, in conjunction with other Satsuma leaders, also sought to invite other high-profile Satsuma men into the navy, in order both to further the political power of the navy and to strengthen Satsuma representation at elite levels in the government. The appointment of Saigō Tsugumichi, whose trajectory into the navy closely resembles Kabayama's, is another case in point. Like Kabayama, Saigō possessed a colorful and decorated military background within the army. Saigō served as the commander of the 1874 Taiwan expedition and had attained the rank of lieutenant general the same year. He later served as army minister, held a post on the army general staff, and moreover served as commander of the Imperial Guard. Saigō's path into the navy differed from Kabayama's, however, in that Saigō became a state councilor in 1881 and served as minister of agriculture and commerce from then until 1884. A year later, owing to the status he gained and the influence he possessed as a civilian minister, Saigō transferred to the navy at the request of Kawamura and Iwakura, and he assumed the position of navy minister. Like Kabayama, Saigō had never served on a warship, let alone commanded one. Besides this, Saigō simply refused to relinquish his rank of lieutenant general for a commensurate rank in the navy, in striking similarity to Leo von Caprivi, who became chief of the imperial admiralty in Germany in 1884.[13] This fact did not go unnoticed by opponents of Satsuma favoritism in the navy.[14]

Many factors contributed to this blatant favoritism and flagrant abuse of power. Initially, in his role as vice navy minister, Kawamura may simply have appointed fellow Satsuma men out of friendship, association, or regional ties. The rise of Nire Kagenori is a case in point. Kawamura had known Nire personally from 1871 onward, when both worked in the Military Ministry. Though Nire had no combat experience whatsoever, his accountancy training and previous position as head of an accountancy section in the Military Ministry made him a valuable asset. That he was from Satsuma added to his appeal. Matsumura Junzō serves as another excellent example. Like Nire, Matsumura was a Satsuma man appointed to the Navy Ministry by Kawamura in the early 1870s. He was a good friend of Nire's, and in fact both had spent time in the Brotherhood of the New Life religious order, along with another Satsuma leader, Mori Arinori.[15] Though no documentary evidence exists that details or accounts for Matsumura's appointment, Satsuma ties, Nire's friendship, and association with both Kawamura and Matsumura most certainly contributed.

It soon became apparent, particularly after 1878, that Satsuma appointments were becoming far more politically motivated. On the advice of other Satsuma men such as Iwakura, Ijichi, Kuroda, Matsukata, and Ōkubo prior to his assassination, Kawamura enhanced Satsuma influence and power within the navy. They did this for two important reasons. In large part, Satsuma men wanted to guarantee that the navy would serve as a Satsuma power base within government, particularly after 1881. In that year, the government announced the eventual opening of parliamentary government in 1890 — an event which many believed would weaken *Satchō* control over politics. Thus, Satsuma dominance over a military service that in many ways would be more immune to parliamentary interference than other organs of state (or so the Meiji oligarchs mistakenly believed) could serve as a bulwark for Satsuma interests. More pointedly, after the 1881 purges of many individuals from the domains of Hizen and Tosa from the government, most notably Ōkuma Shigenobu, the nature of elite-level politics took on a more biaxial character between forces from Chōshū and Satsuma than before.[16] As men from Chōshū had risen to considerable elite-level dominance in the army, Satsuma men sought to balance elite-level representation through dominance in the navy. This they certainly did. Between 1881 and 1906, no non-Satsuma man held the reins of the Navy Ministry. Moreover, three of the four men listed above, Kabayama, Nire, and Saigō, whom Kawamura appointed eventually served as navy minister in his own right. As one Royal Navy officer who was attached to the Japanese naval academy claimed, the navy of 1881 was "an instrument of patronage in the hands of the Satsuma clan."[17] To a large degree it was, and Kawamura's rise and his early appointments support this interpretation. But what did Satsuma domination mean to the navy?

The fiscal and thus ultimately military rewards of Kawamura's effort to bolster elite-level Satsuma dominance over the navy soon became apparent in budgetary negotiations in 1882. For all his strengths as a behind-the-scene administrator and purveyor of Satsuma power, Kawamura, like his predecessor Katsu, proved a less than persuasive or successful advocate for naval expansion within the government. As with his 1873 naval expansion plan, the government rejected a plan that Kawamura submitted in 1881 calling for the construction of sixty battleships over a twenty-year period at a cost of just over ¥40 million.[18] The following year, on advice from fellow Satsuma stalwarts, Kawamura followed a different course of action, utilizing Satsuma ties and elite-level influence: Kawamura approached two high-level Satsuma men, Iwakura and Matsukata, and asked for their assistance in winning over others in the *Dajōkan* to support an eight-year plan calling for the purchase and construction of six warships annually at an annual cost of nearly ¥6 million, or forty-eight warships in all at a total cost of roughly ¥48 million. This figure was in addition to the navy's regular annual operating expenses, which in 1882 amounted to just over ¥3 million. This was, for all intents and purposes, the same plan that Kawamura had submitted a year earlier: a written corollary to his "new" 1882 proposal stated that at the end of the eight-year period, twelve further warships would be added within eight years' time, thus bringing the total to Kawamura's original sixty.[19]

The navy's 1882 plan did not share the fate of the one submitted in 1881, however, in large part because of Satsuma power, influence, and patronage. Between 19 August and 23 November 1882, Satsuma forces, behind Iwakura's leadership, worked tirelessly to secure elite-level support for Kawamura's naval expansion plan.[20] After uniting other Satsuma members of the *Dajōkan*, Iwakura approached the emperor and argued persuasively that naval expansion was critical to Japan's security. Before the Meiji emperor, Iwakura suggested that the standing army of forty thousand men was more than sufficient for homeland security and that the government should therefore direct the lion's share of future defense appropriations toward naval concerns. A powerful navy, Iwakura further commented, was necessary to protect the nation, its citizens, and their assets from foreign powers and would thus legitimize an increase in tax revenue. Iwakura's logic and persuasion struck a responsive chord. On 24 November the emperor assembled select ministers of the *Dajōkan* and military officers and announced the need for increased tax revenues to provide adequate funding for military expansion. An imperial rescript for military expansion followed, and in December, Dajō Daijin Sanjō Saneyoshi approved an annual ¥7.5-million tax increase on *sake*, soy, and tobacco in hopes that these additions would provide ¥3.5 million annually for warship construction, ¥1.5 million for army expansion, and ¥2.5 million for warship maintenance.[21] In February 1883, Sanjō directed further revenues from other ministries to support an increase in the navy's warship construction and purchase budget. Thus, by March 1883, the navy secured the ¥6.5 million required annually to support Kawamura's eight-year expansion plan, the largest the navy had secured in its young existence.[22] It had done so in large part through Satsuma leaders, the elite-level connections they possessed, and the influence they could exert.

Such elite-level backing from members of the Satsuma faction was not a one-off for the navy. Satsuma influence also helped the navy secure another expansion plan submitted by Kawamura the following year, an eight-year, thirty-two-ship program at a cost of nearly ¥27 million.[23] More important, Satsuma-brokered imperial patronage also helped the navy resolve a difficult financial crisis that jeopardized the navy's 1882–83 plan in 1885. In that year, cost overruns associated with the 1882 plan, coupled with fresh requests for further naval increases and an overall decrease in tax revenue, placed the navy's proposed yearly funding commitments well beyond the level budgeted for this service. In the first instance, part of the 1882 plan called for the establishment of naval stations at the ports of Kure and Sasebo, the creation of Marine units (*rikusentai*) at each naval station, and the formation of torpedo-boat squadrons at each naval base. Of these proposals, the cost of transforming Kure and Sasebo into first-class naval installations far exceeded original estimates.[24] While such overruns could potentially have been absorbed by a transfer of funds from the navy's ordinary operating budget—all other factors being equal—a desire to increase the number of warships above the number supported by the original program, in addition to cost overruns associated with the ships already contracted and under construction and decreased revenues, challenged leaders to find a solution acceptable to all sides.

In short, the government and the navy faced two dilemmas, one associated with the type of naval expansion to pursue and the other, more important one, how to pay for agreed-upon expansion. On the one hand, naval leaders claimed they could stay the course and purchase all the remaining ships appropriated for by the 1882 plan in the two-thousand- to three-thousand-ton displacement category without qualitative improvements being carried out on any of these planned warships. This was unsatisfactory, because by 1885 warships ordered in 1882 had been surpassed by newly designed state-of-the-art warships as the core vessels of a large battle fleet.[25] It was pointless from a military standpoint, or so Kawamura and Saigō argued, to continue appropriating money for warships that would be outdated at their time of arrival in Japan. A second option was to purchase state-of-the-art warships that displaced almost twice the tonnage of Japan's previously ordered, yet undelivered warships. Such vessels would require greater appropriations for both construction and operating expenditures if the navy wanted to retain the original number of warships appropriated for under the 1882 plan. Finally, a third option presented itself, which necessitated that the navy expand its forces based on the naval concepts developed by a new school of French naval thinking, referred to as Jeune Ecole, that promoted the construction of cruisers and torpedo boats over heavily armored battleships.[26] This was the course Japan chose, seeking the continued purchase of midsized, lightly armored, but strongly armed cruisers, coupled with further increases in the number of fast torpedo-boat squadrons. Therefore, naval leaders asked for an additional twenty-eight torpedo boats, one first-class ironclad, six first-class and second-class dispatch boats, eight first-class and second-class gunboats, and a number of further support vessels, which all together totaled fifty-four vessels with a combined displacement of 66,300 tons.[27] This, members of the navy argued, would allow Japan to field a strong navy without purchasing a large number of heavily armored, expensive battleships.

Increases in the number of fast torpedo boats, however, like the purchase of the newest heavily armored and armed cruisers, required additional funding, and funding necessitated political support. Though torpedo boats and armed cruisers were dwarfed in size and cost by the largest warships under production in 1885, the addition of fifty-four vessels, however small, requested by the new navy minister, Saigō Tsugumichi, and his deputy, Vice Minister Kabayama Sukenori, still required additional funding. To this end, both Saigō and Kabayama lobbied members of the new cabinet that replaced the *Dajōkan* system in 1885. Again using Satsuma influence, Kabayama and Saigō first approached and gained support from Satsuma cabinet ministers Matsukata Masayoshi, Ōyama Iwao, and Mori Arinori, and the non-Satsuma though entirely pro-navy minister of communications, Enomoto Takeaki. Thereafter, Kabayama, Saigō, and Matsukata secured support from Prime Minister Itō Hirobumi for further naval expansion.[28] Support was one thing; money, another. As the tax-increase plan of 1882 had failed to deliver the estimated revenue to provide for military expansion, Matsukata, Itō, and Kabayama sought an alternative means by which to support fleet expansion.[29] After prolonged discussions, the three ministers proposed the issuance of public bonds to provide the navy with the funds necessary to expand in 1886. With support from the emperor, the government provided a loan to the navy underwritten by public bonds, the first bond campaign of the Meiji state that specifically earmarked funds exclusively for military expansion. The total monetary amount of bonds to be issued was ¥16.7 million divided over three years, with the assumption that roughly ¥5 million or so would be purchased each year. When the first-term bonds were issued, however, Japanese citizens purchased three times the estimated amount. Specifically, the government secured ¥16,642,300 from the public in 1886 alone.[30]

This was not the only way in which citizens could support the cause of naval expansion, however. The bonds proved so popular that the emperor asked the prime minister to establish a fund to which other citizens could donate for naval expansion. Serving as an example, on 14 March 1887, the emperor informed Prime Minister Itō Hirobumi that the imperial family would make an initial donation of ¥300,000 to help assist naval port development and warship purchases.[31] Commenced on 23 March 1887, the naval collection campaign raised more than ¥2 million by that September. Not surprisingly, rich industrialists and aristocrats with Satsuma ties provided large contributions: Prince Shimazu, the former *daimyō* of Satsuma, and Prince Mori, the former *daimyō* of Chōshū, donated ¥100,000 each; Iwasaki Yataro of Mitsubishi shipbuilding and his eldest son, Hisaya, each provided ¥50,000; Kawasaki Hachiroemon of Kawasaki banking and shipbuilding provided ¥50,000; and Hara Rokurō, president of the Yokohama Specie Bank, donated ¥50,000 as well.[32] These donations provided funds to cover purchases as well as the cost overruns associated with the construction of Kure and Sasebo. The navy was, by 1888, becoming a stronger military institution and a burgeoning Satsuma-oriented political force in Japan. By the mid-1880s, Satsuma naval leaders began to master the art of domestic politics and in doing so provided their service with a much firmer fiscal foundation upon which to assemble an impressive naval force. Satsuma ties and influence would remain strong in the navy until the collapse of Yamamoto's cabinet in 1914, but naval leaders could not, after 1890, rely solely on such ties to provide the financial support necessary to accommodate their expansive dreams.

Minami-e: The Early Rhetoric of a South Seas Consciousness

While Satsuma ties and imperial patronage proved instrumental in se-curing elite-level political support, the navy also undertook other efforts to construct an independent military rationale and justification for fleet ex-pansion. An important program revolved around the construction of a South Seas (*Nan'yō*) consciousness in Japan.[33] Working with like-minded individuals and organizations in the late 1870s and throughout the 1880s, certain naval leaders hoped to tie the questions of naval expansion, national defense, emigration, and future economic prosperity to Japanese expansion into the South Seas. In Japanese perception, with the help of the Japanese navy, the *Nan'yō* became a region and a concept as diverse and as expansive as the interests and energies of those who directed their attention toward it.[34] To some disenfranchised ex-samurai, it became a warm tropical par-adise, a territory in which to gain personal achievements and fulfill a sense of adventure. Politicians, journalists, and patriots hoping to plant the Japa-nese flag for national glory mistakenly viewed the South Seas as the one area untouched by Western imperialists and thus the optimal and logical place for the new nation of Japan to acquire colonies. Entrepreneurs and adventurous speculators came to view the South Seas as a resource-rich cornucopia, a potential economic treasure house awaiting exploitation through trade and development. Malthusian-influenced economists saw the South Seas as a relatively empty region, one ripe for Japanese emigration. Many naval leaders, such as Enomoto Takeaki, Saigō Tsugumichi, and, ear-lier, Katsu Kaishū shared these perceptions, but their interests also included what was in the best interest of the navy: naval expansion. While the navy was just one actor among many that helped increase awareness of the South Seas and lobbied for southern expansion during the late nineteenth century, it was the most important and the organization that had the most to gain by Japanese expansion into the *Nan'yō*. Elite-level naval officials and econ-omists such as Taguchi Ukichi believed that with greater awareness of, in-terest in, and eventual expansion into the South Seas, Japan's leaders would feel obliged if not compelled to expand Japan's navy to support and protect its citizens and interests overseas.

In the 1870s, however, few Japanese knew much about or concerned themselves with the Pacific islands that dotted the ocean to the southeast of Japan. Though between seven thousand and ten thousand Japanese lived in overseas settlement communities in the southern regions during the early seventeenth century, the Tokugawa Shogunate restricted any sustained, reg-ularized contact with the outside world after 1639.[35] Early South Seas sojourners and naval officials thus first sought to expand Japan's awareness of the *Nan'yō*. To accomplish this task and to give its naval cadets practical seafaring experience, the navy launched numerous training cruises for its young officers and sailors in the South Seas. Beginning in 1875 and continuing up until the 1920s, these training voyages offered many of Japan's cadets their first exposure to naval operations in the open expanses of the Pacific Ocean, ranging from the Hawaiian Islands and the west coast of North America to New Zealand and Australia, with stops at ports in New Guinea, New Caledonia, Fiji, Samoa, Guam, and at many of the atolls of present-day Micronesia. Once at sea, the navy ordered its cadets to keep a journal of their training cruises and observe and record any information concerning harbor facilities, shipyards, and naval bases they visited. In reference to the islands in the South Seas, cadets were asked to pay particular attention to potential anchorages and provisions, as well as the customs and practices of peoples they visited. Upon return to Japan, these diaries were made available to newly recruited cadets and regularly used for teaching purposes at the academy.[36]

Owing to the tenacity of certain civilians who sought permission to sail with cadets on South Seas training missions, and to the foresight of a few high-level naval officials who granted their wishes, these voyages served as an important vehicle by which to stir the imagination of many Japanese and arouse interest in unknown tropical lands. Indeed, the most important and consistent stream of southern-advance (*nanshin*) publicity that emerged in the late 1870s and 1880s emanated from expansion-minded journalists, writers, adventurers, and intellectuals who rode with or in the wake of the Japanese navy into the South Seas.

One such sojourner was Shiga Shigetaka. From his youth, Shiga possessed a keen interest in maritime affairs, stemming no doubt from the fact at the age of ten his guardian enrolled him in a private school which served as a preparatory school for Japan's fledgling naval academy.[37] Under the guidance of master Kondō Makoto, who served in the *bakufu* navy and later worked as official translator at the naval academy in Tsukiji, and surrounded by pupils destined for the naval academy, Shiga studied maritime science, seamanship, mathematics, English, and other subjects beginning in 1874.[38] Although he never enrolled in the Japanese navy, having left Kondō's school in 1877 because of financial hardship after the death of his benefactor in the Satsuma Rebellion, Shiga never lost interest in maritime pursuits. Though he continued studies in Hokkaidō and took employment in Nagano, and later in Tokyo, he continued to correspond with his former fellow students of the naval preparatory school. Many of his previous comrades, Shiga noted, later enrolled at the naval academy and had gained commissions in the Japanese navy.[39] Utilizing these connections, Shiga gained permission to sail on the training vessel *Tsukuba* to Korea in 1885. The following year, Shiga requested permission from Navy Minister Saigō to accompany the *Tsukuba* on its yearly South Seas training cruise. Soon after receiving Shiga's request, Saigō agreed, and in February 1886 Shiga left Japan for a ten-month-long journey throughout the South Pacific.

Fulfilling the unwritten expectations of his navy sponsors, upon returning to Japan, Shiga published an important and exhaustive work based on his voyage under the title *Nan'yō jiji* (Current conditions in the South Seas). Written at a pace of nearly fifteen pages per day on his return, this travelogue, published in 1887, became an almost instant best-seller, with two additional editions being released in 1889 and a revised and expanded volume appearing two years later. For all its resemblances to a travelogue, other purposes lay behind the writing and publication of *Nan'yō jiji*. For one, Shiga hoped that this book would serve as a wake-up call for Japan, documenting to Japanese average citizens and politicians alike the high degree of foreign colonial development already under way in the South Seas. Reflecting the concerns of many naval officials, Shiga too expressed reservations that Japan knew little of the South Seas and believed that without such knowledge his country would never become an active maritime power. Without maritime power, Shiga concluded, Japan would never reap the potential benefits of commercial and economic expansion in the *Nan'yō*. "At present," he lamented, "only a few books exist on the South Seas."[40] Shiga, therefore, pronounced himself the first individual to discuss the South Seas: "What is the *Nan'yō*? It is the area to which the public have not given attention at all as of yet. . . . I am proud of the fact that I am the first to propose the new subject and substance called *Nan'yō*."[41]

Aside from general ignorance of the South Seas, Shiga worried that many Japanese would, once made aware of the *Nan'yō*, view these territories as of no consequence to Japan. To Shiga, as to many in the navy, the South Seas region was an area of critical importance for future Japanese expansion, and a major theme which ran through nearly all his early works, including *Nan'yō jiji*, is that affairs of the Pacific mattered as much to Japan as those on continental Asia, a theme that many Japanese naval officials would continually reiterate at the highest level in government. Shiga wrote: "At present, our Japan lives in solitude in the Pacific Ocean and borders on the South Sea islands. . . . We should be aware that when whales and crocodiles in the South Seas wave their tails, the waves surge to the foot of

Mount Fuji and shake the mountain."[42] Implicit in this quote, and in many respects throughout the entire travel account, is a warning that Japan might be shut out of the South Seas because of the speed and extent of the European and North American powers' acquisition and development of island territories in the Pacific. It was also of importance for Shiga to voice his concern that control of the South Seas by foreign powers, whether described as crocodiles or as whales, could eventually endanger Japan. Perhaps a less ambiguous warning of the same nature can be gleaned from Shiga's decision to include one poem written by former navy minister Katsu Kaishū in *Nan'yō jiji*:

> A seagull above the Southern Seas
> Sees a bullet shooting up.
> Blue are the waters and the sky.
> Where has the bird gone?[43]

While Shiga may have been the first of a new generation of *nanshin* writers who benefited from the navy's direct support, he certainly was not the last. Hattori Tōru also took part in a number of naval training cruises, and his books *Japan's South Seas (Nihon no Nan'yō)*, written in 1888, and *Policy Toward the South Seas (Nan'yō seisaku)*, published in 1891, echoed many of Shiga's earlier themes. In the same vein, Suganuma Teifū's 1888 work, *Dream of New Japan's Expansion to the Southern Lands (Shin Nihon no zunan no yume)*, and articles and pamphlets written by Taguchi Ukichi, Sugiura Jūgo, Fukumoto Nichinan, and Miyake Setsurei, all supported calls for naval expansion and greater penetration into the South Seas. Through their navy-sponsored or navy-supported travels to the South Seas and the publication of their exploits, these writers played a key role in creating what many historians have claimed was a "South Seas fever" (*Nan'yō nettsu*) in Japan. As the *nanshin* author and journalist Miyake Setsurei later reflected: "At that time the desire for colonies, especially in the South Seas, was strong. . . . We felt Japan had to acquire territory."[44] Sharing this dream in an 1890 publication, Shiga Shigetaka was more specific and forceful, if not more hyperbolic. He wrote:[45]

> Every year on the anniversary of Emperor Jimmu's accession, February 11, and on the anniversary of his passing, April 3 . . . we should ceremonially increase the territory of the Japanese empire, even if it is only by a small measure. On both those days our naval vessels should sail to a still unclaimed island, occupy it, and hoist the Japanese flag. . . . Not only would such a program have direct value as practical experience for our navy, but it would excite an expeditionary spirit in the demoralized Japanese race.

Apart from Shiga, other naval officials also supported the use of military force to secure Japan's place in the sun. No individual was more active in supporting such military adventurism than Enomoto Takeaki, the former *bakufu* navy official who had been brought into the new Meiji government after his abortive naval rebellion in 1869. Over the next twenty-five years, Enomoto would serve various government ministries, including tenures as navy minister, deputy foreign minister, foreign minister, minister of education, minister of communications, and minister of agriculture and commerce. Though Enomoto retained the reputation of being a hard-nosed, quick-tempered man who exacted much out of his subordinates as well as his elite-level colleagues, his bureaucratic credentials were impeccable, and he emerged as a bureaucratic workhorse in the Meiji government. Throughout his political career, Enomoto never let his dream of South Seas expansion evaporate. When, in 1876, though stationed in Saint Petersburg, Enomoto caught word of his own government's plan to suppress a group of rebellious samurai, he suggested that Japan should purchase certain Spanish-held islands in the South Seas, to which the rebels could be exiled.[46] On various Pacific islands, or so Enomoto concluded, the ex-samurai would no longer pose a threat to the government and moreover could channel their energies into establishing permanent overseas Japanese communities in the Pacific.

The 1876 incident was not the only time Enomoto sought to acquire territory for Japan in the Pacific. While serving as navy minister (1881–82), Enomoto himself initiated unauthorized inquiries to the Spanish government concerning its willingness to sell the Marianas Islands and Palau. Later, in 1887 as communications minister, Enomoto placed one of his ministry's survey ships normally assigned to lighthouse duty at the disposal of a group of amateur explorers, including the governor of Tokyo Prefecture. After weeks of exploration, the group discovered a barren island southwest of the Bonin Islands and put in motion procedures that led to the annexation of this island—now known as Iwo Jima—two years later.[47]

Apart from training cruises geared toward building popular interest in the South Seas and clandestine operations to secure information about territory, naval officials also assisted with the formation and development of various societies that encouraged Japanese exploration of and expansion into the South Seas. Working with civilians and coordinating efforts to a shared end did not prove difficult for the navy or civilians associated with these societies, for the simple reason that many naval officials held important positions in many of the most vocal societies that agitated for South

Seas expansion. The Colonization Society (*Shokumin kyōkai*), founded in February 1893, is a perfect example. Though this society was made up of economists, journalists, intellectuals, and politicians, naval officials took the lead in organizing it and held important leadership positions once it was formed.[48] After playing an important role in forming this society, former navy minister Enomoto Takeaki served as its first president, and other naval officials, such as Kabayama Sukenori and Saigō Tsugumichi, attained key leadership positions with the organization. Arguments in support of naval issues, the most important being naval expansion, thus found their way into many pamphlets and journal articles published by the Colonization Society, including its prospectus, which read in part:[49]

> If Japan wants to secure command of the seas, Japan must extend her trade routes . . . [and] strengthen her navy; marine enterprises must accompany her emigration. The navy is useful not only in times of war but also during peace, . . . as the navy helps emigrants and protects ships. Therefore, with the flourishing of emigration and navigation, Japan would feel the need to expand her navy.

The Colonization Society also invited naval officials, returned cadets, and civilian adventurers who had spent time in the South Seas to provide regular lectures on conditions there as well as to lobby on behalf of the twin causes of naval expansion and southern advance. Other societies, such as the Tokyo Geographic Society (*Tokyo Chigaku kyōkai*), founded in 1879, the Oriental Society (*Tōhō kyōkai*), established in 1890, and the Tokyo Economic Studies Association (*Tokyo keizai kenkyūkai*), led by free-trade economist Taguchi Ukichi, likewise supported naval increases because of the benefit a strong navy could provide for Japan's imperial ambitions, whether formal or informal.[50]

In many ways, the relation between Japan's Colonization Society and the navy mirrored the relationship that developed between the German Colonial Society and the Germany navy at approximately the same time in the late nineteenth century. Founded in 1882, the German Colonial Society played an important role in agitating for naval increases, emigration, and colonial acquisition.[51] A far greater symbiotic relationship developed in Germany between these two organizations, with historian Woodruff Smith concluding: "The naval question provided the Colonial Society with a popular issue with which it could arouse flagging public interest in colonial affairs," while the "Colonial Society helped finance the naval propaganda campaign until public contributions could be sought."[52] Like the Japanese Colonization Society, Germany's Colonial Society also invited naval officers to speak on behalf of naval expansion.

In stark contrast to Japan, in Germany the Colonial Society gained support from other established groups that lobbied for naval expansion, including missionary societies, political parties, and shipbuilders employing nearly twenty-five thousand workers in 1882. Each of these actors agitated for increased naval spending by the early 1890s. These groups gave the German navy and the German Colonial Society political muscle that the Japanese Colonization Society lacked. Moreover, while increased awareness of and interest in the navy's potential role as a protector of sea lanes and emigrants may have added a further reason to support fleet expansion, the territorial dreams of the most ardent *nanshin* backers was little more than wishful thinking. By 1890 there were no uncharted territories or deserted islands waiting to be claimed by navy-backed adventurers. Such dreams were but an illusion, a chimaera. Though *nanshin* thinking and a preoccupation with the South Seas would remain closely tied to the navy and its mission up until World War II, these concerns failed to result in territorial acquisition in the early to mid-Meiji period or in subsequent naval increases. Nowhere, in fact, do we find any records of government leaders supporting naval increases in the 1880s in order to facilitate South Seas expansion or protect Japanese adventurers, laborers, or emigrants. Politics, elite-level politics, held primacy over imperial rhetoric, and politics alone ultimately shaped naval development and expansion in Japan. Fortunately for the navy, along with strengthened cabinet-level political clout gained through Satsuma connections, other more pressing strategic concerns gave greater political impetus and priority to naval expansion in the late 1880s and early 1890s than Meiji-era *nanshin* rhetoric ever would.

International Naval Growth, Imperial Expansion, and Continental Concerns

While the navy's efforts to foster a South Seas consciousness in Japan stirred many civilians, adventurers, economists, and journalists, it had little impact on elite-level budgetary considerations or politics. Fortunately for the navy, other factors eventually did. By the middle to late 1880s, international naval growth among the European colonial powers and the United States alarmed many Japanese naval officials, and for good reason. Naval expansion defined military and budgetary politics in many countries during the 1880s. After years of decay following the Civil War, a succession of U.S. naval secretaries urged rapid and thorough expansion of the United States Navy.[53] Partly on account of the U.S. Navy's complete ineffectiveness during Chile's war with Peru in 1881, Secretary of the Navy William Hunt created a naval advisory board that drew up plans for naval expansion.[54] Hunt argued aggressively for the creation of a modern navy comprised of steel-hulled warships and for the elimination of costly and increasingly outdated wooden vessels. In assessing the navy's power in 1881, Hunt admitted before Congress and the president that the U.S. Navy ranked twelfth in the world, behind those of such countries as Chile and China. President Chester Arthur agreed and called for the navy's thorough rehabilitation.[55] The U.S. Congress eventually responded and agreed to support a modernization campaign within the navy, authorizing funding for six new classes of warship. During this modernization phase, naval construction expenditure increased from a paltry $1.6 million in 1885 to nearly $9 million in 1891.[56] Alfred T. Mahan's proposition that the United States must take its rightful place in the world as a commercial, military, and industrial power was, by 1891, on its way to being achieved, at least in the ocean that mattered most to Japan, the Pacific.[57]

The United States was not the only power to undertake naval expansion in the 1880s. In the latter half of this decade, the Royal Navy likewise grew considerably. In 1888, Lord Charles Beresford, naval officer and M.P., argued vociferously for increased naval appropriations.[58] Joining Beresford were a host of other pro-navy propagandists such as W. Laird Clowes, Geoffrey Phipps-Hornby, Charles C. Penrose Fitzgerald, and Alan H. Burgoyne, who argued both at the elite level in parliamentary debates and at the local level through newspapers, naval reviews, warship launches, and fictional accounts of naval wars that the Royal Navy was in the process of losing its supremacy.[59] An element of truth existed in the alarmist claims, as Germany, France, and Italy had undertaken expansion programs in the later half of the 1880s, though the situation was not nearly as dire as propagandists claimed.[60] The pro-navy advocates had succeeded in stirring up a passion for all things naval in Britain, and in 1889 the Salisbury government introduced a sizable expansion plan that provided for the construction of eight first-class battleships, two second-class battleships, nine large and twenty-nine smaller cruisers, four gunboats, and eighteen torpedo boats, at a cost of nearly £22 million.[61] More important, this act also created and codified the Two-Power-Standard formula for British naval defense, suggesting that Britain's naval strength must match the combined strength of the next two naval powers.

International naval development was brought into clear focus at the elite level in Japan's navy by 1887. In the summer of 1886, Navy Minister Saigō

Tsugumichi undertook a yearlong trip to the United States and Europe, where he visited navy yards and naval bases, attended fleet maneuvers, and met with various naval leaders.[62] What Saigō witnessed impressed upon him and other naval officials who accompanied the navy's top bureaucrat that Japan must enlarge and further modernize its navy. Continued naval development, coupled with increasing navy-led imperial and commercial expansion into the Pacific by Germany, France, and the United States, caused Saigō to redouble his efforts to build support for naval expansion. Speaking before the cabinet in February 1888, Saigō made an impassioned speech on behalf of radical naval expansion, couching the proposed increases as necessary for national defense and economic prosperity. Specifically, Saigō introduced a building plan that called for the construction and purchase of 139 vessels, including 16 steel battleships and 48 cruisers. The plan, or so Saigō suggested, could be carried out in three distinct terms over a ten-year period. The costs were astronomical: Saigō budgeted just over ¥65 million for the first term alone. Though the cabinet accepted the need to expand Japan's navy, ministers quickly rejected Saigō's grandiose plan and instead budgeted an extra ¥7 million for naval expansion, which allowed the navy to purchase three *Sankeikan*-class cruisers from France and construct one cruiser, three torpedo boats, and one gunboat at domestic navy yards. Meiji financial realities again dented naval aspirations.

Ironically for the navy and those officials who had attempted to develop a strategic rationale based on a Pacific orientation, continental concerns of the late 1880s and early 1890s gave further credence to calls for naval expansion. While foreign imperial advances into the South Seas concerned many Japanese who, with the backing from the navy, had supported the notion of southern advance, Chinese naval and military development and increasing political turmoil and military insecurity on the Korean Peninsula influenced those individuals who mattered. After China's defeat at the hands of the French in 1884, two of China's most ardent supporters of military "self-strengthening" in the 1880s, Li Hung-chang and Tso Tsugn-t'ang, argued for greater naval development in China and, more important, a centralization of China's naval forces.[63] Though their effort to forge a single national navy failed, Li reorganized the Peiyang Fleet, China's strongest, into a more centralized force along German lines in 1888.[64] In terms of hardware, the Chinese added considerable strength to their naval arsenal after 1885, with the addition of two large German battleships that displaced 7,430 tons each, the *Ting Yüan* and the *Chen Yüan*. These were larger, more heavily armored, and more powerfully armed than any vessel in Japan's navy. Most

TABLE I

Japanese Army, Navy, and National Expenditures
and Military Personnel, 1873–1889

(expenditures listed in yen)

Year	Army expenditures	Navy expenditures	National expenditures	Army personnel	Navy personnel
1873	¥8,733,176	¥1,685,237	¥83,169,237	25,440	2,290
1874	7,262,599	3,552,229	66,134,772	25,440	4,025
1875	6,959,736	2,828,843	69,203,000	25,224	3,750
1876	6,904,829	3,424,988	59,309,000	39,315	4,489
1877	6,087,934	3,167,512	48,482,000	40,859	3,989
1878	7,660,191	2,820,515	60,941,000	41,448	5,023
1879	9,384,320	2,853,614	60,318,000	43,156	8,807
1880	9,061,701	3,415,872	63,141,000	42,315	9,055
1881	8,996,864	3,260,719	71,460,000	43,382	9,056
1882	9,600,000	3,409,554	73,481,000	45,815	8,994
1883	10,849,827	6,160,599	81,031,000	47,065	10,153
1884	11,502,528	6,260,865	76,663,000	151,953	9,847
1885	12,758,674	9,845,592	61,115,000	179,475	11,748
1886	11,956,905	8,908,649	83,224,000	197,363	12,862
1887	12,758,674	9,845,592	79,456,000	64,306	14,224
1888	12,785,101	9,845,592	81,504,000	65,322	13,776
1889	14,339,100	9,363,708	79,714,000	81,178	13,210

SOURCES: For national expenditures and army and navy personnel, see Statistics Bureau, *Historical Statistics of Japan*, 5 vols. (Tokyo: Japan Statistical Association, 1987): 5:524, 527. Navy figures also in Kaigunshō. Kaigun daijin kanbō (Navy Ministry. Navy Minister's Secretariat), *Yamamoto Gonnohyōe to kaigun* (Yamamoto Gonnohyōe and the navy) (Tokyo: Hara shobō, 1966): 401. Army and navy expenditure figures are taken from Ono Gi'ichi, *War and Armaments Expenditures of Japan* (Oxford: Oxford University Press, 1922): 18–24, 41–46.

NOTE: Civilians employed by the Japanese navy are included in the years after 1878.

disturbing to Japanese military men in 1889, however, was the fact that China's Northern Fleet, with its thirty warships, was larger than Japan's entire navy. Chinese army development mirrored its naval expansion programs. Army spending, as a percentage of overall Chinese expenditures, rose from 19 percent in 1880 to 31 percent in 1890.[65] By 1890s, Japanese army generals such as Yamagata Aritomo and Kawakami Sōroku urged naval expansion along with increases in army appropriations as well. In response, Navy Minster Kabayama Sukenori urged one of his brightest subordinates, Lieutenant Saitō Makoto, to devise an expansion plan in 1891 to counter Chinese naval development. Though it enjoyed unanimous support at the cabinet level, a new actor in the budgetary equation, the Diet, did not give this plan immediate support. Japan's parliament would, over the course of the next thirty years, be the navy's most troublesome yet ultimately its most rewarding partner.

Synopsis

The period from Kawamura's accession to the Navy Ministry in 1878 to the expansion program of 1889 was a critical era for the navy. These years witnessed sizable growth in the navy over what it had experienced in the 1870s. Most important, however, the navy emerged as an independent institution that had important clan-based political backing. In Meiji Japan, a state dominated by a small oligarchy, clan connections mattered. Using Satsuma ties and then imperial patronage, the Japanese navy secured backing and then funding which allowed it to undertake the first multiyear naval expansion program in its history. Furthermore, working with civilians who espoused expansion in the South Seas popularized the navy and illustrated its potential utility to economists, intellectuals, journalists, and average citizens. While *nanshin* rhetoric failed to result in any outright territorial acquisitions in the South Seas or any increase in expenditures, such exploits helped the navy establish a strategic identity independent of the army, which increasingly focused its military concerns on the continent throughout the 1880s. Though the navy never gained the support of political parties (as the German navy had in the Reichstag in the 1880s) or with industrialists (since most warships were constructed abroad), such would be the aims of certain astute naval leaders over the coming decades. In time, these ties would prove of critical importance.

Moving into the 1890s, while the overseas threats and concerns over foreign naval developments did not dissipate, important structural political changes in Japan meant that securing funds for fleet expansion required far greater political support than before. No longer would naval officials have to convince just cabinet ministers, clan leaders, or the emperor (or any of or all these in combination); now they must also persuade elected politicians who aimed to exert their own collective power in pursuit of a representative government and their constituents' interests in that government. Thus, the Satsuma monopoly that emerged at the elite level within the navy during the 1880s, a monopoly that considerably strengthened this institution both politically and fiscally, came directly into the crosshairs of many party politicians who had decried *Satchō* domination over government since the mid-1870s. With the opening of parliamentary government in 1890, many of these individuals gained their first real opportunity to challenge *hanbatsu* government and voice their demands for political reform and greater pluralism. As they did so, the "Satsuma Navy," as many liberals saw it, and its budgetary requests for fleet expansion, became an irresistible target for those parliamentarians wishing to rein in the abuses of clique government. Accordingly, naval expansion fell hostage to larger domestic political forces after 1890, providing naval leaders with their most pressing political challenge to date.

CHAPTER THREE

Political Baptism by Fire

The Navy and the Early Diet Sessions,
1890–1894

> With regard to the construction of the two warships and the
> steel factory. . . . What tenable reasons have you for refusing to
> sanction this undertaking?[1]
>> —Navy Minister Kabayama Sukenori

> [The Japanese navy] suffers from dyspepsia much like a bloated
> whale. Until its health is restored, no money can be infused
> into it.[2]
>> —Parliamentarian Suyehiro Shigeyasu

> A strong lever is required to effect reform in the navy. Such a
> lever is to be found with naval appropriations.[3]
>> —Parliamentarian and Jiyūtō leader
>> Itagaki Taisūke

T HE OPENING of Japan's parliament was a momentous occasion
and a political milestone that significantly altered elite-level politics in
Japan. On 29 November 1890, newly elected representatives gathered in the
assembly's main chamber and listened dutifully to the Meiji emperor's
proclamation that opened the Diet, the first elected parliament in East Asia.
Among the 300 representatives present, 171 shared allegiances to Japan's
Freedom and Popular Rights Movement (*Jiyū minken undō*), a political
movement that grew considerably throughout the 1880s from its humble
beginnings a decade earlier. A core principle which united many popular
rights supporters was a desire to expand political pluralism and representative government as encapsulated and articulated in the Charter Oath issued
by the Meiji emperor in 1868. To them, the creation and inauguration of a
parliament with clearly defined powers was an important step in securing
this aim. M.P.'s and *minken* (Popular Rights) supporters also hoped that expanding political pluralism might lead to a reduction in *Satchō* clan-based
political domination over government. Though representatives of the Free-

dom and Popular Rights Movement held a majority of the seats in the lower house during all the early parliamentary sessions, not everyone shared their vision for political reform or desire to restrict clan-based government. On the contrary, conservative members of Japan's ruling oligarchy as well as many progovernment representatives elected in 1890 feared that an unchecked parliament lead by radicals might expose Japan to the rash impulses of representative government and weaken previous policies aimed at forging a strong, centrally directed nation-state.

After the first few Diet sessions, it became apparent to all who participated or followed the proceedings that neither the conservatives' fears nor the radicals' expectations were immediately realized after 1890. Nevertheless, individuals from each side of the political divide, though disappointed with the powers the other side respectively gained or kept in the new framework of parliamentary government, took pride in Japan's institutional accomplishment and viewed the Diet's opening as the beginning of a new chapter in Japan's political, economic, and military emergence. It was, and almost no institution would be more affected than the Japanese navy. With the advent of parliamentary government, M.P.'s exercised considerable control over the government's purse strings, and money determined how quickly and thoroughly Japan's navy could develop. Thus an important political relationship developed and evolved between the navy and the Diet during the tumultuous early sessions of Japan's parliament, when, ironically, the Diet came to exert substantial indirect influence over one of the few institutions it had absolutely no direct legal, political, or constitutional control over, the navy. Parliamentarians in the Diet did so almost exclusively through appropriations, which were, and would always be, the lifeblood of the navy. Though the navy's introduction to parliamentary government would be a baptism by fire, owing to the fact that many naval leaders initially felt that military matters transcended the realm of mere party politics, by 1893 certain farsighted naval leaders saw the Diet as something entirely different, an increasingly important institution whose members were to be courted, respected, and—most important—consulted. By 1893, naval leaders Saigō Tsugumichi and Yamamoto Gonnohyōe had learned an important political lesson that would shape their future political fortunes and those of the navy, namely that parliamentary politics necessitated elite-level pragmatism. While political pragmatism never developed into a full-scale partnership between the navy and a political party in the 1890s as it would later in the Meiji, Taishō, and early Shōwa periods, the eventual pragmatism that naval leaders exhibited by 1893 helped defuse the tensions that surfaced between parliament and the government over naval expansion. Moreover, it established a firm foundation for a stronger, more formalized alliance between the political parties and the navy over the following thirty years.

Prelude to Conflict: Cabinet, Parliament, and the Budget in Theory and Practice

The Meiji Constitution was by its wording and structure a conservative document. Modeled on the Prussian Constitution, it codified the emperor as the physical and symbolic head of state. Specifically, it gave him supreme command of the army and navy, the power to appoint cabinet ministers, and the ability to prorogue or dissolve parliament. The emperor was not the only preserve of power, however. Though the constitution gave few if any initiative rights to the elected assembly, the Diet possessed substantial deliberative influence over the budgetary process. Indeed, the constitution transformed the appropriations process in Japan from a small cabinet-level exercise to an issue of open and transparent national debate. While the cabinet, a group of ministers appointed by and responsible to the emperor, not parliament, drafted and introduced the national budget, passage of the budget required the consent of the Diet. In case the Diet could not agree on a budget, the drafters of the constitution embedded a safeguard, or so they thought, in the form of Article 71. This article stipulated that in the event that parliament refused to accept or pass a budget, the previous year's budget would be reused. While this weakened or at least checked the budgetary power of the Diet in theory, invoking Article 71 in practice was an impractical solution to a government unresponsive to Diet members' desires. If, for instance, the government wanted to increase military or industrial appropriations to finance multiyear expansion programs, relying on the powers given to the government by Article 71 was of no avail. Articulating this point with great clarity and prescience, Inoue Kowashi, an important drafter of the constitution and secretary of the Privy Council from 1890 to 1893, informed Matsukata Masayoshi:[4]

> If military and naval expansion were an absolute necessity for the *hanbatsu* government, it had two choices: either it could seek to force a rectification of the Diet by interfering with elections [after a dissolution of the lower house], or it could attempt to arrange with the Diet some sort of compromise.

Compromise would become essential for the government and the navy, but it took the first Diet sessions to clearly illustrate this point to recalcitrant

Satsuma navy men who believed that military matters transcended the realm of party politics.

Japan's first session of parliament, which ran from November 1890 to March 1891, clearly demonstrated the inevitable conflict and eventual compromise that would become standard procedure for the Diet.[5] As expected, leaders of the main political parties, the Jiyūtō and the Kaishintō, which held a majority in parliament, voiced strong opposition to the government's budget, which called for an increase in government spending over the previous year's level. While not entirely against increased appropriations in theory, party leaders sought to use their institutional influence to reduce the tax burden that the government had placed on agricultural landowners, who were the chief constituents of the political parties. Therefore, the parties wanted an overall reduction in national expenditures to offset the revenue shortfall certain to accompany passage of a land-tax reduction bill.

However important to Diet representatives, the cabinet, led by Prime Minister Yamagata Aritomo, did not share the party members' overriding concern with tax reduction. Consequently, Yamagata refused, at least initially, to support any such initiative. With opposition to the planned spending increases well organized in the lower house of parliament, a budgetary stalemate developed, and Yamagata was left with two realistic options to resolve the dispute. One course of action was to dissolve the lower house of parliament and force new elections in hopes that the composition of the second parliament would be more receptive to increased expenditures. Certain cabinet members doubted whether new elections would fundamentally alter the composition of the Diet. Moreover, they feared that dissolution of the first Diet would set a dangerous precedent, which, in the long run, could undermine the foundations of constitutional government in Japan. The second option open to the cabinet, which, in fact, Yamagata selected, was to negotiate with the political parties over the budget deadlock. After weeks of talks between cabinet ministers and party leaders, both sides accepted a compromise whereby the government agreed to a reduction of expenditures by ¥6.5 million. Neither side could claim absolute victory.

The Navy-Diet Conflicts over Appropriations: The Second Diet Session

Compromise in the first session of parliament aside, ideological differences remained over the nature of national expenditure and taxation. Importantly for the navy, it was within the somewhat volatile political climate that the issue of naval expansion entered into the political debate and further threatened smooth-running and well-ordered constitutional government in Japan during the second and third sessions of the Diet. Indeed, pragmatism, compromise, and conciliation were anything but the dominant features in the second Diet session, which ran from 29 November to 25 December 1891. Conflict, in fact, dogged this session of parliament from its opening day, and naval expansion became a prime target of attack for M.P.'s desirous of reducing or at least limiting state expenditure. While some representatives harbored animosity toward the government for its decision not to reduce the rate of land-tax assessment from 3 percent to 2.5 percent, something M.P.'s sought in the first session of parliament, the primary factor that contributed to the heated and tense atmosphere that hung over almost every parliamentary deliberation during the second Diet was the question of naval expansion.

The driving force behind naval expansion was, as one would expect, the navy minister, Kabayama Sukenori. Kabayama possessed a forceful disposition and a singular focus on expanding the navy's strength and within it Satsuma clansmen. Satsuma ties aside, as an administrator, friends and adversaries alike found Kabayama "honest to a fault," "strong and straightforward," a man "who always kept his word."[6] He was, in many ways, an ideal preparliament Meiji-era bureaucrat, who resolutely championed the navy's interests at the cabinet level. Indeed, for much of the previous decade, Kabayama had used his strong will, tenacity, honesty, and straightforward manner in advancing the navy's administrative and fiscal interests at the cabinet level as vice minister of the navy. Though Kabayama was second in administrative command, contemporary government colleagues referred to the time that he spent in the ministry as the "era of Vice Minister Kabayama," a fitting testament to his political influence.[7] Upon promotion to navy minister in his own right in May 1890, Kabayama wasted little time pushing for further naval expansion. Throughout much of his first months as minister, Kabayama devised, with the assistance of Saitō Makoto, and eventually submitted a substantial plan for naval expansion to the cabinet in September 1890. Kabayama's plan was immense. It called for an increase in the size of the navy from a displacement of 50,000 tons to 120,000 tons over seven years and for upgrades at the new naval station at the port of Sasebo.[8] Not unexpectedly, Kabayama's grandiose plan carried with it a grandiose price tag, roughly ¥70 million over seven years. Though the proposal was costly, Kabayama urged the cabinet to endorse it, claiming that at a mere 50,000 tons' displacement the navy was "insufficient to protect the empire."[9] Moreover, he argued that failure to support this budgetary plan could expose Japan to an increasing military threat posed by China's increasingly strong navy. Anticipating strong resentment to such a large spending increase in the first Diet, Prime Minister Yamagata Aritomo rejected Kabayama's claim and asked parliamentarians to support only the navy's previously proposed continuing budget of roughly ¥5.4 million, from which two cruisers (the *Yoshino* and *Suma*) and a torpedo gunboat (*Tatsuta*) were to be built. Though Yamagata supported naval expansion in theory, he predicted, correctly, that such a grandiose plan would draw the ire of elected representatives in the first session of parliament.

Yamagata's reluctance to champion Kabayama's plan did not deter the feisty Satsuma navy minister. After the Satsuma *genrō* Matsukata replaced Yamagata as prime minister in May 1891, Kabayama redoubled his efforts toward securing support for a naval increase plan. Following earlier accepted building plans that emphasized torpedo boats supplemented by a small number of capital warships, Kabayama completed a plan in June that called for the construction and purchase of eleven capital warships and sixty torpedo boats over a six-year period. Though having completed the plan in June, Kabayama waited for an opportune time to approach his cabinet colleagues to gain their support. The Chinese navy soon provided just such an opportunity.

On 5 July 1891, a visit by China's Northern Fleet to Yokohama sent shock waves through Japan. This "courtesy call," as Chinese naval officials described it, of China's most visually impressive and militarily powerful new warships, including the massive German-built battleship *Chen Yüan* (7,400 tons displacement) resulted in a stream of stories in Tokyo newspapers detailing the Chinese naval development that had occurred since the end of the Sino-French war in 1885. During the vessels' short stay in Japan, thousands of curious Japanese citizens flooded the areas surrounding Yokohama harbor in order to get a glimpse of the Chinese warships. So heated did the political and to a greater extent popular atmosphere eventually become that an unnamed army officer, fearing that naval appropriations would thereafter be prioritized over army spending as a result, submitted a long article to the *Mainichi shinbun* in September. In this article, the officer denounced as "ignorant and unwarranted the excitement caused by the Chinese visit to Japan" and asserted that rather than build warships to match China's growing fleet, Japan should "fortify its coasts" and increase the army garrisons throughout coastal Japan.[10]

At the elite government level, ministers also voiced concern at the apparent growth in Chinese naval power. In early July, government officials approached Kabayama to inquire as to the true strength of the Chinese navy, and more important, Japan's ability to defend itself against Chinese naval power. Kabayama recognized the naval visit and subsequent inquiries about Japanese power as the golden opportunity that it was, and he certainly made the most of it. At an impromptu cabinet meeting on 8 July, three days after the Chinese warships arrived in Japanese waters, the navy minister broached the subject of naval expansion. Believing that the visual display of Chinese naval power would accomplish far more than the dry, intangible facts, figures, and tables concerning the naval strengths of various countries which he had previously used to legitimate his earlier expansion request, Kabayama asked the government to implement his earlier-devised expansion program. Rather than proceed with his usual warnings that Japan was falling behind various other naval powers, the navy minister began his discussion with a simple, if self-evident phrase: "It goes without saying," began Kabayama, "that the construction of battleships is an urgent matter. Despite the large costs, a 120,000-ton navy is necessary to maintain our national power."[11] Following this concise opening, Kabayama introduced his "new" six-year naval plan and urged the prime minister to initiate the program beginning in the next fiscal year. For the rest of that afternoon and for much of the following two months, Kabayama lobbied his fellow ministers and eventually secured their commitment to implement a six-year expansion plan. If such an agreement had been reached at the cabinet level two years earlier, the matter would have been settled, and Kabayama would have likely put his energies toward devising the navy's next expansion plan. It was not, and Kabayama was about to experience firsthand how the advent of parliamentary government had changed everything associated with appropriations.

Keeping to his word and the decision reached by the cabinet in September, Matsukata included the first part of Kabayama's expansion plan in the annual budget he delivered to the Diet in November 1891. Overall, the proposed budget called for a total increase in expenditure by just over ¥10 million.[12] The Prime Minister specifically asked parliamentarians to appropriate ¥5 million for the navy to construct two warships and to establish a steel foundry capable of making armor for warships. Expansion on this scale, out of a total budget of ¥82 million, proved problematic for a vast majority of representatives in parliament, who wanted a substantial decrease in both state expenditures and tax revenue.[13] The vocal opposition of parliamentarians to Matsukata's planned increases transformed into overt hostility when

M.P.'s learned that the prime minister intended to use the budget surplus of ¥6.5 million from the first Diet session to fund the lion's share of the government's proposed expansion plan for 1892, including all the navy's proposed increases.[14]

For many Diet members, Matsukata's financing plan was a monumental slap in the face, an affront to the compromise reached in the first session of the Diet. M.P.s who in that earlier Diet session accepted the compromise that trimmed ¥6.5 million from expenditures, rather than the ¥10 million originally sought, believed that that ¥6.5 million would be used to offset a revenue shortfall thought likely to occur following a proposed reduction of the land tax from 3 percent to 2.5 percent. Matsukata's actions in the second Diet, however, made it clear that no reduction in the land tax would be forthcoming. More amazingly, his actions illustrated that the previous surplus would be consumed by military and industrial expansion. Just as they had been during the first Diet, the lines were thus drawn in late November between a government that favored increased expenditure and party members who favored tax relief and decreased government spending. This time, however, the situation was further complicated by naval expansion.

When the thirty members of the Lower House Budget Committee met on 18 December to discuss the proposed increases, journalists, parliamentarians, and government officials expected a raucous occasion.[15] They were not disappointed. On one side of the debate, Inoue Kakugorō, a leader of the Taiseikai, the progovernment political alliance, urged members to execute their patriotic duty and support much-needed naval expansion. This line of argument met with fierce resistance from the opposition parties. Sugita Tei'ichi, for one, claimed that the fixed costs of ships already in service or in production were already far too high for Japan. If the navy could prune production and operating expenses, the M.P. claimed, then the issue of naval expansion could be revisited, perhaps as early as the next session of parliament. Others argued against naval increases more forcefully. Suyehiro Shigeyasu demanded that all expenditures, including naval and industrial appropriations, be reduced so that tax relief could be granted to Japan's citizens. Such an action, he claimed, was in keeping with the agreement reached in the previous Diet and a policy that was most strongly supported by Japan's taxpayers—or, put more politically, by those Japanese who possessed the franchise to vote. Suyehiro then continued that the navy, like its counterpart the army, needed to undertake administrative retrenchment and reorganization so that funds could be trimmed from the navy's overall operating budget. Two hours of discussions elapsed before the committee closed debate and voted on the navy's proposed expansion. By an over-whelming margin (22-8), the Lower House Budget Committee struck all the proposed naval funding increases from the budget.

When cabinet ministers learned of the budget committee's decision, their reactions were predictable. The Satsuma stalwart Kabayama became incensed at the representatives' actions. He quickly sought Matsukata's permission to speak before the entire lower house prior to the day that parliament had scheduled to discuss the budget committee's proposed reductions to the budget. On 22 December, just after 1:30 in the afternoon, Kabayama addressed the lower house of parliament in what became one of the most notorious speeches delivered in the early years of parliamentary government in Japan.[16] Wearing his most formal navy uniform, Kabayama ascended to the speaker's rostrum and quickly challenged the budget committee for their "unexpected" and "drastic" action of not merely "reducing expenditures, but refusing to grant naval increases at all." Lecturing the M.P.'s in the tone and manner of a Napoleon—or at least so it seemed to Representative Sugita Tei'ichi—Kabayama concluded that members of the budget committee had "no sound reason" for their actions. Met by numerous jeers from representatives who shouted that the navy was too corrupt to receive increases, Kabayama challenged this accusation head-on. Shouting down the representatives' claims of naval corruption, claiming that such accusations were based on a "series of erroneous conceptions," the navy minister pointedly asked: "Do the eighty million eyes that watch us discover so many blemishes?" Interjecting between cries of "Oh, yes, there are many!" and laughter, Kabayama let slip, or perhaps, owing to his strong Satsuma ties, deliberately articulated a statement to the effect that *Satchō* government, which representatives were so quick to criticize, had been responsible for "preserving, without dependence on the forty million people, the tranquility of the country and the peace of the nation." Following this claim but in his same condescending manner, Kabayama argued that the government knew the best course of action concerning military and industrial expansion and that such polices were based on the legitimate defense needs of the country. "Should our country fall or perish," Kabayama warned, "we should be ashamed to face those who had gone before us. It is therefore impossible to be satisfied with the paltry reasons for rejecting our appropriations." Ending with the charged question "Do you understand me?" Kabayama simply refused to obey calls that the president of the lower house made for him to leave the chamber. He exited, and even then only slowly, after an incensed group of M.P.'s led by Arai Shogō charged the speaker's rostrum with the intention of physically removing the well-dressed admiral.

Kabayama's words and actions on 22 December revealed much about his personality and institutional outlook. Unfortunately, they crippled the navy's attempt to restore the pruned expansion expenditures. While Kabayama had, from July to September, taken great pains to convince cabinet ministers of the need for naval expansion, the Satsuma firebrand expended no effort whatsoever attempting to win over supporters in the Diet.[17] Kabayama, like many of his military compatriots in Meiji Japan, felt that matters of military policy transcended the realm of party politics. He was gravely mistaken. More importantly, Kabayama's reference to the merits of *Satchō* or *hanbatsu* government rubbed salt in an open and festering wound, further exposing the navy to an entirely different set of criticisms more controversial and damning than mere wasteful expenditures: Satsuma cronyism and the abuses of *hanbatsu* government. Over the next fourteen months, charges that the navy was rife with Satsuma favoritism and *hanbatsu* corruption became *the* issues that further dogged the navy and united those *minken* politicians who sought to rein in the power of *Satchō* government in Japan. Unfortunately for the navy, opposition leaders claimed that until the navy and the government rectified such abuses and reformed the navy, no appropriations would be given to this service.

The following day in fact, the naval issue again came to the forefront of legislative politics.[18] On 23 December, the entire lower house met to vote on the Budget Committee's amended budget recommendations. As in debate on 18 December, Inoue Kakugorō led the attack on representatives who supported the proposed reductions in naval expenditure. Calling their actions "reckless," Shirai Enpei joined Inoue and reiterated the importance of naval power to Japan as an insular country. In reply, expanding on the theme of naval mismanagement and underhanded practices, opposition M.P.'s introduced a long litany of supposed abuses of power and corruption in the navy at the hands of Satsuma officers, including Kabayama. Ozaki Yukio, a man who for many would come to represent pre-1945 liberalism in Japan, claimed that under such a corrupt ministry, "Any amateur, so long as he happen[ed] to come from Satsuma [could] become [navy] minister."[19] Returning to how corruption equated to finances, Shimada Saburō argued that the Japanese navy was the most expensive in the world, averaging ¥500 per ton while the same ships for the British navy cost roughly ¥300 per ton. Implying underhanded practices such as commission granting, Shimada asked what accounted for this ¥200 discrepancy. Suyehiro Shigeyasu expanded on this point and claimed that the "navy suffer[ed] from dyspepsia much like a bloated whale. Until its health [was] restored, no money could be infused into it." Takagi Masatoshi then suggested that one of the navy's most recent purchases, the *Chiyoda*, a vessel plagued with cost overruns as well as mechanical difficulties, was "useless" to Japan as it could only "steam at one mile per hour when powered by Japanese coal." Though Vice Navy Minister Itō Yūkō responded to Takagi's claim, stating that the *Chiyoda* attained adequate speed when fueled with English coal, this did little to lessen the anger or bewilderment of opposition representatives. Not surprisingly, at the close of this debate, the entire lower house endorsed the Budget Committee's recommendation and stripped all proposed naval increases from the 1892 budget.

Government leaders responded swiftly to the action taken by parliamentarians on 23 December. The following day, Prime Minister Matsukata announced that he and his cabinet would not accept the reductions proposed by the Budget Committee, regardless of whether or not they were supported by a majority of the entire lower house.[20] In response, Sugita Tei'ichi drafted a memorial to the emperor justifying the representatives' actions by documenting the mismanagement of finances within the navy. Before Sugita submitted the draft, however, the prime minister secured an Imperial Rescript dissolving the lower house of parliament. Failure to reach an accord on the naval expansion issue, through either compromise or conciliation, had once again undermined parliamentary government in Japan and kept the navy from expanding its strength and size.

Continuous Turmoil: The Naval Expansion Issue and Politics, January to June 1892.

Dissolution of the Diet, a first in Japanese parliamentary history, did little to extinguish the flames which consumed the naval increase issue. On the contrary, this action further motivated opposition members and strengthened their resolve. Even before the government announced 15 February as the forthcoming election date, opposition leaders began campaigning against the government and specifically targeted the naval expansion issue. On 27 December, Jiyūtō leader Itagaki remarked that despite what many government leaders believed, "the days of autocracy had been replaced by constitutional government and . . . no money would be appropriated for the navy until its abuses of administration had been reformed by parliament."[21] Moreover, during the first two weeks of January, Jiyūtō leaders devised and published their election manifesto for the upcoming contest; not surprisingly, the naval issue received significant attention. Within this long (and, as one would expect, "political") document, three important themes emerged with relation to the navy. First, the Jiyūtō supported naval expansion in theory but would refuse to appropriate funds while the navy was still a "den of Satsuma corruption." Second, Kabayama's endorsement of *Satchō* government was an affront to the emperor, the parties, and the people of Japan, who had worked to preserve Japan since 1868; it therefore required an apology to the emperor and the elected representatives of Japan. Third, if the government reformed the navy in conjunction with the wishes of the Diet, the Jiyūtō would support naval expansion within one session of parliament.[22] The other main opposition party, the Kaishintō, published a similar-sounding election manifesto, with the exception that it offered to support only "gradual increases" in the navy after administrative reforms were executed to the satisfaction of the Diet.

Though given a clear warning by the parties as to the importance they placed on the naval reform issue, naval leaders and cabinet officials refused to compromise. This did not mean that the government and the navy failed to react to the political situation after the second Diet session, however. On the contrary, utilizing progovernment newspapers the government responded with a campaign that condemned the representatives' actions as reckless and dangerous to Japanese national security. If the political parties truly stood for the people, claimed cabinet officials in the progovernment *Tokyo shinpō*, they would appropriate funds for a larger navy.[23] With China and Russia exhibiting clear and unmistakable signs of military self-strengthening, and with territories such as Hawaii, Annam, and Burma coming under foreign control, a strengthened navy was crucial for the continued prosperity of Japan and much more important than any reduction of the land tax; only the unwillingness of the parties to transcend their narrow, sectarian interests, concluded government officials, kept Japan from developing a navy that could guarantee national security well into the next decade.

Criticisms of the representatives' actions aside, the government also undertook more controversial steps, which they hoped would assure passage of a naval increase package in the next Diet. Between the middle of January and February 1892, the government, under the direction of the arch-conservative Home Minister Shinagawa Yajirō, blatantly interfered in parliamentary election campaigns in numerous electoral districts. Formal violations of the election law, 2,652 in total, were unprecedented in scope and extent. Government-sponsored agitators harassed opposition candidates throughout the campaign and surrounded—in some instances overran—polling places on election day. In a less direct though no less controversial manner, Home Ministry officials closed opposition papers, which often served as the most effective and, given the circumstances, least dangerous means by which candidates could publicize their campaign programs.[24] In short, the ballot on 15 February 1892 was the most corrupt election held during the entire Meiji period.

For all intents and purposes, however, such underhanded and, in many instances, criminal acts failed. Despite the scale of antidemocratic activities, the Home Ministry's interventions ultimately proved unsuccessful. Although new members won election to more than half the total seats in the new Diet, 154 out of 300, the progovernment candidates did not possess a clear majority. In fact, members under the *minken* banner retained 135 seats in the new Diet, compared with 108 for the progovernment parties and 57 who classified themselves as independents. As expected, when the third Diet session commenced in May, the atmosphere was anything but cooperative.[25] To make matters more problematic for the navy, Diet members elected Hoshi Tōru as their president. Over the course of the first two Diet sessions, Hoshi had been an outspoken opponent of naval expansion. Moreover, his mistrust of the Navy Ministry was matched only by his dislike for what he perceived as clan government and its strong-arm tactics in the election campaign. This was not a good omen for a smoothly functioning and conciliatory parliament.

As in the previous Diet, the naval expansion issue emerged as one of the most important and contentious issues in the third session. Hoping to draw from the surplus achieved in the first Diet, Matsukata again sought support for the construction of two warships at a cost of ¥2.75 million over seven years and for a steel foundry at a cost of ¥2.25 million over six years, both beginning in 1892. His efforts to secure passage for these appropriations were no more successful than his previous endeavors. This was expected by all but the most obtuse political observers in Japan.

In the weeks preceding the opening of parliament, both the opposition parties and the government publicized their respective aims and objectives for the upcoming Diet session. They were light-years apart. Ōkuma Shigenobu of the Kaishintō and Itagaki of the Jiyūtō issued official proclamations that their respective parties would reject any and all naval increases unless the navy initiated substantial financial, administrative, and personnel reforms.[26] For its part, the government countered by publishing articles that aimed to remind taxpayers and citizens of the grave necessity of securing naval expansion. On 3 and 4 May, the *Tokyo Asahi shinbun* published articles listing the ages of Japan's warships and claimed that if opposition members continued to oppose naval increases, "Japan will one day find herself without ships."[27] Former prime minister and Satsuma statesman Kuroda Kiyotaka also entered the debate, suggesting that the establishment of a steel foundry as proposed by the government would eventually reduce the costs of shipbuilding in Japan.[28] Such claims fell on deaf ears. The simple fact remained that, once again, neither the government nor the navy had done anything to specifically address the demands made by the opposition with regard to naval reform or tax reduction. This was a recipe for confrontation, if not disaster.

In the waning days of May 1892, the government faced the consequences of its inactivity. On 30 and 31 May, the entire lower house of parliament discussed Matsukata's proposed supplementary budget that again provided funds for warship construction and the establishment of a steel foundry. Though the Lower House Budget Committee, comprised of a majority of progovernment and independent M.P.'s, recommended that the entire lower house of parliament adopt Matsukata's proposal, representatives felt no obligation to entertain the committee's findings.[29] The parliamentary actors who led both sides of the debate during the third session of the Diet were nearly to the same as before, with the exception that owing to Matsukata's advice Navy Minister Kabayama did not take part.[30] On 30 May 1892, Sugita Tei'ichi again lashed out at the navy for failing to undertake any reforms to eliminate Satsuma favoritism and at the government for again reintroducing a naval expansion program without demonstrating any willingness to compromise on other important political issues, in particular tax reduction.[31] Sasaki Kyōmei then interjected that the navy needed to reform its policy toward overseas warship purchases, citing the poor performance record and high costs of the recently purchased warships *Chiyoda* and *Chishima*. Though Inoue Kakugorō and Ōoka Ikuzō argued heatedly for the lower house of parliament to pass the expansion requests on grounds of national security, representatives rejected the Budget Committee's recommendation by a vote of 141 to 132 and then quickly removed the entire amount requested for naval expansion by a vote of 141 to 123. The following day, representatives rejected funding earmarked to construct a steel foundry by a similar margin. Parliamentarians had once again challenged the government over the naval expansion issue and won.

What motivated Matsukata to yet again introduce increased naval spending programs to a hostile session of parliament? Metropolitan newspapers were rife with speculation that Matsukata would, as he had done before, use the Diet's intransigence as an excuse to dissolve parliament in hopes that a more amenable membership would be elected. Though such a strategy seemed not improbable, given his earlier actions, Matsukata followed a different if no less politically volatile path. In early June, the prime minister encouraged the House of Peers to reintroduce the pruned expenditures as an amendment in the draft supplementary budget that the lower house of parliament had earlier removed.[32] The Peers' action added yet another layer of political complexity to the naval increase issue. M.P.'s in the lower house immediately cried foul, declaring that such an action was unconstitutional, as only the lower house of parliament possessed the right of budgetary amendment. The Peers, on the other hand, claimed that both houses possessed that right, thus leading to one of the first constitutional crises in Meiji Japan. To resolve the issue, the emperor summoned a full meeting of the Privy Council and listened to members discuss the House of Peers' action. On 13 June, the emperor resolved that both houses possessed the right of budgetary amendment. The supplementary budget, with the naval expansion funds restored, was returned to the lower house of parliament for reconsideration.

This action did not guarantee victory. Despite this highly symbolic political move, the Peers' action did not sit well with representatives in the lower house. A majority of representatives in the lower house saw no need to reverse course and capitulate to the dictates of the upper house, even if they were legitimated by the emperor. Thus, when the supplementary budget again came up for consideration, the lower house rejected the naval increase amendment by an even wider margin, 157 to 123. Confrontation and underhanded political tactics failed to achieve any positive results for the government, and the navy's unwillingness to reform again jeopardized parliamentary stability.

Moving Toward Compromise and Reform: Navy-Parliament-Government Relations to the End of the Fourth Diet Session

In the aftermath of yet another failed Diet session, the government undertook a series of constructive steps that cabinet leaders hoped would lessen the chance for future parliamentary failure. First, Matsukata looked to build from existing members in the Diet a strong progovernment party or association that would unite all the progovernment representatives and forge an alliance strong enough to attract a number of independent M.P.'s to join their fold. If all went according to plan, Matsukata believed that the government could secure a victory on the naval expansion issue through sheer parliamentary numbers. To achieve this aim, Matsukata looked for a skilled organizer and charismatic individual to lead this party. He looked no further than former navy minister Saigō Tsugumichi. In late June, at a meeting aptly held at the Marine Disasters Aid Society in Shiba, Saigō and Shinagawa Yajirō became president and vice president of the Kokumin Kyōkai. Though no small task in and of itself, this was just the first political activity launched by the government.

Following Saigō's appointment, the government initiated a number of cosmetic cabinet changes in hopes that such actions would defuse at least some political tensions that Matsukata had raised with Japan's elected representatives. First, upon Saigō's recommendation, the prime minister encouraged and accepted Kabayama's resignation as navy minister. In his place, Admiral Nire Kagenori assumed administrative command of the navy.[33] Nire, like Kabayama, was a Satsuma man who had served in the military and navy ministries since Kawamura's tenure in the early 1870s, but whereas Kabayama was outspoken, intransigent, and belligerent toward party interference in military affairs, Nire was an unassuming, soft-spoken man who Saigō hoped would not antagonize the Diet as his predecessor had so easily done.[34] After achieving this, Matsukata himself resigned, and when the *genrō* met in August to select a new prime minister, they looked for a man who they thought could broker an agreement between the parties and the government concerning the naval expansion bill and land-tax issues. Their choice was Itō Hirobumi, who had played a key role in bringing about constitutional government. Many government leaders desirous of securing military and industrial expansion while at the same time preserving parliamentary government felt that Itō was the individual best suited to reach a compromise with the opposition parties.

Compromise, of course, required conciliation from both sides, and fortunately for the government, Itagaki also moved in this direction. As the historian Banno Junji has documented, Itagaki led the Jiyūtō slowly away from total opposition to government initiatives, a policy still endorsed by the other main opposition party, the Kaishintō, toward a new policy of constructive engagement with the government.[35] A consummate politician, Itagaki sensed a chance to increase power and influence for the Jiyūtō by forming a vertical alliance with Itō's wing of the *hanbatsu*, a strategy later followed after the Russo-Japanese War by the Seiyūkai in relation to the Satsuma naval faction. Evidence of the Jiyūtō's political shift is found in the

speeches Itagaki delivered at party gatherings and via official policy proclamations published in the *Jiyū shinbun*. On tax reduction, Itagaki warmed to
a gradualist approach. Moreover, the Jiyūtō leader also spoke and wrote at
considerable length about the necessity of expanding Japan's navy, at one
point subscribing to the navy's claim that a force displacing 120,000 tons
was necessary for Japan's security.[36]

One area where the Jiyūtō leadership failed to yield any ground, however, was in relation to naval reform. As a recent convert to large-scale naval
expansion, Itagaki approached the naval reform issue with a newfound zeal.
The Jiyūtō leader therefore suggested that since massive naval expansion
was critical to national defense, a corrupt or mismanaged navy simply could
not be trusted to implement such an important undertaking. At a party
gathering on 15 November 1892, exactly two weeks before the opening of
parliament, Itagaki declared that "while national defense [was] one of the
most important and urgent problems of the day, reform of the navy must
occur" before naval expansion could be implemented.[37] Moreover, Itagaki
articulated that the Jiyūtō had conducted extensive investigations into the
matter and would release its findings and recommendations during the
forthcoming Diet session. A week later, Itagaki repeated this line of argument and stated that the navy's "grandiose expansion [was] supported by
the Jiyūtō in principle" but could be carried out only after parliamentarians
could trust a "reformed and reorganized navy."[38]

Despite such specific warnings, the navy failed to respond to or even
constructively acknowledge the demands of the Jiyūtō. Like his predecessor
Kabayama, the new navy minister Nire either fundamentally misunder-
stood the critically important role that parliament possessed over military
appropriations or genuinely underestimated the resolve of parliamentarians. While Nire was never belligerent to elected representatives, he failed to
engage in any serious dialogue with members of the lower house. For much
of August and September, when a mood of compromise existed, Nire focused his energies on the technical aspects of naval expansion. Owing to the
weakening relationship between China and Japan over Korea, Nire developed an even more ambitious sixteen-year expansion plan than the one that
Kabayama had devised just over a year earlier.[39] Nire directed no similar
diligence or care toward politics, and this was a serious failure. Though
there was a chance for compromise and passage of the navy's budget if its
leaders had responded to the Jiyūtō's calls, the Satsuma-dominated service
again failed to grasp the nettle of naval reform. This would be the last time
naval leaders would repeat this mistake.

Ironically, two unrelated events in late November foreshadowed much of what would transpire in the fourth session of parliament.[40] First, Prime Minister Itō sustained serious injuries during a carriage accident, which kept the statesman, arguably one of the *hanbatsu*'s most skilled negotiators, from attending most of the December sessions of parliament. Second, and more damaging to the navy's program, was a disaster at sea. In the early morning of 30 November, a day after parliament opened, the warship *Chishima* collided with a British P. & O. steamer, the *Ravenna*, in the Inland Sea, off the coast of Ehime Prefecture. Less than ten minutes after the collision, at approximately 3:40 A.M., the *Chishima* sank, claiming 168 lives out of a crew of 184. The *Ravenna*, on the other hand, though badly damaged, continued its voyage to Kobe. Loss of life and prestige aside, politics made the accident doubly damaging to the navy. In an earlier session of parliament, representatives singled out the *Chishima* and the *Chiyoda*, citing their cost overruns and poor performance as evidence in support of their claims of naval mismanagement and corruption. To their credit, M.P.'s did not exaggerate the problems associated with the *Chishima*; they did not have to. During its maiden voyage, from France to Japan, the *Chishima* suffered numerous mechanical difficulties that resulted in a series of unplanned stops for repairs. All together, with repairs and transport expenses added to the total, the *Chishima* cost the navy just over ¥1 million, though the original outlay had been ¥675,000. Its untimely sinking provided opposition M.P.'s with yet more ammunition to fire at the navy in the opening weeks of parliament. Thus the cabinet and the navy entered the fourth Diet session battered, bruised, and further tarnished. Each would receive more in the way of injuries, though of a political nature only, before the end of the fourth Diet.

When parliamentary debate began on 1 December, the government hoped that the atmosphere of budgetary compromise alluded to by Itagaki, would assure passage of the naval expansion program proposed by the Itō cabinet. On that day, Finance Minister Watanabe Kuniaki and Home Minister Inoue Kaoru (on behalf of the injured prime minister) announced that the government would reduce the land-tax burden by roughly ¥3.75 million *if* M.P.'s accepted a naval increase package of ¥16 million over seven years.[41] To offset any budgetary shortfall created by a reduction in tax revenue and increased spending, the government proposed a tax increase on purchases of tobacco and sake, "luxury" taxes which Itagaki had previously stated were acceptable. Though many newspapers in Tokyo, including foreign newspapers which followed politics, viewed the government's announcement as a pragmatic gesture, with a *Japan Weekly Mail* editor claiming that the government had created a "golden bridge for the radicals to retreat across from their stronghold of implacability," the government made no mention of naval reform.[42] This was a serious oversight.

Even before parliamentarians debated the naval increase issue, however, the compromise that Itō so desperately sought seemed in danger. On 16 December, after accepting the government's land-tax-reduction bill, M.P.'s rejected the tax increase for tobacco and sake, claiming that any offset should first be covered by a reduction of administrative expenses (that is, bureaucratic retrenchment). Angered by this turn of events, Finance Minister Watanabe asked members of the upper house not to consider the land-tax reduction until the lower house passed the naval-expansion and tax-increase bills. Despite such political threats, the Jiyūtō refused to capitulate to the government's demands. Moreover, they did so with political flair.

In the latter half of December, Itagaki and the Jiyūtō turned the naval expansion issue effectively against the navy and the government.[43] Reiterating the Jiyūtō's support of naval expansion, Itagaki and other party leaders argued that naval expansion was far too important to be left to a corrupt or mismanaged navy. What guarantees existed that any funds appropriated by the parliament would not be wasted or mismanaged? The events surrounding the *Chishima*, or so the Jiyūtō leader claimed, provided a perfect example of what naval mismanagement could lead to. National defense, Itagaki argued in effect, necessitated naval reform. Claiming that the navy remained a "hotbed of clan influence" and stating that "a strong lever [was] required to effect reform" Itagaki told a cheering crowd of Jiyūtō members that "such a lever has beeen found in appropriations for the construction of warships." Only when the navy accepted the Jiyūtō's reform measures, Itagaki concluded, would parliament lend its support to the necessary cause of naval development.[44]

Unlike the vague calls for reform which it had demanded in earlier parliamentary sessions, the Jiyūtō delivered a tangible, well-articulated, well-reasoned plan for naval reform in the fourth Diet. On 20 December, the day after the House Budget Committee expunged the government's naval expansion request from the budget, M.P. Sugita Tei'ichi submitted a nine-part reform bill.[45] Introducing this measure, Sugita lamented that "the government's failure to eradicate accumulated abuses in the Navy Department prevents the consummation of the much-desired increases of the navy." He thereafter declared that reform was thus the most important issue now facing Diet members. The nine reforms spelled out in the Jiyūtō bill dealt were (abbreviated with a summarized commentary):

The separation of command and administration within the navy. Claiming that "the mixing of command and administration was the source of many evils," Sugita suggested that a separate command organization similar to the Army General Staff, headed by well-trained officers under the control of the emperor, would limit Satsuma appointments based on favoritism. For years, Sugita claimed, Satsuma appointments to command positions by Satsuma navy ministers had more to do with politics than with military merit. This, the Jiyūtō claimed, severely undermined the effectiveness of the navy. Moreover, as administrative affairs did not necessarily require military skill, the Jiyūtō suggested that appointments to the position of navy minister be open to civilians.

Ending the practice of appointing naval officers to civil posts in the Naval Ministry. Sugita argued that naval officers had been appointed to secretarial and other administrative positions in the ministry again on the basis of Satsuma ties. Though appointed to administrative positions, they often did not possess adequate skills to execute administrative duties and were then forced to hire civilian assistants. Why not, Sugita asked, just appoint civilians and thus save money?

Limiting the number of officers above the rank of lieutenant. The navy, claimed the Jiyūtō spokesman, was too top-heavy. Promotion had been too easy for Satsuma officers, and finances suffered as a result.

Reform of officer education to incorporate recent advances in naval science. This reform too was aimed at strengthening the fighting ability of the navy. All officers, the Jiyūtō argued, should undergo continuous retraining as advances were made in naval science. This reform, like nearly every reform suggested, was aimed at those Satsuma officers who attained their positions in the 1870s and 1880s.

Reduction in the number of naval stations in Japan. Japan, or so the Jiyūtō suggested, required two or at most three principal naval bases or districts, not five as the naval leadership argued. Each naval base, the reform bill stated, added needlessly to the navy's overall operating expenses, outlays that could be better used to purchase or build warships.

Creation of a reserve squadron. By creating a reserve squadron comprising half Japan's warships, or so the reform measure stated, Japan could extend the service life of its navy and save a considerable amount on yearly operating expenses.

Greater supervision over the purchase of articles for use on warships. Since furnishing warships with everything from weapons and communications systems to blankets and cutlery required considerable expenses and was a golden opportunity for the procuring officers to reward themselves with sales commissions, a more transparent system of purchases and audits was essential for eliminating costly corruption.

Abolition of the Naval Accounting School and the Naval Medical College. The Jiyūtō suggested that special schools for naval medical officers and naval accountants were wasteful. Medical personnel could be recruited from Tokyo University's medical school, and the navy could likewise recruit accountants trained in civilian schools. Savings from the abolition of these navy schools could be directed toward the construction or purchase of warships.

Reducing appropriations for the Naval War College. The Jiyūtō bill claimed that the Naval War College had at present too few students to warrant the level of its staffing. Therefore the Jiyūtō bill recommended that instructors should be transferred to other duties and staff reduced to facilitate savings.

After providing a summary of the entire measure, Sugita assured the government that the Jiyūtō would support naval expansion if the bill as introduced was acted upon. He then issued a clear warning that betrayed his disillusion with the government's handling of the naval expansion issue in previous Diet sessions. He declared:[46]

> The Diet has already twice rejected the appropriations for the construction of warships because the government has failed to reform the navy. . . .To come before the house again with proposals for warship construction while the navy remained just as it had always been was to betray singular indifference to the view of the house.

The government's unwillingness to implement or even debate the merits of naval reforms as proposed by the Jiyūtō extinguished any hope of compromise that existed at the beginning of the Diet session. Soon after the Jiyūtō introduced their reform bill, Kaishintō representatives pressed the government yet further. Representative Kage Nobumori argued that his party would never support tax increases to pay for naval expansion. If the government wanted funds for naval increases, so Kage suggested, it could reduce the excessive salaries that civil servants, members of the bureaucracy, and military officers received. This, he claimed, amounted to roughly 12 percent of the state's yearly expenses. If redirected toward a reformed navy, such funds could go a long way to support the navy's proposed expansion.[47] In the absence of any substantive response by the government, the lower house of parliament rejected the naval-increase part of the budget by a vote of 154 to 81. Thereafter the government prorogued the Diet for five days, and repeated this action again on 23 January when opposition M.P.'s initiated debate on a vote of no confidence in the cabinet.

With compromise no longer possible, Itō turned his attention toward finding a nonpolitical solution to the crisis that would keep him from dissolving parliament. Itō looked to the emperor. After receiving Itō's appeal, and another submitted by the lower house leadership explaining its position, the emperor presented both sides with a solution.[48] Issuing an Imperial Ordinance, the emperor donated nearly ¥2 million to fund naval expansion over six years. Moreover, he instructed all civil and military officials to return 10 percent of their salaries to the government over the same period to further support naval increases. Led by the emperor's example, the paid members of the House of Peers then agreed to donate a quarter of their salaries over six years to the cause of naval construction and purchases.

Though not ideal, the emperor's solution achieved two important goals. On the one hand, it provided funds for much-needed naval expansion. On the other, the emperor's proclamation, taken together with the previous three failures, convinced Itō that a long-term solution to navy-Diet turmoil over appropriations was critically needed. The answer, Itō concluded, was naval reform that would not only guarantee the navy's institutional, budgetary, and thus military health but also reform that would assure the stability and growth of parliamentary democracy in Japan. Within days of the emperor's announcement and the parliament's passage of Itō's budget, Itō acted on his conclusion.[49] The prime minister approached the Jiyūtō and Kaishintō and assured their leaders that the government would oversee reorganization and reform of the navy once the fourth Diet session concluded.[50]

Navy-Diet Reconciliation: The Naval Reorganization Committee and the Rise of Yamamoto Gonnohyōe

Thereafter, Itō wasted no time in pursuing a course of substantive naval reform and reorganization. True to his word, Itō initiated reforms almost immediately after the Diet concluded. As before, the prime minister's first action was to appoint a new navy minister. On 11 March 1893, Itō replaced the navy's chief administrative bureaucrat, Nire, with an individual who he believed could work successfully with both the naval leadership and the political parties. The astute statesman looked no further than Saigō Tsugumichi, former navy minister (1885–86, 1888–90) and, in March 1893, leader of the Kokumin Kyōkai party in the Diet. Much to the delight and relief of elected officials, Saigō assured representatives in March 1893 that he would use his new post to reform the navy in compliance with the desires of the Diet.[51]

The reforms envisioned by Itō and, of course, the opposition parties went well beyond replacing just the navy's top bureaucrat, regardless of how acceptable he was to M.P.'s. Both the prime minister and the new navy minister understood that substantial reform of naval organization, financial practices, and personnel required a high-profile committee that would at least consult with party leaders. In early April, the prime minister established the Naval Reorganization Investigation Committee, whose members were President of the Privy Council Yamagata Aritomo, Home Minister Inoue Kaoru, Navy Minister Saigō Tsugumichi, Education Minister Inoue Tsuyoshi, Finance Minister Watanabe Kuniaki, former navy minister and current Privy Councilor Nire Kagenori, and Vice Navy Minister Itō Yūkō.[52] Though the government failed to appoint any party politicians to the committee, Itō assured representatives that their views and opinions would be sought and incorporated into the committee's official recommendations to the Privy Council prior to their implementation. Fortunately for all involved in naval reform and parliamentary politics, Itō again stood by his word.

Though the Naval Reform Committee, as it became known in newspapers, conducted hearings and investigations from May to December 1893, it quickly recommended a number of reforms that mirrored suggestions brought forth in the Jiyūtō's parliamentary reform bill presented during the fourth Diet.[53] One of the first recommendations made by the committee concerned separating matters of military command, strategy, and planning from the Navy Ministry, exactly as M.P. Sugita Tei'ichi had earlier articulated. Specifically, the committee called for the abolition of the Naval Command Department and recommended the formation of a independent Navy General Staff following the same organizational model as the army's. With a general staff responsible for all issues of military command and operations, or so the committee and party leaders believed, the Navy Ministry would be free to concentrate exclusively on administration and, importantly, politics.

Following this important institutional reorganization, the committee examined various aspects of the Navy Ministry's administration. In revising the Naval Accounts Supervision Department Act, the Naval Equipment and Purchasing Account Act, and the Naval Base Expenditure and Accounting Act, the Naval Reform Committee addressed other issues that party politicians had repeatedly mentioned in parliament: financial irregularities and mismanagement. In place of these laws, the committee recommended more stringent and transparent controls over finance and, importantly, suggested that a newly created Naval Department of Inspection directly oversee expenditures and conduct audits of Japan's naval bases. The committee also devised laws providing for greater scrutiny over foreign warship orders, commissions given by companies that dealt with the navy, and the purchase of materials for naval depots and warships in Japan, and recommended that naval officers not be appointed to secretarial and general administrative positions in the ministry, which could be filled by civilians. By the end of June, the Naval Reform Committee had more quickly recommended reforms farther-reaching in nature than almost any politician or journalist expected. As one foreign newspaper editorial claimed: "It seems to us that every candid observer must acknowledge that the reforms just effected mark a new epoch in the history of the Japanese Navy."[54] It was a new epoch for the navy, but administrative and organizational reforms were just the beginning of the navy's political transformation.

In addition to administrative and organizational reforms which the Naval Reform Committee recommended to the Privy Council, the navy also began significant personnel reforms. To lead this endeavor, Saigō tapped the resources of a young and energetic naval officer, Yamamoto Gonnohyōe, who in 1893 was just forty-one years old. No other individual would be as important to the navy's political emergence and military development in Meiji-Taishō Japan. With his political skill, military knowledge, administrative ability, and drive, Yamamoto was to the navy what Yamagata Aritomo and Katsura Tarō were to the army. Moreover, Yamamoto possessed charisma and stature, as even the navy's most ardent critics acknowledged.

To Saigō, Yamamoto was the ideal choice to head the navy's personnel reforms. Born in the same neighborhood as naval leaders Kawamura and Saigō, Yamamoto possessed the proper Satsuma pedigree to assume a leadership position in the navy, particularly important if he was to undertake personnel reforms sure to lead to the dismissal of fellow Satsuma clansmen. Unlike some of his compatriots, however, Yamamoto did not rest on his Satsuma laurels. Throughout much of his early career, in fact, Yamamoto challenged Satsuma privilege. In 1880, before undergoing maritime training aboard the *Ryūjō*, Yamamoto submitted a proposal to the Navy Ministry suggesting that all older naval officers, primarily Satsuma appointments, undergo training alongside recent cadets to acquaint these officers with the latest advances in naval science, regardless of whether this would damage their standing with younger cadets.[55] During the 1880s, Yamamoto advanced rapidly as a line officer on board various warships, assuming command of the *Takachiho* in 1890. On every vessel on which he had served, Yamamoto had gained the respect of his subordinates and superiors alike and often, soon after posting to a vessel, had designed plans to improve the operational efficiency of the crew.[56] In 1891, Yamamoto became the Navy Ministry's secretariat and from this time until his appointment by Saigō, Yamamoto urged reform within the Navy Ministry.[57]

When appointed to oversee personnel reform in the navy, Yamamoto had two objectives and approached both with unremitting zeal. On the one hand, as a naval administrator with keen political instincts, Yamamoto understood the importance of eliminating what many outside the navy felt was an appointment and promotion system based on blatant Satsuma cronyism. On the other, as a skilled naval officer, Yamamoto also sought to eliminate "politically appointed" officers to ensure that the most competent and best-trained military personnel held the important command positions in the navy. In short, Yamamoto wanted to improve both the fighting ability and the political standing of the navy. To specifically accomplish each reform, Yamamoto hoped to retire a number of officers, forcefully if necessary, including many from Satsuma who had obtained their positions in large part through personal connections. After a month of investigations, Go-Getter Yamamoto (as the *Chūō shinbun* described him) identified ninety-seven officers, sixty-one of them line officers, including eight admirals—out of thirteen in total in the navy—who he felt should be removed from active duty.[58] Thereafter, Yamamoto persuaded these individuals to "resign from active duty on official suggestion."

While newspapers and party politicians lavished praise on Captain Yamamoto for the zeal with which he undertook personnel reform, military men within both the navy and the army grew concerned over the scale of his activities. After Yamamoto had submitted his recommendations to Navy Minister Saigō, the latter worried that perhaps Yamamoto had gone too far, considering the military tension that existed between Japan and China over Korea.[59] In response, Yamamoto first assured Saigō that an ample number of young professionals existed in the navy, enough to meet any military emergency. Then, sensing the navy minister's persistent concern, Yamamoto suggested that the retired officers could be recalled to active duty if Japan found itself in a protracted conflict. With this final assurance, Saigō accepted Yamamoto's proposal in full.

Following his successful meeting with Saigō, Yamamoto next met with Japan's most important military bureaucrat, Chairman Yamagata Aritomo of the Naval Reform Committee. Like Saigō, the Chōshū general expressed concern over the sheer number of retirements Yamamoto recommended. This was not the only reason for the meeting, however. Having never met before, Yamagata used this occasion to probe deeper into Yamamoto's past and the naval officer's opinions concerning Japan's national-defense priorities.[60] Yamagata came away from the meeting impressed. The following day, Yamagata informed the Naval Reform Committee that Yamamoto was the right man for the job. Thereafter, the two Inoues on the committee, Kaoru and Tsuyoshi, met with Yamamoto, and both came away from their meetings likewise impressed. After his discussion with Yamamoto, in fact, Inoue Kaoru, so the *Hōchi shinbun* reported, approached Saigō to inquire whether Yamamoto could be promoted to vice navy minister.[61] Such was the effect of Yamamoto's professionalism and charm.

The highly political nature of naval reform also encouraged Yamamoto to keep the public and party politicians informed of his actions. This the rising star of the navy accomplished by conducting interviews with newspaper reporters. On 9 June 1893, the *Chūō shinbun* published excerpts from an earlier interview with Yamamoto, the longest yet given by any naval officer in Japan.[62] In it Yamamoto articulated that the parties were indeed correct in claiming Satsuma favoritism existed in the navy, stating that "a man could not control the navy in Kawamura's day unless he was from Satsuma." Coming from a navy man—a Satsuma navy man—this was taken as testament to Yamamoto's honesty. "At present, however," Yamamoto continued, "any respectable and capable man could assume the navy's highest post." In regard to his reforms, Yamamoto claimed that the main purpose was to replace older officers, many of whom did not have the most up-to-date skills, with younger, better-trained individuals. He then invited past critics of the navy to thoroughly scrutinize the service and his reform efforts in the sixth session of the Diet, claiming that he would take full responsibility for his actions as a naval reformer.

Well before the *Chūō shinbun* published this story, though, newspapers raved about Yamamoto's commitment, frankness, and vision for the navy. Newspapers and party politicians alike supported the reforms launched by Yamamoto and the Naval Reform Committee. Both, though in particular Yamamoto's personnel reforms, gave the navy something that it had not recently possessed, good press and support among Japan's elite-level elected politicians. Both were critically important in this age of parliamentary government. They also established a strong foundation for the navy to develop as a national institution wherein promotion to the upper echelons of command was based on merit and ability rather than on clan affiliation or on personal favoritism. Importantly too, through his reforms, Yamamoto gained considerable political experience and greater influence in the Navy Ministry, which would contribute to his later success as navy minister from 1898 to 1906.

Significantly, the administrative reforms recommended by the Naval Reform Committee also benefited the navy. First, the committee's support of a Naval General Staff gave greater political weight to the navy's efforts to establish a separate command organization. Second, acceptance of the reforms placated party leaders who had vowed to block any naval expansion bill unless a reorganization of the Navy Ministry occurred. Between 1893 and 1902, budgetary discussions between the lower house and the cabinet over naval appropriations rarely deteriorated into the raucous political conflicts that had erupted in the second, third, and fourth Diet sessions. Finally, the reforms, and the resultant passage of budgetary increases, placed the navy on a stronger military footing, which would soon pay high dividends during Japan's clash with Chinese maritime forces in the Sino-Japanese War of 1894–95. As he would in almost all political situations, Yamamoto made waves, and moreover he would continue to make his mark on naval politics in Japan up until World War I.

Synopsis

In retrospect, by the eve of the Sino-Japanese War, the Imperial Japanese Navy had undergone a political baptism by fire. Slow at first to respond to the changes associated with the establishment of parliamentary government, the navy faced extensive criticism and attacks by members of Japan's political parties. The question of naval increases, as Itagaki once declared, became a lever by which the parties could implement change within the navy, and the navy was eventually forced to adopt administrative and personnel reforms lest the desire for fleet expansion be dashed. While the reform process was painful, particularly to those such as Kabayama who never fully endorsed or respected the concept that the political parties should influence matters relating to national defense, it ultimately proved beneficial to the navy. At sea, more competent line officers replaced those officers put into command positions on the basis of personal or clan connections. On shore, while corruption and administrative abuses still occurred, the widespread abuses of Satsuma dominance slowly waned after 1893.

Aside from the obvious budgetary rewards gained in 1893 in exchange for a commitment to reform the ministry, the service also gained political experience that would be crucial to the navy's later development. The initial conciliatory maneuvers conducted by Saigō and to a lesser extent Yamamoto certainly helped foster the image that the navy had a pragmatic political elite that was not above working with Japan's other elites, including the burgeoning political parties. In time, these reform-minded servicemen came to realize that the navy had interests to protect and organizational aims that could be best secured by working constructively within the system of parliamentary government rather than continually challenging it. This was the most significant lesson learned by naval officers in the new era of parliamentary government. Indeed, over the next twenty years, the navy would master the art of legislative politics under the leadership of Yamamoto Gonnohyōe, a reformer who had come to the fore at one of the most critically important moments in the navy's early political history.

CHAPTER FOUR

The Rich Rewards and Rivalry of War, 1894–1904

> As a result of this conquest we shall see Japan obliged to strengthen her means of defence considerably more.[1]
> —Baron Albert d'Anthen of Belgium

> The development of the Japanese navy since the war is not to be described as progress; it is a cyclone.[2]
> —Philadelphia shipbuilder
> Charles Cramp

JAPAN'S VICTORY over China in the Sino-Japanese War of 1894–95 was a watershed in Japan's modern emergence. Success on the battlefield, at sea, and at the negotiating table left a tangible imprint on the Japanese nation materially, politically, and psychologically. To Japan's elder statesmen, defeat of East Asia's historically dominant country and civilization further validated the oligarchs' centrally directed state-building and westernization programs launched soon after the Meiji Restoration. For the Japanese people, many of whom wholeheartedly supported mobilization and the war effort, victory further strengthened the bond between citizen, subject, emperor, and state, and heightened a sense of national pride not previously witnessed in modern Japan. On an international level, Japan's military victory and acquisition of colonies transformed the country's standing and image in the West and marked Japan's emergence as a regional military and political power.

Success in Japan's first modern overseas war was no less significant to the Japanese navy. The destruction of China's Peiyang Fleet (Northern Fleet) accomplished what endless reassurances in the Diet had not, namely that the navy was a sound fighting force that had not squandered or mismanaged the nation's resources. Moreover, victory also clearly demonstrated the importance of naval power for national security and for protecting Japan's interests in both East Asia and the Pacific. Rewards gained through conflict for the navy were not limited to the political realm, however, but translated into sizable economic benefits as well. Obtaining nearly ¥360 million as an indemnity from China as a result of the peace settlement created a unique political environment that Saigō and Yamamoto used to lead the navy on a course of further political development and military expansion, the pace of which was best described by a foreign shipbuilder as cyclonic. In short, the decade from 1894 to 1904 was a period of political and military transformation for the navy as well as the country of Japan.

With such rich rewards came rivalry also, both domestic and international. Japan's new stature and postwar naval expansion heightened military tensions in the Far East and increased competition, both naval and political, after 1895. More important for the navy, with its successes at sea and its emergence on shore as an increasingly powerful and well-funded political elite came increased envy from, and rivalry with, its most important domestic competitor, the army. While healthy rivalry had always existed between the services, even when many former army generals such as Kawamura held leadership positions in the navy, interservice competition assumed a far more political and institutional character after the Sino-Japanese War. This would be an endemic and ultimately destructive feature of interservice relations in Japan, shaping both domestic politics and the nature and direction of imperial expansion up until the end of World War II.

Prelude to War for Japan and the Navy

Almost from the beginning of the Meiji period, Japan's military and civilian oligarchs concerned themselves with events in Korea. While Japan did not possess a master plan of imperial conquest that began with Korea, as David Bergammini so long ago erroneously suggested, the peninsular nation assumed a prominent place in Japan's diplomatic, geopolitical, and strategic worldview. As Peter Duus has convincingly demonstrated, Korea's strategic proximity to Japan and its relations vis-à-vis China elevated it to a position of supreme military and political importance in Meiji Japan.[3] The tumultuous relationship of the new era began when many in Japan took Korea's initial refusal to accept Japan's new diplomatic delegation of 1869 as a political insult. Though the new Meiji state wanted little more than to alter the existing diplomatic protocol between the two countries, Korea refused. While this incident and repeated diplomatic slights precipitated debate in Japan about whether to send a military force to punish or subdue Korea, calmer heads prevailed, at least in the early 1870s. In 1875, however,

Japan's leaders adopted a more aggressive stance, endorsing military force, or at least the threat of military force, to open Korea and unilaterally impose Western-style diplomatic practices there. In a move that closely resembled Perry's mission to Japan, a Japanese delegation steamed from Japan on three naval warships and established headquarters on Kanghwa Island, off the western coast of Korea, in February 1876. Negotiating with the Japanese under the threat of invasion, Korea capitulated and signed an unequal treaty with Japan, the Kanghwa Treaty, thus ending the traditional Confucian relationship between Japan and Korea, previously mediated by the Sō family of Tsushima.

While the imposition of an unequal treaty on Korea certainly elevated Japan's diplomatic and military self-confidence and strengthened Japan's ties to that country, it did not sit well with Korea's other important neighbor, China. China had had tributary relations with the Korean Kingdom for much of the previous two hundred years and sought to continue this arrangement despite Japan's diplomatic and political encroachment. From the late 1870s up until the Sino-Japanese War of 1894–95, rivalry over Korea defined Japan's relations with China. From China's perspective, Japan's actions, taken together with the annexation of the Ryukyu Kingdom in 1874, were acts of brazen imperialism launched to pry away tributary states from China's imperium. To halt such activities, China sought to reassert its influence in Korea, first by encouraging the Korean court to open relations with other Western powers—playing barbarians off against other barbarians—and later by supporting a traditional court faction that opposed increased ties to Japan and Japanese-sponsored reforms. The support of rival factions in Korea by China and Japan eventually ignited a powder keg of pent-up antagonism. One explosion occurred in 1882, when soldiers from a traditional Korean army unit launched attacks against rival army units trained by the Japanese. Known as the Imo Mutiny, this revolt brought all three powers close to open conflict. Using the revolt as a pretext, the Chinese government dispatched troops to Seoul and reinforced a pro-Chinese faction at court supported by the Min clan. To Japan, such activities by a country that could not adequately defend itself against foreign powers not only jeopardized Japan's position and the supposed reform polices it supported in Korea but also, leaders feared, would ultimately expose Korea to imperial advances from the Western powers that, in 1882, were still masticating Chinese territory.

Tensions came to a head again just two years later in 1884, when a group of pro-Japanese reformers attempted to overthrow the pro-Chinese Korean court. Japan's military and political leaders agreed that war with China in 1884 was not the most viable or desirable option and instead chose a diplomatic course to resolve tensions. In 1885, Itō Hirobumi and China's Li Hung-chang signed an agreement known both as the Tientsin Convention and the Li-Itō Protocol. Through this accord, both sides agreed to notify the other if either dispatched troops to the peninsula. Moreover, the agreement further stipulated that if one party sent troops after notification, the other had the right to dispatch an equivalent number of soldiers to the peninsula to protect its own interests. Though diplomacy seemingly soothed Sino-Japanese tensions, it did little to guarantee that reforms in Korea would produce a stable polity. Reforms, in fact, had accomplished little, and by the early 1890s many Japanese leaders had lost hope that Korea would ever develop as a strong, independent country as long as China's influence remained paramount. This fact, coupled with increased Russian interest and penetration into the Russian Far East and Manchuria, led many in Japan's military high command to believe that war with China over Korea was inevitable.

The Tonghak Rebellion of 1893 reinforced Japan's dim view of Korea's stability and future prospects. When this rebellion spread rapidly from southern Korea northwards toward Seoul, Japan's leaders feared this might convince China or a Western power to introduce troops to the peninsula on the pretext of reestablishing order. While a weak Korea under Chinese stewardship was problematic for Japan's reform polices there, Japan's leaders viewed the possibility of Korea under the protection or control of a Western power, particularly Russia, as a significant threat to Japanese security. To guard against just such a development, the Itō government agreed on 5 June 1894 to mobilize the army's Fifth Division, the Hiroshima Division, for operations in Korea. Japan's fears were in part realized just two days later, when China's government informed Japan that it had decided to dispatch troops to Korea. Though the Korean court had requested China's military intervention, the Japanese used this as a pretext to send seven thousand troops from the Fifth Division to Korea. From 12 June, the day when Japan's forces landed at Inchon, to 1 August, when Japan formally declared war, both sides prepared for conflict.

For the Japanese navy, initiating hostilities in August 1894 was not ideal. The navy had not yet received the warships ordered as a result of the emperor's intervention in February 1893, namely the battleships *Fuji* and *Yashima*, the cruiser *Akashi*, and the report ship *Miyako*. Though the navy could field four capital ships, one armored cruiser, seven protected cruisers, twelve unprotected cruisers, and twenty-six torpedo boats, the Chinese navy, at least on paper, was numerically superior. Though that superiority, as Mark Peattie and David Evans have documented, was more apparent than real, Japanese naval officers such as Satō Tetsutarō and Suzuki Kantarō possessed deep anxieties over war with China, believing that such a course of action could result in serious losses for the Japanese navy.[4] Such losses, naval leaders understood, would be politically, militarily, and economically devastating to the navy and the nation. Naval officials became so concerned about losses stemming from a war with China that they pressed the cabinet to appropriate extraordinary emergency funds for warship purchases outside normal budgetary channels.[5] In autumn 1894, the cabinet agreed to purchase three battleships from Argentina at a cost of just over ¥9 million and one battleship from Chile at a cost of roughly ¥3 million. With the emperor's backing, parliament endorsed the emergency appropriation once in session.

The Navy and Japan's First Modern War

Fears and cautions aside, the war went remarkably well for the Japanese navy and the nation of Japan. After a small-scale naval exchange on 25 July, five days before Japan declared war, the combined fleet under the command of Admiral Itō Yūkō provided logistical support to the army through much of the first month of hostilities. After prodding by Admiral Kabayama, chief of the Navy General Staff, Admiral Itō turned his attention toward locating and engaging China's Peiyang Fleet in battle. On 17 September, Itō succeeded. That morning and continuing throughout the day, Itō's forces engaged Admiral Ting's fleet in the first significant naval fleet encounter since the Battle of Trafalgar. The Battle of the Yellow Sea, as the engagement became known, left Ting's fleet spiritually demoralized and physically battered, though not completely annihilated. As the battle ended, Itō preferred caution over opportunism. The remnants of Ting's forces limped to China's naval base at Port Arthur, only to leave the port for Weihaiwei weeks later.

Wildly celebrated in Japan, Itō's victory, however limited in a tactical sense, had major implications for the course of the war. After Ting's forces left Port Arthur for Weihaiwei, Itō blockaded Ting's naval forces there throughout the winter of 1894–95. Hemming in the remnants of the Peiyang Fleet allowed the Japanese army to land troops and supplies unmolested in Korea and on the Liaotung and Shantung peninsulas. These landings set the stage for the final and most convincing naval encounter of the war. In February 1895, as Japanese army forces began to overrun the harbor shores of Weihaiwei, followed quickly by two daring torpedo-squadron attacks launched against blockaded Chinese vessels, Admiral Ting ordered a breakout of his remaining seaworthy vessels. This time, Itō did not let caution reduce the totality of Japan's victory. At the Battle of Weihaiwei, Japan sank, captured, or ran aground all but two of China's remaining warships of the once substantial Peiyang Fleet. This time victory was complete, and "the Chinese Fleet," as Baron Albert d'Anethan of Belgium wrote to a European counterpart, "no longer exist[ed]."[6] Disgraced by this total defeat, Admiral Ting committed suicide.

While impressive, success was not limited to the battlefield or the sea. Victory at sea and on shore also translated into success at the negotiating table. At Shimonoseki, Japan's delegation eventually secured a remarkably favorable peace settlement with China. Signed on 17 April, the Treaty of Shimonoseki provided Japan with an indemnity of 200 million taels (roughly equivalent to ¥300 million), territorial rights to Taiwan, the Pescadores Islands, the tip of the Liaotung Peninsula, and important commercial and political rights in China equal to what Western powers possessed. Victory thus provided Japan with much-needed cash, territory, and a degree of equality with the West, at least in relations with China.

Domestically, the war and the favorable settlement were also tremendous political successes for both the government and the armed services. Victory over China provided an almost incalculable boost to Japan's self-perception and moreover validated the state-building course pursued by Japan since the Meiji Restoration.[7] Victories over Chinese forces, as Foreign Minister Mutsu Munemitsu reflected, "intoxicated" the Japanese public with joy and pride, which grew stronger with each reported victory. Enthusiasm reached a crescendo with the announcement of the terms of the Shimonoseki Treaty in April.[8] Importantly too, the war also eliminated most political dissent that had been directed at the government from parliamentarians and popular-rights activists since the opening of the Diet in 1890. The two Diet sessions held during the war, the seventh (18–21 October 1894 in Hiroshima), and the eighth (December 1894 to March 1895), were marked by unanimity of support for the war, both financial and political. Parliamentarians earlier swayed by desires to reduce government expenditures and to lower taxes backed massive increases in military appropriations, nearly ¥150 million to prosecute the war alone, including emergency funds for the navy to purchase warships from Argentina and Chile.[9] War thus went a long way to unite both the elected politicians and the populace behind the government.

Victory-inspired delirium and postwar pride, however, soon dissipated within a week of the Shimonoseki peace. On 23 April, the governments of France, Germany, and Russia united behind a common diplomatic cause, namely that of restricting Japan's wartime gains. Specifically, ministers from these three countries approached Vice Foreign Minister Hayashi Tadasu and suggested in the most unambiguous way that Japan should renounce its claim to the Liaotung Peninsula. Well aware of the naval power these three countries possessed in Far Eastern waters, particularly Russia, Japan's leaders clearly understood the true nature of the suggestion or at least the implications of refusing the established imperialists' requests. Without the diplomatic, political, or military support of either Britain or the United States, Japan faced little choice and retroceded the territory in question to China for an additional 30 million taels (roughly ¥45 million). Victory, while elevating Japan's status in the Far East, further entangled the country in imperial rivalries in East Asia and the Pacific. This factor, combined with the political and popular capital gained as a result of the war, encouraged popular and elite-level support for naval expansion in the postwar world. Naval leaders quickly sought to capitalize on pro-navy sentiment.

Postwar Naval Expansion

With the political and psychological shock of the Triple Intervention still resonating with the public, political, and military elites, the navy wasted no time in preparing postwar expansion plans. In May 1895, Saigō asked Yamamoto, in his new position as Chief of the Naval Affairs Bureau of the Navy Ministry, to compose a study of Japan's future naval needs.[10] Sensing that a great opportunity existed to secure significant fleet expansion, Yamamoto approached this task with unrelenting enthusiasm.[11] Believing that the public would support naval expansion in the wake of Japan's glorious victory, and assuming that political leaders would support it out of obvious necessity after the Triple Intervention, Yamamoto devised a truly revolutionary plan that, if accepted by the cabinet and the parliament, would fundamentally transform the navy into a world-class military fleet.[12] A number of political, budgetary, and military aspects made Yamamoto's plan revolutionary. For one, Yamamoto suggested that Japan purchase and construct a balanced fleet that could act (fight) as a well-unified force. Yamamoto was not, as previous ministers had done, asking for a few battleships or cruisers to augment Japan's existing forces but rather was seeking to assemble a modern fleet from the waterline up. Moreover, Yamamoto understood that all Japan's shore facilities would also need significant upgrades to accommodate and maintain the requested fleet. To oversee this, Yamamoto recommended the establishment of a naval construction bureau to administer and regulate all shore-based development.[13]

The sheer size and modernity of Yamamoto's proposed fleet was revolutionary as well. Quantitatively, Yamamoto's program was immense; the Chief of the Naval Affairs Bureau proposed adding sixteen capital warships to Japan's navy: four battleships in addition to the two already under construction in Britain, six first-class cruisers, three second-class cruisers, and three third-class cruisers.[14] Besides these vessels, the expansion plan called for an additional twenty-three destroyers and sixty-three torpedo boats. Total displacement of all the warships sought was just over 234,000 tons, which equaled a 70-percent increase in the size of the navy as it stood in 1895. Size, however, was not the only revolutionary aspect of the plan. The vast majority of the warships desired by Yamamoto, roughly 90 percent, would be built in British shipyards and would be state-of-the-art. The four battleships proposed in Yamamoto's plan, later named the *Shikishima*, the *Hatsue*, the *Asahi*, and the *Mikasa*, would match any foreign vessel of the same type afloat in 1898.[15] The same held true for the proposed cruisers, destroyers, and torpedo boats. Clearly, Yamamoto's proposal called for a modern fleet that would not only inspire awe and protect Japan's shoreline but also make it possible to extend Japanese power overseas and protect its colonial interests in East Asia. Such a fleet would not come cheap, however. Yamamoto budgeted nearly ¥215 million for the ten years of his proposed program. To put this figure in perspective, ¥215 million was nearly double the entire amount expended on the Japanese navy from 1868 to 1893.

Both Yamamoto and Navy Minister Saigō assumed that securing support for this revolutionary plan would require considerable political effort. To this end, Saigō prepared himself well for debate when he introduced the proposed expansion plan to the cabinet in July 1895. In the months before Saigō introduced Yamamoto's plan, the navy minister asked Yamamoto to prepare a detailed series of position papers with which he could legitimate such a significant naval increase to the government.[16] Yamamoto did not disappoint his superior. After outlining the expansion request, Saigō used the proposals written by Yamamoto to justify his requests to the cabinet. First, Saigō stated that the primary aim of the navy was to command the waters surrounding Japan and its empire, not merely to defend Japan's home islands from possible aggression. To accomplish this, the navy minister asserted, Japan must possess a modern fleet with state-of-the-art battle-ships at its core. To fend off any suggestion that Japan should purchase only battleships, Saigō forcefully argued that battleships alone would be ineffec-tive in providing naval defense. They must, the navy minister argued, be part—a central but not exclusive part—of a balanced battle fleet. This, he claimed, was the lesson of the Sino-Japanese War. Saigō followed his dis-cussion with excruciatingly specific justifications for each type of vessel re-quested, from the battleships down to the torpedo boats. Yamamoto's po-sition papers in support of the fleet-expansion request were remarkable in their detail, logic, and persuasion.

Navy Minister Saigō did not end his discussion at this point, however. After justifying why each type of ship was critically important to Japan, he next legitimated the immense scale of the expansion request.[17] Drawing on another group of papers written by Yamamoto, Saigō argued that Japan must base its navy not just on the strength of its most likely enemy, Russia, but on a combination of two countries that could send their fleets, or part of them, to East Asian waters. Japan, Saigō continued, needed an East Asian two-power standard: this was how the figure of six battleships and support vessels had been decided. Anything less, and Japan's security would be impaired.[18] The specifics appear in Table 2.

While cabinet ministers digested the sheer scale of the proposal pre-sented by the navy minister, Saigō issued an important caveat. This plan, he concluded, if implemented, could safeguard Japan and allow it to establish control of the surrounding sea under *present* circumstances. But, the experi-enced minister stated, "if we increase our [naval] power, so will others. It will be endless."[19] Saigō therefore reasoned or, more precisely, warned that this plan, however expensive, would likely be just the beginning of naval re-quests and certainly not the be-all and end-all of naval expansion in Japan. Japan's development as a naval power in an era of rapidly evolving naval technology and international naval expansion would require a continuing commitment. This was a bold but brutally honest assessment. Once Japan embarked on a course of naval expansion, Saigō reiterated at the close of his presentation, Japan's navy would be compelled to match naval increases adopted by the foreign powers, and if future cabinets ignored future ex-pansion requests, Japan's security could simply not be guaranteed. This was a prescient prediction.

Despite such bold, unambiguous warnings concerning a potential naval arms race, the navy minister's words fell on receptive ears. The cabinet wholeheartedly agreed that Yamamoto's plan must serve as the basis for

TABLE 2

Japanese Warship Construction: Term 1 and Term 2 Naval Expansion Programs Submitted to and Accepted by the Diet in Its Ninth and Tenth Sessions, 28 Dec. 1895 to 29 Mar. 1896 and 25 Dec. to 24 Mar. 1897

Warship type	Number (displacement in tons)
First-class steel battleships	4 (15,500)
First-class cruisers	6 (9,200)
Second-class cruisers	3 (4,800)
Third-class cruisers	3 (3,400)
Torpedo gunboats	1 (1,200)
Torpedo depot vessels	1 (800)
Destroyers	23
First-class torpedo boats	16
Second-class torpedo boats	37
Third-class torpedo boats	10
TOTAL SHIPS	
Capital warships	16
Destroyers and torpedo boats	88
TOTAL COST	¥213,100,964

SOURCE: Ko Hakushaku Yamamoto kaigun taishō denki hensankai (Count Yamamoto biographical compilation association), *Yamamoto Gonnohyōe den* (Biography of Yamamoto Gonnohyōe), 2 vols. (Tokyo: Ko Hakushaku Yamamoto kaigun taishō denki hensankai, 1938): 1:421.

naval defense in Japan. This was indeed a good day for the Japanese navy. Through Yamamoto's considerable efforts, and to a lesser extent Saigō's, it had secured cabinet-level support to assemble a fleet that in just under ten years would decimate the Russian East Asiatic and Baltic squadrons. Less than three months after that political and budgetary victory, true to his warning, Saigō asked for further appropriations to support the purchase of newly designed armored cruisers, warships outside the original plan that Yamamoto had devised in 1895. This plan too, fell on receptive ears, and within the year, both the cabinet and the parliament endorsed the new naval-expansion proposal, referred to as the "Term-Two Naval Expansion Bill."[20] Long dreamed of by every naval leader since Katsu Kaishū, expansions as articulated by the Term-One and Term-Two Expansion Programs were one step closer to reality. All that was left to accomplish was to gain support from Japan's parliament. Given the pre–Sino-Japanese War history of naval dealings with parliament, this looked to be no easy task.

In January 1896, Itō submitted to the Diet the largest military-expansion budget in the history of Japan to that date, an expansion plan with a total price tag of ¥280 million. Out of this total, naval expansion accounted for just over ¥200 million, to be disbursed over the following ten years. Remarkably, with little to no dissent, on 4 February the lower house of parliament endorsed the military-expansion plan.[21] To Saigō and Yamamoto, who had earlier experienced firsthand the effects of a Diet opposed to naval increases, the events of 1896 must have come as a startling though not at all unpleasant surprise. A number of domestic and international factors made naval expansion not only palatable but a priority both within the cabinet and in the Diet after 1895. First, through pragmatic dealings with Itagaki, the leader of the Jiyūtō, Prime Minister Itō secured his commitment to support the government on the issue of military and naval expansion. In July 1895, when the cabinet discussed Saigō and Yamamoto's proposal, Foreign Minister Mutsu called on Takenouchi Tsuna to organize a meeting between Itō and Itagaki.[22] The men met on 27 August, and Itagaki vowed to work with the government in the forthcoming Diet session in exchange for assurances that Itō would select Itagaki for a ministerial position during the next cabinet reshuffle.[23] By the summer of 1895, Itagaki understood the importance of compromise within Japan's parliamentary system. Access to the upper echelons of the polity required the good will and graces of Japan's ruling oligarchs, and in the Diet opposition for its own sake was no way to win elite-level supporters.[24] Itagaki thereafter urged his fellow Jiyūtō members to support the government in all parliamentary proceedings in the ninth session of the Diet (December 1895 to March 1896), particularly in regard to naval expansion, the issue that had so bitterly divided the government and the parliament in pre–Sino-Japanese War Diet sessions. Such political pragmatism and bargaining would yield better results than Itō anticipated. During the last two weeks of November, Itagaki made a series of public and private speeches in which he urged all parliamentarians and citizens to support the forthcoming naval and military expansion proposals. Naval expansion, in the words of Itagaki, was a necessity.[25]

The navy's expansion plan was well received by the rank and file Jiyūtō members for a number of reasons apart from Itagaki's support, however. For one, the government proposed to use money secured from the Chinese indemnity to fund the lion's share of the naval expansion, roughly ¥139 million, with public loans and existing government revenue to provide the rest of the money over the ten years of the program.[26] This meant that no increase in the land tax, at least in 1895–96, was needed to support naval increases, a fact that was critically important in securing widespread parliamentary support. The government did, however, propose a tax increase on sake and tobacco to pay for additional operating expenses that would accompany fleet expansion, but as before, these taxes proved far less controversial, since many M.P.'s saw these taxes for what they were—luxury taxes.

Apart from funding, the other issue that had hindered naval expansion in pre–Sino-Japanese War parliaments, naval corruption, likewise disappeared in the years immediately after the war. With the navy's stunning wartime victories, representatives lost the political will or desire (or both) to question the navy's fighting ability. This is not to say that Yamamoto let his reforming zeal diminish after the war. Rather, building on the earlier personnel reforms, Yamamoto again sought to replace a large number of older officers who had escaped the political purges of 1893–94. With an eye toward expanding opportunities of younger, better-trained officers to fill the navy's expanding fleet, Yamamoto instituted a second round of forced retirements. A remarkable feature of this program was the speed and insensitivity with which Yamamoto eliminated these redundancies. Employing a novel technology, Yamamoto had the retirement notices copied via hectograph, a primitive sort of mimeograph machine, leaving only the officers' names to be written by hand in a blank space near the top.[27] Corruption would not again be a parliamentary issue used against the navy until the Siemens Scandal of 1914.

Political, personnel, and financial considerations aside, military expansion by other countries with interests in East Asia and the Pacific also motivated party politicians to transcend purely parochial concerns and support naval increases. East Asia in the mid- to late 1890s had become a very dangerous and well-armed area of the globe. Throughout 1895–96, Russia reinforced Vladivostok with troops and warships, and this, coupled with concessions the tsar's representatives gained in China through diplomatic negotiations, heightened concern in Japan that Russia sought control over Manchuria, a position from which it could threaten Japan's interests in Korea. Through diplomatic negotiations Russia specifically secured from China permission to extend the Trans-Siberian Railway across Manchuria to Vladivostok. Moreover, the Russians gained the right to build a rail spur from Mukden in Manchuria to Newchang on the Liaotung Peninsula. Last, and most important from a political and psychological standpoint, the Russians secured many of the same rights to the Liaotung Peninsula that Japan had earlier secured through war before being forced under threat to retrocede this territory to China in 1895. Viewed from Japan, Russian expansion in the Far East meant one thing—trouble: not only for Japan's interests in Korea but for the home islands as well if Korea were to fall under Russian control.

A remarkable transformation had thus occurred in Japan. Diet representatives who had in 1893 fought to restrict expansion of the navy by a mere three warships now strongly endorsed the largest expansion plan ever presented, a plan which enlarged the navy by thirteen capital warships and more than seventy-five auxiliary craft. Such was the impact of war, a sizable indemnity, the emergence of elite-level political pragmatism, and continued naval reform along the lines that parliamentarians had requested in the early years of the decade. While naval leaders were quick to capitalize on the auspicious postwar environment, their successes did not go unnoticed by the army, and neither did the fact that in 1897, for the first time in Japanese history, the navy's annual appropriations exceeded the army's. Indeed, many army leaders saw their service's privileged financial and political position challenged for the first time by what they still considered Japan's second service. Such a condition greatly exacerbated existing interservice tensions.

Navy-Army Rivalry, Phase I: Military Organization and War, 1894–1898

Interservice rivalry had existed at one level or another in Japan since the beginning of the Meiji state. During and after the War of Restoration, healthy competition between the two major *han*, Chōshū and Satsuma, influenced relations between the land and maritime forces of the new government. Although many early naval leaders had previously held positions within the army, both services grew increasingly competitive from the mid- to late 1880s onward. As each service grew in size and developed its own distinct strategic identity and outlook, rivalry evolved from a geographically based competition to one which revolved around matters of greater significance: specifically, matters of military organization and command, imperial expansion, and most important of all, budgets.

The first significant area in which rivalry surfaced and developed into an open dispute surrounded military organization, independence, and command. Throughout the 1880s and early 1890s, successive navy ministers, vice ministers, and former ministers, including Kawamura, Kabayama, Nire, and Saigō, pressed for complete organizational autonomy for the navy.[28] Specifically, these leaders argued for the formation of an independent Navy General Staff that was equal in all powers and privileges to the Army General Staff. Though the navy gained administrative independence in 1872, naval commanders held sole responsibility only over military affairs designated as maritime or coastal defense, while the army held responsibility for the larger and more important concern of national defense.[29] The army's chief of staff therefore served as chief of staff for the entire armed forces, and accordingly controlled all naval forces in time of war. To up-and-coming naval leaders, particularly Saigō's protégé Yamamoto, who was trained in modern naval strategy and tactics, such a regulation was a bureaucratic and institutional insult. Seeking complete bureaucratic equality and suggesting that army officers trained in land combat did not possess adequate tactical or strategic training to properly employ naval forces in war, Yamamoto lobbied the government for a change in the existing military organizational structure in 1892–93. Ironically, parliamentarians who assisted Yamamoto in this effort had argued vociferously for the separation of command and administration in the navy during the naval expansion debates between 1891 and 1893. Though army leaders initially balked at such arguments, with Katsura Tarō claiming that the existing system was adequate because, in his opinion, "the army decides the fate of Japan [and] . . . the navy supports [the army]," both services agreed to a compromise in May 1893.[30] Bowing to domestic parliamentary pressure, naval leadership's desires, and common military sense, the government agreed to create an independent Navy General Staff whose leader possessed the right of direct access to the emperor. Importantly for the army, however, the Army General Staff remained responsible for overall national defense planning and retained command and control over naval forces in time of war so as to avoid possible wartime friction between two military staffs planning and directing combat forces.[31] Though not ideal, this settlement provided Yamamoto with a limited bureaucratic victory, and as army leaders soon realized, further independence, however restricted, fostered further rivalry.

Within a year, Yamamoto again pressed for total naval command independence from the army. Timing was not a coincidence. In the spring of 1894, when the military establishment was making preparations for a potential war with China, Yamamoto saw what he believed was an ideal opportunity to exact concessions from the army. Believing that prewar mobilization would give the navy greater leverage to exact concessions from the army, which depended on his service for transport, Yamamoto seized the initiative. In May 1894, Saigō's secretariat lobbied cabinet members to grant full military independence to the Navy General Staff.[32] Army officials and cabinet ministers did not rush to endorse such a purely political and entirely opportunistic move, however. The cabinet, in fact, quickly rejected Yamamoto's request, but this did little to slow Yamamoto. At a cabinet meeting in June 1894, just prior to hostilities with China, Yamamoto expressed both anger and frustration at the cabinet's decision and directed much of his criticism at his childhood friend the vice chief of the Army

General Staff, Kawakami Sōroku. What particularly angered Yamamoto was that Kawakami had devised plans for naval support of army operations without consulting the navy at all. Moreover, upon reading the army's plans, Yamamoto realized that army planners had never considered the necessity of securing command of the sea before sending troop transports from Japan to Korea. This flew in the face of all maritime strategy and deeply unnerved Yamamoto. To show his concern and frustration, Yamamoto pointedly asked Kawakami a simple but loaded question: "Is it true the army has engineers?" Taken aback, Kawakami replied: "Yes . . . of course we do." To this, Yamamoto responded, with no little sarcasm: "Then it should be no trouble [for you] to build a bridge from Yokubo in Kyushu to Tsushima, and then to Pusan in Korea, to now send our army to the continent."[33] Yamamoto followed this exchange with a short presentation aimed as much at revealing the general's lack of maritime expertise or naval experience as at showcasing his own. Throughout, Yamamoto implied that the army leader did not possess the requisite skill or training to command naval forces in war. This fact, Yamamoto concluded, could have devastating consequences in a war with a country that possessed a modern, well-trained, militarily potent navy. Though this presentation did not succeed in securing command independence for the Navy General Staff, it certainly illuminated the growing bureaucratic tension between the two services. Hoping to stem such internal bickering, Emperor Meiji encouraged both services to work together during the war in order to "avoid friction or error."[34]

For the most part, institutional rivalry during the Sino-Japanese War did not significantly hinder Japan's war effort, as General Tanaka Gi'ichi later claimed about operations conducted ten years later during the Russo-Japanese War. Differing strategic outlooks, however, fueled significant debate over the direction and nature of Japan's final push against China.[35] Yamagata Aritomo, commander of the First Army, supported a policy best described as *Advance in the North; Hold in the South*. Specifically, he endorsed a plan whereby troops under his command would advance toward the Chinese capital in autumn 1894. This policy was not well received either by the navy, whose leaders saw little value in further expansion on the mainland, or by certain members of the cabinet, who feared that such a move might invite possible foreign intervention if Japanese troops occupied Peking. Prime Minister Itō thus agreed to support a policy favored by the navy, of advance in the south toward Taiwan and the Pescadores Islands while holding in the north. Believing that Yamagata, commanding the First Army in

Manchuria, might protest any decision that kept his forces from advancing on Peking, on 29 November Itō obtained an Imperial Ordinance recalling Yamagata from the front. With Yamagata back in Japan, the cabinet attempted to forge a clear policy for the remaining military activities of the war. Five days later, members of the Imperial General Headquarters agreed that the army would hold in the north while the navy, with army support, would invade the Shantung Peninsula and the Pescadores Islands as a precursor to an invasion of Taiwan.[36]

This proved to be an important victory for the navy in 1895, one that would have important political and military ramifications well after the war. While Prime Minister Itō's own motives for occupying Taiwan may not have been to gain a stepping stone for further expansion, whether territorial or economic, or to allow the navy a chance to secure further military glory, this was precisely how certain naval leaders viewed the occupation of Taiwan.[37] In contrast to Japan's earlier expedition to Taiwan in 1874, in 1894 the navy played a critical role in the Taiwan operation. From the beginning of hostilities with China, naval officials, particularly Navy Minister Saigō, argued for a military move against Taiwan and the neighboring Pescadores Islands.[38] Having participated in the 1874 Taiwan Expedition, Saigō was desirous of finally securing the rights to these territories.[39] While the navy's imperial ambitions were held in abeyance throughout much of the war, Japanese forces landed on Taiwan on 25 March 1895, five days before Japan and China agreed to a cease-fire. At the ensuing peace negotiations, the navy made clear its determination to retain Taiwan, a territory which naval leaders considered far more vital than the Liaotung Peninsula.[40] At the end of the negotiations, the navy received what it wanted in the Treaty of Shimonoseki, which granted Japan formal rights to the island, whereupon Itō appointed former navy minister Kabayama as Japan's first governor-general of Taiwan. Taiwan thereafter became widely regarded as an important territory within the nebulous confines of the South Seas.[41] Importantly for the navy, whose leaders had since the 1870s demonstrated a keen interest in South Seas exploration and expansion, Taiwan would assume first an imaginary and then a tangible position as a stepping stone for further southern advance.[42] As Takekoshi Yosaburō, southern-advance advocate, Diet politician, and pro-navy enthusiast, would later write in 1907: "As the Southern Cross seems to invite the mariner to investigate the wonders of the Southern Seas, so our successes in Formosa beckon us on to fulfill the great destiny that lies before us, and make our country Queen of the Pacific."[43] Rich in potential, Taiwan and coastal southern China would later be at the center of an intense exchange between Army Minister Katsura and Navy Minister Yamamoto in 1900. But before this, domestic tensions again took center stage.

Navy-Army Rivalry, II: Domestic Politics and Imperial Expansion, 1898–1900

In the years following the Sino-Japanese War, interservice rivalry became far more common and pronounced than it had been prior to that conflict. Less than a month after assuming administrative leadership over the navy as navy minister in Yamagata Aritomo's second cabinet (1898–1900), Yamamoto pushed further for naval equality with the army by proposing an organizational change to the Imperial General Headquarters (IGHQ), an organization assembled in time of war to plan and direct military operations. Specifically, Yamamoto wanted to alter the regulations that governed the appointment of the IGHQ's chief. What precipitated Yamamoto's action was the fact that since the formation of the IGHQ, the chief of the Army General Staff had automatically served as its head, without any formal selection process. This, Yamamoto argued, discriminated against the navy. To remedy this, Yamamoto suggested that the law of appointment be changed so as to allow any general or flag-rank officer (i.e., admiral) to be eligible for the post.[44] The army, however, led by Katsura, immediately challenged Yamamoto's initiative. Katsura argued that it was entirely logical for the chief of the Army General Staff to head the IGHQ, since the army was the main guarantor of national security, and that the navy's primary role was one of support. The actors involved in this performance were the same who had embroiled themselves in the controversy surrounding Yamamoto's attempts to secure complete independence for the Navy General Staff earlier in the decade. Faced with opposition yet again from Katsura as well as Yamagata, Yamamoto took an unusual course of action at this juncture that betrayed both his exasperation with the army and the degree of self-confidence this naval leader possessed. He sent his reform proposal and Katsura's reply directly to the emperor in hopes that he would side with the navy and order the changes that Yamamoto suggested. This was a bold move, and to further legitimate his claims that the navy possessed an independent strategic and military rationale distinct from the army's, Yamamoto included a number of position papers that articulated the navy's emergent navalist ideology, one influenced by the works of Alfred Mahan and John and Philip Colomb.[45] The navy, Yamamoto suggested, was not just a wartime auxiliary to the army but rather an independent organization that possessed a distinct rationale and mission. Moreover, Navy Minister Yamamoto used this opportunity to reiterate three important points: that maritime defense was more critical for Japan's economic security, that a loss of control of the seas around Japan could well lead to devastation of the home islands, and that army-navy cooperation (i.e., army use of navy vessels to transport soldiers) was viable only after the navy had already met and defeated any naval threat to Japan. Thus, in Yamamoto's opinion, naval matters took precedence in peacetime as well as in war. On these grounds, Yamamoto asserted that it was critically important for the IGHQ commander to be fully versed in the most up-to-date theories regarding naval power, as few if any army leaders were in 1898. Emperor Meiji's personal reaction to Yamamoto's proposals is not known, but he soon replied to ministers of both the army and the navy that the issue should be left for future consideration.[46] While Meiji's equivocation ended this chapter of interservice competition, at least temporarily, many other fault lines soon emerged.

An important and unexplored factor that furthered this tension was the terse and often confrontational personal relationship that developed between Yamamoto and Katsura, who became ministers of their respective services in 1898. In his recent biography of Katsura, Stewart Lone suggests that Yamamoto was one of the few people immune to Katsura's charm and political style. While accurate, this is a polite understatement. Yamamoto and Katsura fought bitterly throughout most of their careers. This can be explained partly by the fact that each man, as a rising second-generation military leader in the increasingly bureaucratized state, saw the other as a bureaucratic rival and competitor to his own ministry and service in general. Their rivalry, however, was also personal. Party politician Ozaki Yukio, who described Yamamoto as a formidable adversary whose stature surpassed that of Yamagata, recalled that Yamamoto often exhibited blatant disrespect to Katsura, both in the army leader's presence and behind his back.[47] Moreover, Ozaki claimed that Yamamoto often referred to Katsura by his name without title and at times answered questions asked of Katsura at cabinet meetings before Katsura could answer for himself.

Personal antagonisms came to a head in the spring of 1900 and for a time, significantly altered cabinet politics. In May, Yamagata Aritomo privately announced his intention to step down as prime minister and suggested that Katsura be given the opportunity to form the next cabinet. While Katsura was Yamagata's choice, he was certainly not someone that

Yamamoto supported for the position. Upon hearing Yamagata's recommendation, Yamamoto quickly went on the defensive. Fearing that Katsura's partisanship might threaten naval leaders' initiatives to strengthen both the organization and financial position of the navy, and desirous of keeping his rival from holding the office of prime minister, Yamamoto vigorously campaigned against the army minister's appointment. Clearly hoping to appeal to Yamagata's patriotism, Yamamoto argued that Japan needed a statesman of Yamagata's stature to guide the country while revolution engulfed China during the Boxer Rebellion. Yamagata's leadership, the navy minister suggested, was made all the more necessary by the fact that foreign intervention might result if Chinese authorities could not quell the uprising. In this instance, flattery worked, and Yamagata remained as prime minister.

Yamagata's decision, however, did little to reduce army-navy rivalry. Yamamoto and Katsura again found themselves at loggerheads in the summer of 1900, this time concerning which service would take the initiative and retain operational control in dealing with the antiforeign demonstrations that developed in southern China. In cabinet debates over whether to land troops near Amoy, in Fukien Province, to protect Japanese nationals, Yamamoto at least in the early part of the crisis took a rather cautious approach. In short, Yamamoto feared that large-scale foreign intervention might provoke further antiforeign riots aimed at foreign residents and their political representatives in China.[48] If this in turn led to greater intervention, Japan's defense priorities would shift further to the continent and away from the navy's Pacific and South China Sea concerns. As disturbances became more widespread over late July and August, however, Yamamoto lost faith in China's ability to quell the disturbances and reversed course. At the urging of Vice Navy Minister Saitō Makoto, the navy minister readied marines (*rikusentai*) on ships near Amoy ready to land in order to protect Japanese residents "if some pretext arose."[49] Soon after, Yamamoto took an even more opportunistic line, ordering the captain of the warship *Izumi* "not to lag behind if other foreign powers land[ed] at Amoy" and, if necessary, to "land troops at his own discretion."[50] What made these orders extraordinary was the fact that Yamamoto had issued them without having first secured cabinet approval or consent. When Yamagata and Army Minister Katsura learned of Yamamoto's orders, both men immediately challenged and criticized them. At a meeting which included Prime Minister Yamagata, Navy Minister Yamamoto, Army Minister Katsura, and Chief of the Army General Staff Ōyama Iwao, Katsura bitterly attacked Yamamoto's actions as entirely unjustifiable. Katsura further suggested that if any troops were to be landed at all, they would be army troops dispatched from Taiwan.[51] Yamamoto responded that his intention was not for the marines to occupy Amoy but rather for them to land solely in order to protect consular staff and public officials. This, he claimed, was normal practice and as such did not need cabinet-level endorsement.

Criticism erupted into open hostility on 24 August, when marines landed to protect Japanese officials. Dispatched on the pretext that Japanese citizens were in peril after antiforeign-inspired rebels razed a Japanese temple in Amoy, the landing provoked greater unrest both in Amoy and, importantly, in Tokyo.[52] On 27 August, Army Minister Katsura ordered Taiwan's Governor General Kodama Gentarō to dispatch one infantry battalion, two artillery battalions, and one engineering battalion from the island for operations in and around Amoy.[53] Significantly, following Yamamoto's lead, Katsura failed to consult the navy minister. Once informed, Yamamoto vigorously protested and at a meeting at the foreign minister's residence argued that the marines could handle the situation without interference from the army, something he saw as mere meddling. Implying that the navy's initial action and resultant failure to control the disturbance necessitated army intervention, Katsura looked both to have the army assume operational control over the situation and, importantly, to slight the navy. A terse exchange followed between Katsura and Yamamoto, in which Yamamoto held his ground.[54]

A number of factors motivated Yamamoto to aggressively fend off Katsura's challenge. To begin with, Yamamoto did not want the situation in Amoy to escalate, and he feared that army troops might provoke similar action by other foreign countries. On a more parochial note, the navy minister clearly did not want the army to gain either a foothold in southern China or the glory of protecting Japanese citizens after marines had already landed. Yamamoto therefore first requested and then demanded that Katsura or the army chief of staff revoke the army's dispatch order. Both Katsura and Oyama refused, however, and again reiterated that the initial dispatch of marines had been conducted without the cabinet's approval. Yamamoto again denied that the marines were planning to occupy Amoy, but faced with this opposition the navy minister issued a warning to the army that could be interpreted in only one way: back down. He stated:[55]

> If an imperial battleship were to come across a ship of armed forces steaming toward Amoy and mistake it for a pirate ship [*kaizokusen*] and shots were fired, there would be no grounds for criticizing the action of the battleship. The navy

would be justified in dealing with a pirate ship in accordance with international law.

For a man who Ozaki Yukio claimed could strike terror in one's heart, this was a chilling oration. The following day, 28 August, the government recalled the army transport ships, leaving only vessels of the Imperial Japanese Navy in close proximity to Amoy.[56] Yamamoto's steel resolve silenced the army.

Navy-Army Rivalry, III: Domestic Politics, Military Expansion, and War, 1900–1904

Dispute over South China aside, tensions between Yamamoto and Katsura also seriously complicated domestic politics in the years after 1900. Seeing Katsura's eventual ascendancy to the office of prime minister as inevitable, in 1901, when Katsura again sought this position, Yamamoto followed a different course than the complete opposition and resistance that he had exhibited earlier, in the summer of 1900. In 1901, Yamamoto supported the army general's candidacy, but with one important condition: that Katsura would not only support another proposed naval expansion program but would spearhead the navy's campaign for increased appropriations in the Diet.[57] This was an offer that Katsura could not refuse. If the would-be prime minister demurred, Yamamoto intimated he would refuse to serve as navy minister and, importantly, would prohibit any of his subordinates from filling the position. Since Katsura required a full cabinet to assume power, such an action on Yamamoto's part would thus eliminate any chance for him to form a cabinet. This was an ingenious move, a tactic which the army later used against Prime Minister Saionji in 1912, precipitating the Taishō Political Crisis.

In giving his support to Katsura's cabinet, Yamamoto wanted one thing in return: naval expansion that would commence after the Term-Two Expansion Program ended. Yamamoto's ultimatum placed Katsura in an unenviable political position and widened further, if possible, the political rift between both men. On the one hand, if he wanted to become prime minister, Katsura would undoubtedly need to acquiesce to Yamamoto's demands. On the other hand, Katsura realized that if he accepted the navy minister's conditions, he would face fierce parliamentary opposition to new military expansion. Katsura would therefore be required to expend considerable political capital to secure support for naval expansion. If these difficulties were not enough, two other factors made Katsura's position more problematic. First, Katsura had just three years earlier vociferously challenged a previous expansion plan proposed by Yamamoto that called for the navy to automatically expand up to half the displacement tonnage of all foreign navies which maintained fleets in Far Eastern waters. He, as well as other leaders, rejected this plan on two grounds: first, as a result of this proposed plan, the navy would have been forced to expand to 350,000 tons' displacement, a figure nearly double the size of an already increasingly large navy; and second, it was politically impossible, owing to the budgetary powers of the Diet.[58] Though he expected Yamamoto's new expansion plan for 1902 to be smaller in scale, it would still require significant funding. An about-face by Katsura was sure to be noticed and used by parliamentarians opposed to yet another expensive naval expansion. Therein lay the second difficulty that Katsura faced—money. Estimates put Yamamoto's proposed expansion plan in the neighborhood of nearly ¥115 million, to be dispersed over ten years from 1903 to 1913. This was no small amount, and since most observers believed that funding would have to come from increased taxes because a large portion of the Chinese indemnity had previously been spent on earlier naval expansion, many predicted a bitter parliamentary struggle.[59] This was clearly not the most opportune time for Katsura to form his first cabinet.

Despite bleak parliamentary prospects, Katsura accepted Yamamoto's condition and assumed the office of prime minister in May 1901. When budgetary negotiations commenced in earnest the following year, naval expansion emerged as the issue of concern if not contention within the cabinet. On 27 October 1902, Yamamoto introduced a ¥150-million ten-year expansion plan, to be commenced in 1903.[60] Specifically, the navy minister argued that the money requested would be used to purchase three battleships displacing 15,000 tons each and three armored cruisers displacing 10,000 tons each, and to buy or pay for the construction of various support vessels. The funds requested, so Yamamoto declared, would also be used to upgrade Japan's naval bases and shipyards. When challenged as to why the navy needed yet further expansion two years before the completion of the Term-Two Expansion Program (1895–1905), Yamamoto argued that foreign naval growth was quickly outpacing Japan's. While Japan possessed the world's fourth-largest navy in 1901 in terms of armored battleships and cruisers, Yamamoto suggested that by 1908 Japan would find itself ranked eighth, behind all the major powers, including Italy. Expansion, he thus claimed, was essential on strategic grounds. Yamamoto also raised another point which future naval leaders would continue to raise in support of naval expansion: the economic and industrial benefits of naval growth.[61] Specifically, Yamamoto suggested that the navy's orders for support vessels in domestic shipyards, both navy yards and private yards, would spur the shipbuilding industry in Japan and strengthen Japan's economy.

When the cabinet adjourned that afternoon without reaching any decision on the naval expansion issue, Yamamoto redoubled his efforts. In an unaccustomed maneuver, the navy minister drew up a position paper on behalf of his proposed expansion plan and presented it to the emperor.[62] Admitting that he had assembled his submission in great haste, Yamamoto expressed the grave importance of naval strength to imperial defense. Yamamoto also articulated how grateful he, the navy, and ultimately the nation were to previous imperial interventions that had led to naval increases. This was a bold political move, one that caught Katsura and other cabinet ministers by surprise. In a cabinet meeting on the day of Yamamoto's submission, 28 October, the cabinet agreed to seek Diet appropriations of ¥100 million for naval expansion to be implemented the following year.[63]

Though the cabinet agreed to support the navy's proposal after only two days of debate, securing passage through the Diet proved far more problematic. Even before parliament officially opened, party leaders and M.P.'s expressed concern over how Katsura intended to pay for naval expansion. On 7 November 1902, Hara Kei attempted to persuade the president of the newly formed Seiyūkai political party, Itō Hirobumi, to oppose any increase in the rate of land tax.[64] While Hara expressed no opposition to naval expansion in principle, he argued that funding could be granted after further government and ministerial retrenchment of finances. Hara was not alone in his opposition to increased taxes. Seiyūkai branch committees throughout Japan met in late November, and many passed resolutions against supporting any tax increase.[65] In response, at a cabinet meeting on 28 November, Katsura demanded cabinet unity in the face of what was sure to be united opposition in the Diet.[66] Specifically, Katsura stated that he would seek to make permanent a previously agreed-upon increase in the land tax (from 2.5 to 3.5 percent) that was due to expire, claiming such funds could provide the necessary finances to support naval increases.

When parliament opened on 9 December 1902, M.P.'s went on the offensive against Katsura after he introduced his naval financing bill. On the one hand, earlier opponents of naval expansion such as Sugita Tei'ichi challenged the naval increases on the grounds that the newly signed Anglo-Japanese Alliance of 1902 afforded Japan an opportunity to slow the pace of naval expansion.[67] Sugita was not alone in holding this position. Hara Kei, a pragmatic politician who would come to hold significant—even unmatched—power in the Seiyūkai, also shared Sugita's opinion, at least initially.[68] At a meeting of the Lower House Budget Committee on 10 December, Sugita argued that Britain was now bound to support Japan if the latter were to be attacked by a coalition of two or more powers, thus reducing the urgency for Japan's navy to match a combined threat from Russia and either Germany or France. Was the Anglo-Japanese Alliance not in place to make-up for naval deficiencies of each power? asked Sugita.[69] Later in the session, on 16 December, speaking before the full lower house, other Diet members such as Shimada Saburō and Ozaki Yukio challenged the plan on more practical budgetary grounds. Declaring that he was not opposed to naval expansion in theory, Ozaki demanded that the government find funding for this new expenditure while at the same time reducing the rate of land tax.[70] The land tax, concluded Ozaki, could not be used to pay for increased state expenditures (which he claimed were rising by 20 percent per year) on a continuing basis.

To stem the attack, Navy Minister Yamamoto appeared before parliament on 13 December. During his address, Yamamoto argued that no other source of funding currently existed that could provide the money necessary to implement immediate naval expansion.[71] Moreover, Yamamoto reiterated the urgency of his ministry's request, claiming that future national defense could be secured only through immediate increases in the size of the navy. While M.P. Ozaki again agreed that naval expansion was vital to the nation, he simply demanded that other sources of funding be found to implement the much-needed expansion program.[72] After heated debate, both the Lower House Budget Committee and the entire lower house of parliament rejected Katsura's financing scheme.

Faced with opposition from the Diet and demands from a navy minister who threatened to resign unless naval expansion was approved, Katsura possessed two credible options concerning a resolution of the naval expansion issue. He could either shelve the program and face the collapse of his cabinet from within, or he could prorogue the parliament in an attempt to reach an eventual agreement with the opposition political parties. The prime minister followed the latter course. Throughout December Katsura repeatedly prorogued the Diet to buy time to work out a compromise. During mid- to late December Katsura sought to reach a compromise with party leaders in the Diet. On 25 December, Katsura and Yamamoto met Hara Kei and Matsuda Masahisa of the Seiyūkai and Ōishi Masami and Inukai Tsūyoshi of the Kensei Hontō to hammer out a solution. Though

Kastura suggested that he would be willing to lower the proposed land-tax rate from 3.5 to 3.3 percent, party men still demanded that the rate be reduced back to its original 2.5 percent.[73] Party leaders refused to accept this proposal, and Katsura, unable to reach a compromise, dissolved the parliament on 28 December 1902, hoping that elections would result in a more favorable political environment.[74]

Immediately thereafter, Katsura and other cabinet ministers turned their attention toward reaching a compromise with Itō Hirobumi, president of the Seiyūkai. Katsura and Yamamoto believed that Itō was more committed to the smooth functioning of parliament, and thus would be more likely to reach a compromise, than Hara, Inukai, or Ōishi. Moreover, both believed that Itō's past intervention in 1893, an intervention that helped resolve a navy-cabinet-parliament dispute, might prove beneficial in the 1902 dispute. These were accurate assessments. The day Katsura dissolved parliament, Itō invited Seiyūkai leaders to his residence and informed his fellow party members that he strongly supported the naval increase bill.[75] Four days later, Itō engaged in around-the-clock negotiations with the cabinet to reach a solution that would keep the cabinet together, gain parliamentary support, and provide the navy with funds for naval expansion. Well aware of the difficulties associated with any compromise, on 22 January Itō, Katsura, and Yamamoto reached a compromise they believed would be acceptable to all parties involved.[76] Specifically, Katsura agreed to fund naval expansion through expenditures previously earmarked for railroad construction, and to make up the shortfall in railway funds Katsura sought party support for the issuance of public bonds to pay for railroad expansion.[77] On 25 April, Itō announced the full details of the compromise plan to the Seiyūkai's executive committee and urged its leaders to secure passage of the plan in the forthcoming parliament. Just over a month later, the Seiyūkai rank and file agreed to support the naval expansion and related financing bill.

The May 1903 compromise that led to the Term-Three Expansion Program was not the only naval increase that Yamamoto demanded from Katsura's cabinet, however. Between October and December 1903, as the likelihood of war between Japan and Russia increased, Yamamoto demanded funds for further expansion to support still greater naval expansion. Specifically, Yamamoto demanded funds to cover the immediate purchase of two more battleships and greater funds to increase the pace of construction already undertaken.[78] Though Yamamoto's request angered Kastura greatly, the cabinet agreed to bring the issue up during the next parliament, in December 1903.

Personal and budgetary antagonisms between Yamamoto and Katsura aside, navy-army conflict also emerged in the latter half of 1903 and early 1904 as Russo-Japanese tensions rose. As negotiations with Russia over its failure to remove troops from Manchuria as stipulated by the Boxer Accord of 1900 stagnated and the government prepared for war in late 1903, Navy Minister Yamamoto voiced his opposition to a conflict with Russia. Well aware as navy minister of the difficulties in securing finances for military endeavors, Yamamoto thought it would be virtually impossible to finance a war against Russia. As Okamoto Shumpei has recorded, when Yamamoto was approached by members of the *Kogetsukai*, a secret society comprised mostly of military officers from the Army General Staff who were desirous of war, he asked: "Where will you find the two billion yen necessary to fight a war against Russia?"[79] This important question would dog Japan continuously after hostilities between Japan and Russia broke out in February 1904.

It was not just money that worried Yamamoto; far more serious military considerations also convinced him that war with Russia would be a dangerous undertaking. Drawing on a report compiled by the Navy General Staff, the navy minister believed that a war with Russia would likely result in the loss of half of Japan's warships.[80] With such losses, Yamamoto found it difficult to imagine a Japanese victory. Moreover, if Japan was defeated and forced to pay an indemnity to Russia, Yamamoto rightly feared that Japan would not possess the necessary financial means to rebuild the fleet anytime in the near future, especially as it had taken nearly nine years to construct with ample financial resources. Finally, Yamamoto's maritime-oriented worldview made it more difficult for him to see the necessity of fighting a war with Russia over Japanese interests on the continent. Yamamoto's outlook, which generally reflected the institutional outlook of the navy, was that Japan was a maritime country (*kaikoku*) and, being such, should not entangle itself on the Asian mainland. This important strand of navalist thinking had emerged within the navy and influenced Yamamoto's worldview. When Army Chief of the General Staff Ōyama Iwao in 1903 asked his naval counterpart, Itō Yūkō, to countersign a document for the emperor entitled, "Opinion Regarding the Solution of the Korean Problem," Yamamoto refused to allow Itō to do so. This document, which suggested that Japan should negotiate with Russia over an exchange whereby Russia acknowledged Japan's special interests in Korea and Japan did the same for Russia's interests in Manchuria, also included one clause to which the navy minister strongly objected: that Korea was vital to the security of Japan. In stating the reason for his objection, Yamamoto declared: "What would the

TABLE 3

Japanese Army, Navy, and National Expenditures
and Military Personnel, 1890–1905

(expenditures listed in yen)

Year	Army expenditures	Navy expenditures	National expenditures	Army personnel	Navy personnel
1890	¥15,533,000	¥10,159,000	¥82,125,000	71,099	13,555
1891	14,180,000	9,502,000	83,556,000	71,183	13,532
1892	14,635,000	9,133,000	76,735,000	72,237	12,978
1893	14,721,000	8,101,000	84,582,000	73,963	13,234
1894	10,409,000	10,253,000	78,129,000	104,954	15,091
1895	10,016,000	13,520,000	85,317,000	87,468	16,596
1896	53,243,000	20,006,000	168,857,000	123,913	18,233
1897	60,148,000	50,395,000	223,679,000	144,179	22,176
1898	53,898,000	58,529,000	219,758,000	132,666	23,430
1899	52,551,000	61,662,000	254,166,000	140,000	27,347
1900	74,838,000	58,275,000	292,750,000	150,000	31,114
1901	58,382,000	43,979,000	266,857,000	150,000	34,242
1902	49,442,000	36,327,000	289,227,000	150,000	36,674
1903	46,884,000	36,118,000	249,256,000	150,000	37,434
1904	12,088,000	20,614,000	277,056,000	900,000	40,777
1905	11,109,000	23,412,000	420,741,000	900,000	44,959

SOURCES: Army and navy expenditure figures are taken from Naikaku tōkeikyoku (Cabinet statistics bureau), *Nihon teikoku tōkei nenkan* (Statistical yearbook of the Japanese empire), 59 vols. (Tokyo: Tokyo ripurinto shuppansha, 1962–1967): 43:507 (1924). National expenditures and army and navy personnel are found in Statistics Bureau, *Historical Statistics of Japan*, 5 vols. (Tokyo: Japan Statistical Association, 1987): 5:524, 527.

NOTE: Army and navy expenditure figures for 1894–1895 and 1904–1905 do not include wartime expenditures which fell under extraordinary war expenditures.

loss of Korea mean to us? It will be sufficient if the empire can defend its own territory." As a result, Itō, per Yamamoto's instructions, refused to sign the proposal, which thereafter went to the emperor with only General Ōyama's signature.[81]

Yamamoto's opinions regarding Korea, however, were not shared by all members of Japan's government. Korea remained the most important foreign-policy concern, and in 1904, after a series of failed negotiations, Japan declared war on Russia. Despite dire prewar predictions, the navy did not lose half its battle fleet but instead virtually annihilated both the Far Eastern and the Baltic squadrons of the Russian navy, losses that were critical in Russia's decision to reach a negotiated settlement in 1905. The Japanese naval buildup between 1895 and 1904, which saw the navy purchase a total of eighteen major warships of either battleship or battle-cruiser class, helped Japan establish itself as a dominant regional actor and a world-class naval power. That came with a political cost, however, as relations between the navy and the army grew more tense after 1894. They would worsen from 1905 on, impacting politics throughout late Meiji, Taishō, and early Shōwa Japan.

Synopsis

The decade between 1894 and 1904 was a critically important period for the navy and the nation of Japan. While victory over China seemingly validated the state-building program Japan's leaders had implemented over the previous twenty years, the navy gained more from this war than perhaps any other institution apart from the imperial household. The war transformed the navy's image in many circles from that of an auxiliary force to one of an institution of the greatest importance to Japan's security and international standing. Though army leaders resisted the naval leadership's efforts to gain complete autonomy, the navy would rarely have been seen by anyone but the army as Japan's junior service after the Sino-Japanese War. Image aside, war and a rich peace settlement provided the government with ample funds with which to develop an even greater military-industrial complex than had emerged from the 1880s on. This could not have come at a more crucial time for the Japanese navy. Expansion after 1895 provided a significant boost to the navy's fortunes. Funding, or a lack thereof, which hindered naval development for much of the previous thirty years, was not in short supply between 1895 and 1900, and the navy made the most of the situation.

The interwar years of Meiji Japan also witnessed the development of an important facet in parliamentary politics that would shape and in many ways define politics after 1894: pragmatic compromises. Parliamentarians moved away from outright opposition for opposition's sake after the early sessions, and by 1895 astute leaders such as Itagaki Taisuke or, after 1900, Itō Hirobumi worked to bring their parties into working relationships with other elite actors, including the military services. Though a recalcitrant parliament could foil the government's legislative program through budgetary intransigence, the key to elite-level representation was to forge working relations with Japan's oligarchs. Nowhere did this prove more correct than in the compromises agreed to in support of naval expansion.

Expansion of both the navy's material strength and its political standing was not without consequences. Though many in the army still saw the navy as a supplementary force, to be controlled by the army in times of war, the political reality was that the navy had begun to emerge as a strong competitor to the army. Rivalry between the services, whether based on personalities, strategic outlooks, military priorities, or budgets, would significantly alter domestic politics and foreign relations in Japan. Nowhere would this be more apparent than in the aftermath of the Russo-Japanese War, when calls for greater political pluralism coincided with a precarious economic position, a period in which economic historian Ōhkawa Masazō claimed political actors had different "dreams within the same bed."[82] The navy and army, however, would pursue their respective dreams in very different fashions.

CHAPTER FIVE

War, Pageantry, and Propaganda
in the Service of Naval Expansion, 1905–1910

> Nothing can be obtained without paying a price, and the im-
> portance of this truth is nowhere greater than with the navy, on
> which pivots our nation's rise or fall.[1]
> —*Kokumin shinbun* editorial, 25 October 1905

> It seems inevitable that the navy will bring forward a plan to
> construct dreadnoughts. . . . Newspapers such as the *Jiji* and
> the *Asahi* run articles on it, and the opposition parties, I am
> sure, will jump on the bandwagon and create a disturbance.[2]
> —Prime Minister Katsura Tarō, 12 May 1910

> We ate for the navy in every sense of the word. We do not yield
> an inch to anyone in the sincerity and earnestness with which
> we cling to the belief that the acquisition of naval power should
> be made the basis of our national defense.[3]
> —*Hōchi shinbun* editorial, 11 July 1912

IN THE EARLY HOURS of 27 May 1905, Tōgō Heihachirō, commander of the Combined Fleet, received a cable from the scout ship *Shinano Maru*: "Enemy's fleet sighted in square 203."[4] Though not so emotive
as "Tora, Tora, Tora," the phrase relayed to Admiral Yamamoto Isoroku that
signaled the successful surprise attack on Pearl Harbor, the message from
the *Shinano Maru* in 1905 was no less significant to Japan's navy or empire.
The enemy fleet mentioned was the Russian Baltic Squadron, which, under
the command of Admiral Zinovii Petrovich Rozhdestvensky, departed from
its Baltic home port in October 1904. Hoping that the might of Russia's
most impressive battle squadron could break the blockade of Port Arthur
and decidedly turn the war against Japan, Tsar Nicholas II ordered
Rozhdestvensky to undertake a seven-month transequatorial voyage to
meet the Japanese fleet in the Far East. The gamble did not pay off. On 27
May 1905, both fleets fought the first and perhaps most lopsided decisive
naval battle of the twentieth century. Within twenty-four hours, at a loss of

only three torpedo boats, Japan's navy captured, sank, or grounded thirty-four of Russia's thirty-eight warships, including all the Baltic Squadron's battleships.[5] Heralded by U.S. president Theodore Roosevelt as a victory more overwhelming than the defeat of the Spanish Armada, and by Kaiser Wilhelm of Germany as a battle that ended any chance for a decided turn of the war in Russia's favor, the Battle of Tsushima was the most celebrated and significant victory for the Japanese navy up until December 1941. In just over one day of fighting, Admiral Tōgō and the warships and sailors of the Combined Fleet secured the strategic victory that had eluded Japan's military since the opening phase of the war. As with the navy's actions ten years earlier against Chinese naval forces, victory at Tsushima in 1905 eliminated Japan's chief naval threat and demonstrated the navy's power, status, and importance on a world scale. Tsushima, in the words of Teddy Roosevelt, was the battle that "saved the Japanese empire."[6]

Though known for exaggeration as well as for carrying a big stick in international diplomacy, Roosevelt in his appraisal of Tsushima and its importance to Japan's war effort proved accurate. Often viewed in the same light as Japan's triumph over China ten years earlier, Japan's victory over Russia in 1905, however, was not an unmitigated success. Rather, the Russo-Japanese War taxed Japan heavily in nearly every respect and brought its military-industrial complex and armed forces to the brink of collapse. Apart from the navy's successes at Tsushima and General Nogi Maresuki's capture of Port Arthur on 1 January 1905, Japan's military forces were never able to follow up tactical battlefield successes with an overall strategic victory. In many of the large-scale land battles fought in Manchuria from September 1904 to the war's conclusion, the army could not supply enough troops or material to decisively defeat more numerous Russian forces, leaving tactical victories such as Shaho (September 1904) and Mukden (March 1905) well short of complete. More damaging, the war simply exhausted Japan's financial capabilities, exposing weaknesses in Japan's capacity to fight a strategic war against a larger and richer continental power. Japan's expenditure of nearly ¥1.8 billion on the war, of which ¥800 million was secured from overseas loans, was an immense sum, equivalent to nine times the amount spent in Japan's previous war with China and a figure five times larger than Japan's entire national budget for 1903. Though vast, it was still not enough to secure total military victory.

The peace treaty signed between Russia and Japan in Portsmouth, New Hampshire, clearly reflected Japan's military, industrial, and financial limitations and moreover brought popular political tensions to the forefront of national politics. While Japan's oligarchs eventually secured their primary political objective, including formal Russian recognition of Japan's rights in Korea and a Russian guarantee to withdraw its military forces from Manchuria, the peace treaty failed to secure the objectives that many members of the public and nationalistic societies hoped and expected to obtain through the costly war with Russia. For one, Japan gained no monetary indemnity as it had from China ten years earlier and besides acquired no territory apart from the southern half of Sakhalin Island, a far cry from popular demands for a ¥2-billion indemnity and annexation of the Russian Maritime Provinces. Fed a steady diet of misleading reports that emphasized Japan's military victories, Japanese citizens were unaware of the army's precarious position and expressed great bitterness at what they considered an unjust peace. Such public disillusion and anger expressed itself through popular protest and riots in Tokyo, culminating with the Hibiya Antitreaty Riots of early September 1905. Thus, while a unified, immeasurably strengthened, and popular oligarchy directed Japan on a course of military and industrial expansion after 1895, one paid for by Chinese silver, a more fractured and criticized oligarchic government faced the daunting task of strengthening Japan's military, industrial, and economic foundations in an era of indebtedness and one characterized by increased calls from Japan's elected representatives for further political pluralism.

A wide, almost inseparable gulf thus existed between Japan's postwar positions of 1895 and 1905. One similarity, however, bound the two distinct postwar worlds; a strong desire by both military services to expand their force levels significantly. Accordingly, after 1905 the problem of resolving military expansion with fiscal responsibility and industrial enlargement became a central focus of politics in the years before World War I. To any but the most astute political observer or prognosticator, the prospect of balancing military expansion, fiscal retrenchment, industrial expansion, and greater political pluralism must have seemed destined to fail. Fail it did not, at least from the navy's perspective. Gaining support for naval increases in an environment of indebtedness, austerity, increased pluralism, and acute competition for finite monetary resources necessitated that the navy introduce imaginative and persuasive means to sell its cause on multiple levels after 1905. It did so surprisingly well. Drawing on lessons learned in earlier dealings at the elite political level, building upon the popularity this service had gained as a result of its stunning achievements in the war with Russia, and incorporating public-relations techniques successfully employed by foreign navies, the Japanese navy shaped both public opinion and legislative programs through pageantry, propaganda, and elite-level political pragmatism. In doing so effectively, the navy convinced many fiscally conservative oligarchs and bureaucrats, a tax-weary electorate, and skeptical Diet representatives and party leaders to support the expensive cause of naval expansion in the waning years of the Meiji period with style, substance, and panache.

Postwar Pageantry, Commemoration, and the Selling of Naval Expansion

Less than two months after the Japanese government declared martial law in the nation's capital to quell anti–peace treaty riots, Tokyo was again rife with popular agitation in late October 1905. This time, however, Japanese citizens were not planning to participate in antigovernment rallies but rather were stirring with excitement over the prospect of welcoming home Japan's great war hero, Admiral Tōgō, and the ships and sailors of Japan's Combined Fleet. While government leaders understood the psychological and political importance of commemorating Japan's most successful military leader, the Battle of Tsushima, and Japan's victory over Russia, naval leaders were also aware of the opportunity such an occasion afforded. Recognizing the war as a watershed in the navy's history, naval leaders sought to use the popularity their service had gained in order to strengthen the navy's image as Japan's most important military asset and to build popular support at home for further naval expansion. The navy did so first through well-orchestrated public displays of naval pageantry, commemoration, and power.

During October 1905, the navy orchestrated a triumphal return tour for Tōgō and the Combined Fleet, which exuded military might and political and pro-navy sentiment. Beginning at Nagasaki and continuing up Japan's east coast, Tōgō's fleet made a series of highly publicized appearances at Japan's major ports and naval stations.[7] Unlike the army, whose forces remained in Manchuria and withdrew in piecemeal fashion coordinated with a similar demobilization and withdrawal of Russian forces over 1905 and 1906, the navy returned en masse. This provided the navy with the opportunity "to organize," as one international observer noted, "an effective demonstration," that the navy utilized to full symbolic and political advantage.[8] While Tōgō's tour included stops at Kure, Kobe, and the Grand Shrine of Ise, the highlight of Tōgō's victory tour was the week of festivities planned for the Tokyo-Yokohama-Yokosuka area, the political center of Japan. As David Kertzer and other political scientists have persuasively demonstrated, ritual and symbolism are ubiquitous elements of political life, and their use can bolster incumbent power and allow newly emerging institutions to carve out bases of new political allegiance and influence.[9] As a newly emerging political institution, the navy used the well-orchestrated activities of Tōgō and the Combined Fleet to further its political and budgetary agendas.

The events planned for the weeklong Tokyo-area fete were grand in scale and richly imbued with symbolism, ritual, and politics. Two days after visiting the Grand Shrine of Ise—Japan's most sacred shrine, where Tōgō claimed victory at Tsushima had been secured by "the help of heaven and providence" (*tenyū to shinjo ni yotte*)—the admiral led the Combined Fleet into Yokohama Bay on 20 October, the eve of the centenary of Lord Nelson's victory at Trafalgar. Timing was not a coincidence. Almost immediately upon Tōgō's arrival at Yokohama, local political leaders, including the mayor of Yokohama, Ichihara Morihiro, and the governor of Kanagawa Prefecture, Sufu Kimihara, met Tōgō on his flagship and invited Japan's new hero to a banquet for British admiral Sir Gerard Noel, who planned to commemorate Lord Nelson's victory at Trafalgar with a well-attended gala. Tōgō readily accepted the invitation and upon arrival at the venue, Yokohama's Oriental Hotel, at once became the unofficial guest of honor. In the following day's newspapers, journalists drew significant parallels between Tōgō and Nelson, Tsushima and Trafalgar, with many suggesting that Tōgō's victory was just as important to Japan's national salvation as Nelson's was to England's. No doubt to the delight of naval officials, other editorials suggested that England's long era of naval peace and economic prosperity following Trafalgar rested on Nelson's accomplishments and the maintenance of a strong navy. No paper, however, was so obvious as the *Jiji shinpō*, which emblazoned its front page with photos of both admirals. Underneath ran the caption "Tōgō a hundred years ago, Nelson after a hundred years."[10]

Following a day of closed-door festivities with foreign dignitaries and local politicians, Tōgō assumed a more visible and domestically focused role. After meeting with Emperor Meiji at 11:00 A.M. on Sunday, 22 October, Tōgō rode in an imperial carriage through designated parts of Tokyo that had been, in the words of one foreign journalist, "magnificently decorated with green arches and bunting."[11] As the admiral rode past Hibiya Park, where nearly two thousand citizens congregated to get a glimpse of Tōgō, local authorities ignited a large fireworks display amid shouts of *Banzai!* for

Japan's great hero. Wherever Tōgō went that day, crowds gathered: Shimbashi Station, Hibiya Park, the Navy Ministry Compound, Yokohama Station, the Yokohama docks. Before departing Yokohama jetty to return to his flagship, which like all other ships in Japan that day was dressed in accordance with navy rules of ceremony observed on the sacred occasion of the emperor's birthday, Tōgō expressed gratitude for the welcome he had received.[12] These celebrations, while significant, were just the beginning of the political extravaganza.

The highpoint of Tōgō's triumphal return occurred on 23 October, when the navy choreographed the most impressive naval review in Japan's history to date. Held off the coast of Yokohama, the naval extravaganza intermixed commemoration of Japan's sacrifices in the war with a celebration of the navy's maritime successes and power. More than just a demonstration of Japan's naval might, however, the event clearly communicated and symbolically reaffirmed Japan's political order and clearly calibrated degrees of power within it.[13] Finally, through the visual display of Japanese naval might, coupled with a formal presentation of captured Russian warships to the emperor and nation of Japan, the naval review showcased and validated Japan's previous naval expenditures. It was an event of "stupendous magnitude," as one journalist remarked, that all "classes and nationalities" enjoyed.[14]

The day of the review began with thousands of Japanese citizens streaming into Yokohama from various parts of the Kantō region. By water and land, citizens arrived in Yokohama, congesting both the river and rail-transport systems between Tokyo and Yokohama. While some reporters marveled that the "Sumida and other rivers were as thronged as the Ginza," and others complained that the extra trains proved inadequate to meet the popular demand for the pageant, for the 150,000 citizens who braved the crowds the event was likely well worth any logistical inconvenience. Assembled in Yokohama harbor were 146 warships and twelve large transport vessels, arranged in six impressive lines that measured approximately five miles long and more than two miles across. Resplendent with bunting, formal dress, and smartly dressed sailors and officers, it was apparent to all who viewed these lines of warships that Japan's fleet had indeed returned home as victors.

The political component of the review took center stage in the program soon after the emperor arrived by train from Tokyo. Upon arrival, the Meiji emperor boarded the warship *Asama* to lead the review of the fleet. Once he was settled on the battleship, the navy directed political dignitaries, journalists, and select civilians to board the *Manshū Maru* and the *Yawata Maru*, transport vessels specifically decorated with captured Russian military spoils. These vessels closely followed the *Asama* as it steamed through and around the warship lines. On board the *Manshū Maru*, the second review vessel overall, the navy specifically assembled members of Japan's cabinet, the genrō, and the most important men of both houses of parliament. Following this vessel, the navy filled the *Yawata Maru* with less powerful though no less important parliamentarians, journalists, star pupils, and family members of sailors who had died in the conflict. When these review ships completed their formal, highly ritualized inspection, a process that took upwards of three hours, the navy announced that civilian vessels could, if they would do so in an orderly fashion, likewise inspect the ships of the line, a proclamation that met with widespread enthusiasm. By looking at whom the navy invited to participate in the formal review, it is easy to deduce that the navy sought to symbolically recreate the hierarchical order of Japan's government and society. Not surprisingly, owing to their importance in all matters concerning appropriations, this was the first naval review in which naval officials specifically targeted and incorporated large numbers of parliamentarians into a formal naval-review procession.

If the navy was meticulous in its selection of dignitaries to take part in the review, they also took care in assembling and arranging the warship lines to instill a sense of awe, power, and respect among the participants and spectators. The first vessels that the review ships encountered were a line of small torpedo boats that had played such an important part in the initial attack on Port Arthur in 1904. Next, the reviewers came across two lines of captured Russian vessels, both transport vessels and warships. The first enemy ship encountered was the transport *Sungari*, which the navy had salvaged and refloated. Participants next viewed the destroyer *Biedovy*, the vessel on which Admiral Rozhdestvensky had been captured. Thereafter, the navy revealed to the participants the most important capital ships of the captured Russian fleet, the *Seniavin, Apraxin, Poltava, Peresviel,* and the *Nicolai I,* which Tōgō presented to the emperor and the nation of Japan. Many of the former Russian vessels still displayed the damage inflicted by Japan's warships with one reporter commenting that the *Peresviel* "was pierced in a hundred places," its "funnels riddled like a sieve."[15] Thereafter, to reinforce the navy's previous military achievements, reviewers were shown a number of warships captured by the Japanese navy in the previous war against China, including Admiral Ting's former flagship, the *Chinyen.* Unquestionably, showcasing the captured warships highlighted the navy's

FIG. 1. Souvenir postcard, featuring Admiral Tōgō Heihachirō, of the Imperial Naval Review held in Tokyo Bay in October 1905. This postcard also illustrates the size of the Japanese navy prior to and after the Russo-Japanese War, with the total tonnage also given of Russian warships captured by the Japanese. (Author's private collection)

military prowess and emergence as a world-class military institution and in-strument of empire. The naval review accomplished more than that, how-ever. It provided tangible evidence of Japan's victory to a public that had been thoroughly disappointed by the politically secured spoils of war, and this fact did not go unnoticed.[16] Indeed, the *Jiji shinpō* in a two-day spread on the naval review concluded: "If Japan has failed in diplomacy [through the Treaty of Portsmouth], the glorious navy has done more than make up for such [political] failings."[17]

After exhibiting the spoils of war, the navy charted a course for the re-viewers through Japan's resplendent warships. Viewed directly after the bat-tered former warships of the Russian navy, Japan's formally dressed vessels provided a stark contrast for onlookers and visually reinforced the grandeur of the Japanese navy. At the end of the all-day spectacle, after seafaring rev-elers returned to shore, the navy illuminated important vessels of the fleet, exposed others to floodlights, and invited civilians to tour two of the cap-tured Russian warships. While just over six weeks earlier citizens rioted against the Portsmouth Treaty at Hibiya Park, more than a hundred-fifty thousand citizens turned out in October to celebrate the navy's successes. For those citizens who could not attend the celebration in person, the gov-ernment and the navy produced a series of picture postcards that marked the navy's celebration. While some postcards documented the naval review and others highlighted the captured Russian vessels, the cards most sought after in 1905 and today by collectors were the ones that featured Admiral Tōgō, the most popular cards being one that listed the size of the Japanese navy before and after the war, and one that listed the total tonnage of Rus-sian warships captured by Tōgō and the Combined Fleet. Reflecting on the naval review of October 1905, an editor for the *Kokumin shinbun* applauded the navy for its efforts in both war and peace, remarking that as in Britain, "seawater is the lifeblood of the nation." He urged Japan's citizens therefore to further cultivate a taste and interest in all things naval, and more impor-tant, to support naval expansion. Should Japan's citizens shrink from the costs of furthering naval power, the editor concluded, the people must be reminded that "Nothing can be obtained without paying a price, and the importance of this truth is nowhere greater than with the navy, on which pivots our nation's rise or fall."[18]

Though clearly the high point of the navy's planned activities, the con-clusion of this naval review did not augur an end to the pro-navy festivities. On the contrary, over the following week, politicians, civic groups, and wealthy industrialists hosted functions for Admiral Tōgō, his officers, and sailors of the Combined Fleet. The day after the maritime extravaganza, more than a hundred thousand citizens gathered along a parade route through Tokyo to Ueno Park, where Tōgō received congratulations from Tokyo's mayor, Ozaki Yukio. Not to be outdone or miss the opportunity to be seen with and publicly congratulate the navy and its hero Tōgō, Yokohama politicians celebrated the admiral's return on 25 October. On that day, Governor Sufu of Kanagawa Prefecture, Mayor Ichihashi of Yokohama, Director of the Yokohama Customs House, Hashimoto, and Director of the Yokohama District Court Watanabe, all welcomed Tōgō to Yokohama and expressed their admiration for his selfless service to the nation. As a specific show of gratitude to all Japan's sailors, during the following week Baron Iwasaki Hisaya, the director of Mitsubishi, held two large-scale garden parties for the victorious Japanese sailors. On 29 October and 2 November, Iwasaki entertained over five thousand sailors in total at his Komagome villa with gifts, food, and beer.

Throughout the weeklong celebrations, Japanese newspapers played an important role in furthering interest in all naval matters and channeling popular support and gratitude for the navy into material benefits. On 24 October, the day of the naval review, the *Jiji shinpō* began collecting subscriptions for a "bluejacket entertainment fund" and, following a practice begun during the Sino-Japanese War, published subscriber's names and the amount donated. Soon after, the paper lavished significant praise on both Iwasaki's well-funded garden parties and on a ¥5,000 donation provided by the Mitsui Coporation to the bluejacket fund. Others, such as the Bank of Japan (¥10,000 donation), the Yokohama Specie Bank (¥5,000), the Nippon Yusen Kaisha (¥5,000), and the Furukawa Mining Company (¥2,000), even gained recognition in foreign newspapers for their support of Japan's sailors.[19] Four days later, on 28 October, the *Jiji shinpō* urged Japan's parliamentarians to vote a special ¥1-million award for Admiral Tōgō for his services to the nation. Though the admiral initially argued against such an honorarium, the paper rejected such calls and compelled its readers to press politicians to grant the sum "irrespective of Tōgō's moral idiosyncrasies."[20] Soon, however, Tōgō changed his mind and suggested that the money, if granted, could be put to better use if given to the navy to fund fleet expansion.

Following Tōgō's sea change, the *Jiji shinpō* and the *Tokyo Asahi shinbun* published numerous articles in support of Tōgō's calls for naval expansion. So began one of the navy's most successful and continuous propaganda campaigns of the Meiji and early Taishō eras. As naval leaders well understood, newspapers were the perfect vehicle with which to stir national opinion. Broadsheets became wildly popular in Japan during both the Sino-Japanese and the Russo-Japanese War and, owing to literacy rates increased by compulsory education, served as the optimum medium for reaching large audiences. Indeed, national newspaper circulation increased from 1.18 million newspapers per day in 1904 to 2.77 million in 1909, with readership exceeding publication. Beginning in early November 1905 and continuing intermittently throughout 1906, the *Jiji shinpō*, the *Tokyo Asahi shinbun*, the *Kokumin shinbun*, and the *Nippon* ran pro-navy stories and urged the government to expand Japan's fleet in order to secure the country's new position of importance and responsibility in East Asia. Often based upon information gained from unnamed naval officers or sometimes directly from the Naval Affairs Bureau of the Navy Ministry itself, many of the pro-navy stories mirrored calls made by naval leaders at elite-level cabinet discussions of 1906–7. Immediately before the navy introduced an expansion plan to the cabinet in early September 1906, the *Jiji shinpō* called for the navy to adopt a long-term expansion plan that would establish an "eight-eight-eight" fleet, a battle fleet consisting of eight *Dreadnought*-class battleships as its core with two supporting squadrons of eight armored cruisers each, the same type of fleet that pro-navy papers in England lobbied for at exactly the same time.[21] The publication of such stories in Japanese newspapers was not a coincidence. Soon after newspapers espoused the virtues and necessity of an eight-eight-eight fleet, the navy proposed just such a far-reaching and expensive expansion plan. In fact, an "eight-eight" fleet, as it came to be known after 1907, would be the basis of the navy's expansion requests from 1907 to 1918, and during these years (as later sections of the chapter will show) the navy continued to use newspapers to build support for naval expansion.

The immense popularity of Tōgō and the popular outpouring of interest in naval matters after the war encouraged Navy Minister Yamamoto and eventually his handpicked successor, Saitō Makoto, to implement a number of new policies aimed at furthering navalism, selling fleet expansion, and enhancing the navy's popular image and political stature in Japan. Beginning with great fanfare after 1906, and following a technique employed by many foreign navies after the turn of the century, the navy took great care to market warship launches for vessels constructed in domestic shipyards, imbuing these splendid occasions with a pageantry and formality akin to small-scale naval reviews or grand maneuvers of the fleet.[22] At the launching of the warship *Satsuma* in November 1906 and the warship *Kurama* in October 1907, the navy opened its shipyards to the public and invited thousands of citizens, businessmen, reporters, and politicians to celebrate the twin national achievements of Japanese industry and naval expansion. At the *Satsuma*'s launch in 1906, for instance, Governor Sufu of Kanagawa accompanied the emperor, the navy minister, local politicians, and journalists from Yokohama to Yokosuka, where he thanked the workers who had constructed the vessel and its future sailors who lined the pristine decks adorned with bunting and Japanese flags.[23] To mark the occasion, the navy provided its invited V.I.P. guests with commemorative medallions, lithographed with the vessel's image, which were made of the same material used in the manufacture of the vessel's hull, a policy employed at many subsequent launches. For ordinary citizens, the navy produced special commemorative cards with the vessel's image emblazoned on the front. Finally, the Japanese navy also allowed selected citizens and politicians to board the newly inaugurated warships, where they could discuss naval maters with officers and sailors—and of course, pose for photographs for the newspapers, a practice that mirrored warship launches in England.[24]

Along with launch celebrations, perhaps the most grandiose way in which the navy sought to instill pro-navy enthusiasm in the public, the press, and elected politicians was through grand maneuvers of the fleet. Modeled on the 1905 naval review, fleet maneuvers became the pinnacle of naval pageantry in Meiji-Taishō Japan. Naval reviews made a significant contribution to popular and elite-level support of navalism in Japan. National pride, naval awareness, and confidence were all elevated through public displays of naval power in late Meiji Japan, and moreover naval maneuvers provided the public with tangible evidence of what their taxes had provided. The first large-scale maneuver conducted after the 1905 review occurred in 1908. Held in two stages off Kobe during November 1908, this maneuver followed closely on the heels of the Imperial Army's autumn maneuver conducted outside Kyoto but was much larger in scale. The first part of the maneuver included a large-scale simulated naval battle between two fleet squadrons, one commanded by Vice Admiral Ijuin Goro, who based his forces at Sasebo, and the other commanded by Vice Admiral Dewa Shigeto, whose home port for the battle was Kure.[25] Departing from their respective naval stations during the first week of November, both fleets steamed toward waters off the Eastern Sea of Kyushu and upon arrival engaged in a simulated decisive battle. Timed no doubt to coincide with the visit by the U.S. Navy's Great White Fleet earlier in October, a visit that further heightened naval awareness in Japan, the naval engagement was followed enthusiastically by Japanese newspapers and citizens, many thousands of whom cheered the fleets as they left their home ports for the engagement.

The Grand Naval Maneuver of 1908 did not end with the decisive fleet encounter, however. Rather, after a week of highly publicized naval exercises, both fleets, 124 warships in total that displaced just over 400,000 tons, assembled off Kobe for a Grand Naval Review that was, unlike the army's maneuver and review, open to the public. As with the 1905 review, the emperor and other important political leaders and civic dignitaries reviewed the dressed warships from specially decorated review vessels. To provide citizens who watched the procession from shore a memento and to share the spectacle with others who could not witness the event in person, the navy and the Ministry for Communications produced a series of commemorative cards associated with the event, following the pattern established in 1905. While the card which depicted the emperor's review ship, the *Asama*, was just one of the highly sought-after cards associated with the review, those emblazoned with the likeness of Tōgō, the naval official who received the emperor and directed the review, and cards with images of the two mock battle fleets or pictures of the dueling admirals Ijuin and Dewa also became collector's items almost immediately.

Though an impressive event which furthered public interest and awareness of naval affairs and provided citizens with tangible evidence of what their taxes had provided, the 1908 maneuver was overshadowed in size, scale, and political purpose by other maneuvers, which took place in May 1911 and November 1912.[26] Held in Tokyo Bay, the 1911 and 1912 naval fetes resonated with political meaning; each immediately preceded the introduction of a large-scale naval expansion bill to either the cabinet or the parliament. While naval leaders such as Navy Minister Saitō Makoto and admirals Yamamoto Gonnohyōe, Tōgō Heiharchirō, and Itō Yūkō urged the public to support naval expansion in speeches throughout the spectacles, of particular importance in these pageants is the fact that the navy used these high-profile, popular public events to lavish attention on Seiyūkai leaders such as Saionji Kinmochi, Hara Kei, and Matsuda Masahisa, and by so doing to elevate their stature.[27] Treating such politicians as V.I.P.'s, placing them alongside or at least on the same reviewing ship as the emperor and other elite persons, validated the increasingly important role that Seiyūkai parliamentarians assumed in the late Meiji period. Moreover, participation in these exercises was an outward manifestation of the increasingly close relationship that the navy had begun to forge with the Seiyūkai political party after 1910, a relationship that would give each power and influence where

FIG. 2. Souvenir postcard of the Imperial Naval Review held off Kobe in November 1908. (Author's private collection)

each wanted it most: the navy within the Diet and the Seiyūkai within government and clan circles. Though fully aware of the importance of shaping public opinion through naval pageants, reviews, and maneuvers in a society that was becoming increasingly pluralistic after the Russo-Japanese War, naval leaders clearly understood the potential benefits that could be gained by cultivating an important relationship with Japan's other important burgeoning elite, the Seiyūkai political party. Such a relationship would prove instrumental in the years between 1910 and 1914.

Apart from festive and highly publicized warship launches and maneuvers of the fleet, the navy further capitalized on the nation's memory of the Battle of Tsushima to further pro-navy nationalism and navy political initiatives beginning in 1906. That year, the navy lobbied for and secured from the government the creation of a new national holiday, Navy Day, to commemorate the victory at the Battle of Tsushima. At the first anniversary of Tsushima, despite calls from the *Jiji shinpō* and the *Tokyo Asahi shinbun* to hold another Grand Maneuver in Tōgō's honor, the navy held a smaller though no less political celebration in Tokyo Bay. While thousands of citizens crowded the shores of both Yokohama and Tokyo to see their warships conduct small-scale exercises, the Suikōsha, a navy club similar to a Western navy league, invited more than twenty-five hundred politicians, businessmen, reporters, and imperial representatives to their Tokyo grounds for a banquet in Tōgō's honor.[28] To add national appeal and a further element of propaganda to the event, the navy issued the guests commemorative postcards depicting key participants in the Battle of Tsushima, encouraging them to post these cards to all parts of Japan.[29] For citizens desirous of obtaining a card but not invited to the official ceremony, the navy announced, to much popular fanfare, that it would maintain the post-collection box for three days following the event, allowing ample time for ordinary citizens to enter the navy club's premises, obtain the commemorative cards, have them stamped with the official seal, and post them to friends and relatives throughout Japan.[30] Two years later, to mark Navy Day in 1908, the Suikōsha opened a historical exhibition hall at its Tsukiji headquarters that commemorated Japan's victory in the Russo-Japanese War. Funded in part by donations from the Navy Ministry, the Mitsui Corporation, and annual membership fees, the hall housed trophies from the Russo-Japanese War which the public was invited to view on Navy Day each year.[31] The following year, 1909, Tōgō used Navy Day to publicly unveil at the Suikōsha three bronze statues of the former navy ministers Saigō Tsugumichi, Kawamura Sumiyoshi, and Nire Kagenori. These statues, so Japan's most celebrated admiral declared, honored the men who had secured the naval expansion that made possible Japan's victory over Russia in 1905.[32]

The Suikōsha, often referred to as the Navy Club or the Maritime Friends Association, came to play an important role in pro-navy activities during and after 1905.[33] Supported by the navy since its founding in 1883, the Suikōsha was a club comprised of naval officers, active and reservist, politicians, and industrialists, though the latter were slow to join the ranks of this club, as domestic construction did not begin in earnest until after 1900 for auxiliary vessels and for capital warships after 1914. The association's stated duties were to facilitate friendship among members, provide comfort and assistance to military men in time of war, and promote the navy's profession. Moreover, it came to be a strong pro-navy lobby over the course of the Meiji period. The association's headquarters were located in Tsukiji, the site of the naval academy before it moved to Etajima, but the Suikōsha also had branches at all other major naval ports in Japan, including Kure, Yokosuka, Sasebo, and Maizuru.[34] Each month, this organization published a pro-navy magazine similar to the *Proceedings of the U.S. Naval Institute* entitled *Suikōsha kiji* (Suikōsha news) and soon after this began to publish an illustrated journal entitled *Kaigun* (Navy). Though it never became as strong a lobby or political institution as the Navy League in Germany or in the United States, the Suikōsha nevertheless worked with the navy to sell naval expansion through publications geared toward elites as well as ordinary Japanese citizens.

Efforts and activities launched by the navy, the Suikōsha, and pro-navy or navy-funded publicists helped forge the beginning of maritime or naval consciousness in Japan, something the navy had sought to accomplish since the 1880s. The navy's victory at Tsushima elevated the stature of this service and Admiral Tōgō almost overnight. Capitalizing on the opportunity that victory had provided during the Russo-Japanese War, the navy devised and implemented numerous public-relations activities geared toward building support for naval expansion. The navy, in many ways, emerged from this war, and continued to develop, as a sophisticated elite-level actor in Japan. Budgets, however, were still debated over and decided upon by elites. Almost as soon as the navy's public, political, and budgetary star began to rise, army leaders grew concerned that the navy would, for the first time in Japan's history, overtake the army as Japan's most important and best-endowed military service. The struggle for military and budgetary supremacy that would follow at the elite political level had far-reaching consequences for domestic Japanese politics in the waning years of the Meiji era.

Interservice Rivalry, Budgetary Negotiations, and Attempts to Form a Unified Imperial Defense Plan

Interservice rivalry existed in Japan almost from the creation of the new Meiji state. Influenced initially by differing strategic outlooks, institutional training, and eventually by *Satchō* clan politics from 1880s on, rivalry transformed into outright antagonism over budgetary and military issues. As each service sought larger operating budgets, each feared that the other's requests might jeopardize its own desired expansion. In the fiscally austere years after the Russo-Japanese War, leaders from each service feared that parliamentarians would challenge large-scale expansion programs desired by both military services. Taking this and the navy's increased popularity into consideration, General Tanaka Gi'ichi, chief of the Army General Staff, approached *genrō* Yamagata in 1906 and asked the elder statesman to arrange a return to the prewar situation in which the chief of the Army General Staff assumed military control of all Japan's armed forces in wartime. That was not all, however. Fearing that increased rivalry and naval popularity might undermine army expansion requests, the general also sought to have a unified defense policy created, one which prioritized the army's strategic outlook and budgetary requests over those of the navy.[35] Thus in 1906, when the cabinet discussed Navy Minister Saitō Makoto's naval expansion requests, Yamagata Aritomo and Tanaka Gi'ichi had already initiated discussions on how to give the army the upper hand in postwar appropriations.

Throughout September and October 1906, Yamagata therefore endeavored to create a comprehensive defense policy for Japan. Not surprisingly given his background, Yamagata wholeheartedly accepted Tanaka's suggestion that Japan return to a unified command structure wherein the Navy General Staff would be subordinated to the chief of the Army General Staff.[36] Of further benefit to the army, moreover, Yamagata and Tanaka designated Russia as Japan's primary hypothetical enemy, claiming that a Russian war of revenge was the most probable conflict to threaten Japan in the immediate future. Fully aware that Japan would need more soldiers on the continent to repel such an attack, Yamagata concluded that the formation of new army divisions was the most pressing armaments need, a need far more critical than the purchase and construction of warships as requested by the navy. A final insult to the navy occurred when Yamagata recommended that the navy, which at this time was attempting to solidify its own strategic identity, should serve primarily as an auxiliary to the army and focus its duties on improving and increasing troop transport and communications capacities.

When Yamagata presented his draft proposal to a joint committee comprised of army field marshals and navy fleet admirals in December 1906, navy leaders responded in a swift and predictable fashion. Importantly for the navy, the chief of the Navy General Staff, Admiral Tōgō Heihachirō, led the assault against Yamagata.[37] The hero of the Russo-Japanese War, Tōgō argued that the navy's striking victories in the Russo-Japanese War were testimonies, in part, to the establishment and successful operation of a separate command for the navy. Under no circumstance, the admiral asserted, would the navy relinquish its military-command independence.[38] Admiral Tōgō was a man of few words, but when he spoke he commanded authority. Joining Tōgō, other navy delegates present claimed that the navy possessed its own strategic vision for Japanese security and therefore demanded the right to select its own hypothetical enemy, just as the draft policy allowed the army to do. Naval leaders were particularly concerned that if Russia was selected as the primary potential adversary, the navy would have little justification to support an expensive eight-eight fleet, since the Russian navy of 1907 was in no way a threat to Japan. Consequently, navy leaders declared that the Navy General Staff must reserve the right to determine its own defense doctrine and specifically enumerate the forces necessary to support such plans. Anything less, Tōgō concluded, would simply undermine the navy and Japan's national defense.

Initially underestimating the force and determination with which the navy argued it position, Yamagata continued deliberations with naval officials for over a month, hoping to reach a compromise agreement that could be presented to the emperor. His efforts to construct a single imperial defense plan, however, came to naught. In the end, Yamagata acquiesced to the navy's demands for an autonomous defense plan and endorsed a policy compromise whereby both military services were given the prerogative to formulate their own plans based on their own respective hypothetical enemies.[39] As a result, the army selected Russia and reasoned that a future war with that country would require an increase of six army divisions, from nineteen to twenty-five. The navy on the other hand, chose the largest non-allied naval power, the United States, as its hypothetical enemy. While strategic considerations no doubt influenced this choice, selecting the U.S. Navy was also particularly useful to legitimize navy requests for large-scale expansion; the U.S. Navy in 1907 was, as historian Asada Sadao has argued, a budgetary enemy first, a military one second.[40] A Japanese-American war, or so navy leaders suggested, could be fought and won only if Japan possessed a navy with a total displacement of 500,000 tons, a figure that, if acted upon and secured, would necessitate a doubling of the size of Japan's 1906 navy.[41] In early 1907 the full document was submitted to and endorsed by Emperor Meiji. Though initiated in order to consolidate defense planning and prevent a united front to politicians, albeit one with the army on top, the agreement reached in 1907 did little more than formalize army-navy rivalry at the strategic, political, and budgetary levels. With two distinct hypothetical enemies, defense plans, and force-level expansion plans, it became increasingly more difficult for the army and navy to find common ground on any matter of strategic or foreign policy. More important, their separate plans for the defense needs of the country contributed to increased friction over military appropriations, and this in turn led to acute political disputes and tension throughout the remaining years of the Meiji state.

Yamagata, Tanaka Gi'ichi, and Army Minister Terauchi Masatake were correct in assuming as early as September 1906 that military expansion, interservice rivalry, and budgetary politics would take center stage in postwar policy discussions. In one of his last public pronouncements as navy minister in early 1906, Yamamoto Gonnohyōe told reporters that while the navy had not planned for any large-scale postwar expansion to commence in 1907, other than "making provisions for replacing what the war had destroyed or impaired," he concluded that "it would be necessary to consider what was required in new undertakings" after that point.[42] In new undertakings, Yamamoto had one thing on his mind: state-of-the-art battleships of the new *Dreadnought* class, the largest, most technologically advanced, and consequently the most expensive warships in existence in 1906.[43] Satirizing the "warship of the future," its size, and, of course, its cost, *Tokyo Puck* published a two-page cartoon in its November 1906 issue depicting what one could humorously expect about these warships owing to their exorbitant costs.[44] The warship, which the paper suggested would displace 3.25 million tons, was armed with forty 120-inch guns that could bombard San Francisco from Nagasaki, also included four battleships of the *Satsuma* class (as lifeboats), a public school, a music hall, a vegetable garden, an overflowing theater, and a race course for a semiannual derby for the army divisions that were also stationed on board. *Dreadnought*-class warships, as the cartoon suggested in a wildly exaggerated fashion, would not come cheap and, coupled with army demands for increased troop levels, forced Japan's political leaders to make a number of difficult choices in late 1906.

Elite-level discussions concerning military appropriations began in

FIG. 3. "The Next Year's Budget." This illustration depicts a haggard and melancholy Prime Minister Saionji Kinmochi attempting to compile the budget in an austere room with little cash in the nation's coffers. Waiting in the wings are ambitious ministers of state, led by Army Minister Terauchi Masatake and Navy Minister Saitō Makoto with fresh budgetary demands. (*Tokyo Puck*, 2:24, 10 November 1906)

earnest during the summer of 1906. On 29 June, the Seiyūkai leader Hara Kei, serving as home minister in Saionji Kinmochi's first cabinet, met with former Prime Minister Katsura Tarō, and almost immediately the topic of defense appropriations surfaced.[45] Katsura suggested that naval authorities would insist upon expansion from 1907 on and that the government would likely have to find funds to cover the costs for reasons both of politics and defense. Though he predicted that naval leaders would eventually compromise and not force the collapse of Saionji's cabinet over the failure to expand the navy by as much as they desired, Katsura warned Hara that budget negotiations would prove difficult.

Katsura's prediction proved correct in autumn 1906 when Saionji's cabinet debated the budget for 1907. Difficulties stemmed primarily from the army, however, and not the navy as Katsura had predicted. At a meeting between Saionji, Hara, and Finance Minister Sakatani Yoshio on 14 November, Sakatani argued against any increase in military spending for the 1907 budget, claiming that the financial position of Japan was just too precarious to initiate any new military undertakings.[46] Not wishing to precipitate a cabinet crisis but also not desirous of expanding the military, Saionji and Hara believed the best course of action was to postpone all military requests until 1908. Yamagata and Army Minister Terauchi Masatake refused, at least initially, to consider any postponement in military expansion. Terauchi requested an additional ¥10 million for army expansion in 1907 to begin funding for the creation and deployment of new divisions.[47] Saionji's first cabinet faced enormous difficulties balancing the demands for further military expansion, championed primarily by *genrō* Yamagata Aritomo and Army Minister Terauchi Masatake, and calls for fiscal restraint by Finance Minister Sakatani Yoshio. Saionji's position became so difficult that the magazine *Tokyo Puck* characterized the prime minister's predicament on its 10 November 1906 cover: the illustration pictured a haggard and melancholy Saionji attempting to compile the budget in a austere room with little cash in the nation's coffers while ambitious ministers of state, led by the army and navy ministers, waited outside the hall with a long list of budgetary demands.[48]

Desirous of keeping the cabinet together, Hara, as he would throughout his political career, helped negotiate a settlement, with assistance in this instance from Katsura Tarō and Inoue Kaoru. On 29 November, Hara and Saionji informed Katsura that unless the army moderated its stance, the cabinet would resign, thus jeopardizing the relationship Katsura and Saionji had forged during 1905 in which each alternated as prime minister.[49] After a week of detailed negotiations, army leaders agreed to accept funds to increase the size of their service by two divisions rather than three, and the navy agreed to accept funding that would allow it to refurbish captured Russian warships rather than purchase or build new capital vessels.[50] Compromise in 1906, as it would in future budget negotiations, averted disaster for Saionji's cabinet. Importantly, as Hara recorded in his diary, the navy under Saitō Makoto proved far more amenable to discussion, negotiations, and budgetary pragmatism than the army had, and this fact would not be lost on Hara and other Seiyūkai leaders in the future.[51]

Celebrations were short-lived, however. The following year, Japan's budgetary position worsened, and the cabinet faced two unpopular choices: a reduction of armaments expansion, certain to anger the military, or an increase in personal and business taxes, certain to inflame businessmen, financial experts, landowners, and the political parties. Comprehending that the military would respond poorly to an outright cancellation of the earlier agreed-upon expansion program but that parliamentarians and business leaders would rebel against the government if the prime minister recommended increased taxes, Saionji and Hara again forged a compromise with the military. The cabinet agreed in principle to fund military expansion but asked the army and the navy to postpone the completion of their expansion programs; the army agreed to postpone its two-division increase for three years at a savings of ¥60 million, and the navy agreed to postpone new warship purchases valued at ¥52 million over six years.[52] While the navy accepted this compromise proposal, by 1909, citing increased naval spending in the United States, Germany, Britain, Germany and France, Navy Minister Saitō Makoto was warning parliamentarians that Japan could no longer rely on just refurbishing older warships or those captured during the Russo-Japanese War.[53] Soon after, both services adopted different techniques to secure their respective defense needs, and their differing pursuits fundamentally altered politics over the final years of the Meiji period.

Selling Naval Expansion Through Publications and the Press

Having successfully resisted the army's plans to unify defense planning in 1906–7, naval leaders expanded upon the public-relations campaigns and pro-navy propaganda efforts initiated in 1905 to sell fleet expansion to elites and ordinary citizens. A key component in this pursuit was to further develop and sell a persuasive maritime or navalist ideology upon which formal naval construction plans could be and in fact were based. This was similar to what the American naval strategist Alfred T. Mahan and the German admiral Alfred von Tirpitz had done in the West, and Yamamoto wanted the Japanese navy to formulate and adopt a navalist ideology specifically tailored to Japan's particular geographic and economic situation.[54] In this endeavor, the navy utilized the talents and efforts of Lieutenant Commander Satō Tetsutarō.[55] Satō was, in many ways, an ideal person to research and write on Western navalist thought, naval politics, and navy-parliament relations. For one thing, he was well versed in English and German. Moreover, Satō had also proven his ability as a pro-navy writer, having published earlier in the 1890s a pro-navy pamphlet entitled *Kokubō shisetsu* (Personal opinions on national defense), which came to the attention of both Yamamoto and chief of the Navy General Staff Itō Yūkō. On the basis of this work, his scholarly abilities, and his pro-navy enthusiasm, Itō approached Satō in 1899 and commissioned the young officer to write an official history of the navy for public distribution, believing that such a book would increase popular support for the cause of naval expansion at a time when armaments expansion was again becoming a politically sensitive issue.

Once this project was complete, Satō began a two-year tour of Europe and America to study navalist thought, history, and propaganda techniques employed by foreign navies. Upon returning to Japan in 1902, he produced the first fruits of this project with the assistance of the Suikōsha, publishing a monograph entitled *Teikoku kokubō ron* (On imperial defense).[56] Through extensive use of historical examples he concluded that a strong navy was essential for the defense of any island nation, Japan above all. Moreover, Satō clearly articulated that as the first line of defense for Japan, the navy was far more important to national security than the army, a fact which Satō believed should compel politicians to support fleet expansion.

While doubtless many in the navy and the Suikōsha endorsed Satō's conclusions and found his works both informative and interesting, Satō was for all intents and purposes preaching to the converted. However, his 1902 study, like all his future publications, also served a far more political purpose. The rapid publication of *Teikoku kokubō ron* coincided with a fierce budgetary dispute over military appropriations that erupted in 1902 and continued for much of 1903. While the government, headed by Katsura Tarō, and Diet politicians remained deadlocked over the interconnected issues of naval expansion and land-tax reductions, Navy Minister Yamamoto sent copies of Satō's work to many Diet representatives, the *genrō*, and the imperial household in an attempt to illustrate the importance of the navy's expansionary requests.[57] While it is not known to what extent, if any, Satō's book influenced either the president of the Seiyūkai, Itō Hirobumi, or its

rank-and-file members to accept an eventual budgetary compromise, Yamamoto's political maneuver was the first instance of many to follow in
which the navy minister's office used the power of the pen in an attempt to
persuade Japan's leaders to support naval expansion.

After the 1907 defense decision to allow both services the right to select
hypothetical enemies, the navy continued to publish large quantities of pro-
navy literature geared toward both elite and popular markets. Again, as
with the navy's early publishing endeavors, Satō Tetsutarō played an active
though not exclusive role. Although Satō's publishing career was placed on
hold by events of the Russo-Japanese War, once hostilities ended the officer
vigorously renewed his efforts to formulate and articulate a navalist ideology (*kaigō shugi*) in Japan. In 1908 Satō published a massive, nine-hundred-
page work drawn from his lectures at the Naval Staff College entitled
Teikoku kokubōshi ron (On the history of imperial defense). Again extrapo-
lating from hundreds of historical examples, particularly from England—
which Satō believed most closely mirrored Japan's geographical situation—
he illustrated that naval power was by far the most important aspect of
national defense. "Should the great powers of the world combine against us
and approach these narrow shores with several million men," Satō averred,
Japan would remain unassailable if the enemy was unable to transport such
forces to Japan's shores. Hence, "Japan had no reason to fear an enemy
army" but rather only an enemy's naval power.[58]

As Satō's efforts continued throughout the late Meiji period, his works
were no longer just pro-navy tracts designed to champion the navy's expansionary agenda. Rather, many of his later works increasingly exhibited a
strong critique of the army for its continental aspirations. Satō's later works
began to clearly reflect the mounting institutional and budgetary rivalry
that had developed between the army and the navy after 1905. In his 1912
study *Kokubō sakugi* (A discussion on the national defense policy) Satō remarked: "Our offensive stance vis-à-vis the continent is a tremendous mistake. . . . The military emergency on the continent is a delusion."[59] This
struck at the heart of the army's justification for increased divisions, and
moreover, Satō concluded, "Army strength to protect Japan's position in
Manchuria is of secondary importance or even lower."[60] Only naval power
could guarantee Japan's security, and accordingly Satō argued that it was incumbent upon Japanese politicians to implement a large-scale naval expansion program.

Apart from reflecting the increased rivalry between the army and the
navy, Satō's works also reveal the increased plurality of political decision-

makers in late Meiji Japan; he was no longer just aiming at military bureaucrats and oligarchs. Rather, Satō issued a challenge for parliamentary politicians, members of Japan's chambers of commerce, financial experts, and others who criticized armaments expansion on the grounds of fiscal austerity, to be more open to the necessity of increased naval strength. Satō pleaded with opponents of naval expansion to look beyond their narrow, parochial interests and encouraged them to endorse fleet expansion on the grounds that this was the only means by which to safeguard the Japanese nation. As for the Diet representatives and financial experts who responded with claims that the ambitious scope of the navy's expansion programs was too large for Japan's fragile economy, Satō warned that their shortsightedness endangered Japan: "In our country today, individuals of the 'financial circles' criticize the replenishment of armaments, . . . [but] in short, there are no historical examples of a country that has insured its good fortune by limiting its [naval] armaments."[61] While Satō understood the realities and competing claims of a bureaucratic state, commenting that "educators want [greater funding] for education, religious leaders for religion, and army men for the army," he again asked Japan's politicians to unite, discharge their patriotic responsibility, and support naval expansion.[62]

Satō's works were not the only pro-navy tracts published in the years after 1905. Works geared toward politicians and oligarchs aside, other naval officials also undertook efforts to impress upon the general reading public the importance of and the need for naval expansion.[63] After 1905, the navy likewise produced its own written materials for a mass audience that espoused pro-navy themes. To supplement the journal *Suikōsha kiji*, the navy created the journal *Kaigun*. Through its vivid pictures and neatly packaged articles espousing the importance of continued naval development, *Kaigun*, like its identically named counterpart published by the Suikōsha, served as a mouthpiece for naval expansion. While these publications materials were not so dense, scholarly, or historically based as Satō's contributions, they were nonetheless politically motivated and designed to sell the navy and its political budgetary aspirations.

Quite in contrast to Satō's methodological approach and writing style, other navy personnel tapped into an expanding popular-fiction market to further sell naval expansion to a mass audience. Beginning with the war scare that erupted between Japan and the United States in 1907 that followed the 1906 decision by the San Francisco School Board to exclude Japanese children from regular public schooling, and continuing up through World War I, Japanese authors produced numerous war fantasies and trans-

lated foreign novels of the same genre into Japanese. One of the most popular books of this genre, and by far the most poignant, was written by an
active-duty naval officer, Mizuno Hironori of the Naval Affairs Division of
the Navy Department, under the pen name Kitahara Tetsuo. In his 1913
work, *Tsugi no issen* (The next battle), Mizuno emphasized the importance
of fleet expansion through a fictional account of war between the United
States and Japan. Though his book may not have revealed the fact, Mizuno
had spent only a brief time in the United States as a naval cadet in 1899.
However, his experiences there, in particular the discrimination he witnessed in California against all Asians, left a lasting impact on his thinking
and future writing. Through his work, which is an interesting amalgam of
highly detailed technical naval discussions coupled with emotive, engaging
prose concerning tensions between Asians and Westerners, Mizuno engaged his readers with an imaginative and depressing glimpse of a future
Japanese-American war. Significantly for the navy, and clearly betraying the
reason behind the publication of this book, his war fantasy ends with the
defeat of Japan by the U.S. Navy because Japan's politicians had not supported the navy's requests for fleet expansion.

Mizuno's book was just one work amid a much larger genre that had become increasingly popular in the late Meiji and early Taishō periods.[64]
Other Japanese writers such as Morita Akatsuki also published accounts of
future battles and works that depicted the growing weakness of Japan's
navy when compared with that of other nations. In his 1911 work published
by the navy, *Teikoku Kaigun no kiki* (Crisis of the Imperial Navy), Morita argued, with numerous charts, illustrations, and supporting data to back his
claim, that the navy was at a critical juncture, when the public and the
politicians must unite to support naval growth. Echoing earlier published
newspaper reports, Morita repeatedly told his readers that in comparison
with the world's other naval powers Japan was losing ground so quickly
that without increases the fate of the empire was at stake. Three years later,
in the wake of a naval scandal that exposed naval expansion to severe domestic criticism, Morita published yet another work, *Kokubō to kaigun
jūjitsu* (Naval preparedness and national defense), which reiterated his concerns expressed earlier. However, this 1914 publication went further: Morita
exhorted his readers to support naval efforts to enact a law, similar to England's Fleet Law, that codified naval expansion in relation to what Japan's
naval rivals undertook, thus depoliticizing naval expansion, or at least
shielding it from the angry outbursts of elected politicians.[65] Warships age,
Morita argued, and eventually they reach a point when they are no longer

able to serve the fleet. A fleet law, exactly the same proposal that Yamamoto had raised back in 1898, could guarantee that Japan's navy would never lose its strength.

Along with these Japanese publications, other works written outside Japan added to the war scare of the late Meiji period. Rival translations that appeared in 1911 of Homer Lea's work *The Valor of Ignorance* underscored the popularity of works which depicted a future war between Japan and the United States.[66] Though Lea's work ended on a more positive note for Japan than Mizuno's, these works, together with other print propaganda that the navy produced, served as a military wake-up call, a call to arms rather than mere popular fiction written for entertainment purposes. While Lea's work focused on a Japanese-American war, the works which most closely resembled Mizuno's infamous story had been published in England between 1887 and 1906.[67] Following the large-scale Royal Navy Review of 1887, and in the midst of a fractious debate over naval expansion in England, the *St. James Gazette* serialized the novel *The Great Naval War of 1887*, written by Alan H. Burgoyne and W. Laird Clowes. The primary author, Burgoyne, one of England's chief naval publicists before 1914, Conservative M.P. (1910–22, 1924–29), and founder and editor of the *Navy League Annual*, wrote this novel with the sole intent of revealing the consequences of insufficient naval armament expansion. Erskine Childers' masterpiece, *The Riddle of the Sands*, published in 1903, continued this theme, and in 1906 the *Daily Mail* serialized H. W. Wilson's novel *The Invasion of England* as *The Invasion of 1910*. While the serialized installments were not translated into Japanese, Wilson and Childers' novels were adding yet another dimension to an already well established and popular genre that heightened concern over the state of Japan's naval strength.[68]

Along with novels written by naval officers and others translated into Japanese by pro-navy enthusiasts and organizations, newspapers continued to be one of the most effective means for naval officials to reach a wide audience with a pro-navy message. Unlike the navy-supported newspaper campaigns during 1905–6, which called for expansion in order to secure Japan's victorious postwar position, the post-1907 campaign took a more ominous and threatening tone in an attempt to manipulate public opinion toward supporting naval expansion. From 1907 on, but reaching a crescendo in 1910, naval officials typically provided Japanese newspapers with classified information concerning the Japanese navy. Mirroring stories run in *The Times* at the turn of the century which asked the English public, "Have we lost command of the Sea?" and answered, "Yes, . . . [but] possibly not irreparably," many of Japan's leading newspapers asked similar questions throughout the period 1907–10.[69] While no paper answered yes unequivocally, the result was a stream of reports attributed to anonymous naval officers which more often than not claimed that Japan's naval force was at a dangerously low level by comparative international standards. For instance, in early February 1907, immediately before Navy Minister Saitō warned parliamentarians about the increasing age of many of Japan's most important warships, a number of newspapers published figures and tables that illustrated the graying of Japan's warships and suggested that if expansion was not undertaken soon, the bulk of Japan's forces would become obsolete by 1912.[70] Japan would thus become assailable. Two years later the *Yamato shinbun* and the *Yorozu chōhō* published a similar series of articles arguing that Japan's real naval power had eroded considerably since 1905 and would continue to decrease at an alarming rate if the navy was not allowed to add new vessels.[71] Soon after, the *Tokyo asahi shinbun* entered the fray and published a table that predicted the future naval strengths of Japan, the United States, Britain, Germany, and France, based on current orders and age attrition. For Japan, the paper claimed, the results were startling: by 1920, the Japanese navy would possess a mere eight operational battleships and armored cruisers. When compared to the United States' twenty-six, England's seventy-four, and Germany's thirty-seven, Japan's navy would be by far the weakest naval power, one which could not even defend its homeland from possible invasion.[72] The *Jiji shinpō* in its 30 April number went so far as to claim that Japan could share the fate of Russia and China as losers in a major war if its navy were to weaken any further. After running pro-naval expansion articles for over a week, both the *Jiji shinpō* and the *Tokyo Asahi shinbun* urged their readers to support significant naval expansion, upwards of twenty-five major capital warships, that should begin in 1910 and run through to 1920 at an estimated cost somewhere between ¥400 million and ¥450 million. Within six weeks, Navy Minister Saitō introduced a ten-year naval expansion plan to the cabinet, with an estimated price tag of just over ¥400 million.[73] The public had been well prepared.

Synopsis

By 1910, the increasing effectiveness of the navy's propaganda activities was being felt at the top of Japan's political establishment. The individual most concerned by the navy's elite-level and local-level public relations activities was the army general Prime Minister Katsura Tarō, who stood to lose the most to an increased political role for the navy, particularly if it had the backing of the Seiyūkai and a substantial degree of popular support among the public. Katsura, the newest member of Japan's political estab-lishment to secure the informal title of elder statesmen, *genrō*, had stayed in a position of political power and importance largely because of the com-promise he and the leaders of the Seiyūkai political party, Hara Kei, Mat-suda Masahisa, and Saionji Kinmochi, had reached during the Russo-Japa-nese War. While Katsura held the reins as prime minister, he could count on support from the Seiyūkai majority in the parliament. In exchange for such support, Katsura agreed to recommend and support Saionji as prime min-ister when he himself stepped down.[74] The emergence of the navy as a pop-ular and more politically active force in Japanese politics threatened this position, as Katsura and Hara were well aware. At the height of the 1910 pro–naval expansion campaign led by the *Jiji shinpō* and *Tokyo Asahi shin-bun*, Katsura confessed to Hara Kei his concern that the navy, as the papers suggested, was about to introduce a large expansion program. What wor-ried Katsura most was the prospect that the navy, and specifically his neme-sis Yamamoto, was behind the newspaper campaign and that the admiral possessed two goals: naval expansion well beyond what the government could afford and use of the naval increase issue to undermine Katsura's own relationship with the Seiyūkai.[75] As elite-level political events between 1910 and 1913 would reveal, Katsura was about to be proven correct on both counts.

More than any other event, the victory at Tsushima during the Russo-Japanese War demonstrated the navy's prowess and secured for Japan's ju-nior service recognition as an impressive fighting force. Annihilating the bulk of Russia's vast navy did more than just save Japan's empire. It laid the foundations for the navy to emerge in the public consciousness as the more important military service in Japan. The navy's leaders capitalized on this important opportunity and strove continuously in the last years of the Meiji era to expand the popularity of their service and to transform popularity and prestige into political and thus budgetary capital. The navy thus emerged not only as a strong military actor in the aftermath of the Russo-Japanese War but emerged, moreover, as a politically sophisticated organi-zation that understood the important interconnections between political power, national popularity, budgets, and military strength. Through pageantry, pomp, propaganda, and commemoration, the navy cultivated in-terest in and support for the navy at the rice-roots level. Naval reviews, commemoration ceremonies, publications, warship launches, and Navy

Day celebrations made a significant and fundamental contribution to navalism and naval awareness in Japan. National pride and interest in Japan's
navy rose to new heights after 1905, and public events which showcased
Japan's modern navy and highlighted its past accomplishments provided
the populace with tangible evidence of the benefits associated with naval
expenditure and expansion. Increased popularity had been achieved, and
once this was secured, naval leaders turned their attention to the politicians
who controlled Japan's purse strings.

CHAPTER SIX

Coercion, Pragmatism, and Interservice Rivalry

Elite-Level Politics and Naval Expansion,
1910–1913

> Yamamoto is said to be a strong advocate of naval expansion, and as he is a statesman who calculates every move in his game . . . the only question now is whether he can obtain the support of the Seiyūkai.[1]
>
> —*Niroku shinbun*, 17 June 1910

> The army and the navy not only compete with those of foreign countries but attempt to excel each other at home. . . . They show little regard for the financial condition of their country.[2]
>
> —*Tokyo Asahi shinbun*, 26 October 1912

> The majority of the Seiykai opposed [army expansion], not on principles as did the Kokumintō but from the necessity to give preference to the navy.[3]
>
> —*Jiji shinpō*, 1 October 1912

A DAY BEFORE the opening of the thirtieth parliament, on Christmas Eve 1912, Prince Saionji Kinmochi addressed a gathering of Seiyūkai politicians at the party's Tokyo headquarters. Over two hundred fifty party members, including its most important leaders, Hara Kei, Matsuda Masahisa, Ozaki Yukio, Sugita Tei'ichi, and Motoda Hajime, listened as Saionji, the Seiyūkai president, shared his thoughts on the political situation that engulfed Japan, a situation later referred to as the Taishō Political Crisis (*Taishō seihen*). Though Saionji's previous cabinet (August 1911 to December 1912) had collapsed owing to Army Minister Uehara Yūsaku's resignation earlier in December, a move precipitated by Saionji's acceptance of naval expansion coupled with a refusal to support army expansion, the Seiyūkai leader expressed to the party faithful no regrets concerning his actions.[4] On the contrary, the erudite noble urged the Seiyūkai to push forward his previously planned army retrenchment so that the pruned funds could be used to reduce taxes and, no less important, to expand Japan's navy. Though his remarks brought thunderous applause from the party rank and file and support from the navy, they did not sit well with the army or the new prime minister, Katsura Tarō. Saionji's words following Uehara's resignation simply reconfirmed the fact that the pragmatic political relationship that Katsura had forged with Saionji and Hara during the Russo-Japanese War, an entente that had resulted in cabinet-parliament stability since 1905, was well and truly dead.

The collapse of this working relationship between the Seiyūkai and Katsura did not, however, spell the end of elite-level political pragmatism. Rather, its abrogation and the ensuing political maelstrom can in large part be attributed to the emergence of another important political actor in Japan's increasingly pluralistic polity, the navy. When viewed in this light, Saionji's acceptance of and support for naval expansion do not "defy explanation" as historian Tetsuo Najita has claimed but rather reflect the logical outcome of a new and important political alliance, a navy-Seiyūkai entente that would fundamentally alter elite-level politics in early Taishō Japan.[5] Expanding on its increased postwar popularity and visibility, the navy became further immersed in elite-level politics in late Meiji and early Taishō Japan to secure its budgetary objectives and in doing so emerged as an important pragmatic and at times coercive institutional force in national politics. True to Katsura's fears, as expressed to Hara in May 1910 and again to Saionji six months later, naval and Seiyūkai leaders forged an increasingly close relationship that would eventually pay handsome dividends to both, at the expense of the army and Katsura.[6] A political alliance shaped by the allure of greater political power and influence and forged by a desire to check what each perceived as army-Chōshū dominance in national politics—a point made blindingly apparent during the Taishō Political Crisis—the navy-Seiyūkai entente gave both actors greater power and influence where each sought it most: the navy within the parliament and the Seiyūkai within the bureaucracy and among the Satsuma faction. Moreover, as the navy-Seiyūkai alliance grew stronger, it emboldened both allies to pursue their respective institutional interests more aggressively, and it significantly influenced elite-level politics up until World War I.

Naval Expansion and Katsura's Second Cabinet, 1908–1911

In May 1910, after an extensive pro-navy newspaper propaganda campaign, Navy Minister Saitō Makoto introduced an eight-year naval expansion request to Katsura's cabinet.[7] Specifically, Saitō sought cabinet-level endorsement for a plan that would add fifteen capital warships, twenty-six destroyers, and ten submarines to Japan's navy. At the core of this proposal were seven first-class battleships of the *Dreadnought* class, new, militarily superior, and remarkably expensive vessels that made older capital ships such as the *Mikasa*, Admiral Tōgō's 1905 flagship, increasingly obsolete. In introducing the navy's plan both to the cabinet and later to the parliament, Saitō claimed that Japan's navy was quickly becoming dated in the face of new warship designs and reiterated the fact that no major expansion plan had been approved since the Russo-Japanese War.[8] New warships were necessary, or so Saitō concluded, in order to protect Japan's empire. Not surprisingly, such protection did not come on the cheap. Rather, in this instance it carried the immense price tag of ¥406 million.

Introduced at a time of continued fiscal austerity, the navy's plan put Katsura in a difficult though not entirely unexpected position. The intensity of the navy's newspaper-based public-relations campaign alerted Katsura to an impending spending request, as he admitted to Hara earlier in May. But the level of funding requested nevertheless startled both Katsura and the Seiyūkai power broker Hara.[9] Katsura thus faced a difficult political-military dilemma. On the one hand, he understood the importance of increasing the navy's firepower and moreover predicted that if expansion were not undertaken, the navy would create a political disturbance that might end his current tenure as prime minister. Expansion was therefore desirable for imperial as well as political security. On the other hand, ¥406 million, even if spread out over eight years as requested by the navy, was far more than Katsura believed the government could afford. Katsura's solution, at least the one he divulged to Hara, was to "delay a decision as long as possible" while attempting to find a smaller amount of money with which to placate naval officials, at least temporarily.[10]

The policy of tactical delay was not without its drawbacks for Katsura either in the short term or over the long haul. Throughout much of June and July, naval officers increased their political activities both within the navy and within the cabinet as a whole. Rather than rely entirely on Navy Minister Saitō, who many inside the navy felt might accept a Katsura-sponsored compromise over the expansion plan, officials within both the Navy Ministry and the Navy General Staff engaged in elite-level political maneuvers in hopes of securing passage of the navy's entire expansion plan.[11] On 9 July, three days before the cabinet was set to discuss the navy plan, Vice Admiral Matsumoto Kazu, chief of the Naval Stores Division, met with Vice Navy Minister Takarabe Takeshi, Yamamoto Gonnohyōe 's son-in-law, and expressed his concern that the expansion plan might be whittled away or rejected outright if more pressure was not exerted on Katsura.[12] Almost immediately after this meeting concluded, Takarabe proceeded to visit Admiral Ijūin Gorō, chief of the Navy General Staff, another member of Yamamoto's inner circle. After a short discussion, Ijūin agreed to meet Saitō and intimated that, depending on the outcome, he would proceed if necessary to meet Katsura in person.

Assured by Ijūin's words, Takarabe left the Navy General Staff headquarters, but this would not end the vice navy minister's political involvement. The next day, 10 July, Takarabe visited Yamamoto's personal residence, Daimachi, and related events of the previous two days. Almost immediately, Yamamoto launched a verbal tirade against what he called Saitō's idleness in securing a firm commitment from Katsura to support the navy's entire expansion plan.[13] After this initial salvo, Yamamoto then proceeded to list a long litany of historical examples in which previous navy ministers resolutely championed the navy's interests in the face of seemingly insurmountable political obstacles. He concluded by stating that the navy had (unlike the army) always been forced to fight vociferously for its political and budgetary objectives. He then gave tacit consent for individuals apart from Saitō—implying Ijūin—to approach Katsura directly to discuss the naval expansion plan.

The following morning, Ijūin met Katsura and discussed the navy's full expansion plan, which the cabinet was set to discuss on 12 July. As one would expect from the head of the Navy General Staff, Ijūin offered a number of military and strategic reasons why the navy's plan was absolutely indispensable for Japan. Ijūin did not rely just on military reasoning, however: he also used his charm and political savvy to work on Katsura, claiming that as a military man Katsura was better prepared than any previous prime minister to comprehend the navy's expansion request. In addition to such blandishment, Ijūin also intimated that once naval expansion was completed, his service would lend its support to the army's expansion plans.[14] Though Prime Minister Katsura reiterated his position that the entire amount could not be agreed to, he suggested the possibility that the cabinet would accept a scaled-back expansion plan. Moreover, perhaps attempting to shore up his own position, Katsura further intimated that if he remained in power, he would support further naval expansion after 1913. Though not entirely what the navy desired, the prospect of securing a firm commitment for limited expansion between 1911 and 1913 was enough to keep either Ijūin or Saitō from resigning his position.[15]

At the cabinet meeting on 12 July, ministers agreed in principle to just such a compromise as Katsura had alluded to the day before in his discussion with Ijūin.[16] In the daylong meeting, Katsura endorsed a naval expansion plan of ¥82 million, which would provide funds for limited naval construction and upgrades to battleships already under construction. Two reasons explain why Katsura endorsed naval expansion during a period of overall fiscal austerity, during which the general-turned-prime-minister rejected a smaller expansion request from the army: national defense and domestic politics. Clearly, Katsura could not escape the fact that Japan's navy was falling behind other powers' navies both quantitatively and qualitatively after the emergence of *Dreadnought*-class warships. Tables and figures published by newspapers and given to Katsura by naval officials including Ijūin could not be easily brushed aside. However, domestic politics also played a—if not *the*—critical role in Katsura's behavior in 1910, as it did in most if not all of his actions as prime minister. Katsura sought to remain in power throughout 1910 and into 1911, and supporting the navy's requests in a limited form removed the very real possibility that the navy minister might resign if given no funding increases. Such an action, Katsura understood, would expose his cabinet to collapse if no other naval officer of flag rank on the active list could be found to fill the vacancy. Added to this was Katsura's fear that the navy and the Seiyūkai were gravitating toward one another. Katsura wanted to reduce the likelihood of a navy-Seiyūkai cabinet's emerging either before a revision of the Anglo-Japanese Alliance, or before elections to the House of Peers were concluded, all of which were scheduled to take place in the first half of 1911. What worried Katsura most, at least according to Tetsuo Najita, was that a navy-Seiyūkai cabinet, if it emerged before the upper-house elections, might grant peerage to a large number of pro-Seiyūkai or pro-navy individuals.[17] As those with peerage rank selected from among themselves members to serve in the House of Peers, a large influx of new pro-Seiyūkai or pro-navy peers could influence elections and thus membership of the upper house, which in 1910 was still a preserve of Chōshū, pro-army individuals from the Yamagata faction. Politics thus necessitated compromise on the navy issue.

Katsura's fears of an emergent elite-level navy-Seiyūkai entente were borne out by political developments during 1910 and 1911. On 11 November 1910, Tokonami Takejirō visited Hara and discussed contemporary politics. As a confidant of Hara's, a Seiyūkai member, and a native of Satsuma, Tokonami was an ideal person to serve as a facilitator between the Seiyūkai and the navy, a role in which he excelled. Tokonami began the discussion with a political reference to Yamamoto Gonnohyōe, to which Hara replied that the Satsuma faction under Yamamoto's leadership could "only prosper by allying itself with a political party," since by themselves they were "no match for the Chōshū group."[18] Tokonami then confessed his desire to mediate between both groups, informing Hara that both sides should further discuss the issue. The ever-ambitious Hara readily agreed and admitted that it would be "good for both [Yamamoto through Tokonami and Hara himself] to keep communicating."[19]

Just over two weeks later, communications continued as another Satsuma official with ties to Yamamoto and the Seiyūkai visited Hara, Anraku Kendō.[20] Like Tokonami, Anraku was a Satsuma man, and one who through Hara's political patronage and support had been appointed to and excelled as the commissioner of the Tokyo Metropolitan Police. At their 29 November meeting, Anraku reported a recent meeting with Yamamoto in which the navy kingmaker expressed his conviction that the next cabinet, whoever led it, should include both Hara and his Seiyūkai counterpart, Matsuda Masahisa, with whom Yamamoto had been in contact since July.[21] This was a clear expression of interest on Yamamoto's part, a point that Anraku brought home by confiding to Hara that "Yamamoto looked ambitious" and was desirous of meeting Hara face to face to discuss cabinet politics. To this, Hara replied: "Although I too am desirous to meet Yamamoto, Katsura is very careful about our movements, . . . so I think it would be impossible to meet at this point."[22] Though an elite-level meeting was put on ice, meetings via Satsuma go-betweens continued between Seiyūkai leaders and naval officials up to the formation of the Yamamoto-Seiyūkai cabinet in 1913.[23]

Armed with knowledge of navy-Satsuma ambitions and emboldened by Yamamoto's eagerness to meet concerning future cabinet appointments, Hara stepped up discussions with other Seiyūkai leaders concerning the possibility of forming a future cabinet. In meetings with party members Noda Utarō (27 November and 1, 4, and 11 December), Matsuda Masahisa (5, 12, 14, and 28 December), and Saionji (2, 15, and 18 December), Hara gleaned two important points: first, Saionji would, if called upon to do so, lead another cabinet; and second, other Seiyūkai leaders were as angered by Katsura's refusal to step down as he was and were desirous of seeing a new Saionji-led cabinet formed early in the new year at the latest.[24] Moreover, Hara clearly recognized from his communications with other Seiyūkai men as well as with Satsuma go-betweens that Yamamoto, like many in his party executive, felt considerable animosity toward Katsura.[25]

With such information in hand, Hara met Prime Minister Katsura and needled him over national budgetary concerns, naval expansion, and the state of his cabinet. At their 4 December meeting, Hara played on Katsura's fears, expressed earlier, that parties in the Diet would create a disturbance over the naval increase issue. Hara pointedly asked why Katsura supported naval increases, to which Katsura triumphantly replied that by endorsing limited naval expansion he had "put the navy under his control." Hara, through his discussion with Satsuma intermediaries and by his own observations, knew better.[26] Much to Hara's disappointment, Katsura gave no indication of willingness to step aside for Saionji. The following day, Hara confessed to Inoue Kaoru, a confidant of Katsura's: "It is a pity things have become like this after all these years of friendship . . . an uncertain future will stir up more suspicion."[27] Ten days after their 4 December meeting, Hara and Katsura again exchanged opinions concerning cabinet politics. Though disappointed with Katsura's stated desire to hold power until after all treaty revisions had taken place, or as Hara saw it to hold on to power until after the upper-house elections, Hara departed the meeting in the belief—mistaken in the first instance—that Katsura would neither hold the reins as prime minister again nor support General Terauchi as his successor.[28] On the surface, then, it must have appeared that Katsura's delaying tactic brought stability to national politics. The reality, however, was that the longer Katsura held on to power, the more attractive a Seiyūkai-navy entente became to both Hara and Yamamoto.

At the rank-and-file party level, a navy-Seiyūkai entente was helped considerably by Navy Minister Saitō's behavior before the Diet in late 1910 and early 1911. Indeed, the last piece of the political puzzle that needed to be put into place for the navy to secure its scaled-back ¥82-million expansion program was to gain acceptance in the Diet. Here Saitō excelled. If Saitō's overly pragmatic approach at the cabinet level drew anger and political involvement from members of the Navy General Staff and other officials from the Navy Ministry in June and July 1910, his work in championing the navy's agenda before parliament secured nothing but praise, both from navy colleagues and from parliamentarians. Saitō, once labeled the master of compromise, possessed a distinguished navy career, serving as vice naval minister from 1898 to 1906 under Yamamoto and as naval minister from 1906, a position he would hold until 1914, making his the longest uninterrupted tenure in that office. Much of this he owed to his political skill, pragmatism, and patience. At a Diet Budget Committee meeting on 23 January 1911, Saitō skillfully answered queries raised by Representative Ōishi Masa-

FIG. 4. "Going to Decay: Poor little fellow! His father Saitō can't get enough money to buy new ships for his sonnie, and the old ones are decaying away year after year" and "Dreadnought Rivalry: May Festival coming on, there is a heated rivalry in putting up Dreadnought streamers. Uncle Sam must have the biggest of all." (*Tokyo Puck*, 7:13, 1 May 1911)

mi, a leader of the reform faction in the Kokumintō party. "The navy," declared Saitō in an honest, straightforward manner, "always desired expansion," but owing to financial difficulties in Japan between 1906 and 1909 it had forgone requests for massive increases in naval expenditures.[29] The navy had, as an alternative course, followed a pattern of thrift, upgrading captured Russian warships to supplement Japan's naval strength. The world of naval development had changed, however, and now that warships of the *Dreadnought* class had progressed from the experimental stage to become the standard, Japan needed to follow suit. While the navy desired massive increases in 1910–11, according to Saitō, his service once again accepted the fiscal realities of Japan's economic position and requested only the scaled-back amount of ¥82 million. Saitō continued with such straightforward, seemingly honest, even-tempered language throughout the parliamentary session, and it paid off for the navy. The navy's request passed both houses of parliament with little or no dissent.[30]

Saitō's frank claim that the navy always desired expansion proved true within months of the legislators' endorsing the ¥82-million expansion plan. In May 1911, Saitō introduced a ¥352-million, seven-year expansion plan over and above the funds approved in the previous parliament.[31] This was an explosive issue for Prime Minister Katsura, brought forward by the navy at the most inopportune moment for him. In response, he simply refused to tackle the issue until he had secured treaty revisions and until after the peers' elections. For one thing, Katsura knew that if he refused the navy outright, Saitō would most likely resign or be forced to resign by pressure within the navy. On the other hand, if Katsura accepted the plan, or even a reduced version of the plan, he would most certainly draw strong criticism from two camps: the army, which also sought an expansion program that Katsura had previously shelved in 1911, and parliamentarians not desirous of massive military increases. Katsura therefore followed a path of no resistance by simply not engaging in cabinet-level discussions on the issue. This proved successful, at least for Katsura. When Katsura tendered his resignation in August, the navy question remained unresolved and awaited direction from the new prime minister, Saionji Kinmochi.

Naval Expansion and Saionji's Second Cabinet, 1911–1912

With Katsura's resignation and Saionji's appointment in August, the navy wasted no time in pushing forward discussion concerning the ¥352-million request previously submitted in May. The day after Saionji formally became prime minister, Saitō visited him and submitted the navy's expansion plan.[32] As pragmatic as ever, Saitō admitted the financial difficulties as-sociated with the navy's proposed expansion but reiterated that without further expansion the navy would face grave difficulties in connection with imperial defense. If the request startled the Kyoto aristocrat Saionji, com-ing as it did just months after parliament endorsed ¥82 million in addi-tional funding for the navy, the compromise specialist Saitō offered a way out. Saitō offered to set aside for the time being the specific amount re-quested provided that Saionji would agree in principle that the navy needed further expansion. This the prime minister rejected, knowing full well that it might be used against him when budgetary negotiations progressed more formally in November. All Saionji could offer was his opinion that a deci-sion on expansion in principle, as well in reality, could be made only after a more thorough investigation of state finances.[33] This the prime minister felt might prove difficult, as he wanted each government ministry to reduce overall administrative expenditures by 10 to 15 percent.[34]

Budget-reducing intentions aside, the day after becoming Japan's four-teenth prime minister Saionji faced the exact same problem that had be-deviled many if not all of his predecessors, balancing military expansion requests with other budgetary concerns within a political system that pro-vided military ministers with special political prerogatives. In discussion with Hara concerning Saitō's proposal, Hara and Saionji agreed that unless the navy minister was allowed to introduce his expansion plan to the full cabinet he would likely resign. This jeopardized the cabinet, and moreover, if a new navy minister was found from among the restricted ranks of flag-rank officers on active duty, the new minister would likely introduce the same plan anyway.[35] Both agreed that Saitō should be allowed to make his formal request to the entire cabinet, with Hara adding: "If no finances can be found to support the scheme, we will hold a meeting in the presence of the emperor."[36] While both Hara and Saionji worried about the costs of fi-nancing naval expansion to the extent Saitō envisioned, both realized that allowing Saitō his opportunity was the best way to preserve their cabinet. When informed that he could request the entire amount from the cabinet, Saitō readily agreed.

Saitō indeed submitted the entire expansion plan before the full cabinet on 2 November, and the navy minister did it in his usual pragmatic fash-ion.[37] Aware of the financial difficulties facing Japan—not to mention the internal political difficulties that he himself would be facing if he did not se-cure some form of agreement—the navy minister began his presentation by admitting that expansion costing in the neighborhood of ¥352 million was far too grandiose to request at present. Expansion on this level was necessary but unrealistic, or so Saitō suggested. The navy minister thereafter submitted a scaled-back plan of roughly ¥90 million to purchase three new battleships. Importantly, Saitō claimed that the ¥90-million expansion plan would require no new funding for 1912. When this raised skeptical eyebrows, Saitō informed cabinet ministers that the ¥1.5 million needed to begin construction contracts could be obtained through funds saved by administrative retrenchment within the navy. All it would take from this cabinet, or so Saitō concluded, was ministerial approval to appropriate funds beginning in 1913, roughly ¥88.5 million, to continue with the construction under contract. Though no minister opposed the proposal outright, all agreed that further investigation into state finances would be required before they could endorse any proposal, even one that required no new expenditures for fiscal year 1912.[38]

Soon after the cabinet's first budget meeting, various individuals within the navy began an extensive elite-level lobbying campaign to win supporters over to their expansion plan. While Saitō worked the prime minister on 8 November, again stating that the navy could provide the costs incurred for 1912, Vice Minister Takarabe called on individuals outside the government to add weight and influence to the debate. On 21 November, after a morning of duck hunting with navy colleagues, Takarabe learned and approved of Vice Admiral Matsumoto's attempts to have Admiral Katō Kanji enlist Mastukata Masayoshi's support for the naval expansion plan. Importantly, Katō and Matsumoto decided to contact the elder Matsukata through his son, Matsukata Kōjirō.[39] The third son of the Satsuma *genrō* and former prime minister and finance minister was no disinterested party. On the contrary, the young Matsukata was president of the Kawasaki dockyards, one of the two private dockyards in Japan that were large enough to construct capital warships (excluding vessels of the *Dreadnought* class) for the Japanese navy. Clearly his company would benefit from naval expansion, and many in the navy believed that the elder Matsukata's influence in financial circles could prove decisive for their service's request.

Takarabe also followed a pattern first set by Navy Minister Kawamura Sumiyoshi in 1882 by directly lobbying Satsuma members of the cabinet before ministers agreed upon a final decision. The day after Takarabe endorsed discussions with the Matsukata family, the vice navy minister sent a letter to Admiral Uemura requesting that he contact Agriculture Minister Makino Nobukai and Justice Minister Matsuda Masahisa. While Matsuda did not originate from Satsuma like his ministerial counterpart Makino, he was the leader of the Seiyūkai Kyushu faction (which included Satsuma), a power-ful faction within the Seiyūkai that increasingly supported naval expansion within the Diet. Indeed, from 1904 on, Kyushu became a stronghold for the Seiyūkai, with this party holding every electoral seat for Kagoshima-ken between 1904 and 1917.

The navy's machinations came to light on 24 November, when the cabi-net met to discuss the final budget for 1912. This was a tense moment for the navy and for those officials who had invested considerable effort and time to secure the navy's expansionary designs. So important was this cabi-net meeting for Takarabe that he abandoned the opportunity to witness live-fire exercises off Yokosuka in case "something urgent happened during the day's budget assessment meeting."[40] Takarabe's decision was warranted. As soon as the cabinet ministers agreed on the naval component of the bud-get, Saitō called for Takarabe, and upon his arrival at the prime minister's residence provided him with a handwritten memo which read:[41]

> The cabinet has decided that the naval preparation plan submitted to this meet-ing will be considered after the administrative reform is completed in Meiji 45 [1912]. This decision will be announced to the public. However, it has been un-officially decided that the plan will be commenced in Meiji 46 [1913]. It will be no problem to start [signing] secret contracts, but the cabinet's approval is re-quired before any signing. These decisions are absolutely confidential among those who are in charge.

Takarabe was speechless. To him, this decision initially looked like a failure, as no new funds would be dispersed in 1912 for immediate construction. That evening he confessed his disagreement to Admiral Yamanouchi Ma-suji, former commander of the Kure Admiralty (1905–9) and current presi-dent of the Japan Steel Works, and suggested that for the prestige of the navy either Saitō or a subordinate official in the navy ministry (implying himself) should resign over the failure to gain cabinet approval for imme-diate expansion. Yamanouchi suggested otherwise.

It was not, Yamanouchi suggested, a failure. Although cabinet ministers refused to release funds in 1912 for the entire amount needed to purchase the warships, they agreed that the navy could sign contracts for warships that would be funded from 1913 on. Not only did this remove the issue from parliament in the first instance, but it also committed the cabinet to support naval increases regardless of whatever political and financial diffi-culties might engulf Japan in the following years. It would take an extraor-dinary measure to stop construction once begun. Moreover, reversing this decision the following year would result in protest and resignations from the navy anyway, thus jeopardizing any future cabinet that pursued such a course of action.

Others in the navy agreed with Yamanouchi's appraisal. As a victory was exactly how Saitō viewed the agreement reached by the cabinet on 24 November. In discussion with Takarabe on 25 November, Saitō reiterated this point, claiming that "concrete plans could now be drawn up" for naval expansion.[42] Takarabe begrudgingly accepted this point and encouraged Saitō to begin immediate administrative retrenchment in order that funds saved, upwards of ¥1.5 million, could be channeled to support construction of the three warships in question. This was not the only course of action Takarabe undertook, however. Wanting written assurances from the cabinet that specifically spelled out their support for naval expansion from 1913 on, Takarabe asked Vice Admiral Matsumoto to write a resolution which all cabinet ministers would endorse with their official seal.[43] Importantly, Takarabe wanted specific budgetary numbers included, as well as acceptance in principle of the need to expand the navy by a figure of ¥352 million as originally requested in August. Matsumoto's resolution read:[44]

> The necessity of the naval preparation shown in this plan has been acknowl-
> edged. However, the necessary cost of ¥351.9 million is beyond the capacity of
> the imperial government in view of today's financial situation. Therefore, it has
> been unofficially decided to appropriate an amount of ¥90 million from the
> budgets of Meiji 46 [1913] and after. This is the budget for the construction of
> the three urgently needed battleships. The rest of the preparation cost will be ap-
> propriated from the budgets of Meiji 49 [1916] and after. The annual breakdown
> of the above ¥90 million will be decided after the completion of the entire gov-
> ernment's administrative reform. The navy minister is able to commence the
> construction of the above three battleships from Meiji 45 [1912], by signing se-
> cret construction contracts, after obtaining the cabinet's approval.

When Matsumoto's resolution was presented to the full cabinet (minus Home Minister Hara), the ministers engaged in minimal debate, agreeing to support naval expansion from 1913 on both in principle and as spelled out in the 1911 agreement. The ministers did, however, object to affixing their stamps to a document explicitly stating "by signing secret construction contracts," so the navy removed this phrase from the final draft.[45] Three days later, when the cabinet again discussed the navy's resolution, this time in the presence of Home Minister Hara, he wholeheartedly agreed that "secret" must be removed, but he strongly supported the navy's wish that precise budgetary figures be included in the document.[46]

Before discussion concluded, however, a new political development—
one that would ultimately prove destructive—surfaced within the debate

over naval expansion: army expansion. Not wishing to remain on the sidelines while the navy secured political commitments for future expansion, Army Minister Ishimoto Shinroku asked for and received cabinet assurances that approval of army expansion by two divisions could be expected in late 1912 for the following year.[47] When confronted with this unexpected request and agreement, Hara asked whether army expansion would be made public; Saionji replied: "Certainly." Ishimoto suggested otherwise, believing that it would be best announced after army administrative retrenchment had taken place, to which Hara agreed. Elite-level politics had thus secured political commitments from the cabinet to support both services' expansion at the end of 1912.

The navy's political exploits in 1910–11 resulted in significant budgetary rewards. Mixing coercion and conciliation at the cabinet level, expressing magnanimity before the Diet, and working all the personal connections that remained important in Japanese politics won the navy budgetary victories in a period of overall fiscal austerity. For Saionji and Katsura, the results were less obviously favorable, at least in the long run. Both mortgaged the future by giving political guarantees for future military expansion in exchange for present cabinet stability. Military ministers held special political privileges, and as events of 1912 would show, when they were confronted with what they saw as political backtracking away from previously secured commitments for expansion, cabinet stability evaporated.

Throughout the summer of 1912, Saionji grew more concerned about the upcoming cabinet-level budget negotiations for 1913 and beyond. He did so with good reason. Both military ministries had secured political commitments for expansion beginning in 1913, and both services had undertaken administrative retrenchment to reduce ordinary expenditures. This, the military ministers believed, would make their respective cases for expansion more politically and financially acceptable. Here they both erred. In addition to these political developments, General Uehara Yūsaku's appointment as army minister in April, after the death of General Ishimoto Shinroku, worried Saionji, Hara, and many in the navy.[48] Many individuals within the government and armed forces saw Uehara as a hawk, one who would champion the army's expansion plan while offering little room for compromise.[49] These predictions would prove correct.

Though given Uehara's determination not to be outmaneuvered by the navy or the cabinet one might have expected him to be the one to begin the budgetary battle, it was in fact the navy that first introduced its formal expansion plan to the cabinet in autumn 1912.[50] Unveiled to the cabinet on 5

November, exactly one week before the navy conducted a massive naval review off Yokohama, Saitō sought cabinet-level endorsement of a nine-year, ¥352-million expansion plan, exactly the same one he had presented a year earlier. Viewing acceptance of the plan as part of the overall budget agreement reached in 1911, Saitō concluded by requesting a quick settlement to the issue, which he suggested had already been debated and resolved satisfactorily the previous year. Ministers agreed in principle to Saitō's requests but balked at the ¥352-million cost. The cabinet did, however, support the previously agreed-upon plan for a ¥90-million increase set to commence in 1913.

Though the naval issue had been decided amicably, at least from the navy's standpoint, a quick and favorable settlement to the overall budget issue was complicated by one important factor—army expansion. The seriousness with which army leaders would pursue their expansion requests became known both to Saionji and the navy during the late summer of 1912. In August, upon Hara's recommendation, Saionji discussed army expansion with Katsura, who upon his return from Europe in July had been appointed grand chamberlain and lord keeper of the Privy Council to the new Taishō Emperor.[51] His new imperial position, or so Katsura suggested, kept the experienced statesman from intervening on behalf of Saionji. This was unfortunate, for Katsura had on many previous occasions successfully resisted army expansion requests and thus kept army demands from destabilizing cabinet politics. Barring direct intervention, Katsura suggested that Saionji meet Field Marshall Yamagata Aritomo face to face in order to halt the army's demands, or at least to postpone them for one year. Katsura gravely overestimated Yamagata's willingness to put cabinet stability above army expansion. On 30 August, Yamagata refused to broker or even to support any compromise concerning the two-division increase.[52] As he would later inform the prime minister: "National defense comes first; financial policy, last."[53]

By early autumn, naval officials feared that army intransigence would lead to a budget showdown in which each service might be forced to postpone or reduce the amount requested. Worse yet, Saitō, Takarabe, and Yamamoto predicted that the Saionji cabinet might collapse under such pressure and be replaced by a pro-army, Yamagata-faction prime minister, most likely either General Tanaka Gi'ichi or Terauchi. Either man, so navy leaders believed, would certainly prioritize the army's expansion over that proposed by the navy. On 29 October, Vice Navy Minister Takarabe visited Anraku to learn his opinions concerning the army's machinations, and what he heard further unsettled him. Anraku predicted that Uehara's stubborn insistence on securing expansion at all costs, political or economic, would lead to the collapse of the Saionji cabinet before any agreement could be reached on the naval question.[54] Though Anraku suggested, as he had in the past, that Yamamoto might be the obvious choice to replace Saionji, Takarabe was more realistic in his appraisal of the situation and left the meeting depressed. The vice navy minster believed that the army faction would never endorse Yamamoto's candidacy. Takarabe's fears were confirmed on 26 November, when he met with Minami Hiroshi, chief secretary of the cabinet. During their exchange, Minami confessed that from his point of view the matter of the army's expansion had become more problematic. Yamagata, so Minami believed, had refused Saionji's final request to rein in hard-line expansion supporters within army.[55] This was a sobering revelation.

Aware that the cabinet might soon collapse if the army minister resigned, naval officials increased their political activities in hopes of gaining cabinet-level agreement for their expansion request. On 14 November, Yamamoto met Prime Minister Saionji and encouraged him to "set to work in earnest this time," to which Saionji replied that he would.[56] Nine days later, Takarabe again used his professional ties with Matsukata Kōjirō to enlist the support of the elder, well-respected *genrō* Matsukata. After Takarabe's discussion with the younger, maritime-oriented Matsukata on 25 November, Kōjirō approached his father, and the following day the elder Matsukata asked Minister of Agriculture Makino to introduce a compromise within the cabinet. Thereafter Makino suggested that the cabinet should endorse both the navy and the army expansion requests but that because of the country's financial situation should postpone realization of the army plan for at least one year.[57] The following day, Takarabe met Prime Minister Saionji and again labored to convince him—this time with military reasoning—that naval expansion was far more important to imperial defense than the expansion of the army by two divisions. Expanding the army, so Takarabe concluded, was nothing more than "adding more pawns to a chessboard while neglecting the king, queen, and other important pieces."[58] Takarabe preached to the converted, but Prime Minister Saionji had lost the ability to secure cabinet stability yet again through military compromise, at least when both services were making their demands for expansion to him. Yamamoto was less kind in his appraisal of Saionji's final acts as prime minister, claiming that through his utter "indecisiveness" Saionji had been "forestalled by the army" and had created a "hopeless situation."[59]

The dispute over military expansion reached a crescendo in November and early December 1912. On 9 November, Hara, Saionji, and Finance Minister Yamamoto Tastuo heard from chief of the Army Affairs Bureau Tanaka Gi'ichi the reasons why the army felt it was necessary to expand its force levels by two divisions.[60] The three civilians were not impressed. The following day, Saionji met Yamagata at his personal residence at Odawara. There Yamagata suggested that funds pruned from army administrative retrenchment could be directed to army expansion.[61] Moreover, aware that the cabinet had agreed to support both navy and army expansion the previous year, the Chōshū statesman warned Saionji that "the army would feel uncomfortable if naval expansion was implemented and the army plan rejected."[62] This was an understatement. Regardless of this warning, Saionji, Matsuda, and Hara conferred after this meeting and agreed that they would not support the army's request.

Sensing a political maelstrom, on 16 November Hara met Katsura to see if the former general-turned-prime-minister could mediate between the cabinet and the army. Confessing to Katsura that this issue of a two-division increase was unlike any other political problem he had come across, Hara seemingly begged for Katsura's assistance.[63] Katsura, however, demurred. At the same time, Yamagata worked behind the scenes to win-over Matsukata and other *genrō* to support the army's position.[64] Both efforts at persuasion came to naught, and the cabinet refused to endorse army expansion. On 22 November, Army Minister Uehara introduced an expansion request to the cabinet. Specifically, General Uehara sought funds to support the creation of two new army divisions for deployment in Korea, something army personnel felt was critically important after the 1911 revolution in China and, moreover, something they felt had been decided upon in 1907 during imperial defense negotiations. Though the army requests were far less expensive than the previously supported naval expansion plan, the cabinet approached army expansion with far less enthusiasm. Claiming that Uehara's justifications were poor, the cabinet refused to make any formal decision on 22 November. Six days later, on 28 November, the issue again surfaced, and once again Saionji asked Uehara to justify why army expansion beginning in 1913 was so critical an issue. Well aware that naval expansion had already been agreed upon, the pragmatic Saitō interjected that army expansion might be carried out the following year, after army administrative retrenchment had pruned operating costs.[65] Uehara flatly rejected this proposal. At yet another impasse, the cabinet agreed to further discuss the issue the following day, but again no decision could be agreed upon. Incensed at the cabinet's refusal to endorse army expansion, on 2 December Uehara resigned, and three days later, Saionji's cabinet collapsed. The "two-division issue" had been, in the words of General Tanaka, "transformed into high-level politics," politics which would further unite the Seiyūkai and the Yamamoto-navy-Satsuma factions against the Chōshū-army faction and Katsura.[66] Indeed, within hours of Saionji's resignation, two developments occurred which would have lasting significance to national politics and naval expansion in the early years of the Taishō era: heightened navy political resolve to champion its objectives and party-directed public protest against the Chōshū-army faction.

Naval Politics and the Taishō Political Crisis

Almost as soon as Saionji's cabinet collapsed, Yamamoto and other top naval officials immersed themselves in the politics that surrounded the selection and appointment of a new prime minister. They did so with good reason: naval leaders wanted their previously agreed-to ¥90-million expansion plan to be placed before the Diet by whoever led the next cabinet. No guarantee existed, however, that the next prime minister would support, let alone champion, the navy's concerns. For the first time since 1901, Japan's aging elder statesmen, the *genrō*, met to select the next prime minister. Though navy men had little influence over the deliberations, which ran for the better part of ten days beginning on 6 December, all the navy's senior staffers followed these discussions with great interest. While admirals Itō, Ijūin, and Takarabe expressed concern that a pro-army individual might assume power, thus threatening the navy's 1913 expansion program, Yamamoto worked tirelessly to assure that a navy admiral, himself most of all, would not become prime minister in December 1912. On two separate occasions in early to mid-December, Yamamoto flatly refused to accept an offer of that office and moreover dissuaded any pro-navy Satsuma officials, including Matsukata Masayoshi, from becoming Japan's fifteenth prime minister.[67] Though Matsukata expressed interest in the position, particularly after *genrō* Ōyama Iwao and Inoue Kaoru visited the former prime minister at his Mita residence on 7 December, a visit followed by an extended discussion with Katsura three days later, Yamamoto finally persuaded Matsukata that it would not be good for the Satsuma statesman to "take up the position while Yamagata and his party are based in the palace [implying Katsura's position as grand chamberlain] doing as they please."[68] Matsukata eventually concurred.

A number of factors motivated the former navy minister to reject any offer that would have placed him in a position of national political responsibility. For one, Yamamoto believed that until Yamagata or Katsura resolved or suppressed the two-division-increase issue within the army, cabinet politics would remain as unstable as ever. If Yamamoto had assumed the position as cabinet head without any resolution of the army expansion issue, the Satsuma admiral would have faced three realistic courses of action as prime minister. One, Yamamoto could reject out of hand the army's request for expansion, just as Saionji had previously done in late November. This Yamamoto figured would result in the army minister's resignation. Thus, events of the previous Saionji cabinet would reoccur; not a desirable political beginning for the nation's first admiral-turned-prime-minister. Two, the new prime minister could accept army demands and attempt to force this issue through the Seiyūkai-dominated parliament. This policy was destined to fail, given the public outcry that had developed over the collapse of the Saionji administration, and moreover such heavy-handed tactics would have severely strained relations between Yamamoto and the Seiyūkai party, the one group with which Yamamoto had sought to strengthen his ties in 1912. Finally, at the urging of the *genrō* council, a navy or even pro-navy-oriented prime minister might be forced to temporarily postpone both navy and army expansion in 1913 in hopes that the armed services, the cabinet, and the Diet could reach a compromise by 1914. While this last option might have appealed to many of Japan's elder statesmen, including Matsukata, Yamamoto and the navy had nothing to gain and a considerable amount to lose by following such a strategy. Saionji's previous cabinet had already agreed to support naval expansion, and Hara had given his word that the Seiyūkai would likewise endorse the increase plan in parliament. Yamamoto would not have endangered the navy's position by serving as a mediator between the army and the political parties, nor would he agree to postpone naval expansion that had previously been agreed upon just to placate the anger of army officials. Although desirous of expanding his power base, Yamamoto possessed keen political instincts and the foresight not to delve into the political dispute at such an early and unresolved stage. "The Chōshū leaders are responsible for this political chaos"—or so Yamamoto informed both Matsukata and Yamagata—"let them be responsible for restoring order."[69] Finally, from an entirely parochial standpoint, Yamamoto and the navy had everything to gain from a worsening of the relationship between the army-Chōshū faction and the political parties. The prolonged dispute over the two-division expansion made a formal navy-Seiyūkai entente more attractive to both sides.

While Yamamoto distanced himself from accepting any position of national political responsibility in December 1912, he made every effort to strengthen the navy minister's resolve to fend off any political attempt to reduce or retract the previously agreed-upon ¥90-million expansion plan that was set to commence in 1913. Yamamoto predicted that the next *genrō*-appointed prime minister might approach Saitō, perhaps with imperial backing, in an attempt to forge a compromise whereby the cabinet would postpone both army and navy expansion requests until 1914. Such a policy might appeal to the new prime minister, Yamamoto believed, as it would eliminate current political antagonism over military increases and greatly reduce army anger and jealousy over the rejection of the two-division increase on the grounds of fiscal retrenchment. Yamamoto clearly articulated these fears in a letter given to admirals Saitō, Ijūin, and Takarabe on 14 December, which stated:[70]

> Because of the current difficulties in organizing a new cabinet, there is a possibility that a second-class or third-class politician may come to power. In such a case, a dispute may arise with the intention of postponing the naval preparation along with the postponement of the army division increase. However, the question of whether the navy should be expanded, or whether a division increase should be postponed, belongs to the responsibilities of the ministers of state. It is by no means a question in which *genrō* should meddle; as far as I believe, even the emperor should not interfere with the issue. This matter needs serious consideration. We should not commit ourselves, without thorough consideration, to the opinion that the naval expansion issue is the same as the army division issue. I would like you to be very careful about it, or we will be forestalled by rivals and put in a very difficult position.

Yamamoto's predictions would prove prescient. On 17 December, the *genrō* selected Katsura as the next prime minister, and at 11:00 A.M. Katsura received an imperial request to reassume the office. Within hours of this announcement, Katsura requested a formal meeting with Saitō to discuss the naval expansion issue and to see if the former navy minister would himself serve or recommend another admiral to serve as navy minister. Anticipating just such a move, Yamamoto relayed a far sterner warning to Saitō than the one he had issued on 14 December, informing the navy pragmatist: "When you meet Katsura, if the issue of your successor is raised, never recommend anyone. It would be better that way, considering the power struggle within the navy."[71] Through this statement, delivered to the navy minister by Takarabe, the vice navy minister and Yamamoto's son-in-law, Yamamoto warned both Saitō and by extension Katsura that the naval expansion issue was not negotiable and that if pressed on this issue, the navy might well withhold a ministerial appointment, mirroring the army's tactics earlier in the month.

Budgetary discussion between Katsura and Saitō commenced the next day and continued for the better part of a week. As Yamamoto predicted, Katsura began his first meeting with Saionji by outlining a political compromise.[72] Katsura first suggested that navy and army expansions be postponed for one year. When Saitō expressed displeasure over this suggestion, the wily Katsura gave assurances that shipbuilding could proceed without appropriating the navy's full ¥350-million expansion plan, or even the previously agreed-to ¥90-million component set to begin in 1913. This was akin to the earlier suggested, though rejected, plan of the Saionji cabinet in which secret contracts would be signed and the money diverted from a current account and reimbursed after the full expansion plan had been approved by the Diet the following year. When Saitō rejected this proposal outright, Katsura suggested another approach. Katsura assured Saitō that the cabinet would introduce a ¥3-million expansion plan to the upcoming Diet with which the navy could begin construction on three battleships.[73] The full ¥350-million package, including the ¥90 million already agreed upon by the previous cabinet to begin in 1913, Katsura argued, simply could not be realized given the current political and financial situation surrounding military expansion requests. The politics surrounding appropriations needed to be reformed, or so Katsura suggested, and to accomplish this Katsura went on to outline a plan to establish the Military Defense Council. This group, composed of representatives from the army, navy, Finance Ministry, and cabinet, would at least in theory coordinate army and navy expansion requests prior to their introduction to the Diet.[74] Such an organization, Katsura believed, would eliminate the political instability associated with military appropriations and the interservice rivalry that had become more severe since the 1907 Imperial Defense Conference. Katsura was not alone in this assessment. At the beginning of the Taishō Political Crisis, Hara referred to the increased rivalry over appropriations that had contributed to the collapse of the Saionji cabinet as an "evil practice."[75]

When Saitō revealed the nature of his early discussions with Katsura to other top naval officials, the results were swift and predictable. Almost immediately, Takarabe argued that Katsura's so-called compromise would be unthinkable for the navy to support.[76] Admiral Ijūin relayed the same message to Katsura directly, and soon after this Yamamoto endorsed the hardline position suggested by both these subordinates. Faced with such strong political opposition within the navy and mindful of Yamamoto's veiled threat, Saitō informed Katsura that he could not accept the proposed compromise. Compromise, however, pumped through Saitō's as well as Katsura's veins. The following day, Saitō met Katsura and Finance Minister

Wakatsuki Reijirō under the pretense of informing the prime minister that they could not serve in the proposed cabinet. Removed from naval subordinates, Saitō succumbed to Katsura's charms and logic and agreed to the previously suggested compromise: the full ¥350-million expansion plan would be brought before parliament in early 1914, and ¥3 million would be appropriated in 1913 to begin the construction of three battleships.[77] Later that evening, when criticized by his navy subordinates, Saitō announced that he had changed his mind and agreed to accept Katsura's offer, claiming: "I was determined to resign, but Katsura was here for more than two hours. We reached a basic agreement whereby the navy plan would be commenced from next year and I would remain in my position as navy minister."[78] Takarabe immediately challenged the wisdom and desirability of the compromise, claiming that it would be difficult to secure the entire ¥350-million plan in 1914 and that in the next year Katsura could easily go back on his word.[79] Matsumoto added that it would be next to impossible to sign contracts for warship construction without a firm guarantee of cash and that ¥3 million was simply not enough.

Faced with this resistance, Saitō left the Navy Ministry that afternoon and met Katsura. At this juncture, Saitō revoked his commitment to serve in the cabinet. Katsura had anticipated just such a development and refused to accept Saitō's resignation. When Saitō persisted, Katsura informed the admiral that he had already informed Emperor Taishō of the navy minister's earlier decision and that to reverse course now would be highly problematic.[80] Upon returning to the Navy Ministry at 11:00 P.M. Saitō found admirals Takarabe, Ijūin, Fujii, and Matsumoto waiting, anxious for word as to how Katsura responded to Saitō's resignation. When Saitō informed the admirals that Katsura had thwarted his attempt to resign, both Takarabe and Matsumoto offered their immediate resignations. Saitō refused to accept either subordinate's offer and moreover encouraged each to give serious thought to his decision to resign.[81] The following day, the *Tokyo Asahi shinbun*, citing highly placed but unnamed naval officers, published an article said to represent the views of prominent naval officers who believed Katsura's compromise was insulting.[82]

If facing unruly, determined subordinates and a crafty prime minister was difficult enough for Saitō, matters became more uncomfortable for the navy minister the following day. After his 11:00 P.M. meeting with Saitō, Takarabe informed Yamamoto of Saitō's political missteps, and this compelled the navy's most important admiral to intervene. On 20 December, Yamamoto met Saitō, and the father of the Japanese navy informed the navy minister in no uncertain terms that it would be "undesirable for him to remain in his post given the current political atmosphere in the navy."[83] Saitō acquiesced to Yamamoto's demand and informed Katsura of his "final decision" that afternoon.[84] Katsura was not moved. The general-turned-prime-minister had also anticipated this action and had earlier secured an Imperial Rescript compelling Saitō to remain in the cabinet as navy minister, thus undercutting the navy's ability to coerce Katsura into accepting navy demands by withholding a ministerial appointment.[85] This was a bold, daring, unprecedented move that left Yamamoto and the navy with no real room to maneuver, at least officially. Responding to this development, Yamamoto relayed a message to Saitō that read:[86]

> Your negotiation with Katsura has been behind the scenes. From now on, you must bring our original plan to cabinet meetings and emphasize that the plan should be approved. Now that you have received the emperor's order, you have to do it; otherwise your service to him could not be considered sufficient. If you emphasize the necessity of the plan to the utmost, we will be able to have the money, because Katsura is already considering increasing the ¥3 million to ¥6 million or even ¥10 million. Then we will be able to start preparing for the construction of the three battleships. This way, we can preserve the dignity of the navy.

The day after, Yamamoto assembled all flag-rank officers from the Kantō area at the Navy Ministry headquarters and told them that owing to the emperor's desire the navy must stand behind Saitō and work with him to secure the political objectives necessary to secure naval expansion in the future.

Having lost the ability to coerce Katsura, Yamamoto encouraged the navy to follow a pragmatic approach and exhorted naval administrators to direct their energies into expanding the size of the naval commencement budget from ¥3 million to ¥10 million. On 22 December, Katsura agreed to budget an additional ¥3 million for the commencement of battleship construction in 1913. Although this was a far cry from the ¥90 million previously agreed upon by the Saionji cabinet, naval leaders had little choice but to follow the pragmatic route, since Katsura had used the emperor to secure the navy's political compliance. As Takarabe wrote in his diary the day after the emperor issued the imperial rescript "Katsura's shrewdness is quite impressive."[87] Katsura's victory, however, was pyrrhic. His return to national politics and his use of an imperial rescript to stabilize his position vis-à-vis the navy over the expansion issue unleashed a torrent of popular protest and anger, which the navy used to further cultivate a base of support within

the Seiyūkai. Though not there yet, even though he had previously been offered the position of prime minister, Yamamoto's day, and the navy's, was
still to come.

Popular Protest and the Political Emergence of Yamamoto

Katsura's use of imperial rescripts to secure Saitō's position in the cabinet further energized an already agitated party-based antigovernment popular protest movement. Since the collapse of the Saionji cabinet in early December, metropolitan newspapers such as the *Jiji shinpō*, *Chūō shinbun*,
Tokyo Asahi shinbun, and the *Tokyo Nichi nichi* not only lionized Saionji for
standing up to the army's demands but strongly criticized the army for anticonstitutional behavior. Anger increased throughout much of early to
mid-December as the *genrō* met and eventually selected the next prime minister. Throughout the nearly two-week process, Seiyūkai branch offices in-
undated the Tokyo headquarters with petitions of support against the
abuses of "clique government" and encouraged national leaders to resolutely stand behind the principle of constitutional government.[88] Katsura's
selection to head the next cabinet further strengthened the resolve of opposition forces that had previously banded together under the Movement for
Constitutional Government. Officially launched at a public rally in Kabuk-
iza, Tokyo, this movement, led by Seiyūkai and Kokumintō leaders such as
Ozaki Yukio, Inukai Tsūyoshi, and Sugita Tei'ichi, rallied opposition politicians and the general public against Katsura.[89] With slogans such as "Protect the Constitution" and "Destroy Clique Government," Ozaki and
Inukai used the Seiyūkai party structure to organize popular rallies
throughout the country and urged the people to reelect their current Diet
representatives if Katsura dissolved parliament. More damaging to
Katsura's agenda, however, was the fact that his partisan actions to secure
Saitō's position helped solidify the navy-Seiyūkai alliance. Members of a
newly formed Protect the Constitution Movement, particularly Seiyūkai
members, made numerous references to the different approaches that the
navy and army took to secure their objectives, with the navy receiving considerable praise for pragmatism in working with the previous Saionji cabinet. "The navy was now feeling its past errors," declared Ozaki at a public
rally in late December, "and was now trying to stand on the confidence of
the people, unlike the army, which was following the will of the Chōshū
clansmen."[90] Ozaki and others made no public references to the navy's earlier coercive behavior against Saionji or its anticonstitutional act of not vol-

untarily providing a cabinet minister. Moreover, at the height of the early crisis surrounding Saitō's appointment, many newspaper editorials wrote in favor of the navy, its leaders, and the naval expansion issue.[91] Naval expansion was far more popular and far less controversial than army expansion with many parliamentarians; and Chōshū-faction behavior during the Taishō Political Crisis did nothing but reinforce the navy's popular image as pragmatic. Precisely as Yamagata had predicted in November when he warned Tanaka, Uehara, and Katsura that party men would "use against us convenient slogans such as the army versus the people, the ruling cliques versus the people, the bureaucrats versus the people, and carry on this fight with renewed vigor," the struggle over military appropriations had been transformed into a national political debate.[92]

Faced with strong opposition from both the Diet and the navy, Katsura strove to strengthen his position vis-à-vis parliament before its scheduled opening in January. Realizing that the opposition Seiyūkai and the Protect the Constitution Movement at large would likely obstruct the government's efforts during the forthcoming session of parliament, Katsura took two controversial steps. First, the prime minister postponed the opening of the Diet from 21 January to 5 February with the assistance of the new emperor.[93] Time, Katsura believed, would afford his cabinet with the opportunity to build support among non-Seiyūkai members of the Diet. Second, to this end, Katsura announced the formation of a new political party, the Dōshikai, which he hoped would eventually counter the monopolistic control wielded by the Seiyūkai in the Diet. Both moves, however, drew widespread criticism from various camps; party men challenged the prime minister for proroguing the Diet, and the Yamagata faction expressed its displeasure at Katsura's desire to form a political party, whether progovernment or not. Moreover, Katsura's decision to form a political party to counter the Seiyūkai made a Seiyūkai-navy-Satsuma entente all the more appealing to Saionji, Matsuda, and Hara. Through early December, Hara believed that Katsura would attempt to reach some compromise with his party and Saionji, but Katsura's actions soon convinced Hara that the prime minister was about to wage an intense political "battle with our party."[94] He was correct, and when Katsura's Dōshikai party attracted forty-four members of the Kokumintō party, Hara and Saionji began to think more seriously about the merits of allying with the navy-Satsuma faction.[95]

Though suspending the Diet and forming a new political party were bold actions, they did not stave off the inevitable. When the Diet finally convened in early February, Seiyūkai and Kokumintō representatives strongly challenged Katsura. On the first day of the new parliament, representatives openly questioned the prime minister's motives and condemned his continued reliance on imperial rescripts to secure the government's desired political ends. Party men claimed that Katsura's behavior was disrespectful to the new emperor and an affront to constitutional government. If citing ideals had no effect, representatives also challenged Katsura on technical legal grounds, arguing that the rescript used to postpone the Diet had not been properly countersigned by a minister of state or the lord of the Privy Seal.[96] To party men who publicly asked whether the prime minister had overstepped his authority, the answer was a spirited yes. As Katsura's response did nothing whatsoever to silence the opposition, that afternoon the Seiyūkai introduced a resolution of no confidence that had been drafted by Hara and Motoda Hajime on 16 January.[97] It read:[98]

> Prince Katsura Tarō has, in receiving his appointment, frequently troubled the sovereign for rescripts. He has confounded the palace and the government, abused his official power to raise a private party, suspended the Diet in a wanton manner just at the point of its opening. He is acting against the true principle of constitutional government and putting obstacles in the path of the country's administration, which is contrary to the requisite means for maintaining the dignity of the imperial household on the one hand and promoting the happiness and prosperity of the people on the other. Be it resolved, therefore, that this house finds itself unable to place confidence in a cabinet like the present one.

Following the Seiyūkai's no-confidence resolution, M.P. Ozaki delivered an impassioned speech—in which he asked, "Do they not intend to destroy their enemies by using the throne as a parapet and imperial rescripts as bullets?"—at which representatives in the Diet exploded with thunderous applause and shouts of support.[99] Hara had assembled every Seiyūkai representative except Itō Yōzo, including the aged Haseba Junkō, a fact which Takarabe, who witnessed the turbulent proceeding on 5 February, described as truly impressive.[100] Sensing an embarrassing defeat, Katsura denied representatives the right to vote on the no-confidence measure. Once again the prime minister used an imperial rescript and postponed proceedings in the Diet for another five days. Katsura's shrewdness was indeed impressive, but it was wearing thin.

Proroguing parliament in the face of the no-confidence resolution resulted in widespread protest. Major public rallies erupted in Tokyo and Osaka that strengthened the position of the Seiyūkai. Heightened criticism of the government's reckless belligerence extinguished the chance of a negotiated settlement, and as a consequence the prime minister possessed few options to resolve the crisis, none of which held out much promise or was without controversy. One option was for Katsura to dissolve parliament in hopes of breaking the Seiyūkai majority through elections. Unless Katsura was willing to use the Home Ministry to shape the election's outcome, as was done in 1892, this option held little chance of success. A second option was to fight a head-on battle in the parliament, but this held out even less of a chance for victory. A final option involved the issuance of yet another imperial rescript. On 9 February, Katsura secured a rescript that compelled Saionji, as president of the Seiyūkai, to withdraw the vote of no confidence that party leaders had introduced on 5 February. While Saionji agreed to follow the rescript and predicted that victory would be Katsura's, the emboldened Seiyūkai rank and file would have to accept this decision, and their doing so was not a given.

It was at this juncture that Yamamoto descended into the maelstrom of the Taishō Political Crisis. In one of Katsura's futile attempts to reach a compromise with the Seiyūkai earlier in January, Akiyama Teisuke approached Yamamoto on the prime minister's behalf and asked him to impress upon Saionji the need to "not oppose Katsura's policies too strongly." Yamamoto had no reason or desire to serve as mediator and informed Akiyama that "it was too late to ask for third-party assistance." Yamamoto concluded that this crisis, if resolved by mutual concessions or compromise at this stage, was likely to result in a "double suicide."[101] Yamamoto did not seek to fashion an agreement between Katsura, Saionji, and the Seiyūkai but rather sought to exploit the situation to further his own and the navy's political agenda through closer ties with the Seiyūkai.

Yamamoto's determination crystallized over 9 and 10 February 1913 as national political events accelerated to a climax. After a heated discussion within the Seiyūkai leadership, Hara and the party's executive committee agreed to abide by Katsura's latest imperial rescript on 9 February. That night, before rank-and-file party members voted on the matter, Satsuma go-between Tokonami Takejirō met Hara and informed the party leader that he would approach Yamamoto, as he had done in the past, to see if the Satsuma admiral could resolve the crisis.[102] Early the next morning, after learning of Katsura's latest rescript the night before from Tokonami, Yamamoto met Katsura. Yamamoto lit into his longtime nemesis and political rival, blaming him for the political chaos that gripped the nation.[103] A frail and haggard Katsura replied that he was either going to call an election and abide by its results or resign outright if a suitable successor could be found. This set Yamamoto's mind racing. Armed with this knowledge, Yamamoto quickly proceeded to the Seiyūkai party headquarters. There, party men were discussing the no-confidence resolution, and Yamamoto's arrival further energized the meeting. Yamamoto's disclosure and Saionji's response hardened Seiyūkai resolve and encouraged both Yamamoto and the rank-and-file members to stand up to Katsura. Informing Yamamoto that he would not again assume the office of prime minister, Saionji encouraged the Satsuma admiral to "stand up and come to power."[104] Yamamoto thus returned to the prime minister's residence, but upon his arrival Katsura denounced his meddling in national politics. Yamamoto left, but the damage that Yamamoto's actions inflicted had already been done. Informed of Katsura's supposed willingness to resign, Seiyūkai party members voted overwhelmingly to ignore Katsura's latest imperial rescript and reintroduce the no-confidence resolution when parliament opened later that day. Before such an embarrassment came to pass, however, Katsura resigned.

The following day, the *genrō* once again met to select a prime minister. Knowing full well that the Yamagata faction would reject his suggestion that the Seiyūkai be allowed to form a party cabinet, Saionji next recommend Yamamoto. Ōyama Iwao seconded Saionji's nomination of Yamamoto, and the *genrō* unanimously agreed that the Satsuma admiral and father of Japan's navy be allowed to form the next cabinet. The elder statesmen thereafter ended the meeting, making it clear to Saionji that it was up to Yamamoto and the Seiyūkai to reach some working relationship in the next session that would avoid the political and popular disturbances that had developed during Katsura's previous cabinet. After the *genrō* meeting ended, Saionji informed Yamamoto of his selection as Prime Minister, and the navy kingpin "accepted the nomination as if he was overjoyed."[105] Yamamoto's political intrigues helped bring to a close one of the shortest and perhaps most controversial cabinet ministries in Meiji-Taishō Japan. Yamamoto would quickly turn to gain the support of the Seiyūkai for a cabinet he believed would hold great promise for the navy, the Seiyūkai, and the nation.

Synopsis

The collapse of the Saionji-Katsura entente that had been a mainstay of elite-level politics between 1905 and 1912 opened up a world of opportunity for Yamamoto, the navy, the Satsuma faction, and the Seiyūkai. Building on the public popularity this service had secured in the Russo-Japanese War, naval leaders skillfully established the foundations to emerge as an elite-level political force in Japan that matched their military force at sea. Through co-ercion, compromise, pragmatism, and propaganda, the navy championed its cause at the elite level and in doing so forged increasingly strong ties with the emergent Seiyūkai political party. Early budgetary successes, how-ever, brought about increased political and budgetary rivalry with the army. Rather than hindering an eventual Seiyūkai-navy entente, this development accelerated that alliance considerably. When juxtaposed with the army's be-havior in bringing about the downfall of Saionji's second cabinet, the navy's involvement in national politics seemed tame by comparison, at least from the outside. Moreover, as army intransigence grew and Chōshū army gen-eral Katsura returned to national politics with a desire to establish a new po-litical party to counter the Seiyūkai, a navy-Seiyūkai alliance seemed logical and desirable to most party men and navy bureaucrats. Though the Seiyūkai and the navy were not perfect political partners, few political partnerships were in pre–World War II Japan. Though the proposed Yamamoto-Sei-yūkai cabinet of early February 1913 held great political promise, as events of 1914 would show, such a partnership offered an equal political peril as well.

CHAPTER SEVEN

The Rise and Fall of Navy Political Fortunes, 1913–1914

> I want to use this opportunity to pay tribute to you and to give you assurances of my profound respect for the principles and pronouncements of your party and to declare my opinion that political affairs should be managed in accordance with the spirit of these principles.[1]
> —Yamamoto Gonnohyōe to Seiyūkai party

> This house [the House of Peers] proposes to cut ¥70 million out of the naval estimates because it does not like the Yamamoto cabinet.[2]
> —Murata Suneyoshi

> It would be ridiculous to fall into the trap of the opposition and allow the cabinet to be overthrown. Let's endure together until we reach our limit and then decide what to do with the future of the cabinet.[3]
> —Yamamoto Gonnohyōe to Hara Kei

ON 22 FEBRUARY 1913, Yamamoto Gonnohyōe delivered one of the most emotive, articulate, and calculated speeches of his political career. Gathered before the confident admiral-turned-prime-minister, more than two hundred members of the Seiyūkai political party praised Yamamoto for his openly expressed commitment to "respect the principles and pronouncements" of their party.[4] The ascendency of Yamamoto, a rise intimately linked with Seiyūkai support, marked the beginning of a formal navy-Seiyūkai entente that gave power, influence, and greater political status to both groups where each sought it most. Through hard work, pragmatism, and compromise, over the course of 1913, the navy and the Seiyūkai secured a number of initiatives which each had long sought: administrative, bureaucratic, and financial reforms desired by party men, and for the navy, budgetary increases that would have ultimately provided funds for the long-cherished "eight-eight" fleet. In the wake of the Taishō Political Crisis, the navy and the Seiyūkai emerged as powerful political players in Japan's increasingly pluralistic polity and forged an alliance that heralded a new orientation in Taishō politics.

The formal navy-Seiyūkai entente, however, was short-lived. Beginning in January 1914 and continuing throughout February and early March, revelations concerning navy corruption, referred to as the Siemens scandal, resulted in large-scale public demonstrations against the navy and the Seiyūkai-backed government. As initial investigations revealed corruption on a far more egregious scale than first reported, opposition politicians, many of whom had strongly condemned Uehara's resignation and Katsura's return to politics in late 1912, vociferously challenged the navy-Seiyūkai government to resign in order to "protect" the spirit of "constitutional government" in Japan. Moreover, echoing calls made in parliament between 1891 and 1893, opposition Diet members again in 1914 demanded that the navy be "cleansed" before funds could be appropriated for expansion. Both groups, those desirous of protecting constitutional government and those wishing merely to reform the navy, worked together and organized large-scale public rallies in Tokyo to bring public pressure upon Yamamoto's ministry.[5] The tide of popular support for the new alliance ebbed, and political commentators, journalists, and high-ranking officials in both the navy and the Seiyūkai grew concerned over how rank-and-file Seiyūkai parliamentarians would respond to the Siemens scandal and the public outcry associated with it. Many individuals questioned whether rank-and-file Seiyūkai party members would join the opposition and pass a vote of no confidence in Yamamoto's cabinet, thus ending the first Seiyūkai majority cabinet, or if they would support the government that had given them greater influence in national politics than they had ever before enjoyed.

If such attacks and potential political pitfalls were not problematic enough, Yamamoto and the Seiyūkai also faced similarly determined opposition from other, more powerful sources apart from the public and the lower house of parliament. The Siemens scandal and the public outcry it engendered allowed the Yamagata-backed Chōshū-army faction, the one group most opposed to the Seiyūkai-navy entente, to attack the newfound political alliance from the one institution in which neither the navy nor the Seiyūkai had any base of support, the House of Peers. The peers' goal was the destruction of the Yamamoto-Seiyūkai cabinet, and Yamagata faction members used the Siemens scandal to attack the navy's expansion budget, the raison d'être of the entente from the navy's perspective. If the Taishō Political Crisis transformed the army's two-division issue into high-level politics that developed into a struggle between Chōshū and the nation, the

Siemens scandal similarly transformed a navy corruption issue into high-level politics that pitted the navy-Seiyūkai cabinet against a strange alliance of popular agitators, opposition parliamentarians, and the members from the House of Peers. Politics in the increasingly pluralistic world of Taishō Japan were easily supercharged, and the political attacks launched in 1914 ultimately proved as disastrous to the navy and the Seiyūkai as events of 1912–13 had proven to the army and the Chōshū faction.

Elite-Level Politics and the Formation of the Yamamoto-Seiyūkai Cabinet, February 1913

Though virtually every Seiyūkai member rejoiced at the downfall of Katsura's cabinet in early February 1913, not all of the rank-and-file party members rushed to endorse Hara, Matsuda, and Saionji's plan to forge a cabinet with Admiral Yamamoto. For the better part of ten days beginning on 12 February, Seiyūkai leaders deliberated over the necessity and efficacy of sharing power with members of the navy-Satsuma group. Had not, asked many political protestors and agitators, the downfall of Katsura marked the end of oligarchic rule, clan politics, and ushered in the beginning of Taishō democracy? Opposed to Hara and Matsuda's pragmatic, tactical approach to politics, hard-line Seiyūkai members such as Ozaki and Okazaki agitated for the creation of a pure party cabinet, reiterating calls made by members of the Protect the Constitution Movement during the Taishō Political Crisis. Hara and other Seiyūkai pragmatists thus faced the difficult task of maintaining party unity and upholding their principles while at the same time working together to forge a coalition with the navy-Satsuma faction. Fortunately for the Seiyūkai leaders, Yamamoto too was a pragmatist who proved amenable to many of their demands.

Discussions between Hara and Yamamoto began in earnest on 12 February, the day after Yamamoto received imperial backing to organize a new cabinet.[6] From the beginning of the meeting, it became clear that Yamamoto wanted both Hara and Matsuda to be ministers in the new government. The farsighted admiral correctly assumed that if these individuals had a clear political attachment to the cabinet, they would be far less likely to agitate against the government from the lower house. This would be essential to Yamamoto, as his chief political objective was to eventually secure a commitment from the lower house to pass the navy's coveted ¥350-million expansion plan. Although both Seiyūkai leaders initially refused, claiming they could better lead the party from outside the government and fearing that their formal inclusion in the cabinet might elicit resignations from radical Seiyūkai men, Yamamoto remained adamant that both men must serve as cabinet ministers. Both eventually agreed, and Yamamoto suggested that Hara was the obvious choice to serve as home minister and Matsuda to serve as justice minister.

After both sides reached this agreement, discussions became more problematic. With Hara and Matsuda's support secured, Yamamoto outlined other individuals whom he saw as potential and desirable cabinet ministers. Specifically, Yamamoto envisioned appointing Mishima Yatarō, president of the Yokohama Specie Bank, as finance minister, Chinda Sutemi, Japan's ambassador to the United States, as foreign minister, and Makino Nobukai as the imperial household minister.[7] The Seiyūkai pragmatists balked at these suggestions, however. For one reason, Hara and Matsuda wanted a cabinet comprised exclusively of Seiyūkai members, except for the service ministers, who were barred by law from having any party affiliation. Second, both party leaders felt it was necessary to include the outspoken proponent for constitutional government, Inukai Tsūyoshi, in the cabinet. While Yamamoto declared that he would show some flexibility in many of the cabinet positions, he flatly disagreed over including Inukai.[8] As leader of only a moderate-sized party in the Diet, Yamamoto figured that Inukai could make more trouble within the cabinet than he could from the floor of parliament, even if his party sided with the newly created Dōshikai party, a highly unlikely event so soon after the Taishō Political Crisis. The Seiyūkai men figured differently. Both Hara and Matsuda feared that unless Inukai assumed a position in the cabinet, he would continue to snipe at the government and perhaps appeal to dissatisfied members of the Seiyūkai and encourage their defection.[9] While agreeing to moderate his demands concerning the finance, foreign, and imperial household ministers, Yamamoto would not acquiesce to this last demand and returned to the Navy Ministry at 3:00 P.M. after hours of talks ended in deadlock.

Cabinet-oriented discussions did not end with Yamamoto's departure from Saionji's private residence. Upon the navy leader's return to the Navy Ministry headquarters, Yamamoto spoke at great length with Saitō about the negotiations. Then, Yamamoto invited Makino Nobukai, the second son of the great Satsuma restoration leader Ōkubo Toshimichi, to the ministry to discuss the current impasse.[10] Once there, Makino suggested that Yamamoto give in to the Seiyūkai's demands concerning the number of current party men they wanted to include in the cabinet, three, but he gave little advice on the question of Inukai's appointment. Shortly thereafter,

Admiral Yamanouchi Masuji and Vice Minister Takarabe seconded Makino's suggestions, arguing that Yamamoto should accept Hara's conditions if such an agreement could result in a quick compromise. Without Seiyūkai support, they claimed, naval expansion would be difficult if not impossible to secure. After a brief discussion, Yamamoto accepted Makino's suggestion.

There were, however, limits to how far Yamamoto would go to secure a coalition cabinet. These limits were defined soon after Makino departed. At the urging of Hara, two uninvited Seiyūkai members with maritime and Satsuma connections, Kikuchi Takenori (former general affairs chief of the Kyushu Railway) and Fukuzawa Momosuke (Tokyo agent for the Hokkaidō Colliery and Steamship Company), arrived at the Navy Ministry. After discussing the potential benefits that a coalition could have for the navy, both men lobbied Yamamoto to join the Seiyūkai party and lead the cabinet as a party man. This, of course, would require Yamamoto's resignation from the navy, but both suggested that such a gesture would allow Yamamoto to unite all members of the Seiyūkai and thus establish a firm foundation upon which to implement changes and secure naval expansion. As a politically aware admiral, Yamamoto had expected such calls for him to join the Seiyūkai, but on this occasion, as he would again do the following day, he informed Seiyūkai hard-liners that he would not, under any circumstances, resign his active service position within the navy. Though Yamamoto was a pragmatist, willing to accept certain Seiyūkai demands, he remained a navy man and would not, as Katsura had done, retire from active service to lead a political party.[11]

While Yamamoto was meeting with some of his closest confidantes and listened to hard-line Seiyūkai representatives, so too did Hara and Matsuda. Earlier in the day, when cabinet discussions were conducted at Saionji's residence, Seiyūkai representatives from each of the party's eight regional branch offices met and eventually passed a resolution which demanded that the forthcoming cabinet be party-based. If representatives agreed to support Yamamoto as prime minister, they declared they would do so only if the admiral retired from active service and joined the party.[12] This resoluteness did not bode well for the party executive meeting scheduled for later that evening. Indeed, at the Seiyūkai executive meeting, factions within the party emerged with Oku Shigesaburō, Motoda Hajime, and Itō Daihachi backing Hara and Matsuda's call for compromise with Yamamoto, while Okazaki Kunisuke and Ozaki Yukio opposed it on grounds of party and constitutional principle.[13] When this meeting concluded, it became apparent to Hara and Matsuda that a compromise with Yamamoto would be more difficult to organize and attain than either had at first imagined.

If this growing split within the Seiyūkai executive between moderates and hard-liners was troublesome to the two chief pragmatists, what transpired next caused further concern. At approximately 10:00 P.M. a group of young hard-line party men visited Hara at home and expressed their collective outrage over the leadership's negotiations conducted earlier with Yamamoto.[14] When Hara challenged the agitators, the group handed the Seiyūkai leader a resolution which demanded that Inukai Tsūyoshi, Ozaki, and Okazaki be appointed to any future Seiyūkai-backed cabinet. Moreover, the resolution also stipulated that the signatories would refuse to support a coalition unless all other cabinet ministers, including the prime minister, were party men.[15] Finally, and most problematic of all, the agitators claimed they would actively work against any coalition government formed on Yamamoto's terms. After asking the group to leave his home, Hara recorded in his diary that opponents of a compromise with Yamamoto were beginning to make "quite a stir," and the worried leader expressed concern that unless an agreement could be reached quickly, the Seiyūkai might fracture or Yamamoto might lose the opportunity to form a cabinet altogether.[16] A formal entente, or so Hara concluded, would then be meaningless to both sides.

Fearing the formation of a bureaucratic cabinet if the Seiyūkai could not reach an accord with Yamamoto quickly, Hara and Matsuda redoubled their efforts to win hard-liners over to their pragmatic cause. After resuming talks with Yamamoto on the morning of 13 February, both men met with parliamentary and nonparliamentary members of the party in the late afternoon. At that meeting, Matsuda urged representatives not to feel betrayed by the party executive's plan and not to oppose a compromise with Yamamoto on the grounds of constitutional or party principle. Matsuda also took it upon himself to arrange one-to-one meetings with some of the most outspoken critics of the negotiations with Yamamoto to assure them that neither he nor Hara had "sold out" the principles of the Seiyūkai.[17] He and Hara had the best interests of the party at heart and were working with Yamamoto, or so Matsuda claimed, to further the cause of constitutional government and, more important, Seiyūkai power.

Hara, who followed a somewhat different approach than his colleague Matsuda, also undertook to win over hard-liners the following day. Whereas Matsuda empathized with recalcitrant hard-line members and encouraged them to see the mid- to long-term potential strategic benefits of working with Yamamoto, Hara challenged the hard-line position with simple, tactical, political logic and fear. In discussions with members from the Tōhoku branch of the Seiyūkai, Hara issued a stark warning to the captive audience: if a coalition cabinet was not agreed upon soon, Katsura might make a political comeback. If such a revelation was not disturbing enough, Hara reiterated the simple fact that no one from the *genrō* would recommend either Hara or Matsuda as the next prime minister if talks with Yamamoto failed, and without such backing a party cabinet would be impossible to form. Moreover, Hara further articulated that if the party did not support Yamamoto, whom Saionji had recommended in the *genrō* council, then Saionji's power and influence within this body, and thus that of the Seiyūkai, would decrease considerably. Given these facts, Hara concluded, there simply was no viable political alternative to forming a cabinet with Yamamoto and working within the confines of the cabinet to further party initiatives and the pursuit of power.[18] This was the best opportunity, and one that might not present itself again in the immediate future if Yamamoto failed. Though well reasoned and articulated, such tactical political rhetoric did not sway all the hard-liners to support the leadership's position. Later in the evening, Ozaki and Okazaki met with Inukai after a group of radicals from both parties banded together and presented a resolution to the Seiyūkai leaders demanding the formation of a pure party cabinet.[19] Events were not going as planned for either Hara or Matsuda.

After a day in which hard-liners relentlessly expressed their anger and vented their frustrations with Hara and Matsuda, Hara again met with Okazaki and Ozaki on 16 February.[20] Each side again reiterated its position, but after an hour the hard-liners gave Hara three specific conditions, which they sought before they could support a Yamamoto-Seiyūkai cabinet. They were: first, that all ministers in the cabinet, excluding army minister, the navy minister, and the prime minister, must be party men; second, that Inukai must be included in the cabinet; and third, that the cabinet must undertake policies to reform the bureaucracy and limit the powers of the Privy Council. Though Hara accepted these conditions and told both men that he would argue these points at his next meeting with Yamamoto, he also stated unreservedly that he could not guarantee success. Emboldened by a group of young party agitators who arrived outside the meeting hall during the negotiations, the hard-liners informed Hara that unless these conditions were secured, they would demand the resignations of Hara, Matsuda, and Motoda. When informed of these developments, Takarabe expressed in no uncertain terms that the "situation had worsened."[21]

Throughout much of 17 and 18 February, Hara and Matsuda worked to reach a compromise within the party that could be given to Yamamoto in hopes of resolving the political deadlock.[22] For over an hour on 17 February, party leaders within the parliamentary committee deliberated over the hard-liners' conditions given to Hara and Matsuda the day before and agreed that these points should form the basis of negotiations with Yamamoto. The Satsuma admiral accepted the proposal to support Seiyūkai policies but would not give ground on the issue of Inukai. Yamamoto did not want Inukai in the cabinet and moreover argued that the foreign minister, along with the military ministers and the prime minister, must be free of any political-party connection. These were the admiral's final conditions, and this rebuff worried Hara. Later, after the Seiyūkai leaders departed, Ogawa Heikichi, Seiyūkai M.P. from Nagano, arrived at Navy Ministry headquarters and urged Yamamoto not to withdraw from negotiations, suggesting that a compromise could be reached whereby the Seiyūkai would agree that the future foreign minister would not be required to be a party man.[23] This was what Yamamoto wanted to hear, and a compromise now looked possible if the Seiyūkai rank and file could be persuaded to accept this position.

The next day, Hara reported Yamamoto's response to the hard-liners' three conditions at a Seiyūkai executive meeting. Yamamoto, or so Hara proclaimed, had moderated his position, thus making an agreement possible. Specifically, Hara reported that Yamamoto agreed: first, to follow the principles of the Seiyūkai; second, to appoint three current Seiyūkai members to the cabinet; and third, to require that all other ministers, excluding the two military ministers, the foreign minister, and the prime minister, join the party.[24] This was the best the party could hope for, and Hara concluded that such a compromise was a significant victory for the Seiyūkai. Though discussions continued for much of the afternoon, at 4:10 P.M. Seiyūkai parliamentarians held a general meeting, and a majority voted to accept the compromise. Common ground had been reached. Angered, Ozaki and Okazaki resigned from the party with twenty-four other core members of the hard-line faction and formed the Seiyū Club. While damaging, the loss of twenty-six defectors was not enough to eliminate the Seiyūkai plurality in the Diet, though they did lose their absolute parliamentary majority.[25] Two days later, at Seiyūkai headquarters, Yamamoto pronounced his commitment to Seiyūkai principles and polices and afterward treated his newfound allies to a lavish dinner party that impressed many members.[26] Ironically, on that very day Okazaki began to negotiate his return to the party, and within a month over half of the defectors had returned to the fold of their pragmatic mother party, the Seiyūkai. Political power and the allure of even greater political rewards were too tempting for even the most outspoken, principled party men to ignore.

Though the establishment of the Yamamoto-Seiyūkai cabinet was the logical outgrowth of elite-level political maneuvering undertaken by both the navy and Japan's chief political party, its creation was not without difficulties. Hara and Matsuda had angered a vocal minority within the Seiyūkai over their willingness to reach a compromise with the emergent navy-Satsuma faction in a "speedy grab of power."[27] Hara's pragmatism struck at the heart of what many self-proclaimed principled party men had fought for in their demonstrations and attacks against the previous Katsura ministry. Hara, and to a lesser degree Yamamoto, saw the political world differently. Both believed that a pragmatic alliance could further the aims of each group far more than remaining in continued opposition, or in the case of the navy, remaining as Japan's second service in both a political and a budgetary sense. The new alliance, both believed, offered considerable political and budgetary prospects that more than compensated for any short-term difficulties that emerged from the sentiments and activities of party radicals. Unlike the Seiyūkai, no one in the navy protested against a compromise with a political party. Though military men had been warned and later proscribed from engaging in political activities or joining political parties by the 1878 Admonition to Soldiers and Sailors and the 1882 Imperial Rescript to Soldiers and Sailors, politics determined the budget, and the budget determined how far and how quickly Japan's navy could expand as a military force. Fortunately for this service, the navy was led by two of Japan's most able, pragmatic bureaucrats, Saitō and Yamamoto, men who thrived in politics and excelled in the increasingly pluralistic environment of Taishō Japan. Given the nature of budgetary appropriations, the navy's second-tier leaders, such men as Takarabe, Ijūin, Fujii, and Matsumoto, understood better than many military bureaucrats the potentially rich rewards of having as their chief political ally the party that dominated the lower house, the institution that controlled the purse strings of the empire. The Seiyūkai, as the strongest party in parliament, was the long-sought ally the navy had cultivated since just after the Russo-Japanese War, and it is therefore not surprising that the first test of this new alliance occurred over the navy's proposed expansion budget.

The First Parliamentary Test: Naval Expansion

Yamamoto, Japan's first admiral to serve as prime minister, wasted no time in introducing the navy's expansion budget before the Seiyūkai-dominated lower house. Two days after the reopening of parliament on 27 February, Yamamoto submitted the navy's ¥6-million expansion plan for discussion during the lower house of parliament's general budget meeting.[28] Claiming that the previous Katsura cabinet had already agreed upon the urgency of the navy's expansion program, Navy Minister Saitō asked for a speedy acceptance of the proposal put before parliament. Moreover, the calculating minister also reminded parliamentarians gathered that this figure was far less than what Saionji's previous cabinet had agreed to support before it was brought down by Army Minister Uehara's resignation in December 1912. Supporting this program, therefore, would be in keeping with what the last pro-Seiyūkai cabinet had sought. While some Seiyūkai men accepted this reasoning, others did not. Almost immediately, Kokumintō representative Moriya Konosuke asked if this ¥6 million was just the first stage of a larger ¥350-million to ¥400-million plan that the government hoped to introduce during the next legislative session. If so, Moriya concluded, the government should admit to harboring such long-term, ambitious, expensive expansion plans. The naval leadership, in short, should come clean and outline their vision for future naval expansion and give representatives a clear indication of what would be asked of them in forthcoming sessions of parliament. When Saitō responded with a vague and formulaic response as to the necessity of naval expansion, Moriya interjected and pointedly asked if the government would specifically call on M.P.'s to support future expansion as a result of endorsing the ¥6-million program in 1913. If the ¥6-million expenditure was, as the government suggested, to commence battleship construction, how much, the feisty M.P. asked, would be needed to complete the job? Challenged, Saitō acknowledged that the ¥6-million request was indeed seed money for large-scale fleet expansion that would cost upwards of ¥350 million over the period between 1914 and 1921. The Kokumintō orator now had a clear answer, but his hopes for further challenges from representatives evaporated when Seiyūkai men entered the debate — or, more precisely, ended it. Though the Seiyūkai championed administrative retrenchment for both service ministries, no Seiyūkai member criticized the whopping ¥350-million plan alluded to by Japan's experienced navy minister. Power and naval popularity outweighed principle.

Three days later, representatives again took up the naval expansion issue within the larger framework of national defense, and again Seiyūkai members failed to challenge or even question the efficacy of naval expansion or the means wherewith to pay for such an expensive undertaking. Opposition members therefore followed another line of questioning. At a Lower House Budget Subcommittee meeting, anti-Seiyūkai representatives Inukai and Oishi Masami inquired as to the government's overall defense policy and relations between the two armed services.[29] No doubt desirous of embarrassing the new government, Oishi, a recent convert to Katsura's Dōshikai party, prodded the new army minister, Kigoshi Yatsusuna, about his plans for future army expansion. When the army minister replied that the current government endorsed the 1907 Imperial Defense Policy, which stipulated division expansion for the army, Oishi asked on what military or strategic grounds the government based this policy. After the army minister opined that developments in China necessitated army expansion, Oishi immediately questioned why the government had not then proposed army expansion, if strategic factors necessitated it. Was the government not derelict in its responsibility? Clearly, Oishi desired to drive a political wedge between the army and Yamamoto's cabinet, or perhaps he sought to further exacerbate army-navy tensions in hopes of precipitating a cabinet breakup. Suspecting such motives, Yamamoto himself entered the debate and forcefully declared that while it was stated policy to expand the army, funds were not available to carry out expansion in 1913. Naval expansion was more urgent, and in a era of limited funds naval expansion had to take priority. To silence any further criticism from either parliament or the army, Yamamoto concluded that the cabinet would investigate whether funds could be found in 1913 so as to begin army expansion in 1914. This was the desire of the government: army expansion, but expansion tempered by fiscal restraint. No such restraint, however, restricted naval expansion.

Having their respective challenges again blocked in parliament, opposition M.P.'s continued in their efforts to challenge Yamamoto's budget and weaken Seiyūkai unity. One such occasion occurred on 10 March, when the Lower House Budget Subcommittee again discussed the navy's proposed expansion plan.[30] At this meeting, Kokumintō representative Takagi Masutarō led the charge, specifically asking the navy minister how much M.P.'s would be expected to grant the navy over the following years as part of the navy's overall budget scheme. Concerned that once the "set" program was approved, the navy leadership would seek to further enlargement, as they had done in the past, Takagi pressed Saitō to give specific figures, or at least a rough estimate, of the yearly expenditures that the navy would require between 1914 and 1921 to complete the ¥350-million plan. Saitō refused to give exact figures but informed the M.P. that the navy's yearly requests would not, under normal circumstances, exceed ¥60 million, a figure that was still 60 percent of the navy's total operating budget in 1913 and thus no small amount. To reassure Takagi, the navy minster promised to provide specific figures concerning the navy's long-term expansion plan when Diet members would vote on the overall plan in 1914.

Noticeably absent yet again within all final budget discussions concerning the navy were any critiques or challenges issued by Seiyūkai members. For the most part, throughout Yamamoto's first parliament, Seiyūkai members supported their new alliance partner en masse, and this proved critical to the navy's budgetary successes. Without Seiyūkai defections, opposition M.P.'s could not block any Seiyūkai or navy initiatives. On 13 March, the budget subcommittee endorsed the navy's request by a vote of five to three, and the following day the House Budget Committee followed suit by a razor-thin margin of one vote, thirty-one to thirty.[31] The next day, 15 March, the entire lower house accepted the government's proposed budget by a margin of 186 to 181.[32] Seiyūkai support proved decisive. On 29 March, the budget passed both houses of parliament, and the navy received its additional ¥6 million.[33] Acknowledging the support of his new formal parliamentary allies, the day after the budget passed the lower house Yamamoto hosted a banquet to thank all Seiyūkai parliamentarians, at which the stately prime minister thanked each member for his support.[34] Maintaining Seiyūkai support and using it to secure naval expansion was the first successful test of Yamamoto's ability to work effectively with the Seiyūkai. Following this, Yamamoto turned his energies toward solidifying Seiyūkai support through a variety of political and administrative reforms sought by the party executive as well as the rank and file. For the Seiyūkai, bureaucratic, administrative, and fiscal reforms were paramount and were the basis upon which further parliamentary support for Yamamoto would rest. For Yamamoto, securing the reforms sought by the Seiyūkai was a means by which to maintain party support for the next round of budget negotiations, scheduled for autumn 1913. These negotiations, from the navy's standpoint, would be crucial, as Yamamoto planned to introduce the entire ¥350-million naval expansion plan originally put forward in 1911.

Solidifying the Navy-Seiyūkai Relationship: Administrative Reform and Retrenchment

Throughout March 1913, while Saitō persuaded parliamentarians to support the navy's budget requests, Yamamoto worked with Hara and Matsuda to secure one of the Seiyūkai's most cherished reforms; reform of the law that governed the appointment of military-service ministers. In 1913, only generals or admirals on the active military list could serve as army minister or navy minister, a practice that had been codified in law in 1899 at Yamagata's urging. Such restrictions on eligibility angered party politicians on two grounds. First, active military men could not have any political-party affiliation, owing to an earlier imperial rescript again drafted by Yamagata. Second, restrictions on eligibility gave the military services even greater powers to influence and potentially blackmail cabinets to support military expansion, as a cabinet could not function without its full complement of ministers. When a prime minister was thus faced with a recalcitrant service minister who refused to continue in his post or who refused to recommend a successor from the active list, he faced three undesirable alternatives: acquiesce to the military's demands, usually budgetary; resign; or secure an imperial rescript that compelled an admiral or general to serve as a service minister. Between 1910 and 1913, Saionji and Katsura both faced such a political situation and were forced to follow one of the three above-mentioned courses of action. Seiyūkai leaders thus believed that expanding ministerial eligibility would restrict the military's ability to coerce cabinets and thereby further strengthen constitutional party-based government.

Well aware of the tenacity with which the military would fight this reform, Hara and Matsuda believed that Yamamoto, as a military prime minister, would have the stature to revise this law. Fortunately for both, Yamamoto proved amenable. On 6 March, the day after the Lower House Budget Subcommittee discussed naval expansion, Hara and Matsuda met the prime minister and made a case for revision.[35] While both agreed that this would assist the smooth running of government, Hara also suggested that this bureaucratic reform would go a long way to defuse public antagonism toward the military that had arisen during the Taishō Political Crisis. Yamamoto concurred, confessing to the Seiyūkai leaders that he had already broached this issue with the service ministers, Saitō Makoto and Kigoshi Yasutsuna, but that he needed a few more days to contemplate the best course of action to secure revision.

Desirous of striking while the iron was hot, Hara pushed ahead and brought the issue up for discussion just two days later. On 8 March, Hara again asked Yamamoto for his thoughts on the issue, and Yamamoto replied that he had secured both the army minister's and the navy minister's consent to revise the law governing military appointments. A formal announcement, or so Yamamoto claimed, would follow at the next cabinet meeting, scheduled for 10 March.[36] Astonished and delighted, Hara asked the prime minister if the decision could be leaked to party members, as this, the leader assumed, would assure passage of the government's budget. Moreover, Hara believed that securing victory on this issue would guarantee Okazaki's return to the Seiyūkai, which Hara felt would also compel many other defectors to return to the party. This reform and its timely announcement could thus be used to secure many political objectives. Though Yamamoto gave no reply to Hara's request for a calculated leak of information, the Seiyūkai leader met with Anraku later that evening and discussed how this political reform could be used to recruit new party members and strengthen the Seiyūkai.

Celebrations, however, were short-lived. At the 10 March cabinet meeting, deliberations did not go according to plan. While Navy Minister Saitō readily accepted the revision, Army Minister Kigoshi demurred. Kigoshi refused to accept the proposal until after he had further consultations with chief of the Army General Staff Hasegawa Yoshimitsu, a well-known and outspoken opponent of revision.[37] Through his indecision, Kigoshi found himself in a unenviable position between a cabinet and public that sought reform and army men who staunchly rejected such calls. Though the army minister appealed to the father of the army, Yamagata, to support his acceptance of this revision, claiming that the army should not involve itself yet again in another political conflict, Yamagata refused to intervene in the dispute.[38]

Well aware that divisions existed in the army that could, if brought to the surface, potentially threaten the cabinet if Kigoshi resigned, Yamamoto worked to secure acceptance of the revision proposal throughout much of April. That month, Yamamoto met with individuals from both the Army Ministry and the Army General Staff in an attempt to persuade them to support his revision proposal. Neither effort worked. On 17 April, Kigoshi informed Yamamoto that his efforts to win over hard-liners in the army had failed and that Hasegawa had threatened resignation if the government implemented the reform.[39] Unfortunately, this was not the worst of it. Earlier in the week, before Kigoshi admitted his failure, Takarabe learned from Cabinet Secretary Yamanouchi Kazutsugu that other individuals in the army were planning to use this dispute to bring down the Yamamoto cabinet.[40] Chief among the instigators, or so Yamanouchi claimed, was General Nagaoka Gaishi, Commander of the Sixteenth Army Division, based at Kyoto. Fearing that Kigoshi might cave in to Yamamoto's plan, Nagaoka and members of the Army General Staff drafted a memo urging retention of the current law and submitted it directly to the emperor, bypassing the cabinet, the army minister, and the prime minister.[41] This added yet another layer of complexity to an already tense and difficult political situation.

After admonishing Kigoshi for his lack of leadership and his inability to control army hard-liners, Yamamoto quickly came to the realization that he possessed only one realistic option to guarantee passage of the reform measure and preserve his cabinet. On 8 May, Yamamoto submitted a counter-appeal to the emperor that detailed his support of the planned revision. That was not all, however. Yamamoto also recommended to the young emperor that he completely disregard the position paper submitted by the army officers.[42] This was a bold move that significantly increased the stakes in the dispute. If he failed, Yamamoto knew, he would be seriously undermined as prime minister, but if he succeeded, he would completely undercut the army's attempts to stop his reform and destroy his cabinet. Yamamoto, a military man of great stature, succeeded. With the emperor's endorsement, both the Privy Council and the army accepted Yamamoto's planned revision. Yamamoto's involvement proved critical, and the admiral had through considerable effort secured a tremendous symbolic victory in championing one of the Seiyūkai's most sought-after reforms. With this victory, Yamamoto further strengthened his political relationship with the Seiyūkai. Significantly, however, he also further strained relations between the government and the Chōshū faction.

Though revision of the eligibility requirement for military ministers was of high symbolic value, one lauded throughout the popular press and within the Seiyūkai, Yamamoto's other reform initiatives proved far more important in strengthening the Seiyūkai as a political party. Specifically, the Seiyūkai wanted more opportunities to expand their power within the bureaucracy, the center of the Yamagata faction's power. Here Yamamoto's support for reform again proved critically important. From 1899 on, individuals within Japan's bureaucracy from the position of vice minister down were determined by the result of civil-service examinations. Hara and other party leaders hoped to open these positions to party patronage by granting cabinet ministers the right to personally select vice ministers and other lesser officials such as chief secretaries, bureau chiefs, and councilors from the ranks of the bureaucracy.[43] If a minister was a party man, or so Hara figured, and he possessed the right of free selection, able and ambitious bureaucrats within a ministry would join a party for fear that if they remained outside party politics they would be bypassed for selection to the upper echelons of a ministry by bureaucrats with party ties. Such a reform, Hara believed, could over time transform the make-up of Japan's bureaucracy. Civil servants, or so Hara hoped, would no longer be just bureaucrats, but rather party politicians.

Hara was not alone in recognizing the impact that such a reform might have on Japan's bureaucracy. Members from Yamagata's faction also comprehended this point and attempted to stall the Seiyūkai-backed reform proposal of Yamamoto. On eleven occasions in early summer 1913, the Privy Council, the organization responsible for any alterations to the laws governing civil-service regulations, discussed Yamamoto's proposal, and each time members rejected it outright. In response to this intransigence, Yamamoto intimated that he would yet again appeal directly to the emperor as he had done with the law regarding the appointment of military ministers. The prime minister also upped the ante by suggesting that he would, if forced to follow this course of action, recommend that members of the Privy Council be replaced if they remained obstinate in the face of needed national reform. Faced with Yamamoto's perseverance and veiled threats, and well aware of the public outcry that might develop if the reform measure was not accepted, within a month of Yamamoto intimation the Privy Council accepted Yamamoto's proposal. Yamamoto had again accomplished a long-cherished Seiyūkai initiative, one that many party men believed struck at the heart of the Yamagata faction. By early September, seven bureaucrats of vice-ministerial rank joined the Seiyūkai party, and a number of lesser officials in each ministry followed suit as Hara had indeed predicted.

A final policy which Yamamoto undertook in large part to further solidify support within the Seiyūkai was financial in its emphasis. Almost immediately after forming his cabinet, Yamamoto publicly endorsed the Seiyūkai's stated policy of administrative fiscal retrenchment. On his first day standing before parliament as prime minister, Yamamoto endorsed retrenching the central government's administrative expenditures and, more important, suggested that the overall individual tax burden be reduced.[44] This was music to the Seiyūkai members' ears. Claiming that he would eliminate long-standing abuses in connection with the management of government institutions, Yamamoto matched his rhetoric with actions. In June

1913, Yamamoto announced his planned administrative retrenchment program and highlighted the savings; roughly ¥66 million, of which ¥35 million was trimmed from ordinary expenditures (including ¥14 million from the military ministries) and ¥31 million from extraordinary expenditures. Yamamoto's government also streamlined the bureaucracy by eliminating just over five thousand civil-service positions. The prime minister's retrenchment and redundancy program drew immediate praise from party men, the Tokyo and Osaka chambers of commerce, and virtually every metropolitan newspaper in Japan, including the *Tokyo Asahi*, *Jiji shimpō*, *Tokyo Nichi nichi*, and the *Hōchi*.[45] More important to Seiyūkai representatives, this ¥35-million reduction in ordinary expenditures afforded Yamamoto the opportunity to reduce income-tax revenue by nearly ¥7 million.[46] Since the opening of the Diet in 1890, political parties had consistently lobbied for tax reduction but more often than not faced opposition from both the government and the bureaucracy. An admiral turned national politician on the inside of government who was committed to the policies of the party yet again secured results that had hitherto been impossible to obtain.

Solidifying the Navy-Seiyūkai Relationship: Pork-Barrel Naval Spending, Pageantry, and Budget Negotiations

As successful as Yamamoto was in obtaining Seiyūkai political objectives, the savvy admiral did not rest on his early accomplishments believing that these alone would secure the necessary support for his long-sought naval expansion program. Rather, the prime minister actively campaigned on behalf of the navy's initiates. Furthermore, the prime minister was assisted by the emergence of a private navy-industrial establishment that made appropriating funds for naval expansion far more attractive to Seiyūkai politicians desirous of reinforcing bastions of electoral support through a positive industrial policy. For a growing number of Seiyūkai politicians, naval expansion came to be viewed as a way in which to further the expansion of industry in Japan, particularly in Kyushu, home of the Mitsubishi shipyard, where the Seiyūkai had a virtual stranglehold on political power.[47] Power, and the expansion of power, was at the base of much of the Seiyūkai's political initiatives.

In the late Meiji and early Taishō period, shipbuilding underwent a transformation in Japan, spurred on in large part by naval construction. Between 1906 and 1910, Japanese shipyards produced 78 percent of the navy's warships. This was a significant percentage, but the figure is somewhat misleading. Only 2 percent of this overall 78 percent was constructed in private shipyards, the other 76 percent being produced in navy-owned arsenals in Yokosuka, Sasebo, Kure, and Maizuru.[48] By 1913, however, private shipbuilders provided 37 percent of the navy's total production, 5 percent more than navy-owned, navy-operated arsenals produced. As the two largest private shipbuilding firms in Japan, the Mitsubishi shipyard at Nagasaki and the Kawasaki shipyard at Kobe, were the primary beneficiaries, securing large-scale expensive orders from the navy provided jobs and an influx of state money for M.P.'s' constituent bases and stimulated industrial expansion in allied areas associated with shipbuilding. For Seiyūkai party leaders who looked to increase party support through a positive industrial policy, championing naval spending at private firms was an ideal vehicle by which to stimulate economic growth and political support.[49] It dovetailed well with other Seiyūkai-backed expansion programs such as harbor development, rail expansion, and the expansion of other industrial enterprise, and moreover the expansion carried out by private shipyards to accommodate naval orders also laid the foundation for future expansion in the nonmilitary shipbuilding categories as well.[50] Finally, naval orders encouraged the diffusion of technological know-how from domestic naval arsenals to private shipyards and from overseas shipyards to private Japanese yards. In 1911, the navy sent a handful of construction engineers from the Kawasaki shipyard to work with Vickers shipbuilders in England on the construction of the naval warship *Kongō*; there the engineers gained valuable experience that was put to use in later naval orders for the superdreadnought *Haruna*.[51] Expanding capacity and production in private shipyards was a win-win situation both for the navy and for the Seiyūkai, as leaders from each side understood.

Evidence of Seiyūkai concern over the percentage of warships produced by private firms surfaced in parliamentary discussions over naval expansion. As early as 1910, Navy Minister Saitō fielded questions concerning the percentage of warships that were ordered from private shipyards in Japan.[52] Saitō responded by claiming that the navy hoped to transfer as much construction to domestic shipyards as possible but that at present Japan's domestic capacity was not sufficient to meet naval demands. Naval expansion, Saitō suggested, could spur development within the Japanese domestic shipbuilding industry. Another instance when the question of domestic production arose occurred in 1912, when Seiyūkai member Nakamura Junkurō questioned Navy Minister Saitō over the percentage of naval funding that was being contracted to private shipbuilders. On this occasion, as he would whenever this question appeared in discussions within the Lower House Budget Committee, its subcommittee, or on the floor of the full parliament, Saitō claimed that naval policy was to transfer as much as possible to private yards so as to stimulate shipbuilding capacity in Japan. The following year, Vice Navy Minister Takarabe reiterated these claims at a meeting of the Lower House Budget Subcommittee and moreover argued that the navy's standard policy was to purchase as many components for navy-made ships from private industry as possible, including iron plate.[53] Strengthening the navy was thus strengthening Japan as an industrial power. Two years later, in 1915, Seiyūkai leader Noda Utarō echoed these concerns and urged the navy to further promote private warship construction so as to benefit the nation and the economy.[54] While links between Japanese industrial concerns, the navy, and parliament were not as pronounced as they were in Germany in the era preceding World War I, owing significantly to lower levels of industrial capacity, Seiyūkai men could more convincingly justify and more readily accept naval expansion that encouraged private industrial growth and technological development over army expansion that did little to promote either.[55]

A final means by which Yamamoto hoped to solidify members of the Seiyūkai and public to support naval expansion surrounded the continued use of naval pageantry. In his capacity as prime minister, Yamamoto helped organize a series of impressive pro-navy celebrations throughout November and December 1913, the period when the cabinet and parliament began to debate the government's proposed budget for 1914. On 1 December, the navy held a commemorative celebration to mark the launching of the *Dreadnought*-class battleship *Kirishima* from Mitsubishi shipyard at Nagasaki, to which all Seiyūkai members from the Kyushu faction were invited as V.I.P.'s. Less than two weeks later, on 14 December, the navy organized an even larger celebration to launch the *Dreadnought*-class battleship *Haruna* at the Kawasaki shipyard at Kobe. On each occasion, naval leaders publicly thanked the politicians, industrialists, and workers who had contributed to the navy's expansion and reiterated their value to the nation. As with other launches, special dignitaries, including many Seiyūkai representatives, received commemorative medallions to mark the launch, and by their presence at such occasions with military leaders, bureaucrats, and representatives of the imperial family, Seiyūkai men were given greater political clout and stature.[56] These events mirrored the celebrations conducted in November 1913, when the navy staged a well-publicized ceremony to mark the arrival of the British-built battleship *Kongō*, the largest battleship afloat at that time.[57] For its arrival on 5 November the navy staged a two-day fete, with newspaper reporters and select party officials allowed to board the vessel with the navy minister as he welcomed the ship to Japan.

While impressive, these exercises paled in comparison with the extravaganza associated with the navy's Grand Maneuver of the Fleet, which took place on 10 November. In all, fifty-five vessels of the Imperial Navy, including the newly arrived *Kongō*, conducted military maneuvers off Yokosuka. As with previous Grand Maneuvers, the emperor attended, having been escorted from Tokyo to Yokosuka via train by high-ranking naval officials and select cabinet ministers, including Hara Kei, as well as a number of local dignitaries and Seiyūkai officials.[58] As part of the fleet exercise, the emperor, in a highly visible and symbolic ceremony, bestowed upon Admiral Itō Yūkō the Grand Cordon of the Chrysanthemum for his service to the empire. Afterwards, as Emperor Meiji had done earlier, Emperor Taishō viewed the maneuvers from the battleship *Kattori*. Finally, the maneuver was concluded with the announcement that from 1913 on the navy would conduct a similar fleet exercise for the emperor and the public every year. This announcement prompted one reporter from the *Tokyo Asahi* to comment that such maneuvers were, and would continue to be, nothing more than a means for the navy to build public and political support for expansion.[59] He was, in many respects, correct.

Like the naval review held the year before, the November 1913 review coincided perfectly with the navy's budgetary agenda. Earlier in October, Saitō had submitted a ¥352-million budget proposal to Yamamoto, which covered the years from 1913 to 1921.[60] Specifically, the plan called for the construction of seven *Dreadnought*-class battleships (three of which were already under construction that had begun with the ¥6-million budget approval in March), two first-class cruisers, five second-class cruisers, twenty-six destroyers, and ten submarines. When completed in 1921, Japan would possess an "eight-six" fleet. Not unexpectedly, Yamamoto quickly endorsed the plan and informed Saitō that he would introduce the navy's request to the cabinet in early November just prior to the navy's planned festivities. On 4 November, the cabinet discussed the preliminary budgets, including Saitō's proposal. At this meeting, Finance Minister Takahashi Korekiyo agreed in principle to support the navy's program and informed Saitō that he would give a firm commitment after calculating the other ministries' requests.[61] From Saitō, Takarabe, and Yamamoto's standpoint, budgetary matters looked extremely promising for the navy.

Hara, however, saw things slightly differently. Meeting Saitō five days

TABLE 4

*Japanese Army, Navy, and National Expenditures
and Military Personnel, 1906–1914*

(expenditures listed in yen)

Year	Army expenditures	Navy expenditures	National expenditures	Army personnel	Navy personnel
1906	¥67,870,000	¥61,876,000	¥464,276,000	200,000	46,676
1907	126,043,000	72,272,000	602,401,000	220,000	51,551
1908	141,803,000	71,579,000	636,361,000	225,000	52,824
1909	106,803,000	71,046,000	523,894,000	225,000	52,687
1910	101,323,000	83,840,000	569,154,000	225,000	54,731
1911	105,000,000	100,463,000	585,375,000	225,000	56,887
1912	104,125,000	95,486,000	593,596,000	227,861	59,777
1913	95,440,000	96,446,000	573,634,000	227,260	55,940
1914	87,700,000	83,700,000	648,420,000	231,411	60,914

SOURCES: National expenditures and army and navy personnel are found in Statistics Bureau, *Historical Statistics of Japan*, 5 vols. (Tokyo: Japan Statistical Association, 1987): 5:525, 528. Army and navy expenditure figures are taken from Naikaku tōkeikyoku (Cabinet statistics bureau), *Nihon teikoku tōkei nenakan* (Statistical yearbook of the Japanese empire), 59 vols. (Tokyo: Tokyo ripurinto shuppansha, 1962–1967): 43:507 (1924).

later, on 9 November, Home Minister Hara, who always had one finger on the pulse of the Seiyūkai and one on national politics, expressed considerable caution.[62] Hara's concern did not stem from any dissent he gleaned from his party, but rather from the army. While Hara freely admitted that the Diet and the navy were on "quite good terms, unlike the army," the Seiyūkai leader feared army reaction to a budget which provided funds for significant naval expansion while at the same time ignoring army requests for much smaller increases. Though Saitō responded that the government would initiate army expansion in 1915, Hara warned the navy minister to be more patient with his service's own requests in order to maintain harmony between the services. Hara clearly wanted the Yamamoto cabinet to avoid the fate of Saionji's last cabinet, which had been brought down by an intransigent and jealous army minister hell-bent on expanding the army's budget.

Not unexpectedly, therefore, discussions over naval expansion took center stage at the cabinet budget meetings held on 21, 25, and 27 November.[63] After providing each minister present with a highly detailed position paper justifying the expansion request, Saitō won over Finance Minister Takahashi.[64] Though Takahashi believed the expensive request could be divided into three parts, with the first part being accepted outright and the last two sections being agreed upon in principle, Hara again voiced his concern and suggested a lesser amount for naval expansion, roughly ¥90 million.[65] Saitō then countered with a ¥230-million proposal, which was followed with a ¥160-million compromise being suggested by the prime minister that would cover expansion from 1914 to 1919.[66] This was a figure everyone could agree upon. Though it was less than the navy originally requested, ¥160 million was still the largest single increase package agreed upon since the Russo-Japanese War. Best of all, or so naval leaders and Seiyūkai cabinet officials presumed, owing to the close relationship that had developed between the navy and the Seiyūkai, parliamentarians would raise only token opposition to the government's budget. Events, however, would show that while the cabinet had not overestimated the level of support the Seiyūkai's rank and file would give to the government, both parties underestimated the level of animosity the navy-Seiyūkai entente had created within the Chōshū bureaucratic faction, the army, and the newly formed Dōshikai party. Given this tense political situation between forces of the old order and the new guard, a bribery and blackmail scandal that resulted in the rejection of the government's proposed naval expansion budget was all that was needed to once again reorient national politics in early Taishō Japan.

The Siemens-Navy Scandal

When Yamamoto submitted his government's budget to parliament in January 1914, the admiral had good reason to believe that his legislative agenda, including the massive naval expansion program agreed upon by the cabinet, would sail through parliament. The lower house was still dominated by the Seiyūkai, and Hara had given the prime minister assurances that the party rank and file would follow the lead of the cabinet and support all government initiatives. On 23 January 1914, the same day that the House Budget Committee began formal consideration of Yamamoto's massive naval expansion program, hopes for a quick acceptance of the government's budget and a controversy-free parliamentary session evaporated. That morning, Tokyo newspapers reported on a verdict handed down by a German court against Carl Richter, a former Siemens employee in Tokyo.[67] The German court sentenced Richter to two years' penal servitude for theft and attempted extortion of fellow Siemens employees in Japan. The property in question, which Richter stole from the Siemens Tokyo office, was a series of documents that revealed corrupt business practices conducted between Siemens officials and well-placed officers in the Japanese navy. Specifically, the documents detailed commissions that Siemens had paid to individuals in the Japanese navy, officers who had been instrumental in securing orders for the company with their service. Publication of details concerning the Richter verdict and allusions to the stolen documents he produced at his trial called into question the scruples of certain Japanese naval officials and cast doubts over the efficacy of granting new appropriations to a seemingly corrupt navy. The Siemens-Schückert scandal, as it was to become known, provided forces opposed to the Seiyūkai-navy entente with the opportunity that they had desired to attack the government, and this they did with remarkable tenacity.

In brief, the events leading to the eventual exposure of naval corruption dated back to the early spring of 1913. At that time, Richter, a stenographer who had become increasingly dissatisfied with his ¥125 monthly salary and with the Siemens Corporation in general, uncovered materials that documented the payment of commissions to Japanese naval officers who had been instrumental in securing orders for the German-based corporation with the Japanese navy. Realizing their potential worth, Richter removed the documents from the company office and stored them at his residence in Tokyo. Anything but the model employee, Siemens fired Richter on 17 October 1913 for habitual lateness and continued underperformance. Angered over his dismissal, the following day Richter returned to company headquarters in Tsukiji with the intention of blackmailing his former employers. Specifically, the disgruntled stenographer asked to meet his former boss, Victor Hermann, who in 1913 served as the managing director of the Tokyo Siemens office.[68] As Hermann was away on business, Richter agreed to see the acting director, Takagi Chōsaburō. During their exchange, Richter disclosed the content of the documents in his possession and produced an extortion letter in which the former employee demanded payment of ¥25,000 in exchange for the safe return of the documents. If Takagai refused, or so Richter threatened, the documents would be sold or given to the press. Unaware of how to handle such a volatile, illegal, and potentially damaging development, Takagi asked Richter to await Director Hermann's return. Unexpected travel complications delayed Hermann's return, however, and time propelled Richter along another trajectory.[69] Fearful that Takagi would inform the police of the extortion effort, Richter proceeded to find another buyer for the documents and looked no further than Reuters correspondent Andrew Mabel Pooley. On 3 November both men met at the Reuters office in the Nippon News Agency Building in Kyōbashi, Tokyo, and discussed the contents of the documents held by Richter. After examining the materials later that afternoon, Pooley immediately offered Richter ¥750 for the documents and told Richter that payment could be arranged within twenty-four hours. While a considerably smaller sum than he originally wanted, Richter agreed to Pooley's offer, hoping to conclude his involvement in the blackmail affair quickly so that he could leave Japan. Both men agreed to the price offered, and immediately afterwards Pooley proceeded to meet George Blundell, the top Reuters official in Tokyo, and persuaded him to authorize the agreed sum to secure the transaction. Trusting Pooley, Blundell agreed, and on 4 November the transaction between Pooley and Richter took place. Money and documents changed hands.

Recognizing the sensational nature of the documents and desirous of removing them from any location under the jurisdiction of Japan's law-enforcement agencies, Pooley and Blundell posted the documents to their branch office in Shanghai on 5 November. Once the documents reached Shanghai, Pooley approached the Siemens company himself and met with the recently returned Victor Hermann on 14 November. Like Richter before him, Pooley threatened to uncover the corrupt dealings that the Siemens company had engaged in with the navy unless the company paid a substantial ¥250,000 in exchange for the documents. While Hermann had previously viewed Richter as a minor inconvenience, the Siemens director felt that A. M. Pooley, with his firmly established press connections, was obviously a major threat to the special relationship that the Siemens Corporation had developed with certain naval officers. Although initially startled at the excessive price asked by Pooley, Hermann agreed to issue a money order for the sum from the Deutsche-Asiatic Bank of Yokohama once the papers were returned to the Tokyo office.

Feeling that negotiations had been successful, Pooley dispatched Reuters agent Hashiguchi Jihei to fetch the documents from Shanghai. Hermann, however, was less satisfied with the agreement. Not wishing for the Tokyo office to pay the entire sum, Hermann conspired to devise a plan by which Siemens could offset at least part of the ¥250,000. To this end, on 17 November, Hermann met with Navy Minister Saitō and informed him of the particulars of the case.[70] Hoping to receive funds from the navy to cover the ¥250,000 settlement, Hermann suggested to Saitō that the publication of such documents would have a devastating effect on the navy's political standing, not to mention any future dealings between the navy and his company. Such tactics did little to impress Saitō, however, and the meeting ended with the navy minister refusing to cover any expenses associated with the blackmail affair. Afterwards Takarabe informed Anraku, the superintendent of the Tokyo police, to deal harshly with Hermann if he persisted in his demand that the navy provide funds to cover the payment to Pooley.

On his own, Hermann contacted Pooley and told him that a new figure would have to be agreed upon. A little over a week after discussing the matter with the navy minister, the Siemens managing director informed Pooley that he could pay only ¥50,000 for the documents. Faced with no real alternative and desirous of ending his involvement in the blackmail affair, Pooley acquiesced and accepted the reduced figure in exchange for the stolen documents. After informing Saitō that the matter had been resolved favorably, Hermann proceeded to the German consulate, where he burned the documents, believing that this was the end of the matter and that through his actions he had successfully preserved the secret and illegal relationships previously established with the high-ranking officers in the Japanese navy. On 27 November, Hermann informed Anraku that negotiations with Pooley had been settled amicably, and afterwards Anraku relayed the good news to the Navy Ministry. Everyone involved breathed a sigh of relief and felt that a political disaster had been avoided.

In this, Hermann and officials in the Navy Ministry were badly mistaken. Richter had outfoxed the Siemens corporation yet again. Before selling the documents to Pooley, on 3 November Richter had made photographic reproductions of the documents in question at the Hirano Photographic Studio in Tokyo. Unaware of Richter's action, Hermann had sent a copy of the former employee's extortion letter to officials in Germany and asked that he be arrested upon his return to Germany. German officials obliged, and Richter was arrested upon arrival. At his trial Richter produced the photographic copies as part of his defense strategy, a final swipe at the German corporation. Unfortunately for all parties involved, the documents, most of which were detailed in Japanese newspapers via correspondents in Berlin and London, clearly revealed the special relationship that Hermann had cultivated with several well-placed naval officers through two intermediaries, Yoshida Shūkichi, a former Siemens employee, and Captain Sawasaki Takehiro of the Japanese navy. To briefly illustrate the pattern of that relationship: in 1909 the Siemens Corporation placed a bid with the navy to construct a wireless telegraph station at Funabashi in Chiba for approximately ¥750,000. In order to gain an advantage over its competitors, the Siemens director agreed to give a certain percentage of the original contract estimate to two admirals involved in the selection process, Matsumoto Kazu (director of the Naval Stores Department) and Murakami Kaku'ichi (chief of Naval Construction Department), through two intermediaries, Sawasaki Takehiro and Yoshida Shūkichi.[71] Along with this specific instance, Richter's papers also made reference to a long-term relationship that Siemens had cultivated with Japanese naval officers stationed in Europe to oversee the construction and outfiting of Japanese warships. One such example involved Admiral Fujii Mitsugorō, who the documents stated was an active commission hunter and a good friend of the Siemens Corporation whose palms should always be kept warm. This was an accurate appraisal. Not only had Fujii, who in 1914 was head of Kure Naval Station, helped arrange orders for the construction of the battleship *Kongō* from Vickers (for which he received payments totalling just over ¥400,000) but he also took commission bribes in relation to the procurement of turbine engines for warships produced in Japan. Other naval officers, such as Captain Sawasaki Hirotake of the Naval Stores Department, were also implicated in Richter's documents. Detailing these underhanded practices extensively in the newspapers made it seem as if the navy were full of corrupt officers; one newspaper referred to them as "battleship millionaires."[72]

The Siemens-Navy Scandal: Protest and High-Level Politics

For Yamamoto, the navy, and the Seiyūkai, news of the Siemens scandal could not have come at a less auspicious time. Parliament had just convened, and discussions on the navy's new budget had commenced. Opposition M.P.'s thus seized upon the revelations of corruption to attack the government and question the desirability of supporting the navy's expansion program.[73] At the Lower House Budget Committee meeting on 23 January, Shimada Saburō of the Dōshikai party lashed out strongly at the navy. Shimada claimed that the foreign and domestic press reports of the scandal cast doubt upon the moral integrity of the navy and moreover soiled Japan's reputation abroad. More troubling to the government, Shimada next linked the corruption issue with the navy's expansion requests before the parliament and asked aloud how Japan's citizens would feel about granting increases to a seemingly corrupt navy. Shimada then confessed that he, as a representative of the people, would have trouble supporting naval expansion, even if surplus revenue existed, until the corruption controversy was settled. The fiery oration ended when the Dōshikai representative asked the navy minister to divulge all information concerning the scandal and to give assurances that the corruption outlined was an isolated phenomenon. Navy Minister Saitō assured representatives that while he had learned of the theft of the Siemens documents through a November meeting with Victor Hermann, the payoffs were an isolated incident and the navy had already begun to investigate the matter.[74]

Saitō's admission of the November meeting with Hermann allowed the opposition to expand their attacks against the government. Why, asked Hanai Takuzō (Chūseikai) at a general meeting of the lower house on 29 January, did the government not involve the police after Hermann approached the navy minister?[75] Shimada and Hayashi Hiriku then followed this line of inquiry and asked Navy Minister Saitō what had transpired between Siemens representatives and himself in November. Had Siemens representatives asked for a payment? Was one given? As a follow-up, both M.P.'s asked why Home Minister Hara had not taken a more determined, visible, active role in the investigation. Both Hara and Saitō responded that not enough was known in November to make any arrests but that a full inquiry was at present under way. Ozaki Yukio (Chūseikai) then asked the government how parliamentarians could trust a corrupt navy to investigate its own corrupt dealings.[76] Answering his own question, Ozaki replied that the government could not be trusted to investigate the matter and seconded calls made earlier in the week for the establishment of a parliamentary investigatory committee.[77]

Spurred on by growing public disquiet and the publication of further acts of wrongdoing by a number of other naval officers, opposition M.P.'s became more belligerent toward the government. On 5 February, following the arrests of Andrew Pooley and Victor Hermann by officers from the Tokyo Metropolitan Police Department, leaders from the Dōshikai, the Kokumintō, and the Chūseikai began to draft a no-confidence resolution against Yamamoto's ministry.[78] Aware of the growing public discontent and the hardening political opposition, and confronted with further stories of naval corruption, Justice Minister Okuda Yoshindo warned Hara that the Seiyūkai should be careful about giving unqualified support to the navy.[79] The next day, at a Seiyūkai party budget meeting, parliamentary representatives asked Hara questions concerning the government's proposed naval expansion budget.[80] Though some M.P.'s suggested that the party should side with opposition calls to reduce or at least hold off on the increases until the controversy passed and the navy was exonerated or cleansed, a majority of members agreed to follow Hara's lead.

Sensing unease within the party, Hara broached the budget question with Yamamoto and Saitō the following day.[81] At the prime minister's residence, Hara predicted that while he had secured the support of a majority of Seiyūkai members, voting for the entire expansion plan might damage the Seiyūkai unity and thus the navy-Seiyūkai partnership over the long haul. Pointedly, Hara asked Yamamoto if he would be willing to reduce the original expansion estimates. Testing the waters, Yamamoto replied that the navy would not be happy with such a development. Hara immediately shot back: "Do you want to make things convenient for the navy, or do you prefer the [political] security of choosing a course likely to avoid causing bad feelings among the Seiyūkai party? You must think carefully." After this frank rebuttal, Yamamoto suggested that Hara speak directly with Saitō. When confronted with Hara's suggestions, the pragmatic Saitō offered a compromise. Though Saitō admitted to wanting the entire estimate passed, the navy statesman declared that he would be willing to accept a revised budget that trimmed ¥30 million from the overall plan, the cost of one battleship that was to be constructed in 1917.[82] Hara believed that this act of conciliation would more easily allow Seiyūkai representatives to vote with the government. The following day, Hara informed the party executive of his discussion with Saitō and received unanimous support to pursue the reduction.[83] On 9 February, the Seiyūkai introduced a measure to the Lower House Budget Subcommittee reducing the navy's proposed budget by ¥30 million.

Hara's move was timed brilliantly to weaken the opposition. On 10 February, forces opposed to the Yamamoto cabinet launched a two-pronged attack against the government. First, opposition members rallied more than thirty-five thousand citizens to protest against the government. United by calls to protect the constitution and cleanse the navy, the group massed outside the Diet and demanded that members introduce a vote of no confidence in the government. Inside the Diet, opposition M.P.'s did exactly that. Demanding that Yamamoto take responsibility for the navy's corrupt dealings and for the public outrage and disorder that these revelations had caused, President Inukai Tsūyoshi of the Kokumintō introduced a measure of no confidence in the government.[84] Looking exhausted, Yamamoto challenged the opposition's bill, claiming that it would be irresponsible for any government official to resign in the midst of investigations. Though this was a weak defense, Yamamoto did not have serious reason to worry. The Seiyūkai, as expected, backed the government and rejected the no-confidence measure by a vote of 205 to 164.[85] The government had survived the first challenge brought about by the disclosure of naval corruption.

The government did not survive unscathed. On 12 February, the lower house passed a revised naval expansion budget incorporating the ¥30-million Seiyūkai-sponsored reduction resolution. This reduction was just the beginning of budgetary troubles for the navy. On 14 February, the House of Peers began deliberations over the government's proposed budget with Egi Senshi, Den Kenjirō, and Murata Tsuneyoshi attacking the government on two grounds: failure to take responsibility for the corruption scandal and ignoring the army's requests for a two-division increase so that the government could divert further monetary resources to the navy.[86] The tenacity with which the peers challenged the government convinced Hara and Yamamoto that the upper house might attempt to reduce the navy's budget further than the lower house had done earlier in February.[87] If the peers followed this course of action, a joint interhouse budget committee would be called to reach a decision.

Hara and Yamamoto's prediction proved correct. Desirous of punishing the navy and bringing about a collapse of navy-Seiyūkai unity, the House of Peers Budget Subcommittee reduced the navy's proposed expansion request by ¥70 million, ¥40 million more than the lower house had supported.[88] Four days later, the Upper House Budget Committee followed suit by a vote of 48 to 7, with the full house supporting the decision by a convincing margin of 240 to 44 on 13 March.[89] The peers struck at the navy's most cherished political objective, and they did so with vengeance. Introducing new budgetary cuts beyond the ones agreed upon by the lower house, the peers now forced the amended budget back to the Seiyūkai-dominated lower chamber. When members rejected this revised budget, a joint-chamber conference committee was held to resolve the budgetary dispute.

Events that transpired next gave both the Seiyūkai and the navy cause for celebration. By a vote of ten to nine, the conference committee agreed to accept the budget proposed by the lower house, the one that called for only a ¥30-million reduction.[90] When the lower house's budget went back to both chambers for approval, the representatives quickly endorsed their earlier-proposed budget. Celebrations ended here, however. Uncustomarily, the upper house refused to abide by the joint budget committee recommendation.[91] Lacking the endorsement of both houses of parliament, the budget failed, and Yamamoto was left with two alternatives: he could, as the constitution provided, use the previous year's budget for the forthcoming fiscal year, or he could resign in hopes that a new government would succeed where he had failed. As the budget for 1913 did not include any provisions for new expenditures desired by the navy, Yamamoto tendered his resignation to the emperor on 24 March, claiming that failure to secure a budget was "one of the most regretful events" in his life.[92] The hard work and effort Yamamoto expended to build support within the lower house of parliament had succeeded, but his best-laid plans had been foiled by the House Peers, the citadel of conservative, pro-Yamagata-faction followers who had most strongly opposed the navy-Seiyūkai entente, what it represented, and the reforms which it had implemented.

Although weakened politically by Yamamoto's resignation and the disclosure of naval corruption, naval leaders sought to influence national politics in hopes of furthering the navy's budgetary agenda. Upon submitting his resignation to the emperor, Yamamoto recommended Hara Kei as the next prime minister.[93] Claiming that he, as well as Katsura, had reached the conclusion that the era of transcendental cabinets (non–party-based cabinets) was over, Yamamoto suggested that Hara, as president of the majority party in the lower house of parliament, was the obvious choice to lead the next government. Privately, Yamamoto harbored the belief that Hara and the Seiyūkai would continue to support naval expansion and that Prime Minister Hara would counter Yamagata's forces, which had been responsible for undermining his cabinet. Hara, when told of Yamamoto's recommendation, became overjoyed; his long-sought desire seemed close at hand.

Unfortunately for Hara, not everyone supported Yamamoto's recommendation. In the aftermath of the Siemens scandal, Yamagata sought to reorient national politics back toward his conservative bureaucratic faction. In April, the Chōshū leader convened a meeting of the *genrō* council to select the next prime minister. After immediately rejecting Hara's nomination, Yamagata and Ōyama recommended Kiyoura Keigo to form the next cabinet. Kiyoura was the archetypal Yamagata-faction member who had served as justice minister and home minister in previous cabinets led by Yamagata and Katsura. As such, Kiyoura openly professed his belief in, and expressed the merits of, transcendental cabinets, and sought to create one in 1914.[94] Fearing that as a pro-army Yamagata-faction bureaucrat Kiyoura would look upon naval expansion unsympathetically, the naval leadership worked to block his candidacy or at least to secure a commitment from the would-be prime minister to support naval expansion. Specifically, Admiral Katō Tomosaburō, the naval officer put forward to take over for Saitō, demanded that Kiyoura call a special session of parliament to reinstate the naval expenditures pruned by the House of Peers. This was the condition upon which Katō's service would hinge. Believing that Katō would back down rather than face the public wraith sure to develop when word leaked of the navy's political and bugetary intransigence, Kiyoura refused to accept

Katō's demands. Here, Kiyoura underestimated Katō's resolve. Katō simply refused to serve in the cabinet, and unable to find any other eligible person to serve as navy minister, Kiyoura withdrew from the task of forming a cabinet. Though no longer in a position to influence politics pragmatically from inside the government, naval leaders still found it possible to exert leverage over cabinet politics through coercion.

Blocking the formation of a cabinet and derailing the smooth working of constitutional government much as the army had done during the Taishō Political Crisis was a huge political gamble for the navy, particularly after the popular outcry that had erupted against the navy in reaction to the disclosure of the Siemens scandal. Indeed, Kiyoura was counting upon such calculations to dissuade the navy from following just such a course of action. Here, however, Kiyoura overestimated the public's reaction to the navy's maneuvers. Owing to Kiyoura's background and his desire to strengthen the Yamagata faction's power through a transcendental cabinet, few individuals from the party movement, liberal intellectual circles, or the popular Protect the Constitution Movement expressed any outrage over the navy's actions. Had the navy elite blocked the formation of a party-based cabinet, the primary repercussion might well have been a further weakening of the navy's political position and greater public outrage at the navy. But Kiyoura was no party man.

After Kiyoura's attempts to form a government failed, the *genrō* nominated Ōkuma Shigenobu, a man backed by the Dōshikai, to head the next cabinet. As a historic figure in the early party movement, Ōkuma enjoyed widespread public support. Moreover, his gesture of inviting outspoken party members Ozaki and Inukai into his cabinet seemed to confirm his commitment to party involvement in cabinet-level politics.[95] But significantly, like Kiyoura before him, Ōkuma initially had difficulties securing a navy minister, and the issue again revolved around naval appropriations. Katō would likely put the same demands to Ōkuma as he had to Kiyoura, and the would-be prime minister refused to give any assurance that he would fight to reinstate the ¥70-million naval expenditure demanded by the navy. Ōkuma therefore turned his attention to other eligible candidates and with the help of Katō Takaaki, his foreign minister–designate, decided upon Admiral Yashiro Rokurō, who in 1914 was the commander of Maizuru Naval District. In normal circumstances Yashiro would have been an unlikely choice, as he was well down on the seniority list and considered by many as an outsider to the Yamamoto faction. These attributes, along with the fact that no officer from the Maizuru district had been implicated in any scandal, played to Yashiro's advantage. Moreover, Yashiro and Katō were good friend since their days as students at the Aichi English School in Nagoya. Most important, however, his position as an outsider who had called for rapid and thorough reform of the navy while the Siemens scandal unfolded convinced Ōkuma that Yashiro not only would be more willing to thoroughly cleanse the navy but was also an individual who might be willing to assume the position of navy minister without making exorbitant budgetary demands as a precondition to serving in the cabinet.

In this assumption, both Ōkuma and Katō were partly correct. Given that the navy-Seiyūkai alliance had collapsed, the reform-minded Yashiro wished to develop a cooperative working relationship with Ōkuma and the Dōshikai. But no less than Katō Tomosaburō, Yashiro was determined to advance the fiscal interests of the navy. He, like Katō before him, therefore sought assurances from Ōkuma concerning naval finances as a precondition to joining the cabinet. However, whereas Katō had requested a special Diet session to restore the entire ¥70 million which the peers had cut from the navy budget, Yashiro demanded far less. Specifically, Yashiro demanded only a special parliamentary session to appropriate between ¥6 million and ¥9 million, which he argued was necessary to continue with the construction of three warships already under contract in Japanese shipyards. Though not pleased with the prospects of blocking a cabinet with party support, even if the party in question was the Dōshikai, the naval leadership faced a remarkably difficult position that Yashiro was willing to fight for in 1914. The rejection of the navy's budget in 1913 not only kept the navy from implementing fleet expansion, but it also forced the navy to stop construction already under way on three battleships, two of which had been contracted to the private shipyards of Kawasaki and Mitsubishi. A bare minimum demand of Yashiro, and realistically anyone who would be asked to serve as navy minister, therefore, was that the next cabinet would appropriate funds so as to allow for the continued construction of the three battleships in question.

Internal political developments within the navy and the government pushed the navy toward accepting the reduced figured put forward by Ōkuma. As negotiations between Yashiro and Ōkuma unfolded, a new series of allegations concerning commissions paid to naval officers arose.[96] During investigations related to the Siemens affair, both military and civilian prosecutors found overwhelming evidence that implicated a number of high-ranking naval officers in contracts between Vickers's corporate agent in Japan, the Mitsui Corporation, and the Japanese navy. With yet another major scandal coming under public scrutiny, Yashiro was quick to take Ōkuma at his word that he would hold a special session of the Diet to secure the funds necessary to continue construction of the vessels in question. In return, Yashiro agreed to cleanse the navy thoroughly and to support Justice Minister Ozaki's prosecution of civilians associated with the scandal, reiterating his earlier statement that even Yamamoto or Saitō would "be brought before the law" if he were guilty.[97] Nine days later Yashiro placed both Yamamoto and Saitō on the reserve list and launched investigations into their conduct, though no charge was ever brought against either individual.[98]

The navy minister's words were matched by his deeds. During Yashiro's tenure in office the speed of navy courts-martial increased, and he made certain that the press and political parties were kept well informed of developments surrounding the Mitsui-Vickers scandal.[99] As a result of naval and civil investigations, prosecutors found sufficient evidence to prosecute five civilians in connection with the Siemens case and seven in relation to the Mitsui-Vickers affair. As with the Siemens affair, the Mitsui-Vickers case concerned commissions paid to Japanese naval officers.[100] As Yashiro directed, the navy quickly prosecuted those officers associated with the Siemens and Vickers scandals. On 7 May the courts-martial of Captain Sawasaki and Admiral Matsumoto began, followed the next day by pretrial proceedings for Admiral Fujii. After three weeks of deliberations, naval justices sentenced Matsumoto to a three-year prison term, fining him ¥409,800 and gave Sawasaki a one-year prison term and a ¥11,800 fine.[101] After a lengthier trial, Fujii was sentenced to a prison term of four and a half years and ordered to pay ¥368,306.

Both the press and politicians who had attacked the navy earlier in the year over the scandals lauded the new minister for his efforts to prosecute and punish corrupt officials and restore public confidence in the navy. Ōkuma and other cabinet ministers were also pleased with Yashiro's high-profile efforts, because they reduced the chance that opposition parties and the press would challenge the government over the issue of remaining naval corruption during the special session of the Diet. To further ensure his parliamentary success, Ōkuma waited to ask representatives to approve the disbursement of funds to continue naval construction until after the commencement of civilian trials associated with the Siemens and Vickers cases. Three days after the opening of the Siemens trial, in fact, Ōkuma invited representatives from both houses to his official residence to discuss the navy's financial request. The prime minister urged officials to support an extraordinary spending request that would give the navy nearly ¥6.5 million, informing parliamentarians that the money was absolutely essential to the navy and national defense.[102] Ōkuma also understood that the only way to guarantee the cabinet's stability was to work with both military services and parliament. While Ōkuma reiterated the urgent necessity of naval expansion, the prime minister also made a concerted effort to assure disgruntled peers that army expansion would be a priority in the next parliamentary session.[103] Importantly, Ōkuma assured a number of pro-army peers that the overall long-term policy of his cabinet would be to find balance between the army and the navy. The prime minister's assurances, coupled with Yashiro's tireless efforts to win support among parliamentarians, proved successful. By the end of June both houses had endorsed the prime minister's proposal, and on 30 June, the ¥6.5-million supplementary expansion program for the navy received imperial approval.

Synopsis

Yamamoto's tenure as prime minister, at least from the navy's perspective, could best be described as a government of unfulfilled potential. Throughout much of 1913, Yamamoto and Hara had worked together and strengthened the Seiyūkai's position within government, and in exchange the navy had gained parliamentary support for naval expansion. This was exactly what each had wanted in the relationship. The cautious relationship that had emerged over the course of the late Meiji period and solidified as a formal alliance in 1913 in the wake of the Taishō Political Crisis gave power and influence where each party had wanted it most. While Yamamoto used his newfound political position to implement a number of the Seiyūkai's most desired administrative reforms, the naval leadership lost the opportunity to gain what they most wanted from the alliance, naval expansion. They failed not because of a collapse of the alliance in the wake of popular outcry against the navy over the Siemens scandal but rather because of the powerful enemies they had further antagonized by their early successes. Indeed, while the Seiyūkai supported the navy during the period of its greatest unpopularity prior to World War II, Japan's majority party could not preserve the government in the face of entrenched conservative opposition. Displeased by the administrative reforms implemented at the behest of the Seiyūkai and enraged over Yamamoto's one-sided defense-appropriations bills, the peers used the Siemens scandal to bring about fundamental changes in the government. Interservice squabbles, interfactional rivalries, and military appropriations had once again transformed high-level politics in Japan. They would continue to do so until the end of World War II.

Indeed, as Ōkuma Shigenobu would soon find out, whoever held the reins of government, and from whatever faction or institution he drew support, the question of military appropriations would continue to bedevil Japanese politics, at least in peacetime. Though the new prime minister had secured his post by giving a guarantee to the navy that he would support limited naval expansion, the larger question of naval finances remained unresolved in late spring 1914. For a government that did not plan to raise taxes, the question of how to pay for expanding the navy and army that would be demanded of the cabinet in autumn 1914 was a major dilemma that Ōkuma knew he would face. How, if at all, Ōkuma could balance and accommodate military demands with those of state finance was the most important issue for the prime minister to resolve if he was to remain in power. Others too knew that the military appropriations budget was *the* issue facing the new cabinet, with one foreign newspaper editor predicting on 1 August 1914: "The reported naval demand . . . is going to be a very heavy strain on national finance. How this is to be adjusted with the fiscal policy under contemplation by the present government is the Gordian knot for Count Ōkuma to cut."[104] It was, but fortunately for the navy and the nation of Japan, dramatic events in Europe soon provided a golden opportunity for the government to increase expenditures for military expansion and to do so *with* popular support. In 1894 and again ten years later, in 1904, a successful war provided Japan's leaders with the means and motives to increase military spending and the ability to do so with the support of a majority of the population. World War I was no exception. Rather, in the end, it proved to be Japan's most lucrative war.

CHAPTER EIGHT

Opportunism, Expansion, and Limitation

The Imperial Navy and Japan's Great War,
1914–1922

> The South Seas islands are to be made the occupied territory of the Imperial Navy. Keep this in mind, and execute your duties in accordance with this aim.[1]
> —Navy General Staff Order of 15 October 1914

> It is simply impossible for us to build any further warships in our domestic yards, and moreover we have been forced to import construction materials from overseas.[2]
> —Hara Kei, January 1918

> Even if we tried to, it is a foregone conclusion that we are simply not up to [a naval arms race with the United States]. . . . my policy is to build up an adequate defensive force within the limits of Japan's national power.[3]
> —Katō Tomosaburō, February 1919

WELL REMOVED from the foul trenches of Western Europe, the inclement Eastern Front, and the nerve-racking convoy operations carried out across the treacherous North Atlantic, the cataclysmic event that forever altered European history was a war, if not *the* war, of opportunity for Japan. Though Japan's direct military commitments to World War I were negligible in terms of size, Britain's East Asian ally reaped seemingly incalculable rewards from this conflict. World War I transformed Japan, and of all the many institutions and organizations that benefited from it none did so more than the navy. Acting opportunistically in the opening months of the war, initially without the consent of the cabinet, the navy used the war to further its institutional, strategic, and budgetary aims, and did so with astonishing success.[4] The war provided the navy with the opportunity

to secure its long-sought South Seas possessions and, through its operations in the eastern Mediterranean, global experience and further international recognition. Moreover, the war precipitated a massive naval development program in the United States, and the Japanese navy used all these
phenomena to further justify greater naval expansion in Japan. Japan, as
many admirals argued, simply had to increase the size of its navy to protect
its empire, new and old, to uphold its military commitments to Britain, and
to defend against the threat posed by U.S. naval increases. Politicians motivated in part by foreign naval development but more thoroughly by domestic political concerns agreed and backed naval expansion on a level previously unknown in Japan.

Fortunately for the proponents of fleet expansion, World War I provided
not only the motives but also the means to support extensive naval development. The war infused the Japanese state with money that could be directed toward naval expansion. After an initial recession that covered the
first few months of the conflict, Japan's economy expanded markedly between 1915 and 1919. Money gained from selling manufactured goods to
markets previously dominated by the European imperial powers in South
and Southeast Asia and profits accrued by selling war materials to the Entente powers turned Japan from a debtor nation to a creditor for the first
time in this country's history. Japan's balance of trade between 1915 and 1918
totaled just over ¥1.48 billion in surplus, while foreign specie holdings by
the Bank of Japan and the Japanese government topped ¥1.3 billion in 1919.
Telling too, Japan's national expenditures rose from ¥618 million in 1914 to
¥1.6 billion in 1921.[5] In a world awash with yen, the navy did surprisingly
well. Naval spending as a percentage of total state expenditure rose from
just under 13 percent in 1914 to just over 21 percent in 1918. Peace, however,
did not slow the pace of naval construction. On the contrary, by 1921 naval
expenditures alone consumed an obscene 33 percent of Japan's national
budget. To admirals who had devoted much if not all of their time to the
pursuit of naval expansion, the war must have indeed seemed like "divine
aid."[6]

By 1920, however, not all admirals greeted these numbers with the glee
and gratitude that one would expect. While monetarily rewarding beyond
almost all comprehension, the period of seemingly unlimited naval growth
exposed significant weaknesses in Japan's ability to provide adequate defense against a stronger and richer adversary, the U.S. Navy. While Japan
could produce warships of outstanding quality that easily matched vessels
produced in U.S. and British shipyards, it could not produce enough of

them to keep pace. The war clearly demonstrated the limits of Japan's industrial capabilities as well as its dependence on natural resources from overseas. Japan could not in 1921, any better than it could in 1941, win a naval race against the United States, let alone a total or unlimited war in which industry, resources, and logistics were as fundamental to victory as military prowess and spirit. This was a harsh realization, and no one within the navy understood this better than Katō Tomosaburō, the resolute navy minister who had in July 1920 secured parliamentary commitment for the navy's long-desired eight-eight fleet at a cost of ¥750 million to be spent between 1920 and 1927.[7] Comprehending the correct lessons of World War I and the naval expansion that accompanied and followed it, Katō faced significant difficulties convincing fellow naval personnel that limiting naval growth within an international treaty system was the most rational if not the only means by which to strengthen Japan's national defense. Unlimited naval growth might have enriched the navy's budgetary coffers and strengthened this institution in the narrowest sense, but it was not a guarantor of national security. This went against everything that almost every naval officer who had pursued fleet expansion believed, and therefore it did not sit well with all in the Japanese navy. Katō thus channeled his energies at home and abroad into securing pragmatic naval limitations and in doing so unleashed pent-up antagonisms that had been previously subordinated to the cause of naval expansion, *the* cause of the navy from 1868 to 1922.

Southern Advance in the Context of Japanese Opportunism

On 18 August 1914, British Foreign Secretary Sir Edward Grey wrote to the British ambassador in Japan, Sir Conyngham Greene: "There are many things going on in many places that I do not at all like: it is an inevitable consequence of being engaged in a huge war—everyone outside it will try to take advantage of the situation."[8] Whether or not Grey had Japan in mind, it is certainly the case that Japan entered World War I at Britain's request with a great deal of opportunism. In the opening days of the European war, Japan's Anglophile foreign minister, Katō Takaaki, relayed to Grey through Greene that Japan would define its attitude toward the European war only after it had an intimation of what Great Britain thought Japan should do.[9] "If called upon to do so," Katō added, his country would assist Great Britain "with all her strength," while "leaving it entirely to His Majesty's Government to formulate the reasons for, and nature of, the assistance required."[10] Katō, in an attempt to reinforce the sincerity if not the finality of his position also stated that he had conveyed this position to the German ambassador in Tokyo the previous day.[11] During the first week of August, then, while Grey assessed the political and military benefits and consequences of requesting Japanese assistance, Katō repeatedly indicated his government's willingness to render such support if called upon to do so.

On 6 August, the British government sought just such assistance, but its request was tempered by the realities of Britain's precarious position and divergent interests in Asia. On the one hand, certain members of the British government, namely in the Admiralty Office, strongly desired Japanese naval assistance.[12] On the other hand, British diplomats in China and Hong Kong believed that Japanese participation would diminish Britain's "future political influence in China and our prestige in Asia generally" and "would involve deplorable complications now and hereafter."[13] Therefore, Grey's communiqué of 6 August clearly defined the limited assistance he was requesting. Specifically, Grey asked for naval assistance only to "hunt out and destroy German armed merchant cruisers in East Asian waters."[14] The next morning, Grey informed Japan's ambassador in London, Inoue Katsunosuke: "His Majesty's government would gladly avail themselves of proffered assistance of the Japanese Government in the direction of protecting British trading vessels."[15]

Though Britain's request was more restrictive than he had hoped for, Katō nevertheless proceeded to obtain cabinet approval to enter the war. On the evening of 7 August, he met with Prime Minister Ōkuma at his private residence in Waseda and convinced him to support Japan's entry into the conflict.[16] Ōkuma then convened an extraordinary session of the cabinet to discuss Katō's proposal, and at 2:30 A.M. on 8 August the other ministers endorsed Katō's proposal to enter the war on the broad basis of the Anglo-Japanese Alliance. Katō left Waseda at 5:30 A.M. to advise the emperor, then at Nikkō, of this decision. He returned to Tokyo later that day and attended a second cabinet meeting, this time in the presence of the most influential *genrō*, Yamagata, Matsukata, and Ōyama, to inform them of the decision for war.[17]

Within thirty-six hours after receiving the British request, the cabinet, the emperor, and the most influential *genrō* had been informed of and had endorsed Katō's policy, albeit begrudgingly.[18] From that point on, the language of Katō's communiqués changed considerably. Specifically, he was no longer willing to "leave it entirely to His Majesty's Government to formulate the reasons for, and nature of, Japanese assistance required."[19] On 9 August, Katō sent an aide-mémoire to Grey that stated: "Japan cannot restrict her action only to the destruction of hostile armed merchant cruisers, but it will become necessary for her to resort to all and every possible means."[20] Furthermore, Katō concluded that such actions would necessitate an independent declaration of war against Germany.[21] The tone of this and nearly all subsequent messages resonated with Katō's newfound confidence. That sureness arose not only from the fact that he had obtained the domestic political support needed for participation but also because he believed Great Britain's military position in East Asia was such that Grey's government had no choice but to acquiesce to Japan's military and diplomatic freedom of action. Katō's actions in early August 1914 were masterstrokes of diplomatic opportunism.

Foreign Minister Katō and to a lesser though no less important extent Prime Minister Ōkuma saw significant opportunities in Japan's entry into the European war. Both saw within this larger, attention-diverting conflict a unique chance to further Japan's interests in China. Prior to 1914, Katō had sought to extend the Japanese territorial leasehold in China, informing Foreign Secretary Grey in 1912 that he would wait for the "right psychological moment" to renegotiate the issue with Chinese leaders.[22] After returning to the Foreign Ministry in 1914, Katō criticized the China policy of maritime-oriented Prime Minister Yamamoto Gonnohyōe, stating that "questions between both countries had lined up in a row on the shelves, dust had collected on them, and no one had disposed of them."[23] Katō believed that seizing Germany's territorial possessions in Shantung during the opening stages of the war might provide the leverage needed to extend Japan's economic and territorial interests in China.[24]

An examination of Japan's official diplomatic communiqués drafted in the first weeks of the war as well as the statements issued by the government further reveal Katō and Ōkuma's overriding interest in China. After Katō received Great Britain's military request on 6 August, the foreign minister communicated to Greene "that an attack upon Tsingtau [*sic*] would be the quickest way of settling business."[25] Moreover, Japan's 15 August ultimatum to Germany further illustrated that the government's territorial ambitions lay clearly on the continent. Article 2, the only article that mentioned any German territory, specifically advised the German government: to "deliver on a date not later than 15 September 1914, to the imperial Japanese authorities, without compensation, the entire leased territory of Kiachou [*sic*], with a view to the eventual restoration of the same to China."[26] Three days later, when meeting with a group of Japanese businessmen, Ōkuma declared the official reason behind Japan's ultimatum: "Japan's object is to eliminate from the continent of China the root of German influence, which forms a constant menace to peace in the Far East. . . . Japan's wartime operations will not, therefore, extend beyond the limits necessary for the attainment of that object."[27] Continental aspirations drove Katō and Ōkuma. Neither, however, shared a similar desire to expand the war to the Pacific. To most members of the cabinet, the German-held islands of present-day Micronesia were of little immediate or potential value. Not everyone in Japan shared this view.

Long a dream of many naval personnel since the late 1870s, the acquisition of a South Seas territorial empire had never been more than that: a hollow dream. The aspirations of many *nanshin* advocates foundered simply because Japan's navy lacked any realistic opportunity to carve out and secure a place in the sun. No uncharted islands of any significance existed in the 1880s waiting for intrepid explorers or naval personnel to claim them for Japan, and the occupation of charted islands would have resulted in military conflict with a previously established colonial power: Spain, Germany, Britain, France, or the United States. This was not a realistic option. The opportunity presented by World War I, however, afforded Japan just such an opportunity to acquire Pacific territory within the larger framework of providing assistance to the Entente powers.

The chance to seize territory through naval operations in the Pacific arose when at Britain's request Japan agreed to locate and destroy the remaining nucleus of Admiral Maximilian von Spee's East Asiatic Squadron, which had fled its home port at Tsingtao in the opening days of the war. Believing that von Spee's vessels lurked somewhere in the vast waters adjacent to Germany's Pacific island territories, the Japanese navy formed two separate task forces to commence operations in the Pacific, one led by Admiral Yamaya Tanin and the other by Admiral Matsumura Tatsuo.[28] Yamaya's task force put to sea on 14 September. It did so, however, with restrictive orders. Following Foreign Minister Katō's suggestions, Yashiro and Vice Navy Minister Suzuki Kantarō urged discretion in all operations in the Pacific, telling Yamaya: "The foreign minister feels that occupation of any German territory in the Pacific would lead to an extremely unfavorable diplomatic situation. Therefore, even if by chance you stop and must land military personnel, do not acquire the islands and hoist the Japanese flag. If marines [*rikusentai*] become necessary, you must recall them expeditiously."[29] Yashiro and Suzuki's timidity was not well received.

By the end of September, Yashiro changed his mind and endorsed a more aggressive policy. A host of factors motivated Yashiro to recommend against following the wishes of his close friend Katō and the stated policy of the cabinet. First, a cacophony of voices within the navy challenged the restrictive orders recommended by Yashiro. The first to voice concern was Captain Katō Kanji, the infamous Katō who would later challenge Katō Tomosaburō over the desirability of naval limitations at the Washington Conference. In September 1914, Katō was commander of the battleship *Ibuki*, which had been assigned to joint operations with British and Australian vessels in the Indian Ocean. Almost as soon as the navy minister issued the restrictive orders, Katō communicated his profound disbelief that the navy would not use the wartime opportunity to acquire territory in the *Nan'yō*.[30] Determined not to let this opportunity pass by, Katō sent another, more belligerent telegram to naval headquarters again on 29 September urging immediate occupation of Germany's South Seas islands.

Katō was not alone in voicing his concern and displeasure. Shortly before putting to sea, the commander of the Second South Seas Task Force, Matsumura, met with Admiral Akiyama Saneyuki of the Naval Affairs Division of the Navy Ministry, one of the strongest southern-advance proponents in the service.[31] Akiyama boldly suggested that perhaps Matsumura did not necessarily have to pay attention to the minister's orders.[32] He argued that it would be impossible to locate the small number of German vessels in the vast Pacific without occupying potential German bases. Akiyama further declared: "If you do a job that expends large sums of money, at least get some profits."[33] He then lamented that the First South Seas Task Force had accomplished nothing and, moreover, had wasted valuable resources.[34] Akiyama therefore suggested that it might be profitable if Matsumura occupied phosphate-rich Angaur Island. Akiyama clearly did not want this opportunity for Japan to gain a foothold in the South Seas to slip away. Occupation, he figured, could lead to further southern expansion and legitimate fleet growth.[35] After his meeting with Akiyama, Matsumura proceeded to the Navy General Staff headquarters, where Vice Chief of Staff Admiral Inoue Yoshika sided with Akiyama. Inoue, in fact, more explicitly condemned Yashiro's restrictive orders, musing aloud: "Do you think that you will be able to accomplish what the navy minister wants in time of war?" He then said pointedly: "As long as the islands are enemy territory, what should you be afraid of? I do not think it is the rule of war to withdraw."[36] An aggressive and opportunistic policy was gaining adherents within the navy.

As Matsumura subsequently put to sea with his force of one battleship and two cruisers, Admiral Yamaya, commander of the First South Seas Task

Force, took matters into his own hands. On 30 September 1914, Yamaya violated his restrictive orders, dispatched a landing force to Jaliut Atoll, and thereby seized what was Germany's commercial headquarters in the central Pacific.[37] Occupation had begun. Upon notification, naval headquarters, at the request of the Navy Ministry, ordered a complete withdrawal of the forces that had landed. Yamaya complied and recalled his troops but did so only begrudgingly. Yamaya's actions as well as Matsumura's earlier discussions and Katō's sharp telegrams brought about debate within the navy between 30 September and 3 October 1914 over what course Japan's navy should follow.[38] The debate focused on whether the navy should follow the restrictive course recommended by the foreign minister, the cabinet, and the navy minister and see the German-held islands in the Pacific fall into the hands of Australian forces or whether the navy should seize the opportunity that had for so long been nonexistent. An important factor in the final decision may well have been budgetary. Yashiro changed his mind and sought cabinet approval for the navy's occupation of German territories in the North Pacific one day before both service ministers were to present their wartime budget requests to the Military Affairs Council.[39] This was done, it must be remembered, within the context of the army's moving toward the German stronghold on the Shantung Peninsula. Further, Yashiro knew as well as everyone else in Ōkuma's government that the army would again make fresh demands for budgetary increases that would allow the army to expand by two army divisions. Though Foreign Minister Katō resisted Yashiro's overture, Yashiro persisted, and eventually both agreed that the navy could temporarily occupy German territory in the Pacific. Within three weeks, the navy had expanded Japan's colonial empire by an area covering 2,700 miles from east to west and 1,300 miles from north to south.[40] Southern advance was no longer a dream but a reality, and one that would indeed enrich the Japanese navy.

War and the Politics of Naval Expansion

Even before Yashiro made his formal request for naval expansion in early October, the navy used the war to gain appropriations from the Diet. On 4 September, just weeks into the conflict, Prime Minister Ōkuma called a special session of parliament to approve a supplementary war budget.[41] Specifically, the navy asked for ¥38 million to cover costs associated with initial naval operations, and from this total the navy requested that just over ¥10 million be directed to the construction of ten first-class destroyers.[42] The request for destroyers allowed Yashiro to point out in no uncertain terms the advanced age of Japan's fleet and thus the necessity for further expansion known as "replenishment." Though Yashiro freely admitted that the navy possessed fifty destroyers in 1914, he articulately pointed out that forty-two of the fifty were at least nine years old. Before parliament on 5 September 1914 Yashiro therefore argued that the majority of Japan's destroyers not only were outdated but more dangerously were at the end of their operational lifespans. This endangered Japan's naval forces and could potentially restrict operations that Japan might find itself called to undertake by its ally Great Britain. Expansion of Japan's destroyer forces was, or so the navy minister concluded before parliament, a military and political necessity. On 9 September parliamentarians agreed, and within the month the navy had placed orders for ten new destroyers.

Though parliament had readily agreed to the destroyer appropriations in September, the additional ¥10 million this entailed was just the beginning of the navy's wartime expansion requests. Since August, Yashiro and his close subordinates in the Navy Ministry had begun preparations on their next large-scale expansion plan, which they hoped to submit to the cabinet in November. However, naval officials realized they would also have to gain the support of the newly formed Military Affairs Council prior to cabinet discussion as well as before submission to parliament. This, Yashiro believed, could further complicate the politics of military appropriations. The Military Affairs Council was the brainchild of Prime Minister Ōkuma, though Katsura had briefly flirted with the idea of such an organization in his ill-fated last cabinet.[43] Ōkuma's goal was to bring about stability to cabinet politics by closely coordinating military expansion requests between the armed services, the Finance Ministry, and the Foreign Ministry.[44] Well aware that the politics of military appropriations had destroyed the previous three cabinets, Ōkuma created an organization that he believed could balance military requests from both services and do so within the financial means of the state. The Military Affairs Council thus included the prime minister, each service minister, the chiefs of the two military general staffs, the finance minister, and the foreign minister.

While the council helped coordinate military expansion planning, it was by no means a panacea. The council met four times between 2 July and 6 August 1914, and at each meeting both military services submitted and discussed expansion proposals.[45] As expected, when the council met in October, Yashiro first argued on behalf of the eight-eight fleet and requested endorsement of the ¥351-million plan that had been originally discussed in

1911. Army leaders followed shortly thereafter, asking for ¥12 million to organize two new army divisions and deploy them in Korea.[46] Once deliberations began, Yashiro quickly acknowledged that state finances would not accommodate such sweeping naval requests and pragmatically offered to pursue only an additional ¥90 million, which would provide continuing expenses for three battleships already under construction, six further destroyers, and two submarines.[47] This pragmatic, conciliatory approach was quite opposite of Army Minster Oka Ichinosuke's tactic. Oka remained adamant that the military expansion as requested by the army be carried out in total. Moreover, Oka strongly refuted claims made by Finance Minister Wakatsuki Reijirō that army expansion would eventually bankrupt the state.[48] Army expansion thus proved more difficult to resolve than that brought forward by the navy. Army Minister Oka thereafter continued to make strong demands for his appropriations request and simply refused to compromise, despite challenges again being issued by the finance minister.[49] To resolve the deadlock, Ōkuma capitulated and endorsed the army minister's proposal. The Military Affairs Council still could not rein in a recalcitrant military minister determined to expand his service's budget. Events of early October thus illustrated to Ōkuma the council's limited powers.

In December, the prime minister discovered an even greater systemic weakness of the council. It simply failed to consider the most important actor in the appropriations process: the Diet. This was a significant oversight. When parliament convened in early December, military expansion budgets, as they had in the past, took center stage. The Seiyūkai remained the strongest party in the parliament and used military appropriations to settle political scores with the Ōkuma government. Though the finance minister assured representatives that army and navy expansion could be carried out without destroying the finances of the state, parliamentarians disagreed. Owing to their previously established ties with the navy and the pressing need for naval expansion, parliament endorsed the navy's request but again refused to support the army's two-division increase package, despite the unanimous recommendation of the Military Affairs Council.[50] Thus Ōkuma faced a similar situation to that which had undermined the Yamamoto cabinet in 1914. Rather than resign, however, the prime minister followed another course of action. Ōkuma dissolved parliament and called new elections for 25 March.

Ōkuma did everything in his power, both legal and extralegal, to assure that the next parliament would be more amenable to his government's programs. In one of the most corrupt elections since 1892, Ōkuma and his government decimated the Seiyūkai at the polls.[51] The Seiyūkai lost seventy-two seats, and progovernment parties increased by eighty-three. Though the new parliamentary make-up made passage of the army's expansion request more likely, the loss of Seiyūkai power worried Navy Minister Yashiro and others in the navy. Yashiro therefore dispatched Vice Navy Minister Suzuki Kantarō to build alliances within the new Diet, and the skilled bureaucrat did just that.[52] Despite four want-of-confidence measures introduced by oppositions M.P.'s over the course of the three-week session that began on 15 May, Suzuki's hard work helped secure passage of a ¥94-million expansion plan that covered the continuing construction costs of the three battleships first ordered in 1911 and the construction of eight new destroyers and two submarines.[53] Even with backing from the cabinet and the Military Affairs Council, securing parliamentary support was still the key to military expansion, and naval leaders still comprehended this point.

Almost immediately thereafter, Japan's new navy minister, Katō Tomosaburō, endeavored to secure elite-level political support for the navy's next enlargement package. Born in Hiroshima in 1861, Katō rose through the navy quickly and gained a reputation as a true administrative professional and a remarkably able bureaucrat. He served as vice naval minister to Saitō (1906–9) and commanded the Kure Naval Admiralty (1909–14), and his sea postings included stints with Admiral Tōgō during the Russo-Japanese War. Katō was also appointed commander in chief of the First Fleet in December 1913. Though cadaverously thin, to the point of looking frail, Katō possessed a will of iron that he used to further the navy's institutional interests in government. Indeed, four months after the navy obtained an additional ¥94 million, Katō argued on behalf of a ¥364-million eight-year expansion program when Ōkuma's cabinet met in September 1915 to discuss the budget for 1916.[54] Specifically, Katō asked for an additional ¥43 million for 1916, with a firm budgetary and political commitment to dispense ¥321 million between 1917 and 1923 for continued naval expansion. The additional funds, or so Katō argued before the cabinet, would allow the navy to assemble an eight-four fleet, which he and other naval officials claimed was essential for the empire's security.[55]

When parliament convened in December 1915, Ōkuma set the tone for discussions concerning military appropriations. Speaking on 7 December, the prime minister informed M.P.'s that the cabinet strongly supported the navy's request and urged parliamentarians "not to let another day pass" without first appropriating funds for naval expansion.[56] Moreover, when

M.P.'s pressed the prime minister about the financial implications associated with yet another new naval undertaking, Ōkuma immediately responded with assurances that naval expansion was in "harmony" with national finances. Katō followed this line later that same day in response to questions raised by M.P. Seiki Naohiko, who asked what the navy's true long-term intentions were in relation to naval expansion. Katō, as he had done in the past, claimed that securing money with which to assemble an eight-eight fleet was still the desired long-term objective but that he had asked for a considerably smaller sum for an eight-four fleet in order to keep his requests in line with the nation's finances.[57] On 24 February 1916 parliament endorsed the navy's expansion request.

With funding for one year of the larger eight-year plan in place, Katō proceeded to secure the entire continuing budget (¥262 million) in the following session of parliament. After cabinet ministers agreed to fund the entire amount with no opposition being voiced, the program proceeded to parliament first in January 1917 (38th session) and then again in June 1917 (39th session) after the prime minister dissolved the thity-eighth parliament prior to acceptance of the budget.[58] A number of factors pointed to success in the Diet. First, elections held in April 1917 returned the pro-navy, pro-industrial Seiyūkai as the largest party in parliament, with 162 seats out of a total of 381. Seiyūkai-industry-navy links had increased as the navy had directed more naval production to private shipyards, and during 1916 Hara Kei had spoken at shipyards throughout Japan urging greater naval expansion as a means to facilitate industrial growth.[59] Moreover, both the new prime minister, Terauchi Masatake, appointed in October 1916, and his finance minister, Katsuta Kazue, took great pains in the Diet to assure parliamentarians that naval expansion could easily be accommodated within the nation's finances. Domestic political concerns aside, passage of the 1916 Naval Act in the United States, a bill that appropriated $588 million for the construction of 157 warships over a three-year period, provided a further degree of strategic legitimacy to the navy's contention that naval expansion was a necessity for Japan's security.[60] Parliamentarians concurred, and in July 1917 the Diet appropriated the ¥262 million for naval expansion. Katō had secured his first significant multiyear budgetary victory.[61]

Katō did not wait long to build upon his early successes. Just ten days after parliament endorsed the navy's eight-four fleet expansion scheme, the navy minister approached Prime Minister Terauchi with a fresh expansion request. On 26 July, Katō urged the Chōshū army general–turned–prime minister to endorse another fleet expansion plan and to introduce it to the next session of parliament.[62] Specifically, Katō sought ¥182 million for additional construction and roughly ¥43 million for upgrades to warships already under construction in Japan.[63] Rather than just claiming that further expansion was a necessity for Japan's national security, Katō used a number of new justifications in support of his latest expansion plan. For one, Katō claimed that the effectiveness of cruisers in commerce-raiding operations during the war required that Japan undertake new expansion in this area, and he suggested that ¥182 million be directed for the construction of cruisers. For another, the development of high-speed heavily armored battle cruisers in the United States mandated that Japan follow suit and upgrade the two battle cruisers already under construction in Japan at a cost of ¥43 million. Katō did not stop there, however. After discussions with Finance Minister Katsuta Kazue on 10 October 1917, the naval leadership requested a further ¥66 million to construct two more battles cruisers, thus giving Japan, when all expansion plans were completed by 1923, an eight-six fleet.[64] In autumn 1917, Terauchi agreed with Katō's logic and assured the navy minister that he would fight on behalf of the navy at the next session of parliament.

Katō well understood the politics of military appropriations in Japan, and after he submitted his request to the cabinet, the naval leadership lobbied M.P.'s to back the proposed expansion plans. Parliamentarians needed little convincing. Naval expansion had become increasingly popular during World War I, which enriched Japan and led to worldwide increases in naval spending. Throughout 1916 and 1917 newspapers such as the *Jiji shinpō* and the *Tokyo Nichi nichi* published numerous articles on naval development in the United States and just as many editorials suggesting why Japan must increase its naval strength to match.[65] At public engagements, naval officers reiterated these same themes. Speaking before an assembly of local governors and politicians in June 1917, Captain Yamamoto Eisuke, the nephew of Yamamoto Gonnohyōe and chief of a naval research bureau that examined the European war, argued that Japan needed to match U.S. naval expansion.[66] Many M.P.'s actively endorsed this argument and actually criticized the government for not appropriating enough money for necessary military expansion. In late 1917 and into 1918 Kokumintō M.P. Inukai Tsūyoshi urged the government not only to spend more on naval defense but also to enlarge Japan's military-industrial complex as a means of strengthening Japan's economy.[67]

A final factor that made naval expansion as desired by Kato more likely to pass parliament in the fortieth session (December 1917 to March 1918) was the reemergence of the Seiyūkai as a strong parliamentary force in Japan. After having secured a plurality of seats during the April 1917 lections, Hara moved to cooperate with Terauchi's cabinet in order to secure more power and influence for himself and for his party.[68] Hara and the Seiyūkai rank and file therefore supported the Terauchi cabinet on a number of domestic and international issues, including naval expansion. In March 1918, parliament endorsed all Katō's various expansion schemes. In just over nine months, from July 1917 to March 1918, Katō had added more than half a billion yen to the navy's coffers, and as a result Japan's shipyards would soon be operating at full capacity.[69]

Uncharted Water: Postwar Expansion and the Attainment of the Eight-Eight Dream

The cessation of hostilities in Europe did little to dampen the navy's expansionist agenda. In the months after the armistice, Katō directed his energies to the attainment of the eight-eight fleet.[70] The iron-willed admiral and his closest advisors drafted a mammoth plan that called for the construction of four battleships, four battle cruisers, twelve cruisers, thirty-two destroyers, an aircraft carrier, various submarines, and numerous support vessels.[71] Katō believed that construction costs alone would entail ¥761 million over an eight-year period from 1920 to 1927, but warship construction was not the only expense associated with the plan.[72] Owing to the size and scope of the eight-eight plan, Katō and his closest advisors agreed that shore-based naval infrastructure and industrial facilities would require expansion as well. Earlier during the fortith session of parliament, Katō informed M.P.'s that a shortage of raw materials and industrial capacity could restrict naval expansion even if the government continued to appropriate funds for further warship construction.[73] Thus a key aspect of the eight-eight-fleet plan was a massive increase in spending earmarked for shore-based naval industry. While this was a military-industrial necessity, it was also a political masterstroke. Appropriating such a large percentage toward shore spending, which normally constituted between 5 percent and 8 percent of previous expansion budgets, sat well with pro-industry-minded Seiyūkai representatives.[74] Finally, the eight-eight-fleet plan provided funds for the Japanese navy to invite French and British naval aviators to Japan to serve as naval flight instructors. Though minor in comparison with the costs of building four superdreadnought-class capital ships, the scope of this plan added to its appeal. Increasingly divergent elements in the navy—

aviators, capital-ships proponents, submariners, and those who argued for greater shore-based spending—could all find aspects of this plan that were appealing. No one in the navy could realistically fault this plan.

The breadth of this plan, particularly its emphasis on shore-based facilities, also appealed to pro-industry Seiyūkai M.P.'s. Hara, as leader of the Seiyūkai, needed little convincing. The navy's political and economic agenda received its most significant boost ironically after hostilities ended at the hands of Japan's first party cabinet, headed by Seiyūkai leader Hara Kei. Hara became prime minister in September 1918 after the Rice Riots had helped bring down Terauchi Masatake's cabinet. Heralded by many contemporary observers and later historians as the beginning of responsible party government in Japan, Hara's tenure as prime minister was marked and was in many respects in fact defined by military expansion (most significantly naval expansion), pragmatic dealings with Japan's most senior and conservative elder statesman (Yamagata Aritomo), and an expansion of Seiyūkai party power. All three were intimately interrelated. As the experienced, pragmatic, politically driven opportunist par excellence, Hara understood the inherent difficulties of securing the reins of the prime ministership as a party leader and remaining in power long enough to be effective. Hara understood that to become prime minister he would have to win over Yamagata, the conservative and staunchly promilitary *genrō* who in 1918 could still, if he so desired, influence the selection of the prime minister, as Hara in fact recorded in his diary: "Today, the maker of cabinets is Yamagata."[75] Moreover, to remain in power long enough to implement his own political reforms and to return the Seiyūkai to the majority in parliament through these measures, Hara knew he would have to win over the military ministers. To secure both aims, Hara therefore made a series of important tactical compromises with the military and Yamagata in order to gain a long-term strategic victory for himself and the Seiyūkai. In negotiations leading up to his appointment as prime minister, Hara announced in public that strengthening national defense—"perfecting national defense," as his party referred to it—would be a foundation of his cabinet.[76] "The premiership carried with it the burden of compromising with the parties as well as with non-party elites," as Peter Duus has written with such eloquence, "a post which only the foolhardy or those with a keen sense of political balance were likely to covet."[77] Hara was just such an individual.

Hara's commitment to defense increases helped win over both Yamagata and the military services, and in his capacity as prime minister Hara worked to implement domestic political reforms that would further strengthen

Seiyūkai power. Specifically, Hara sought reforms that would lead to the creation of small electoral districts, which he believed the Seiyūkai could dominate in the next election. Furthermore, the Seiyūkai leadership expanded rural infrastructure projects, not only to reinforce old Seiyūkai electoral strongholds but also to forge new bases of party power in rural Japan.[78] Hara thus approached naval expansion with enthusiasm, as military expansion could provide political stability that would allow the Seiyūkai prime minister the opportunity to secure political reforms that would give him and his party more power and influence.

Throughout much of October and November 1919, budgetary discussions focused on military appropriations. Finance Minister Takahashi shuddered over the requests presented by the navy and the army, but Hara encouraged him to find a way to provide funds to support both, claiming that national defense was the first priority of the budget.[79] Hara worked with both service ministers to prune back expansion though not eliminate it from the budget. Hara and Army Minister Tanaka agreed to reduce the army's proposed expansion plan from a fourteen-year exercise to an eight-year program that importantly would not begin until 1921, rather than 1920. For the navy, Hara gained Katō's approval to trim appropriations for support vessels and submarines as well as commitments to redirect some of the savings to further support the expansion of shore-based industrial facilities. In order to provide for such increases, Hara and Takahashi agreed to use funds from the previous year's surplus, raid the bond-sinking fund, and increase taxes on sake. None of these, Hara predicted, would create any political controversy, and thus, in effect, each could be used to buy off the military for cabinet-level stability. On 3 November, the cabinet approved the budget.[80] The eight-eight fleet was one important step closer to fruition.

The final piece of the political puzzle that stood between the eight-eight plan and the acquisition of the warships was of course parliament. Though the Seiyūkai did not hold an absolute majority in the Diet, Hara believed that he could count on the support of more than enough opposition M.P.'s to gain a majority to back his pro-military expansion budget. To this end, Katō lobbied M.P.'s throughout December and January, and again in July.[81] Parliamentarians, however, became far more concerned over a universal-male-suffrage proposal than naval expansion in the course of the parliamentary session.[82] Tensions and tempers both inside and outside the Diet became so severe and inflamed over the suffrage debate that Hara used the maelstrom to his own political advantage. In late February, Hara dissolved parliament and called new elections. In spring, the Seiyūkai hammered the

TABLE 5

Japanese Army, Navy, and National Expenditures
and Military Personnel, 1915–1922

(expenditures listed in yen)

Year	Army expenditures	Navy expenditures	National expenditures	Army personnel	Navy personnel
1915	¥84,699,978	¥84,974,783	¥583,270,000	242,230	62,881
1916	94,813,114	116,625,000	590,795,000	248,175	67,962
1917	123,436,576	162,435,084	735,024,000	251,600	69,428
1918	152,081,959	215,903,389	1,017,036,000	255,887	73,328
1919	221,268,029	316,419,080	1,172,328,000	260,753	77,626
1920	246,557,000	403,202,000	1,359,978,000	275,028	83,668
1921	246,979,000	483,590,000	1,489,856,000	284,819	88,161
1922	230,909,000	373,892,000	1,429,690,000	292,612	78,837

SOURCES: National expenditures and army and navy personnel are found in Statistics Bureau, *Historical Statistics of Japan*, 5 vols. (Tokyo: Japan Statistical Association, 1987): 5:525, 528. Army and navy expenditure figures are taken from Naikaku tōkeikyoku (Cabinet statistics bureau), *Nihon teikoku tōkei nenkan* (Statistical yearbook of the Japanese empire), 59 vols. (Tokyo: Tokyo ripurinto shuppansha, 1962–1967): 43:507 (1924).

opposition and returned as the majority party in parliament. Electoral victory sealed the fate of the eight-eight fleet. Seiyūkai representatives were not about to vote against the leader who had just returned them to power en masse, and when the forty-third parliament convened in July 1920, M.P.'s overwhelmingly endorsed the navy's eight-eight-fleet plan.[83] Hara and Katō had good reason to celebrate.

The Chimera of Naval Defense and the Pragmatism of Limitation

Unlimited naval expansion was not in and of itself a means of guaranteeing national security. This was perhaps the most obvious but also the most troublesome lesson of World War I for naval officers who had expended considerable effort to pursue this cause, *the* cause of the navy. "National defense," or so declared M.P. Inukai, the president of the Kokumintō, did not involve just "defense provided by the army and the navy" but involved a "coordinated approach whereby commerce and production" were devoted to the cause as well.[84] Inukai was correct. Though this was an obvious lesson that military leaders could have drawn from the Russo-Japanese War, World War I reinforced the totality of modern warfare in the minds of both military men and politicians as well. Inukai aside, others drew this lesson too, including naval personnel. The navy's Temporary

Naval Affairs Research Committee established in October 1915 and led by admirals Yamaya and Takeshita Isamu reached similar conclusions.[85] Victory in war, or so this committee's findings suggested, was as much about economic, industrial, and civil mobilization as it was about force levels at a front or on the sea. Their findings were supported by naval officers who had traveled to Europe during the war such as Akiyama Saneyuki, who concluded that industrial strength and a large independent resource base were as fundamental to victory as modern warships in great numbers.[86]

The war, however, exposed a significant weakness in Japan's industrial capacity and its reliance or near dependence upon imports of natural resources and steel. The eight-six fleet, which parliament approved in early 1918, pushed private navy yards and the navy's own arsenals to the brink of 100 percent of their capacity. Without greater capacity, money earmarked for warship construction could not be utilized. This was why naval officers set aside an uncustomarily large percentage of the eight-eight budget to support industrial expansion. Importantly, naval leadership's efforts to enlarge capacity were matched by efforts launched by the private sector as well. Mitsubishi invested nearly ¥21 million in its Nagasaki shipyard to accommodate further naval orders, and Kawasaki followed suit. Kawasaki, however, expended far greater sums, roughly ¥100 million between 1919 and 1921.[87] While impressive, an increasing number of naval officials questioned whether or not such expansion would be enough to provide the navy and Japan with adequate industrial capabilities to engage in a naval arms race with the United States, even if vast quantities of capital existed to build warships.

The answer to this question can best be contextualized by looking at the resources needed to build and eventually operate such warships regardless of shipbuilding capacity. Warships required two vital commodities, high-grade steel and oil, though the majority of naval vessels in 1918 still used coal. Coal-powered warships, however, were being phased out after World War I, and this too caused considerable anxiety in Japanese naval circles. Japan was poorly endowed with both oil and the materials needed to make high-grade steel. Though Japan's dependence on foreign steel in World War I was not so acute as its dependence on foreign oil would be in the late 1930s, shipbuilders and thus the navy suffered when the flow of steel slowed. Imports of British and U.S. steel slowed to a standstill in the later years of the war, the former out of domestic necessity and the latter from a politically motivated embargo.[88] At its most vulnerable point in 1917, more than 90 percent of Japan's shipbuilding steel came from the United States, and when exports stopped, shipbuilders and the navy suffered. While firms such as Kawasaki and Mitsui pressed Japan's government for direct negotiations with President Woodrow Wilson to lift the steel embargo, some firms, including Kawasaki, approached U.S. steel makers on their own in an attempt to acquire steel for production.[89] Neither action influenced U.S. policy makers, and the U.S. government refused to modify its position. More disturbing, however, was Katō's growing realization that owing to Japan's lack of resources, limited shipbuilding capacity, and the vast richness of the United States in both these regards, Japan simply could not defend against or match U.S. naval increases in a traditional way—that is, with unlimited naval expansion—given the state of Japan's industrial capacity. As early as February 1919, Katō admitted as much to Diet representatives who questioned him about—or, more precisely, criticized him over—the navy's inability to keep pace with naval increases.[90]

World War I exposed the limitations that Japan's lack of resources and industrial capacity (when compared with the U.S.A.'s) imposed on its economy and military. This would be devastating in a long, drawn-out war of attrition, which by 1918 naval planners believed would in all likelihood be the nature of a war against the United States.[91] By 1919, then, Katō had begun to understand that an unlimited naval race with the United States meant trouble. The U.S. naval expansion program of 1916, coupled with postwar plans for greater fleet enlargement, worried Katō and other naval leaders considerably. Katō believed that unlimited naval expansion by the United States could "create such a disparity" in power between Japan and that country that the Pacific might be "reduced to an American lake."[92] Hyperbole aside, Katō's concerns were not unfounded. Japan could not win a naval arms race with the United States, and completion of the eight-eight fleet might well spur on such an unsustainable and potentially disastrous armaments race and thus make Japan's position vis-à-vis the Americans more precarious than before.

There was, Katō believed, another option. Naval limitations within an international system, coupled with strict agreements proscribing U.S. fortification of advance Pacific island bases such as Guam or the Philippines, offered Katō, the navy, and the nation of Japan a potentially pragmatic solution to the difficulties all faced. If Katō had begun to realize the drawbacks of stiff naval competition with the United States and the possible benefits of naval limitation, a report issued by the Navy Ministry's League of Nations Affairs Research Committee (*Kaigun kokusai renmei kankei jikō kenkyūkai*) in July 1921 may well have solidified his opinions.[93] This committee's findings suggested that limitations coupled with proscriptions on U.S. fortifications could actually improve Japan's naval position against the United States. On the other hand, an unlimited naval race against the United States would by 1925 reduce the overall ratio of Japan's capital ships to those of the United States to a level far below the 70 percent that many in the navy, including the committee members, believed was critical to the security of Japan's home islands and empire. Pragmatism, or so Katō came to believe, as defined by limitations within an international framework, was the surest and most stable way to guarantee Japan's long-term military, economic, and political security.

Not everyone in the Japanese navy shared Katō's opinions concerning naval limitation, however.[94] Foremost among Katō's critics was Katō Kanji (no relation), who in 1921 was a vice admiral within the Navy General Staff. Katō Kanji, a sea admiral with a sharp military mind, agreed with Katō Tomosaburō and with most other naval leaders that World War I had clearly demonstrated the overwhelming industrial and military potential of the United States, particularly as compared with Japan's. In Katō Kanji's mind, this necessitated that Japan possess a powerful peacetime fleet that could in a time of war inflict an early, complete, and decisive victory against the U.S. Navy.[95] Japan, in Katō's opinion, could not win a war of attrition against the United States and could not build a fleet as quickly in time of war. Therefore, he argued, Japan must possess a standing fleet large enough to inflict a decisive naval victory early in any future war with the United States, and limitations went counter to this logic.

Politics went a long way to determine the resolution of the limitation issue that split the two Katōs. After receiving an invitation from the U.S. government to discuss naval limitations in Washington, Prime Minister Hara appointed Katō Tomosaburō as Japan's chief delegate, the only chief delegate among the powers assembled who was an active-duty naval officer. In Hara's mind, the pragmatic Katō, the navy's most successful administrator and a champion of previous fleet expansion programs, was one of the few men in Japan who could successfully negotiate naval limitations that would be accepted by the Japanese navy. Hara was correct. Throughout the Washington Conference, Katō faced strong criticisms and challenges from Katō Kanji, who was appointed by the Navy General Staff to serve as the chief naval specialist to the Japanese delegation. Though Katō Kanji initially argued that any limitations agreement that did not result in parity with the Americans would be a political insult and a military disaster for Japan, he eventually accepted the fact that parity would not be politically or militarily acceptable to the Americans. He thus channeled his energies into convincing Katō Tomosaburō that Japan must accept nothing less than a 70-percent ratio compared with the American and British navies. Seventy percent was the magic ratio, first developed and articulated by Lieutenant Commander Satō Tetsutarō just after the Russo-Japanese War, which Japanese navy strategists believed would allow Japan to be victorious in a trans-Pacific naval engagement with the U.S. fleet.

Katō Kanji and Satō were not alone in their fixation on the 70-percent ratio. The Naval Affairs Research Committee for the League of Nations concurred with Satō's earlier findings and recommended against accepting any ratio that was less than 70 percent, suggesting that "there can be no room whatsoever for compromise on this issue."[96] The committee also warned that Japan's position in the western Pacific could be severely threatened by continued U.S. naval expansion and fortifications of facilities at either Guam or in the Philippines. While Katō Tomosaburō refused to commit to any firm ratio, the committee's recommendation vis-à-vis U.S. fortification resonated with Katō's own beliefs, and the navy minister decided to hold out for a nonfortification clause in any agreement reached that limited naval armaments.

Though angered by Katō Tomosaburō's willingness to accept a 60-percent ratio if it accompanied a nonfortification clause for advance U.S. bases in the western Pacific, Katō Kanji had little room to maneuver in Washington. The resolute Katō Tomosaburō had been given considerable flexibility by Hara to reach any agreement he deemed reasonable, and the senior Katō followed pragmatism in Washington as he had done previously in budgetary negotiations in Tokyo. Katō Tomosaburō simply refused to accept the junior Katō's recommendations and followed a course which he saw as a military necessity. Reflecting later that he had been guided by intuition and acted within the mindset that avoidance of hostilities with the United States through diplomatic means was the surest means to provide for Japan's security, Katō Tomosaburō signed the treaty that aborted the eight-eight fleet.[97] This was a pragmatic end to the long-cherished eight-eight fleet that had been achieved through extensive political engagement.

Synopsis

World War I was, for the Japanese navy, a war with two distinct yet interrelated outcomes. On the one hand, the navy attained two of its most cherished goals, commitments for fleet expansion that would culminate in the eight-eight fleet, and a South Seas empire. Naval admirals acted opportunistically in the opening months of the war to acquire the latter, while Katō, and to a lesser extent Yashiro, worked tirelessly to achieve the former throughout the conflict as their predecessors had done, by political engagement. Acting opportunistically and at other times pragmatically in the domestic sphere, Katō emerged as one of the navy's most successful administrative leaders, more so perhaps than Saitō or even Yamamoto. Katō, however, was greatly assisted by a series of prime ministers each of whom clearly understood that mastering the art of military appropriations was fundamental to his own political success if not survival. Moreover, the money that flowed into Japan during the war, just as in the aftermath of the war with China twenty years earlier, eliminated serious parliamentary critiques of grotesquely proportioned military expansion plans. It was the ideal climate in which to champion naval expansion, and Katō succeeded.

Katō's and thus the navy's successes, however, were tempered by the other, more troubling realizations made clear by the war. The nature of warfare in the early twentieth century had changed, and no longer was a nation's rise or fall necessarily dependent on one or even a series of impressive battles, such as the Battle of Tsushima, regardless of how total or complete they might be in a narrow tactical sense. War had become an industrial, economic, and social exercise as much as a strictly military phenomenon. This had tremendous implications for a newly industrializing power such as Japan that had limited natural resources and an industrial capacity that was far less than that of its most likely future enemy. The pursuit and attainment of naval expansion, if it resulted in an unlimited naval arms race with the United States, would simply never provide the security that Japan's military and political leaders desired. Fortunately for the Japanese state, naval leaders such as Katō Tomosaburō understood that the cause of naval expansion, which had motivated if not driven naval leaders almost from the navy's inception, could no longer be the only political pursuit for this service.

Conclusion

JAPAN'S FLEET on the eve of the Washington Naval Arms Limitation Conference was an impressive instrument of war and a complex and sophisticated organization of state. As the third largest fleet in the world and with its history of stunning military successes, it commanded respect both in Japan and abroad. The navy's exploits in peace and war instilled national pride, secured and defended Japan's colonial interests, and demonstrated to the world that Japan had emerged as a modern industrial and imperial power. The navy's development from a ragtag collection of "soldiers," as Yamamoto Gonnohyōe described the early Meiji navy in 1893, to the awe-inspiring fleet that patroled the waters of East Asia by 1922 mirrored, symbolized, and influenced the rise of modern Japan.[1] It did so perhaps better and more thoroughly than almost any other state institution.

Behind the impressive fleet, its well-trained sailors, and its formidable warships lay vast fiscal outlays. International naval recognition and maritime security came at an enormous price for the Japanese state, but it was a price that Japan's politicians and civilians were willing to pay. By mastering the politics of appropriations Japan's admirals secured the vast sums needed to develop, employ, and maintain a militarily impressive fleet. Political engagement and the money that flowed from it determined how quickly, thoroughly, and successfully Japan's navy could emerge as a potent military force and floating symbol of nationalism. Money provided the means to acquire and build warships, train sailors, and fight wars, but it took the mastery of politics to ensure that money flowed in the navy's direction. The pursuit of ever-increasing appropriations became *the* domestic focus if not the sole preoccupation of Japan's leading admirals and naval statesmen between 1868 and 1922. This overlooked political process has been the focus of my book.

In the course of the Meiji-Taishō era, Japan's admirals succeeded remarkably well in convincing their fellow statesmen, party politicians, and the public to support naval expansion. The navy succeeded first and foremost in the political arena because the leaders who emerged within this institution were pragmatists who adapted to and manipulated the politics that surrounded national finance. During the years covered by my study, the navy eventually accepted and endorsed the changing dynamics that accompanied the political transformation of the Japanese state from an oligarchy to a parliamentary democracy, albeit one with paternalistic and conservative tendencies in which military men and Japan's *genrō* retained political privileges. As the budgetary process expanded from an oligarchic exercise carried out behind closed doors to a more transparent parliamentary process, the navy expanded its political efforts to match this transformation. After 1890, naval leaders could no longer rely exclusively on elite-level Satsuma oligarchic ties to gain political and monetary support but rather were forced to work with Japan's elected politicians. These leaders did so not because they were champions of democracy or increased political pluralism, or proponents of constitutional government per se but rather out of a perceived and real institutional necessity. In reaching out and engaging in wider political activities, however, the navy found a number of beneficial allies willing to support massive naval increases.

In gaining political allies, none was more important or more consistent in its support as the Seiyūkai political party. The Seiyūkai emerged as the chief parliamentary force in late Meiji–early Taishō Japan, and it is not at all surprising, given the budgetary powers of Japan's parliament, that the navy looked to build ties with this organization. Importantly, naval leaders such as Yamamoto Gonnohyōe, Saitō Makoto, and Katō Tomosaburō found that the Seiyūkai was receptive to their political overtures. Like the navy under these three leaders, the Seiyūkai under the stewardship of Itō Hirobumi, Saionji Kinmochi, and Hara Kei followed a similarly pragmatic course, and pragmatic opportunism was the key to the navy-Seiyūkai entente. In a world where the Seiyūkai and the navy each viewed the Chōshū-backed Yamagata-army faction as its most dangerous and powerful political adversary, both hoped together to form a counter to this political group. Their entente was more than just a reactive alliance against conservative forces, however, as it also provided significant opportunities for each to gain and to expand power where they desired it most. This gave the relationship endurance. While navy leaders used their service's constitutional privileges to coerce prime ministers and prospective prime ministers on a few occasions, they did not, nor could they, effectively, coerce parliamentarians and party politicians. The navy needed parliamentary support, and fortunately for naval leaders they did not have to resort to political aggression to win over party politicians. The Seiyūkai, under the cabinets of Yamamoto, Hara, and Saionji, supported naval expansion primarily because of the political stability that working with the navy brought to politics and also because party leaders quickly realized the need to accommodate and work constructively with nonparty elites in order to gain further access to positions of power and influence, above all the prime ministership. With political stability and an important nonparty elite ally, the Seiyūkai obtained greater power and once in a position of elite-level influence implemented policies their leaders desired and programs they coveted geared toward further increasing party power. The Seiyūkai was not comprised of "principled pacifists" in late Meiji and Taishō Japan (1900–1926) any more than it was in the early Shōwa period.[2] It was a party of pragmatic opportunists, a trait the Seiyūkai shared with the navy.

The navy did not cultivate just elite allies. In an effort to build support for the expensive cause of naval expansion, navy men cast their nets wider than just over parliament. Naval leaders were quick to recognize that winning political support for a sizable navy was a national exercise. Navy men understood that they would need not only the cooperation but also the support of the public in their expensive undertakings. To facilitate the public's backing the navy became a producer of pro-navy propaganda and pageantry with the intent to popularize their service and expansionary agenda. In producing naval launch cards, organizing naval reviews, and producing vast amounts of pro-navy written material, from pamphlets and newspaper articles to popular fiction, navy leaders not only succeeded in popularizing their service but also became important purveyors of nationalism in the process. That they did so as effectively as they did also demonstrates just how sophisticated their institution had become and the degree to which the wider population had come to support navalism. The Seiyūkai and other elected officials supported naval expansion—though not always to the full extent that navy wished prior to World War I—not just for elite-level pragmatic purposes but also because the navy and the cause of naval expansion had become more acceptable and popular within the public sphere, certainly more popular than the army. This in itself, within a country that possessed no naval tradition, was a significant achievement for naval leaders.

If Japan's navy served as a mirror that reflected the dynamic political and social conditions of late Meiji and early Taishō Japan, it also reflected Japan's military and industrial limitations, which became all the more apparent when compared with the military and industrial capacity of the Japanese navy's chief hypothetical enemy, the United States. British shipyards provided the lion's share of Japan's capital warship fleet until 1914. When naval production shifted exclusively to domestic shipyards and naval expansion increased significantly during World War I, private and navy-owned shipyards and arsenals experienced considerable difficulties filling demand. This was a disturbing revelation to Japanese admirals who correctly understood the economic, industrial, and political-military lessons of World War I. It became all the more ominous when viewed alongside the U.S. Navy's building programs of 1916 and 1919. The picture that emerged was clear to those admirals who approached it with objectivity: in a naval race Japan simply could never overtake or even match the United States, a country rich in resources that possessed significant industrial capacity. Naval arms limitation, coupled with restrictions on the United States' ability to fortify its western Pacific bases, was, as Katō Tomosaburō concluded, the surest way to guarantee Japanese naval and thus national security.

加藤友
三郎

Not all naval personnel saw events of World War I or its lessons so clearly as Katō Tomosaburō. Naval limitation fostered considerable resentment within certain elements of the Japanese navy. Naval limitations simply went against everything that most naval officials had worked, argued, and fought for over the previous fifty years: naval expansion. If the pursuit of naval expansion and larger budgetary appropriations became the political cause of the Japanese navy and thus the glue that bonded and united this service, naval limitations went a long way to tearing this cohesion apart from the mid-1920s on. Through internal purges and capitalizing externally on a public sense of crisis, officers opposed to naval limitations replaced and marginalized the more pragmatic naval politicians such as Takarabe Takeshi, Yamanashi Katsunoshin, and Hori Teikichi.[3] Once in positions of influence and power within the navy and national government, officers of this so-called fleet faction allowed the naval limitation treaties to expire and returned the navy and the nation of Japan wholeheartedly to the expensive pursuit of unlimited naval expansion. This was their collective vision of how best to obtain naval and national security. In the 1930s, the pursuit of appropriations to fund such enormous increases in expenditures again became the central, overriding focus of Japanese naval politics. But more than this, naval personnel let the pursuit of increasing budgets shape strategic priorities and military planning. Expansion to the south became naval policy not just because of the resources Japan could obtain—resources critical to the navy as much as any other actor in Japanese politics—or because of the links the navy had previously established with civilians who advocated *nanshin*. Southward expansion, led and protected by the navy, and the conflict this might precipitate with the naval powers of the United States and Britain were also used to justify further fleet expansion.[4] Asked by the army's Colonel Suzuki Tei'ichi in 1934 whether the navy seriously contemplated and planned for a war with the United States, Vice Chief of the Navy General Staff Admiral Suetsugu Nobumasa replied: "Certainly, even this is acceptable if it will get us a budget."[5] And get budgets they did. From the mid-1930s on, naval leaders succeeded in securing the funds necessary to develop one of the most impressive naval fighting forces in the world. Military spending reached an astonishing 70 percent of Japan's total overall expenditures by 1938.

But did these officers of the fleet faction overthrow constitutional government and destroy liberalism and democracy to achieve their aims any more than Saitō or Yamamoto did earlier in Meiji-Taishō Japan? Certainly the image of a government hijacked by military men leading Japan into a dark valley still persists in some quarters today. Naval leaders of the 1930s, however, like naval leaders of the 1910s and 1890s, continued to receive support from the political parties who annually approved the navy's massive increases in expenditures. The political parties of Japan in the 1930s, like their Meiji and Taishō antecedents, could have more aggressively fought and resisted military expansion through the power they had in the budgetary process. They chose not to: doing so would have seriously undermined their political positions and hindered their pursuit and attainment of greater power. Ironically, in the earliest sessions of parliament, at the height of what many consider Meiji authoritarianism, parliamentarians did indeed use their legislative authority and power to thwart naval expansion on grounds of political and moral principle.[6] They would rarely do so again in Meiji-Taishō or early Shōwa Japan. As the leaders of the political parties became more ambitious and the parties themselves became stronger, their leaders sought to manipulate politics, as the naval leadership did, more aggressively to secure their own objectives. To do so, party politicians sought alliances with nonparty elite actors in Japan, the military services above all. In 1930, in an act of pure political opportunism, the Seiyūkai, along with Admiral Katō Kanji, publicly condemned the London Naval Arms Treaty in a brazen attempt to embarrass and bring about the collapse of the Minseitō cabinet of Prime Minister Hamaguchi; their actions were as much motivated by domestic political opportunism as they were based on strategic military grounds.[7] Parliamentarians who voted for and at times strongly championed military increases in Meiji-Taishō Japan, like later parliamentarians who acted similarly in the 1930s, share considerable blame for the emergence of strong, well-funded, and politically active military services in pre–World War II Japan.

In the course of prewar Japanese history, the naval leadership did not hijack, overthrow, or circumvent politics or the political process. Rather, naval leaders accepted, endorsed, and mastered the art of politics. The navy was not a silent, apolitical service, but rather the naval leadership was a politically active elite that forged alliances with other elite and nonelite actors in Japan. Naval leaders simply had to engage in politics in order to secure the funding for the fleet expansion they desired in the functioning pluralistic parliamentary democracy that Japan became during the Meiji and Taishō periods. The navy's emergence as a political elite, one which worked at both the local and the elite level in society in the pursuit of greater budgetary appropriations, made waves in pre–World War II Japan. As a result, this service, described by one foreign observer at the turn of the century as the "recognized market for the disposal of obsolete and worn-out ships of every degree, both mercantile and naval," emerged as one of the strongest navies afloat in the first half of the twentieth century.[8] The Japanese navy's emergence at sea and on shore significantly influenced Japanese domestic politics and Japan's development as a regional power. In doing so the Japanese navy shaped the modern history of East Asia and the Pacific, and that of its most important prewar rival, the United States.

REFERENCE MATTER

Notes

Introduction

1. Specifics of this plan as presented to the cabinet by Navy Minister Saitō Makoto can be found in Ko Hakushaku Yamamoto kaigun taishō denki hensankai (Count Yamamoto biographical compilation association), *Yamamoto Gonnohyōe den* (Biography of Yamamoto Gonnohyōe), 2 vols. (Tokyo: Ko Hakushaku Yamamoto kaigun taishō denki hensankai, 1938): 2: 1014–1015. The cabinet decided upon the navy's budget at a 27 November cabinet meeting. For details of the discussion, see Hara Kei'ichirō, ed., *Hara Kei nikki* (Diary of Hara Kei), 6 vols. (Tokyo: Fukumura shuppan, 1965): 27 Nov. 1913 entry, 3: 367; and Banno Junji, ed., *Takarabe Takeshi nikki* (Diary of Takarabe Takeshi), 2 vols. (Tokyo: Hara shobō, 1983): 27 Nov. 1913 entry, 2: 233–234. For newspaper quote, see *Tokyo Asahi shinbun*, 10 Nov. 1913: 1.

2. Albert Craig, *Chōshū in the Meiji Restoration* (Cambridge, Mass.: Harvard University Press, 1967): 9.

3. Uzaki Rojō. *Satsu no kaigun, Chō no rikugun* (The Satsuma navy and Chōshū army) (Tokyo: Seikyōsha 1911): 6.

4. Eckart Kehr, *Battleship Building and Party Politics in Germany, 1894–1901*, transl. and introd. Pauline R. Anderson and Eugene N. Anderson (Chicago: University of Chicago Press, 1973); originally published in 1930 as *Schlachtflottenbau und Parteipolitik, 1894–1901*.

5. Another work by Eckart Kehr that relates to this topic is "The German Fleet in the 1890s and the Politico-Military Dualism in the Empire," in Gordon A. Craig, ed., *Economic Interest, Militarism, and Foreign Policy: Essays on German History* (Berkeley and Los Angeles: University of California Press, 1977): 1–21.

6. Paul E. Pedisich, "Congress Provides a Navy: The Emergence of a Modern Navy as a Force in Congressional Politics, 1882–1916," Ph.D. dissertation, State University of New York at Stony Brook, 1998.

7. Mark Shulman, "Institutionalizing a Political Idea: Navalism and the Emergence of American Seapower," in Peter Trubowitz, Emily Goldman, and Edward Rhodes, eds., *The Politics of Strategic Adjustment: Ideas, Institutions, and Interests* (New York: Columbia University Press, 1999): 79–101; Peter Trubow-

itz, "Geography and Strategy: The Politics of American Naval Expansion," ibid.: 105–138.

8. John F. Beeler, *British Naval Policy in the Gladstone-Disraeli Era, 1866–1880* (Stanford: Stanford University Press, 1997): 150–170, 191–260.

9. David A. Rosenberg and John T. Sumida, "Machines, Men, Manufacturing, Management, and Money: The Study of Navies as Complex Organizations and the Transformation of Twentieth-Century Naval History," in John Hattendorf, ed., *Doing Naval History: Essays Toward Improvement*, U.S. Naval War College Historical Monograph Series, 13 (Newport, Rhode Island, 1995): 35.

10. Military and technological studies on the Japanese navy abound. See, for instance, Hayashi Katsunari, *Nihon gunji gijitsu shi* (A history of Japanese military technology) (Tokyo: Haruki shobō, 1972); Chihaya Masataka, *Nihon kaigun no senryaku hassō* (Strategic concepts of the Japanese navy) (Tokyo: Purejidentosha, 1982). In English, see Paul S. Dull, *A Battle History of the Japanese Navy* (Annapolis: Naval Institute Press, 1979); Itō Masanori, *The End of the Imperial Japanese Navy*, transl. Roger Pineau and Nadrew Y. Kuroda (New York: W. W. Norton, 1962).

11. David C. Evans and Mark R. Peattie, *Kaigun: Strategy, Tactics, and Technology in the Imperial Japanese Navy, 1887–1941* (Annapolis: Naval Institute Press, 1997): xxi.

12. See Roger Dingman, *Power in the Pacific* (Chicago: University of Chicago Press, 1977); Stephen Pelz, *The Race to Pearl Harbor: The Failure of the Second London Naval Conference and the Onset of World War II* (Cambridge, Mass.: Harvard University Press, 1974); Kobayashi Tatsuo, "The London Naval Treaty, 1930," in James W. Morley, ed., *Japan Erupts: The London Naval Conference and the Manchurian Incident, 1928–1932* (New York: Columbia University Press, 1984): 11–117.

13. Hatano Sumio, "Shōwa kaigun no nanshinron" (The navy's southward advance in the Shōwa period), *Zōkan rekishi to jimbutsu: hishi-Taiheiyō sensō* (Special issue of history and personalities: secret episodes of the Pacific War), Dec. 1984: 277–285; Hatano Sumio, "Nihon kaigun to nanshin: sono seisaku to riron no shiteki tenkai" (The Japanese navy and southward advance: the historical develoment of its policies and theory) in Shimizu Hajime, ed., *Ryōtaisenkanki Nihon-Tonanjia kankei no shosō* (Various aspects of Japanese-Southeast Asian relations between both world wars) (Tokyo: Ajia keizai kenkyūjo, 1986)): 207–236; Hatano Sumio and Asada Sadao, "The Japanese Decision to Move South (1939–1941)," in Robert Boyce and Edmond Robertson, eds., *Paths to War: New Essays on the Origins of the Second World War* (New York: St. Martin's Press, 1989): 383–407; Tsunoda Jun, "The Navy's Role in the Southern Strategy," in James W. Morely, ed., *The Fateful Choice* (New York: Columbia University Press, 1980): 241–296.

14. Tsunoda Jun, "Nihon kaigun sandai no rekishi" (Three periods of history in the Japanese navy), *Jiyū* 11: 1 (Jan. 1969): 90.

15. Asada Sadao, "The Japanese Navy and the United States, 1931–1941," in Dorothy Borg and Okamoto Shumpei, eds., *Pearl Harbor as History: Japanese-American Relations, 1931–1941* (New York: Columbia University Press, 1973): 230.

16. Koike Sei'ichi, "Taishō kōki no kaigun ni tsuite no ichi kōsatsu" (Examination of the Japanese navy in the late Taishō era), *Gunji shigaku*, 25: 1 (1989): 35–53. Though published in 1957, Imai Sei'ichi's article is still valuable for Taishō-era

politics: Imai Sei'ichi, "Taishō ki ni okeru gunbu no seijiteki chii" (The political position of the military in the Taishō period), *Shisō* 339 (Sept. 1957): 3–21; ibid., 402 (Dec. 1957): 106–122.

17. See works by Matsushita Yoshio, *Meiji gunsei shiron* (A historical discussion of the Meiji military establishment) (Tokyo: Yūhikaku, 1959), *Nihon gunsei to seiji* (Politics and the Japanese military system) (Tokyo: Kuroshio shuppan, 1960), *Nihon gunbatsu no kōbō* (The rise and fall of Japan's military cliques), 3 vols. (Tokyo: Jinbutsu ōraisha, 1967); Imai Sei'ichi, "Taishō ki ni okeru gunbu no seijiteki chii" (The political position of the military in the Taishō period), *Shisō* 339 (Sept. 1957): 3–21, and ibid. 402 (Dec. 1957): 106–122. In English, see Stewart Lone, *Army, Empire, and Politics in Meiji Japan: The Three Careers of General Katsura Tarō* (London: Macmillan, 2000); Roger Hackett, *Yamagata Aritomo in the Rise of Modern Japan* (Cambridge, Mass.: Harvard University Press, 1971); and Richard Smethurst, *A Social Basis for Prewar Japanese Militarism: The Army and the Rural Community* (Berkeley and Los Angeles: University of California Press, 1974).

18. Lone, *Army, Empire, and Politics in Meiji Japan*, 89.

19. Peter Duus and Gordon Berger have convincingly demonstrated the flaws associated with this skewed portrayal of the political parties as principled champions of liberalism in pre–World War II Japan. See Gordon Berger, *Parties Out of Power in Japan, 1931–1941* (Princeton: Princeton University Press, 1977); and Peter Duus, *Party Rivalry and Political Change in Taishō Japan* (Cambridge, Mass.: Harvard University Press, 1968), and "The Era of Party Rule: Japan, 1905–1932," in James Crowley, ed., *Modern East Asia: Essays in Interpretation* (New York: Harcourt Brace, 1970): 180–206.

Chapter 1

1. Summary of report issued by Japanese Military Ministry in 1870. For details of entire plan, see Kaigunshō, Kaigun daijin kanbō (Navy Ministry, Navy Minister's Secretariat), *Kaigun seido enkaku* (History of naval organization): 26 vols. (Tokyo: Hara shobō 1971–1972), 2 (2): 37–41.

2. Quoted in Roger Hackett, "The Meiji Leaders and Modernization: The Case of Yamagata Aritomo," in Marius Jansen, ed., *Changing Japanese Attitudes Towards Modernization* (Princeton: Princeton University Press, 1965): 254.

3. Gaimushō (Japanese Foreign Ministry), *Gaikō bunsho: Nichiro sensō* (Diplomatic documents: The Russo-Japanese War) (Tokyo: Nihon kokusairengō kyōkai, 1957–1960): no. 5, 731. Quoted in Okamoto Shumpei, *The Japanese Oligarchy and the Russo-Japanese War* (New York: Columbia University Press, 1970): 119.

4. For a description of the early administration of the Japanese armed forces, see Nihon kindai shiryō kenkyūkai, eds. (Historical records study association of modern Japan), *Nihon rikukaigun seido, soshiki, jinji* (The personnel, organization, and institutions of the Japanese army and navy) (Tokyo: Daigaku shuppankai, 1971), 1–81. Hereafter cited as *NRKSSJ*.

5. Taniguchi Naomi, "Kaigunkyō Hakushaku Kawamura Sumiyoshi no kōgyō" (The achievements of Navy Minister Count Kawamura Sumiyoshi), in Hirose Hikota, ed., *Dai kaigun hatten hishi* (The secret history of the great navy's development) (Tokyo: Kōdōkan tosho, 1944): 27.

6. It is often assumed that a strong centralized state emerged almost immediately after the Meiji Restoration of 1868. Political, military, and economic centralization began in earnest only after 1870.

7. Taniguchi Naomi, "Kaigunkyō Hakushaku Kawamura Sumiyoshi no kōgyō," 35–37.

8. For a general discussion on the early Meiji navy, see Ikeda Kiyoshi, *Nihon no kaigun* (The Japanese navy), 2 vols. (Tokyo: Isseidō, 1967).

9. Kaigun rekishi hozonkai (Navy historical preservation association), eds., *Nihon kaigunshi* (A history of the Japanese navy), 10 vols. (Tokyo: Hatsubai Dai'ichi Hōki shuppan kabushiki kaisha, 1996): 1: 59–60.

10. Taniguchi, "Kaigunkyō Hakushaku Kawamura Sumiyoshi no kōgyō," 27–28.

11. Taniguchi, "Kaigunkyō Hakushaku Kawamura Sumiyoshi no kōgyō," 29.

12. Kawamura would make similar arguments for the creation of an independent Navy General Staff. See Taniguchi, "Kaigunkyō Hakushaku Kawamura Sumiyosh no kōgyō," 78–80.

13. Kaigunshō, Kaigun daijin kanbō, *Kaigun seido enkaku*, 2 (2): 33–35.

14. Kaigun rekishi hozonkai, *Nihon kaigunshi*, 1: 59–61.

15. Kaigunshō, Kaigun daijin kanbō, *Kaigun seido enkaku*, 2 (2): 8.

16. Saitō Makoto, "The Navy," in Alfred Stead, ed., *Japan by the Japanese*: 2 vols. (Washington, D.C.: University Publications of America, 1979): 1: 121–141.

17. Joseph H. Langford, "The Growth of the Japanese Navy," *The Nineteenth Century and After*, 54: 319 (Sept. 1903): 474. Also quoted in Peter Cornwall, "The Meiji Navy: Training in an Age of Change," Ph.D. dissertation, University of Michigan, 1970: 42.

18. Figures taken from Kaigunshō, Kaigun daijin kanbō (Navy Ministry. Navy Minister's Secretariat), *Yamamoto Gonnohyōe to kaigun* (Yamamoto Gonnohyōe and the navy) (Tokyo: Hara shobō, 1966), 400–401; Ogawa Gotarō, *Conscription System in Japan* (Oxford: Oxford University Press, 1922): 16–17; and Statistics Bureau, *Historical Statistics of Japan*, 5 vols. (Tokyo: Japan Statistical Association, 1989): 5: 527.

19. Yamamoto gave this description to a *Chūō shinbun* reporter in 1893. See *Chūō shinbun*, 3 June 1893. Reprinted in Ko Hakushaku Yamamoto kaigun taishō denki hensankai, *Yamamoto Gonnohyōe den*, 1: 345. Italics are mine.

20. Kawamura's bureaucratic skills will be highlighted in the next chapter. Kawamura would return as navy minister in 1878 and thereafter played a critically important role in turning the navy into a bastion of Satsuma power in the early Meiji years.

21. Kaigun rekishi hozonkai, *Nihon kaigunshi*, 1: 237–242.

22. Report contained in Katsu Kaishū, *Katsu Kaishū zenshū* (The collected works of Katsu Kaishū), 24 vols., reprinted edition (Tokyo: Hara shobō, 1967): 8: 253–272. See also Kurihara Ryūichi, *Bakumatsu Nihon no gunsei* (The military system in *bakumatsu* Japan) (Tokyo: Jinbutsu ōraisha, 1972), 141–142; and David C. Evans, "The Satsuma Faction and Professionalism in the Japanese Naval Officer Corps of the Meiji Period, 1868–1912," Ph.D. dissertation, Stanford University, 1978: 15.

23. Kaigunshō, Kaigun daijin kanbō, *Kaigun seido enkaku*, 2 (2): 37–41. One

important and often overlooked aspect of this plan, which would recur in virtually all future expansion plans, was the inclusion of figures detailing the naval strength of foreign navies as a justification for Japanese naval development

24. Taniguichi, "Kaigunkyō Hakushaku Kawamura Sumiyoshi no kōgyō," 29–37.

25. Taniguchi, "Kaigunkyō Hakushaku Kawamura Sumiyoshi no kōgyō," 29–31.

26. Kaigunshō, Kaigun daijin kanbō, *Yamamoto Gonnohyōe to kaigun*, 277–280; Taniguchi, "Kaigunkyō Hakushaku Kawamura Sumiyoshi no kōgyō," 35–37.

27. Ono Gi'ichi, *War and Armament Expenditures of Japan* (London: Oxford University Press, 1922), 32–34.

28. Led by Saigō Tsugumichi in May 1874, 3,658 Japanese soldiers were sent to the island of Taiwan. See Watanabe Ikujirō, "Seiban jiken to kindai Nihon no kensetsu" (The Formosan expedition and the building of modern Japan), *Ōkuma kenkyū* 5 (1954): 1–95.

29. A considerable amount of material has been written on Meiji-era naval training and the social and geographic origins of the Japanese navy. In English, see Evans, "The Satsuma Faction"; and Cornwall, "The Meiji Navy."

30. Kaigun rekishi hozonkai, *Nihon kaigunshi*, 1: 100–108.

31. Kaigun rekishi hozonkai, *Nihon kaigunshi*, 1: 237–242.

32. Matsushita Yoshio, *Nihon gumbatsu no kōbō* (The rise and fall of Japan's military cliques), 3 vols. (Tokyo: Jinbutsu ōraisha, 1967): 1: 53–57; and *NRKSSJ*, 81–121.

33. Taniguchi, "Kaigunkyō Hakushaku Kawamura Sumiyoshi no kōgyō," 62–64.

34. Quoted in Evans, "The Satsuma Faction," 16.

35. Ikeda, *Nihon no kaigun*, 1: 58.

36. Evans, "The Satsuma Faction," 48.

37. This school, often referred to as the Japanese Naval Academy, was established by the new Meiji government in 1869 on the grounds of the former Tokugawa *bakufu* naval studies center at Tsukiji in Tokyo. It was eventually moved to Etajima, an island in the Inland Sea, close to the Kure Navy Yard in 1888.

38. While theoretical teaching was basic, the Dutch also gave the *bakufu* a steamship, the *Soembing*, which served as a training vessel under the name *Kankōmaru*. Shortly after the *bakufu* opened this center, it called for each domain to send prospective students to study alongside *bakufu* students. By 1856, in fact, enrollment totaled more than a hundred and fifty students. A year later, because of the success of the Nagasaki center, the *bakufu* opened a branch of the Nagasaki training school in Edo.

39. Conrad Totman, *The Collapse of the Tokugawa Bakufu, 1862–1868* (Honolulu: University of Hawaii Press, 1980): 180–186, 254–256. For a greater source of material on Dutch naval assistance in the *bakumatsu* era, see, Katsu Kaishū, *Katsu Kaishū zenshū*, vols. 8–10, *Kaigun rekishi* (A history of the navy), reprinted (Tokyo: Hara shobō, 1967).

40. Evans, "The Satsuma Faction," 52–53. Discussed in much greater detail in Kaigunshō, Kaigun kyōiku honbu (Navy Ministry, Chief of naval education), *Tei-*

koku kaigun kyōiku shi (A history of education in the Imperial Navy), 7 vols. (Tokyo: Kaigun kyōiku honbu, 1911): 1: 109–112.

41. Kaigunshō, Kaigun kyōiku honbu, *Teikoku kaigun kyōiku shi* 1: 200.

42. For a more detailed discussion on this topic, see David C. Evans, "The Recruitment of Japanese Navy Officers in the Meiji Period," in Robert W. Love, Jr., ed., *Changing Interpretations and New Sources in Naval History* (New York: Garland, 1980): 231–239.

43. Kaigunshō, Kaigun kyōiku honbu, *Teikoku kaigun kyōiku shi* 1: 154. Also quoted in Evans, "The Satsuma Faction," 53.

44. Ikeda, *Nihon no kaigun*, 1: 66–68.

45. Evans, "The Satsuma Faction," 61–66.

46. Kaigunshō, Kaigun kyōiku honbu, *Teikoku kaigun kyōiku shi* 7: 4–5. Also discussed in Cornwall, "The Meiji Navy," 115.

47. Evans, "The Satsuma Faction," 85–89.

48. When Japan was divided into four naval districts in 1901, each district was responsible for filling the quota established by the navy minister. The naval barracks at Kure, Sasebo, Yokosuka, and Maizuru became the four headquarters for naval recruitment in the Meiji and Taishō periods.

49. Cornwall, "The Meiji Navy," 208–211.

50. Cornwall, "The Meiji Navy," 212.

51. For further details, see Ogawa, *Conscription System in Japan*, 188–189. Ogawa's figures suggest that the average salary for an N.C.O. in the navy in 1910 was ¥224, while his army counterpart received ¥114. Also, the average pay per year of all enlisted ranks in the navy came to ¥64 per year, while the army's average was ¥20. See also Matsushita Yoshio, *Chōhei seiteishi* (A history of the establishment of the conscription system) (Tokyo: Gogatsu shobō, 1981) [reprint of 1943 edition].

Chapter 2

1. Ozaki Yukio, *The Autobiography of Ozaki Yukio: The Struggle for Constitutional Government in Japan*, transl. Hara Fujiko (Princeton: Princeton University Press, 2001): 124.

2. Taguchi Ukichi, "Nan'yō keiryaku ron" (On South Seas expansion), *Tokyo keizai zasshi* (Tokyo Economic Journal), no. 513 (1890): 353. In Taguchi Ukichi, *Teikan Taguchi Ukichi zenshū* (Collected works of Teiken Taguchi Ukichi), 8 vols. (Tokyo: Teikan Taguchi hakkōkai, 1927–1929).

3. Details of this plan and the discussions which Iwakura initiated in 1882 are mentioned in Kaigun rekishi hozonkai, *Nihon kaigunshi*, 1: 237–242.

4. Evans, "The Satsuma Faction," 129–130.

5. A considerable amount of information on Kawamura and his role in the early Meiji navy can be found in Taniguchi Naomi, "Kaigunkyō Hakushaku Kawamura Sumiyoshi no kōgyō," 23–123.

6. Taniguchi, "Kaigunkyō Hakushaku Kawamura Sumiyoshi no kōgyō," 47–52.

7. Ko Hakushaku Yamamoto kaigun taishō denki hensankai, *Yamamoto Gonnohyōe den*, 1: 62–65.

8. Evans, "The Satsuma Faction," 136–137.

9. Evans, "The Satsuma Faction," 137; Matsushita Yoshio, *Nihon gunsei to seiji*, 151.

10. For a discussion of Kawamura's involvement in suppressing the Satsuma Rebellion, see Kaigun rekishi hozonkai, *Nihon kaigunshi*, 1: 228–237.

11. For a brief English-language overview of Kabayama's career prior to joining the navy in 1883, see Evans, "The Satsuma Faction," 145–146.

12. The ranks of the Tokyo police were largely comprised of ex–midlevel samurai from Satsuma. It therefore became a tradition to appoint a "strong" Satsuma character to the post of commissioner.

13. Lawrence Sondhaus, *Preparing for Weltpolitik: German Sea Power before the Tirpitz Era* (Annapolis: Naval Institute Press, 1997): 150–153.

14. Saigō later relinquished his army title in 1894, when he was promoted to the rank of full admiral, Japan's first. Ozaki Yukio launched the most critical attacks against the navy for its blatant Satsuma favoritism, and the opening quote at the beginning of this chapter is one of many critiques that Ozaki launched against the navy both in private and later on the floor of the Diet.

15. Cited in Evans, "The Satsuma Faction," 149; and discussed in greater detail in Ivan Hall, *Mori Arinori* (Cambridge, Mass.: Harvard University Press, 1973): 106, 125.

16. Of the growing bifurcation of the government between Chōshū and Satsuma power, Ozaki wrote: "The coup of 1881 also meant that the Meiji government was entirely purged of Tosa and Hizen influence, and it now became the exclusive preserve of the two powerful clans of Satsuma and Chōshū." See Ozaki, *The Autobiography of Ozaki Yukio*, 55.

17. John C. Perry, "Great Britain and the Emergence of Japan as a Naval Power," Ph.D. dissertation, Harvard University, 1961: 130.

18. Historian Matsushita Yoshio claims failure of this plan was due largely to Kawamura's inability to sway fellow ministers to support his requests. See Matsushita, *Nihon gunbatsu no kōbō*, 1: 92–93.

19. Kaigun rekishi hozonkai, *Nihon kaigunshi*, 1: 237–242.

20. Details of the 1882 plan and elite-level effort to secure its passage are located in Matsushita Yoshio, *Meiji gunsei shiron*, 2: 33–42.

21. Kaigun rekishi hozonkai, *Nihon kaigunshi*, 1: 240–242.

22. With adoption of this plan, the navy obtained the following warships: *Naniwa* (3,708 tons), *Takachiko* (3,708 tons), *Uneme* (3,615 tons), *Takao* (1,778 tons), *Yamato* (1,500 tons), *Katsuragi* (1,500 tons), *Musashi* (1,500 tons), *Tsukushi* (1,371 tons), *Atago*, *Chōkai*, and *Maya* (all 621 tons). Note: the *Uneme* was lost at sea on its maiden voyage from France to Japan.

23. Kaigun rekishi hozonkai, *Nihon kaigunshi*, 1: 241.

24. Kaigun rekishi hozonkai, *Nihon kaigunshi*, 1: 242.

25. The H.M.S. *Inflexible* dwarfed in size and firepower warships that were state of the art in 1882, displacing 11,800 tons while the core warships ordered under the 1882 plan displaced on average only 3,800 tons. Reflecting on the role that technological innovation had on making older warships obsolete, Laird Clowes wrote, "[the] best ship existing in 1867 would have been more than a match for the entire British fleet existing in 1857, and . . . the best ship existing in 1877 would have been almost, if not quite, equal to fighting and beating the entire fleet of only ten years earlier. By 1890, the ships of 1877 had become well-nigh obsolete; and by

1900 the best ships, even of 1890, were hardly worthy of a place in the crack fleets of the country." See William Laird Clowes, *The Royal Navy: A History from the Earliest Times to the Present*, 7 vols. (London: Sampson Low, Marston, 1897–1903): 7: 68; also cited in John Curtis Perry, "Great Britain and the Emergence of Japan as a Naval Power," *Monumenta Nipponica*, 21: 3–4 (1966): 310.

26. For a discussion on the impact of the Jean Ecole school of naval thinking on the Germany navy, see Sondhaus, *Preparing for Weltpolitik: German Sea Power before the Tirpitz Era*, 15.

27. Kaigun rekishi hozonkai, *Nihon kaigunshi*, 1: 301–302.

28. Kabayama took a leading role in lobbying on behalf of the navy as vice minister under Saigō Tsugumichi. Japanese military historian Matsushita Yoshio claims that Saigō's tenure should be known as the era of Vice Minister Kabayama. See Matsushita, *Nihon gunbatsu no kōbō*, 1: 161. For discussions of this expansion plan and the cabinet negotiations, see ibid., 1: 163; Evans, "The Satsuma Faction," 144–147; and Kaigun rekishi hozonkai, *Nihon kaigunshi*, 1: 301–305.

29. In 1882, the government increased taxes on soy, tobacco, and sake. Dajō-kan ministers believed that these taxes would raise ¥16.4 million over three years running from 1883 to the end of 1885. Actual revenue realized amounted to only ¥10.1 million, thus leaving a shortfall to provide for naval expansion. See *Tokyo Nichi nichi shinbun*, 20–22 July 1886.

30. Kobayashi Ushisaburō, *The Armament Loans of Japan* (London: Oxford Univ. Press, 1922): 34–36; and Kaigun rekishi hozonkai, *Nihon kaigunshi*, 1: 303–5.

31. Kaigun rekishi hozonkai, *Nihon kaigunshi*, 1: 301–303.

32. The *Tokyo Nichi nichi shinbun* published a list of the major contributors to this fund. See *Tokyo Nichi nichi shinbun*, 14 April 1887. The *Japan Weekly Mail* also published the names of industrial contributors to the naval fund.

33. In the first years of the Meiji period, the term *Nan'yō* referred to the islands of the central Pacific that were located southeast of Japan, specifically the territories of the Marianas, Caroline, Marshall, and Gilbert islands. Over the course of the later Meiji period and up to World War II, the *Nan'yō* expanded to include Pacific islands south of the equator and territories including New Guinea, Australia, New Zealand, the Hawaiian Islands, the Dutch East Indies, and the colonies of Southeast Asia.

34. The best studies in English on the general ideology of southern advance and Japan's involvement in the South Seas are Mark R. Peattie, *Nan'yō* (Honolulu: University of Hawaii Press, 1988): 5–20; Henry P. Frei, *Japan's Southward Advance and Australia* (Honolulu: University of Hawaii Press, 1991): 31–47; Shimizu Hajime, "*Nanshinron*: Its Turning Point in World War I," *Developing Economies* 25: 4 (Dec. 1987): 386–402; J. Charles Schencking, "The Imperial Japanese Navy and the Constructed Consciousness of a South Seas Destiny, 1872–1921," *Modern Asian Studies* 33: 4 (Nov. 1999): 769–796; and Akira Iriye, *Pacific Estrangement: Japanese and American Expansion, 1897–1911* (Cambridge, Mass.: Harvard University Press, 1972). The best studies in Japanese are Yano Tōru, *Nanshin no keifu* (A genealogy of southern advance) (Tokyo: Chūō shinsho, 1993): 9–47; and Yano Tōru, *Nihon no Nan'yō shikan* (Japan's historical view of the South Seas) (Tokyo: Chūō shinsho, 1979).

35. For a detailed overview of Japanese trade, see Robert L. Innes, "The Door

Ajar: Japan's Foreign Trade in the Seventeenth Century," Ph.D. dissertation, University of Michigan, 1980: 58–62. See also Iwao Sei'ichi, *Nan'yō nihonmachi no kenkyū* (A study of Japanese settlement communities in the South Seas) (Tokyo: Chijin Shokan, 1940; reprint: Iwanami shoten, 1966); Henry Frei, "Japan in World Politics and Pacific Expansion, 1870s–1919," in John A. Moses and Christopher Pugsley, eds., *The German Empire and Britain's Pacific Dominions, 1871–1919* (Claremont: Regina Books, 2000): 173–196.

36. Kaigunshō, Kaigun kyōiku honbu, *Teikoku kaigun kyōikushi*, 7, Supplement: 13–17. Training cruises are discussed in greater detail in Cornwall, "The Meiji Navy," 137.

37. For insight into the early works and years of Shiga's life, see *Shiga Shigetaka zenshū* (Collected works of Shiga Shigetaka), ed. Shiga Fujio, 8 vols. (Tokyo: Shiga Shigetaka kankokai, 1927–1929). For a recent English-language monograph on Shiga that touches upon this time in his life, see Masako Gavin, *Shiga Shigetaka, 1863–1927: The Forgotten Enlightener* (Richmond: Curzon Press, 2001): 48–50.

38. More than three hundred Japanese naval officers who experienced combat in the Sino-Japanese and Russo-Japanese wars attended the *Kōgyoku juku*. See Miwa Kimitada, "Crossroads of Patriotism in Imperial Japan: Shiga Shigetaka, Uchimura Kanzō, and Nitobe Inazō," Ph.D. dissertation, Princeton University, 1967: 14. See also Gavin, *Shiga Shigetaka*, 50.

39. Shiga Fujio, ed., *Shiga Shigetaka zenshū*, 7: 5. Also discussed in Gavin, *Shiga Shigetaka*, 62.

40. Shiga Shigetaka, *Nan'yō jiji* (Current conditions in the South Seas) (Tokyo: Maruzen, 1887): 4.

41. Text taken from Shiga Fujio, ed., *Shiga Shigetaka zenshū*, 3: 105.

42. Shiga, *Nan'yō jiji*, 2–3.

43. Poem quoted in Miwa, "Crossroads of Patriotism," 156; and Gavin, *Shiga Shigetaka*, 75. Gavin suggests that the gun in Katsu's poem represents civilization and that this is a warning that unless Japan becomes a modernized, civilized country it will be as defenseless as a seagull. I would argue that given Katsu's role in the early Japanese navy, the "message" of the poem is more closely related to naval concerns, highlighting the critical need for increased naval strength.

44. Miyake Setsurei, *Daigaku konjaku tan* (University reminiscence) (Tokyo: Gakansha, 1946): 142–143. I would like to thank historian Henry P. Frei for brining this quote to my attention. Also cited in Frei, *Japan's Southern Advance and Australia*, 45.

45. Shiga Shigetaka, *Nihonjin* (The Japanese people), 3 April 1890: 12. Also cited in Frei, *Japan's Southern Advance and Australia*, 45; and Peattie, *Nan'yō*, 9.

46. See letters dated 12 September 1876 and 1 January 1877 regarding the requests to government officials to purchase the islands. Enomoto Takeaki, *Shiberia nikki* (Siberia diary), 3 vols. (Tokyo: Kaigun yūshūkai, 1935).

47. Enomoto's exploits are discussed in Peattie, *Nan'yō*, 6–9.

48. A complete membership list is published in the first journal published by this society in 1893. See *Shokumin kyōkai hōkoku* (Transactions of the Colonization Society): 1: 1 (Feb. 1893).

49. "Shokumin kyōkai setsuritsu shuisho" (Colonization Society prospectus), *Shokumin kyōkai hōkoku*, 1: 1 (Feb. 1893): 109–111.

50. Taguchi Ukichi, "Nan'yō keiryaku ron" (On South Seas expansion), *Tokyo keizai zasshi* (Tokyo Economic Journal), 513 (1890): 353.

51. Woodruff D. Smith, *The German Colonial Empire* (Chapel Hill: University of North Carolina Press, 1978): 119–150, 169–170; and Richard V. Pierrard, "The German Colonial Society, 1882–1914," Ph.D. dissertation, University of Iowa, 1964: 178–180.

52. Smith, *The German Colonial Empire*, 172–173.

53. Paolo E. Coletta, *A Survey of U.S. Naval Affairs, 1865–1917* (New York: University Press of America, 1987): 32–36.

54. Pedisich, "Congress Provides a Navy," 15–16.

55. Ibid., 16.

56. Coletta, *A Survey of U.S. Naval Affairs*, 238.

57. Excerpts of Mahan's 1890 article published in the *Atlantic Monthly* are quoted in Coletta, 42–43.

58. Beeler, *British Naval Policy in the Gladstone-Disraeli Era, 1866–1880*, 268–270.

59. W. Mark Hamilton, *The Nation and the Navy: Methods and Organization of the British Navalist Propaganda, 1889–1914* (New York: Garland, 1986): 81–90: Arthur J. Marder, "The Origin of Popular Interest in the Royal Navy," *Royal United Service Institution Journal* 82 (1937): 763–771; and Steven R. B. Smith, "Public Opinion, the Navy and the City of London: The Drive for British Naval Expansion in the Late Nineteenth Century," *War and Society* 9: 1 (May 1991): 36–38.

60. The most worrisome development for Britain, and one which also concerned Japan's admirals, was the accession of pro-navy Wilhelm II in 1888. See Ivo Nikolai Lambi, *The Navy and German Power Politics, 1862–1914* (Boston: Allen and Unwin, 1984): 31–49.

61. Hamilton, *The Nation and the Navy*, 143; and Marder, "The Origin of Popular Interest in the Royal Navy," 766.

62. Kaigun rekishi hozonkai, *Nihon kaigunshi*, 1: 302–303.

63. John L. Rawlinson, *China's Struggle for Naval Development* (Cambridge, Mass.: Harvard University Press, 1967), 129–153

64. Chia-Chien Wang, "Li Hung-chang and the Peiyang Navy," *Chinese Studies in History*, 25: 1 (1991): 59–60.

65. Peter Duus, *The Abacus and the Sword: The Japanese Penetration of Korea, 1895–1910* (Berkeley and Los Angeles: University of California Press, 1995): 62.

Chapter 3

1. The entire text of Kabayama's speech can be found in Nihon teikoku gikai (Japan's imperial parliament), *Dai Nihon teikoku gikaishi* (A parliamentary history of imperial Japan), 18 vols. (Tokyo: Nihon teikoku gikaishi kankōkai, 1926–1930): 1: 1491. Hereafter cited as *DNTG*.

2. For the full text of Suyehiro's 23 December oration, see *DNTG*, 1: 1495–1497.

3. *Kokkai*, 24 Dec. 1892: 1.

4. Cited in Banno Junji, *The Establishment of the Japanese Constitutional System*, transl. J. A. A. Stockwin. (London: Routledge, 1992): 50.

5. See Uchida Kenzō, Kanahara Samon, and Furuya Tetsuo, eds., *Nihon gikai*

shiroku (The history of parliamentary government in Japan), 6 vols. (Tokyo: Dai'ichi hoki shuppan, 1990): 1: 87–93. For two excellent English-language studies which thoroughly discuss the issues which divided the government and the political parties in the first Diet, see Banno, *The Establishment of the Japanese Constitutional System*, 9–80; and George Akita, *Foundations of Constitutional Government in Modern Japan, 1868–1900* (Cambridge, Mass.: Harvard University Press, 1967): 76–89.

6. These epitaphs are courtesy of parliamentarian Ozaki Yukio, ironically one of Kabayama's most outspoken critics. See Ozaki, *The Autobiography of Ozaki Yukio*, 124, 162.

7. Military historian Matsushita Yoshio wrote that Kabayama was one of the most skilled bureaucratic leaders in the early Meiji navy. See Matsushita, *Nihon gunbatsu no kōbō*, 1: 161–165. For a discussion on Kabayama's Satsuma favoritism within the navy, see Evans, "The Satsuma Faction," 121–162.

8. Details of this plan are found in Kaigun rekishi hozonkai, *Nihon kaigunshi*, 1: 303–306.

9. Kaigun rekishi hozonkai, *Nihon kaigunshi*, 1: 306.

10. *Mainichi shinbun*, 17 Sept. 1891; *Japan Weekly Mail*, 19 Sept. 1891, 330.

11. Kaigun rekishi hozonkai, *Nihon kaigunshi*, 1: 308.

12. Banno, *The Establishment of the Japanese Constitutional System*, 45–46.

13. As early as May 1891, Itagaki Taisuke, leader of the Jiyūtō political party, warned the government that his party would follow a "negative" policy—i.e., a reduction of expenditures and tax revenue—in the second Diet session. See the Jiyūtō manifesto written in early May and published in three parts in the newspaper *Jiyū shinbun* between 9 and 17 May 1891.

14. Ko Hakushaku Yamamoto kaigun taishō denki hensankai, *Yamamoto Gonnohyōe den*, 1: 320–322.

15. A large portion of the debates concerning naval appropriations in the second session of parliament can be found in the Diet transcripts found in *DNTG*, 1: 1441–1492.

16. Kabayama's entire speech and representatives' responses to it are recorded in *DNTG*, 1: 1491–1494. All quotes in the following paragraph are taken from this source.

17. See Ōtsu Jun'ichirō, *Dai Nihon kenseishi* (A constitutional history of Japan), 12 vols. (Tokyo: Hobunakn, 1927–1928): 3: 630.

18. Deliberations in the house on 23 December 1891 are recorded in *DNTG*, 1: 1492–1497. All quotes in the following paragraph are taken from this source.

19. Ozaki, *The Autobiography of Ozaki Yukio*, 124.

20. See *Tokyo Nichi nichi shinbun*, 25 Dec. 1891.

21. Speech recorded in the newspaper *Jiyū shinbun*, the Jiyūtō political organ, on 27 December 1891. For a more general discussion about Itagaki's position during and after the second Diet session, see Shinba Eiji, *Itagaki Taisuke: Jiyū minken no yume to haiboku* (The aspirations and setbacks of the popular-rights movement) (Tokyo: Shinchōsha, 1988): 227.

22. The Jiyūtō Election Manifesto was published in two parts during the first two weeks of January by the newspapers *Jiyū shinbun* and *Kokkai*. See the editions of 6, and 7 Jan. 1892.

23. See *Tokyo shinpō*, 16 Jan. 1892: 7.

24. Peter Duus, *Party Rivalry and Political Change in Taishō Japan* (Cambridge, Mass.: Harvard University Press, 1968): 9. Specifically, 2,652 violations of the election law were reported, as opposed to just 153 submitted during the first parliamentary elections in 1890. Moreover, the Home Ministry reported that 25 people died as a result of campaign violence, and more than 375 were wounded. For a firsthand account of the tactics employed by the government, see Ozaki, *The Autobiography of Ozaki Yukio*, 125–129.

25. Uchida et al., eds., *Nihon gikai shiroku*, 1: 117–122.

26. See *Mainichi shinbun*, 30 March 1892, for Kaishintō proposals; and *Jiyū shinbun*, 3 May 1892, for Jiyūtō proposals.

27. *Tokyo Asahi shinbun*, 3 and 4 May 1892.

28. Kuroda made this and other pro-navy remarks at a party attended by a number of newspaper reporters and journalists. Kuroda's comments even made their way into foreign newspapers in Japan. See *Japan Weekly Mail*, 14 May 1892, 644.

29. The *Mainichi shinbun* reported the Budget Committee as follows: Jiyūtō, 10; Kaishintō, 5; independents, 12; and pro-government, 18. See *Mainichi shinbun*, 7 May 1892

30. Vice Navy Minister Itō Yūkō answered questions raised by opposition members.

31. For Sugita's remarks and all other statements made by M.P.'s and government officials, see *DNTG*, 1: 1999–2011. All quotes in the following paragraph are taken from this source.

32. Discussed briefly in Andrew Fraiser, "The House of Peers," in Andrew Fraiser, R. H. P. Mason, and Philip Mitchell, eds., *Japan's Early Parliaments* (London: Routledge, 1994): 20–22.

33. Uchida et al., eds., *Nihon gikai shiroku*, 1: 125.

34. Matsushita, *Nihon gunbatsu no kōbō*, 1: 187–189.

35. Banno, *The Establishment of the Japanese Constitutional System*, 59–64.

36. Shinba, *Itagaki Taisuke*, 239–242.

37. *Jiyū shinbun*, 16 Nov. 1892: 1.

38. *Jiyū shinbun*, 23 Nov. 1892: 1.

39. The plan proposed the construction of nineteen warships with a combined displacement of 87,800 tons. Nire included calculation for Japan to purchase the largest battleships available from England, warships that displaced 11,400 tons, to serve as a counter to China's largest German-built warships. See Kaigun rekishi hozonkai, *Nihon kaigunshi*, 1: 310–315.

40. Details of these two events are taken from the *Jiyū shinbun*, *Hōchi shinbun*, *Mainichi shinbun*, and the *Japan Weekly Mail*, which reported both stories in great detail during between the last week of November and the second week of December 1892.

41. *DNTG*, 2: 360–367.

42. "Golden bridge" quote found in the political editorial of the *Japan Weekly Mail*, 10 Dec. 1892, 718.

43. Quotes from Itagaki in this paragraph are taken from *Jiyū shinbun*, 24 Dec. 1892: 1.

44. *Kokkai*, 24 Dec. 1892; *Japan Weekly Mail*, 31 Dec. 1892, 811.

45. For the entire bill, see *DNTG*, 2: 616–619. All quotes in the following paragraph are taken from this source.

46. Speech contained in *DNTG*, 2: 619–622.

47. For the debates over naval appropriations in January and February 1893, see *DNTG*, 2: 747–758, 856–873.

48. See Ko Hakushaku Yamamoto kaigun taishō denki hensankai, *Yamamoto Gonnohyōe den*, 1: 323–328; and *DNTG*, 2: 879.

49. Kaigun rekishi hozonkai, *Nihon kaigunshi*, 1: 312–315.

50. Ko Hakushaku Yamamoto kaigun taishō denki hensankai, *Yamamoto Gonnohyōe den*, 1: 329–330.

51. Ikeda, *Nihon no kaigun*, 1: 113.

52. Ko Hakushaku Yamamoto kaigun taishō denki hensankai, *Yamamoto Gonnohyōe den*, 1: 330.

53. Kaneko Kentarō, *Itō Hirobumi den* (Biography of Itō Hirobumi), 3 vols. (Tokyo: Shunpō Ko Tsuishōkai, 1940–1941): 2: 904–906; Ko Hakushaku Yamamoto kaigun taishō denki hensankai, *Yamamoto Gonnohyōe den*, 1: 329–333; and Hayashi Shigeru and Tsugi Kiyoaki, eds., *Nihon naikaku shiroku*, 1: 208–209.

54. *The Japan Mail*, 8 June 1893: 276–277.

55. Ko Hakushaku Yamamoto kaigun taishō denki hensankai, *Yamamoto Gonnohyōe den*, 1: 98–104.

56. Evans, "The Satsuma Faction," 181.

57. Ko Hakushaku Yamamoto kaigun taishō denki hensankai, *Yamamoto Gonnohyōe den*, 1: 330–331.

58. The *Chūō shinbun* applied the term "go-getter" to Yamamoto. See *Chūō shinbun*, 28 April 1893; and Ko Hakushaku Yamamoto kaigun taishō denki, *Yamamoto Gonnohyōe den*, 1: 339.

59. Ko Hakushaku Yamamoto kaigun taishō denki hensankai, *Yamamoto Gonnohyōe den*, 1: 333–334.

60. Ko Hakushaku Yamamoto kaigun taishō denki hensankai, *Yamamoto Gonnohyōe den*, 1: 334–337.

61. *Hōchi shinbun*, 3 June 1893.

62. Excerpts of the interview can be found in Ko Hakushaku Yamamoto kaigun taishō denki hensankai, *Yamamoto Gonnohyōe den*, 1: 344–348, while the entire interview is published in the 9 June 1893 *Chūō shinbun*. All quotes in this paragraph are taken from these two sources.

Chapter 4

1. George Alexander Lensen, *The d'Anethan Dispatches from Japan, 1894–1910* (Tokyo: Sophia University Press, 1967): 45.

2. Quoted in U.S. Naval Institute, *Proceedings*, 23: 84 (1897): 766. Also quoted in Cornwall, "The Meiji Navy," 52.

3. Peter Duus provides a thorough analysis of Japan's early relations with Korea in terms of Japan's larger foreign and domestic policy considerations. See Peter Duus, *The Abacus and the Sword: The Japanese Penetration of Korea, 1895–1910* (Berkeley and Los Angeles: University of California Press, 1995): 29–65. Much of

my discussion of pre–Sino-Japanese War diplomacy between China and Japan over Korea is drawn from this source.

4. Kaigun rekishi hozonkai, *Nihon kaigunshi*, 1: 314–315. See also Evans and Peattie, *Kaigun*, 37–39; and Toyama Saburō, *Nishin, Nichiro, daitōa kaisen shi* (A naval history of the Sino-Japanese, Russo-Japanese, and Greater East Asian wars) (Tokyo: Hara shobō, 1980): 74–75.

5. Ko Hakushaku Yamamoto kaigun taishō denki hensankai, *Yamamoto Gonnohyōe den*, 1: 410.

6. Lensen, *The d'Anethan Dispatches from Japan, 1894–1910*, 39.

7. For an excellent study that examines the social, psychological, and cultural effects of victory, see Donald Keene, "The Sino-Japanese War of 1894–95 and Its Cultural Effects in Japan," in Donald Shively, ed., *Tradition and Modernization in Japanese Culture* (Princeton: Princeton University Press, 1971): 121–175.

8. Mutsu Munemitsu, *Kenkenroku: A Diplomatic Record of the Sino-Japanese War, 1894–1895*, transl. Gordon M. Berger (Princeton: Princeton University Press, 1982): 106–113.

9. In October 1894 the cabinet and parliament agreed to purchase three Argentine warships at a cost of nearly ¥9 million. Though this purchase fell through, the government used ¥3.3 million of these funds to purchase the Chilean warship *Esmeralda*. This vessel arrived in Japan in February and was renamed *Izumi*. Ko Hakushaku Yamamoto kaigun taishō denki hensankai, *Yamamoto Gonnohyōe den*, 1: 410.

10. Tsunoda Jun, "Nihon kaigun sandai no rekishi" (Three periods in the history of the Japanese navy), *Jiyū* 11: 1 (Jan. 1969): 93.

11. Kaigunshō, Kaigun daijin kanbō, *Yamamoto Gonnohyōe to kaigun*, 346–349.

12. Kaigunshō, Kaigun daijin kanbō, *Yamamoto Gonnohyō to kaigun*, 346–349; and Ko Hakushaku Yamamoto kaigun taishō denki hensankai, *Yamamoto Gonnohyōe den*, 1: 411–412.

13. Ko Hakushaku Yamamoto kaigun taishō denki hensankai, *Yamamoto Gonnohyōe den*, 1: 423–424.

14. Ko Hakushaku Yamamoto kaigun taishō denki hensankai, *Yamamoto Gonnohyōe den*, 1: 421.

15. For military specifications of these warships, see Evans and Peattie, *Kaigun*, 59–61.

16. A summary of these papers is found in Ko Hakushaku Yamamoto kaigun taishō denki hensankai, *Yamamoto Gonnohyōe den*, 1: 412–419.

17. Ko Hakushaku Yamamoto Kaigun taishō denki hensankai, *Yamamoto Gonnohyōe den*, 1: 415–416; and Kaigunshō, Kaigun daijin kanbō, *Yamamoto Gonnohyōe to kaigun*, 351–352.

18. Kaigunshō, Kaigun daijin kanbō, *Yamamoto Gonnohyōe to kaigun*, 351–352.

19. Ko Hakushaku Yamamoto kaigun taishō denki hensankai, *Yamamoto Gonnohyōe den*, 1: 414.

20. For details of this plan, see Ko Hakushaku Yamamoto kaigun taishō denki hensankai, *Yamamoto Gonnohyōe den*, 1: 418–420.

21. *DNTG*, 3: 1587–1592; and Ko Hakushaku Yamamoto kaigun taishō denki hensankai, *Yamamoto Gonnohyōe den*, 1: 419–421.

22. See *Takenouchi Tsuna jijoden* (Autobiography of Takenouchi Tsuna), in *Meiji bunka zenshū* (The complete works of Meiji culture) (Tokyo: Nihon hyō-

ronsha, 1927–1930): 22: 447–448. I would like to thank the late Marius Jansen for bringing this source to my attention.

23. For discussions on cabinet-parliament relations in the ninth Diet session, see Kaneko, *Itō Hirobumi den* 3: 254–268.

24. Robert Scalapino, *Democracy and the Party Movement in Prewar Japan: The Failure of the First Attempt* (Berkeley and Los Angeles: University of California Press, 1953): 168–170.

25. See *Jiyū shinbun*, 23, 24, and 25 Nov.; *Tokyo Nichi nichi shinbun*, 23 Nov.; and *Jiyū Tōhō*, 25 Nov.: 1–2.

26. The Chinese indemnity was distributed as follows: naval expansion, ¥139,157,097; redemption of war expenses, ¥78,957,165; army expansion, ¥56,781,708; supplementary fund for naval expansion, ¥30 million; funds transferred to the imperial household, ¥20 million; funds transferred to general accounts in 1898, ¥12 million; education fund, ¥10 million; reserve fund for calamities, ¥10 million; extraordinary war expenses, ¥3,214,485; and funds for the naval iron foundry, ¥579,762.

27. For a discussion of this affair, see Evans, "The Satsuma Faction," 190; and Matsushita, *Nihon gunbatsu no kōbō*, 1: 271–272.

28. In 1883, Kawamura proposed a detailed plan for complete naval administrative autonomy. Reproduced in Taniguchi, "Kaigunkyō Hakushaku Kawamura Sumiyoshi no kōgyō," 27–28.

29. Evans and Peattie, *Kaigun*, 22–23.

30. Tsunoda, "Nihon kaigun sandai no rekishi," 95.

31. Tsunoda, "Nihon kaigun sandai no rekishi," 92–96; and Gow, "The Evolution of a General Staff System in the Imperial Japanese Navy," 82–84.

32. Tsunoda, "Nihon kaigun sandai no rekishi," 93.

33. Ko Hakushaku Yamamoto kaigun taishō denki hensankai, *Yamamoto Gonnohyōe den*, 1: 358–359.

34. Kunaichō (Imperial household agency), *Meiji Tennō ki* (Chronicle of the Meiji Emperor), 13 vols. (Tokyo: Yoshikawa kobunkan, 1968–1975), 8: 495.

35. For the best in-depth description of this in English, see Lone, *Japan's First Modern War*, 164–177.

36. Kaneko, *Itō Hirobumi den*, 3: 134–138.

37. For an overview of the factors that motivated the Itō government to occupy Taiwan, see Edward I-Te Chen, "Japan's Decision to Annex Taiwan: A Study of Itō-Mutsu Diplomacy, 1894–95," *Journal of Asian Studies* 35: 1 (Nov. 1977): 61–72.

38. Chen, "Japan's Decision to Annex Taiwan," 62–67.

39. For an English-language overview of the 1874 expedition, see E. H. House, *The Japanese Expedition to Formosa in 1874* (Taipei, Taiwan: SMC Publishing, 1984) [reprint of 1875 edition].

40. Mutsu, *Kenkenroku*, 144.

41. Yano, *Nanshin no keifu*, 148. See also Katayama Kunio, "The Expansion of Japanese Shipping into Southeast Asia before World War I: The Case of O.S.K.," *The Great Circle: Journal of the Australian Association for Maritime History*, 8: 1 (Apr. 1986): 1–2.

42. Tsurumi Yūsuke, *Gotō Shimpei* (Official biography of Gotō Shimpei), 4

vols. (Tokyo: Gotō Shimpei denki hensankai, 1937–1938): 2: 414–421. For a discussion of Katsura Tarō's interest in southern expansion from Taiwan, see Lone, *Army, Empire, and Politics in Meiji Japan*, 45–50.

43. Takekoshi Yosaburō, *Japanese Rule in Formosa*, transl. George Braithwaite (London: Longmans, Green, and Company, 1907), 11.

44. Tsunoda, "Nihon kaigun sandai no rekishi," 92–94.

45. For excerpts of Yamamoto's plan, which he sent to the emperor, see Bō eichō Bōei Kenshūjō Senshishitsu (Self-Defense Agency, Self-Defense Research Institute, War History Office), *Dai Hon'ei Kaigunbu, rengō kantai* (Imperial Headquarters, Navy Division and Combined Fleet Headquarters) (Tokyo: Asagumo shinbunsha, 1975): 73–75.

46. Tsunoda, "Nihon kaigun sandai no rekishi," 96.

47. Ozaki, *The Autobiography of Ozaki Yukiko*, 351, 280.

48. For an overview, see Marius Jansen, "Opportunists in South China during the Boxer Rebellion," *Pacific Historical Review* 20: 3 (Aug. 1951): 241–250; Ian Nish, "Japan and the Boxer Disturbances," 449–461; Saitō Seiji, "Amoy jiken saikō" (A reconsideration of the Amoy Incident), *Nihonshi kenkyū*, 305: 1 (Jan. 1988), 31–46; and Lone, *Army, Empire, and Politics in Meiji Japan*, 83–87. For Yamamoto's initial caution, see Gaimushō, *Nihon gaikō bunshō*, 33: 3, no. 2369: 941.

49. Saitō, "Amoy jiken saikō," 32–33. Saitō urged Yamamoto: "We should place two or three large warships in Amoy . . . and when the time arrives, have them (marines on board) occupy the vital point of Amoy." See also Tsurumi, *Gotō Shinpei*, 2: 457.

50. Ibid. See also Gaimushō, *Nihon gaikō bunsho*, 33: 1, no. 889, Yamamoto to Aoki: 911; and Nish, "Japan and the Boxer Disturbance," 452.

51. Gaimushō, *Nihon gaikō bunsho*, 33: 1: 945–946.

52. Jansen, "South China and the Boxer Rebellion," 246.

53. Saitō, "Amoy jiken saikō," 37.

54. For this series of exchanges between Yamamoto and Katsura, see Gaimushō, *Nihon gaikō bunshō*, 33: 3, no. 2369: 945–947.

55. Gaimushō, *Nihon gaikō bunshō*, 33: 3, no. 2369 (supplementary document no. 43): 946.

56. The Japanese naval historian Itō Masanori cites this quote but gives no reference for its location in the Japanese Foreign Ministry Archives. Itō states that Yamamoto declared: "Army troop-laden ships on the high seas without cause will be sunk as pirates by the Japanese navy. Please understand that this is in accordance with international law." See Itō Masanori, *The End of the Imperial Japanese Navy*, transl. Roger Pineau (London: Weidenfeld and Nicholson, 1962): 206. A transcript of this meeting is located within a larger file contained within Gaimushō, *Nihon gaikō bunshō*, 33: 3, no. 2369: 940–953. See pages 946–947 for Yamamoto's oration.

57. Kaigunshō, Kaigun daijin kanbō, *Yamamoto Gonnohyōe to kaigun*, 123–126.

58. Evans, "The Satsuma Faction," 255–256; and Tsunoda, "Nihon kaigun sandai no rekishi," 94–95.

59. See discussion in the Diet concerning the scale of Yamamoto's requests that were placed before parliament in December 1902. See *DNTG*, 5: 1876–1880, 1883–1886.

60. Ko Hakushaku Yamamoto kaigun taishō denki hensankai, *Yamamoto Gon-nohyōe den*, 1: 505–510.

61. Ko Hakushaku Yamamoto kaigun taishō denki hensankai, *Yamamoto Gon-nohyōe den*, 1: 510–513.

62. Ko Hakushaku Yamamoto kaigun taishō denki hensankai, *Yamamoto Gon-nohyōe den*, 1: 505–506.

63. Tokutomi Ichirō, *Katsura Tarō den* (Official biography of Katsura Tarō), 2 vols. (Tokyo: Hara shobō, 1967): 2: 27–28.

64. Yamamoto Shirō, *Shoki Seiyūkai no kenkyū* (A study of the early years of the Seiyūkai) (Osaka: Seibundo, 1975): 225.

65. *Jiji shinpō*, 27 Nov. 1902.

66. Tokutomi, *Katsura Tarō den*, 37–38.

67. *DNTG*, 5: 1859–1868.

68. *Hara Kai nikki*, 29 Oct. 1902.

69. For a discussion of the broader topic of the Anglo-Japanese Alliance and the navy, see J. Charles Schencking, "Navalism, Naval Expansion, and War: The Japanese Navy and the Anglo-Japanese Alliance," in Phillips O'Brien, ed., *The Anglo-Japanese Alliance* (London: RoutledgeCurzon, 2004): 122–139.

70. *DNTG*, 5: 1880–1881.

71. *DNTG*, 5: 1876–1877.

72. *DNTG*, 5: 1879–1881.

73. Yamamoto, *Shoki Seiyūkai no kenkyū*, 237.

74. Yamamoto, *Shoki Seiyūkai no kenkyū*, 233–237.

75. Yamamoto, *Shoki Seiyūkai no kenkyū*, 242.

76. Yamamoto, *Shoki Seiyūkai no kenkyū*, 243–244.

77. *Hara Kei nikki*, 19 and 20 May 1903: 2: 60; and Tokutomi, *Katsura Tarō den*, 2: 70–77. For debate in the Diet, see *DNTG*, 5: 1938–1942, 1989–1990.

78. Ko Hakushaku Yamamoto kaigun taishō denki hensankai, *Yamamoto Gon-nohyōe den*, 1: 518–519.

79. Okamoto, *The Japanese Oligarchy*, 75.

80. Okamoto, *The Japanese Oligarchy*, 101.

81. Tsunoda, "Nihon Kaigun sandai no rekishi," 97; and Okamoto, *The Japanese Oligarchy*, 76.

82. Ohkawa Masazō, "The Armaments Expansion Budgets and the Japanese Economy after the Russo-Japanese War," *Hitotsubashi Journal of Economics* 5 (Jan. 1965): 68–83.

Chapter 5

1. *Kokumin shinbun*, 25 Oct. 1905. This editorial was also published in the *Japan Times*, 26 Oct. 1905.

2. Prime Minister Katsura Tarō speaking to Seiyūkai leader Hara Kei. See *Hara Kei nikki*, 12 May 1910: 3: 23–26. Hara's understanding here was that Katsura was worried that Yamamoto would ride a wave of pro-navy sentiment with the opposition parties "on his shoulders" and destroy the relationship that Katsura had forged with the Seiyūkai.

3. *Hōchi shinbun*, 11 July 1912: 9; *Japan Weekly Mail*, 13 July 1912, 41.

4. Quoted in John Albert White, *The Diplomacy of the Russo-Japanese War* (Princeton: Princeton University Press, 1964): 207. See also Ogasawara Nagayo, *The Life of Admiral Tōgō* (Tokyo: Seito shorin, 1934): 334.

5. For the military specifics of this battle, see Evans and Peattie, *Kaigun*, 124. In terms of human loss, 4,830 Russian sailors died, and 5,917 were captured. Japan lost 110 men killed.

6. Gaimushō, *Nihon gaikō bunsho: Nichiro sensō*, no. 5: 731. Quoted in Okamoto Shumpei, *The Japanese Oligarchy and the Russo-Japanese War* (New York: Columbia University Press, 1970): 119.

7. The following information concerning Tōgō's triumphal return tour is taken from newspaper accounts, namely the *Jiji shinpō*, the *Tokyo Asahi shinbun*, and the *Tokyo Nichi nichi shinbun* from 12 October to 29 October 1905.

8. See *Japan Weekly Mail*, 21 Oct. 1905: 482.

9. A lucid account of the interplay between ritual, pageantry, symbolism, commemoration, and politics is David Kertzer, *Ritual, Politics, and Power* (New Haven: Yale University Press, 1988). In the field of Japanese history, such themes are discussed in relation to the emperor in Takashi Fujitani, *Splendid Monarchy* (Berkeley and Los Angeles: University of California Press, 1996).

10. *Jiji shinpō*, 21 Oct. 1905. Much of the information contained in this paragraph was drawn from the *Jiji shinpō*, *Tokyo Asahi shinbun*, and *Kokumin shinbun*.

11. *The Japan Times*, 23 Oct. 1905.

12. See the *Jiji shinpō*, *Tokyo Asahi shinbun*, *Kokumin shinbun*, *The Japan Times*,and *The Japan Weekly Mail* for details concerning Tōgō's movements and public reception on 22 October 1905.

13. David Kertzer uses two military pageants conducted by the former Brazilian government and the government of the former Soviet Union to demonstrate how such events have been used to communicate power and the hierarchical distinctions of a polity. The 1905 naval review in Japan was no exception. See Kertzer, *Ritual, Politics, and Power*, 30–31, 73–74.

14. *Japan Weekly Mail*, 28 Oct. 1905: 475.

15. *Japan Times*, 24 Oct. 1905.

16. These vessels were renamed *Mishima*, *Okinoshima*, *Tango*, *Sagami*, and *Iki*.

17. *Jiji shinpō*, 23 Oct. 1905; Japan Times, 24 Oct. 1905.

18. *Kokumin shinbun*, 25 Oct. 1905.

19. *Japan Times*, 28 Oct. 1905.

20. See *Jiji shinpō*, 28 Oct. 1905. See also *Japan Weekly Mail*, 28 Oct. 1905: 473.

21. See *Jiji shinpō*, 13, 14, and 15 Sept. 1906.

22. For an excellent description of how the British Royal Navy marketed itself to politicians and the general public in the late nineteenth and early twentieth centuries, see Marder, "The Origin of Popular Interest in the Royal Navy," 763–771.

23. *Jiji shinpō*, 16 Nov. 1906; and *Japan Weekly Mail*, 17 Nov. 1906: 531.

24. Hamilton, *The Nation and the Navy*, 50.

25. Both admirals had served in the Russo-Japanese War, and each received a Golden Kite for his services, Ijuin receiving a First-Class Golden Kite, and Dewa receiving a Second-Class Golden Kite. Details concerning the 1908 naval review are drawn from the *Jiji shinpō* and the *Tokyo Asahi shinbun*.

26. W. Mark Hamilton has written similarly of naval reviews and maneuvers conducted by the Royal Navy between 1887 and 1897. See Hamilton, *The Nation and the Navy*, 80–91.

27. See Ko Hakushaku Yamamoto kaigun taishō denki hensankai, *Yamamoto Gonnohyōe den*, 2: 1012, 1013–1014, 1014–1015; *Takarabe Takeshi nikki*, 12 Nov. 1912: 2: 100; ibid., 10 Nov. 1913: 2: 228–229; and *Hara Kei nikki*, 10 Nov. 1913: 3: 359.

28. *Jiji shinpō*, 28 May 1906.

29. During the Russo-Japanese War the navy also issued other cards, including a series of warship cards commemorating the Meiji emperor's birthday. For images of these and other cards, see *Japanese Philately* 41: 4 (Aug. 1986): 152–158.

30. See *Jiji shinpō*, 29 May 1906. The *Tokyo Asahi shinbun* and *Chūō shinbun* also reported extensively on this event.

31. *Japan Weekly Mail*, 30 May 1908: 609; and *Jiji shinpō*, 28 May 1908.

32. *Japan Weekly Mail*, 27 May 1909: 735; and *Jiji shinpō*, 28 May 1909.

33. The best source in English on the Suikōsha is a file contained within the Office of Naval Intelligence Reports for 1907. See United States Navy, Office, Records of the Chief of Naval Operations, Record Group 38, Office of Naval Intelligence, Registers 1886–1923, File no. E-7-d 07-180, "Suikōsha, or Naval Club of Japan."

34. For information concerning the Kure branch office of the Suikōsha, see Kure shishi hensan iinkai (Kure city history compilation association), *Kure shishi* (History of Kure city), 6 vols. (Kure: Kure shiyakushō, 1964–1995): 3: 226–232.

35. In the immediate postwar period, General Tanaka Gi'ichi repeatedly argued that the navy's command independence had allowed the navy to pursue its own objectives during the war—namely the destruction of Russia's naval forces—while at the same time deemphasizing naval assistance that the army required, particularly the transport of troops. Discussed in Tsunoda, "Nihon kaigun sandai no rekishi," 97–98. In Tsunoda's monograph *Manshū mondai to kokubō hoshin* (National defense policy and the Manchuria problem) (Tokyo: Hara shobō, 1967), the author claims that according to Army Vice Chief of Staff Nagaoka Gaishi the navy balked at the army's plan to use naval vessels in a supporting role to capture Vladivostok. Moreover, the navy hedged its support of the Sakhalin occupation even after the defeat of the Russian Baltic Fleet. Cited in David Evans, "The Satsuma Faction," 248.

36. Tsunoda, "Nihon kaigun sandai no rekishi," 98. See draft defense policy in Bōeichō bōei kenshūjō senshishitsu, *Kaigunbu Rengō kantai*, 109–110.

37. The series of meetings began on 24 December 1906. See Bōeichō bōei kenshūjō senshishitsu, *Kaigunbu rengō kantai*, 110–111.

38. Tsunoda, "Nihon kaigun sandai no rekishi," 98.

39. For text of the Imperial Defense Policy of 1907, see Bōeichō bōei kenshūjō senshishitsu, *Kaigunbu rengō kantai*, 112–118.

40. Asada Sadao claimed that in 1907 the United States was nothing more than a "budgetary enemy." Asada Sadao, "The Revolt against the Washington Treaty: The Imperial Japanese Navy and Naval Limitation, 1921–1927," *Naval War College Review*, 46: 3 (Summer 1993): 83–84.

41. See the document entitled *Kokubō shoyō heiryokuryō* (The forces necessary

for defense), in Bōeichō bōei kenshūjō senshishitsu, *Kaigunbu rengō kantai*, 116–120.

42. *Japan Weekly Mail*, 13 Jan. 1906: 28.

43. The *Dreadnought*-class warship is discussed in Evans and Peattie, *Kaigun*, 152–154.

44. *Tokyo Puck* (2: 4), 10 Nov. 1906: 384–385.

45. *Hara Kei nikki*, 29 June 1906: 2: 183–184.

46. *Hara Kei nikki*, 14 Nov. 1906: 2: 207.

47. *Hara Kei nikki*, 22 Nov. 1906: 2: 208.

48. *Tokyo Puck* (2: 4), 10 Nov. 1906: 377.

49. *Hara Kei nikki*, 29 Nov. 1906: 2: 210.

50. Ohkawa Masazo, "The Armaments Expansion Budgets and the Japanese Economy after the Russo-Japanese War," 76–77.

51. *Hara Kei nikki*, 3 Dec. 1906: 2: 211–212.

52. Ohkakwa, "The Armaments Expansion Budgets and the Japanese Economy after the Russo-Japanese War," 79–80.

53. Saitō shishaku kinen kai (Viscount Saitō commemorative society), *Saitō Makoto den* (Biography of Saitō Makoto), 4 vols. (Tokyo: Saito shishaku kinenkai, 1941): 2: 54–59.

54. Eckart Kehr, *Battleship Building and Party Politics in Germany, 1894–1901*, ed., transl., and introd. Pauline R. Anderson and Eugene N. Anderson (Chicago: University of Chicago Press, 1973): 73–95.

55. For a brief description of Lt. Commander Satō Tetsutarō, see Evans and Peattie, *Kaigun*, 133–136.

56. Satō Tetsutarō, *Teikoku kokubō ron* (On imperial defense) (Tokyo: Suikōsha, 1902).

57. Ko Hakushaku Yamamoto kaigun taishō denki hensankai, *Yamamoto Gonnohyōe den*, I: 505–507.

58. Satō Tetsutarō, *Teikoku kokubōshi ron* (On the history of imperial defense), 2 vols., reprinted edition (Tokyo: Hara shobō, 1979): I: 144. Quoted in Evans and Peattie, *Kaigun*, 138

59. Satō Tetsutarō, *Kokubō sakugi* (n.p., 1912): 19–20.

60. Satō, *Kokubō sakugi*, 26–27.

61. Satō, *Kokubō sakugi*, 36.

62. Satō, *Kokubō sakugi*, 36.

63. Indeed, like the writings of Mahan and Colomb, Satō Tetsutarō's works were geared for an elite-level audience. For a discussion on elite-level writers such as Mahan and Colmb, see Marder, "The Origins of Popular Interest in the Royal Navy," 768.

64. Mark R. Peattie, "Forecasting a Pacific War, 1912–1933: The Idea of Conditional Japanese Victory," in James White, Michio Umegaki, and Thomas Havens, eds., *The Ambivalence of Nationalism* (New York: The University Press of America, 1990): 119–120. Also see Shōichi Saeki, "Images of the United States as a Hypothetical Enemy," in Akira Iriye, ed., *Mutual Images: Essays in American-Japanese Relations* (Cambridge, Mass.: Harvard University Press, 1975): 101–108. See also John J. Stephan, *Hawaii under the Rising Sun* (Honolulu: University of Hawaii Press, 1984), 56–59.

65. Morita Akatsuki, *Teikoku kaigun no kiki* (Crisis of the Imperial Navy) (Tokyo: Teikoku kaigun no kikki hakkōjo, 1912), and *Kokubō to kaigun jujitsu* (Naval preparedness and national defense) (Tokyo: Teikoku kaigun no kiki hakōjo, 1914).

66. Homer Lea's original work was published by Harper & Brothers in 1909. The two rival Japanese translations were *Nichi-Bei hissen ron* (The inevitable Japanese-American war) by Mochizuki Kotarō and *Nichi-Bei sensō* (The Japanese-American War) by Ike Kyōkichi. For details see Saeki, "Images of the United States as a Hypothetical Enemy," 102. For a short biography of Homer Lea, see Stephan, *Hawaii under the Rising Sun*, 56–57.

67. Two good discussions about war-scare literature in England during this period are found in Hamilton, *The Nation and the Navy*, 166–168; and Ignatius. F. Clarke, *Voices Prophesying War, 1763–1984* (London: Oxford University Press, 1966).

68. I would like to thank Elizabeth Malcom, Professor of History at the University of Melbourne, for bringing Childers' war-fantasy novel to my attention.

69. *The Times*, 20 Oct. 1900. Cited in Hamilton, *The Nation and the Navy*, 75.

70. *Mainichi shinbun*, 6 Feb. to 9 Feb. 1908. Saitō spoke before both houses of parliament and answered questions concerning the age of Japan's fleet. See *Japan Weekly Mail*, 15 Feb. 1908: 162.

71. *Yamato shinbun* and *Yorozu chōhō*, 18 and 19 Apr. 1910.

72. *Tokyo Asahi shinbun*, 30 Apr. 1910. The paper reached these numbers by using the formula that the operational life of a battleship or armored cruiser was approximately twelve to fifteen years.

73. Ko Hakushaku Yamamoto kaigun taishō denki hensankai, *Yamamoto Gonnohyōe den*, 2: 1011.

74. For a detailed description of this relationship, see Tetsuo Najita, *Hara Kei in the Politics of Compromise* (Cambridge, Mass.: Harvard University Press, 1967).

75. *Hara Kei nikki*, 12 May 1910: 3: 23–26.

Chapter 6

1. *Niroku shinbun*, 17 June 1910. Reprinted as "Political Forecast" in *Japan Weekly Mail*, 18 June 1910: 909.

2. *Tokyo Asahi shinbun*, 26 Oct. 1912.

3. *Jiji shinpō*, 1 Oct. 1912. The newspaper attributed this statement to an unnamed leader in the Seiyūkai, most likely Hara Kei or Saionji Kinmochi. Also cited in *Japan Weekly Mail*, 5 Oct. 1912: 577.

4. Speech quoted in Kobayashi Yūgo, *Rikken Seiyūkai shi* (History of the Seiyūkai), 8 vols. (Tokyo: Rikken Seiyūkai shuppan kyoku, 1925): 5: 600–602. Though Saionji did apologize to the emperor in his speech, he made no concession to the army's demands.

5. Najita, *Hara Kei in the Politics of Compromise*, 96. Najita wrote that acceptance of the navy's program "was contrary to the cabinet's retrenchment programme and defied explanation." This policy decision taken by Saionji is also discussed in Lesley Connors, *The Emperor's Adviser: Saionji Kinmochi and Pre-War Japanese Politics* (London: Croom Helm, 1987), 38–39.

6. *Hara Kei nikki*, 12 May 1910: 3: 23–26; ibid. 12 Nov. 1910: 3: 53–54.

7. For details of this plan, see Ko Hakushaku Yamamoto kaigun taishō denki hensankai, *Yamamoto Gonnohyōe den*, 2: 1011–1015.

8. Saitō shishaku kinen kai, *Saitō Makoto den*, 2: 137–142.

9. *Hara Kei nikki*, 12 May 1910: 3: 23–26.

10. Ibid.

11. *Takarabe Takeshi nikki*, 9 July 1910: 1: 109.

12. Ibid. A number of naval officials expressed concern that Saitō, whom Admiral Nomura Kichisaburō would later call the "master of compromise," might accept a lesser expansion plan than the ¥402 million requested. See Ikeda, *Nihon no kaigun*, 2: 21–22.

13. *Takarabe Takeshi nikki*, 10 July 1910: 1: 109–110.

14. Ijūin's discussion with Katsura was relayed to Yamamoto through Takarabe. See *Takarabe Takeshi nikki*, 11 July 1910: 1: 110–112.

15. Both Matsumoto and Takarabe believed that if the cabinet shelved naval expansion in 1910, both Navy Minister Saitō and the chief of the Navy General Staff would resign. *Takarabe Takeshi nikki*, 9 July 1910: 1: 109.

16. Ko Hakushaku Yamamoto kaigun taishō denki hensankai, *Yamamoto Gonnohyōe den*, 2: 1011.

17. Najita, *Hara Kei in the Politics of Compromise*, 85–86.

18. *Hara Kei nikki*, 11 Nov. 1910: 3: 52–53.

19. *Hara Kei nikki*, 11 Nov. 1910: 3: 53.

20. *Hara Kei nikki*, 29 Nov. 1910: 3: 58.

21. Yamamoto's discussions and meetings are discussed by Takarabe. See *Takarabe Takeshi nikki*, 9 July 1910 1: 109.

22. *Hara Kei nikki*, 29 Nov. 1910: 3: 58.

23. Yamamoto Shirō, *Yamamoto naikaku no kisōteki kenkyū* (Research into the formation of the Yamamoto cabinet) (Kyoto: Kyoto Joshi Daigaku, 1982): 53–93.

24. On 2 December Saionji informed Hara of his willingness to head a new cabinet. See *Hara Kei nikki*, 2 Dec. 1910: 3: 59–60.

25. At a 17 November 1909 meeting between Yamamoto Tatsuo, Anraku, and Hara, Hara reflected, "I have heard that Yamamoto Gonnohyōe is so indignant about the depredations of Yamagata and the Chōshū faction that he once complained to Itō about the situation." See *Hara Kei nikki*, 17 Nov. 1909: 2: 385–386.

26. Hara's diary entries are full of references to Satsuma-Chōshū, navy-army tensions. On 22 November 1910, Hara went to a garden party held to commemorate the fiftieth wedding anniversary of Mr. and Mrs. Matsukata Masayoshi. Hundreds of people attended, including the cabinet members. Hara reflects that it was amusing to see the Chōshū people—Katsura, Inoue, Terauchi, et al.—sitting together while the Satsuma group—Yamamoto, Kabayama, Tōgō, et al.—sat together at another table. See *Hara Kei nikki*, 22 Nov. 1910: 3: 55–56.

27. *Hara Kei nikki*, 5 Dec. 1910: 3: 64–65.

28. *Hara Kei nikki*, 14 Dec. 1910: 3: 67–72. At this meeting Katsura confessed that his current cabinet would be the last.

29. Saitō shishaku kinenkai, *Saitō Makoto den*, 2: 137–139.

30. Saitō shishaku kinenkai, *Saitō Makoto den*, 2: 139–141.

31. Ko Hakushaku Yamamoto kaigun taishō denki hensankai, *Yamamoto Gonnohyōe den*, 2: 1012

32. *Hara Kei nikki*, 29 Aug. 1911: 3: 160–161; and Saitō shishaku kinenkai, *Saitō Makoto den*, 2: 168. Military specifics of the plan can be found in Ko Hakushaku Yamamoto kaigun taishō denki hensankai, *Yamamoto Gonnohyōe den*, 2: 1012.

33. As relayed to Hara. See *Hara Kei nikki*, 29 Aug. 1911: 3: 160–161.

34. Roger Hackett, "Yamagata and the Taishō Crisis, 1912–1913," in Sidney D. Brown, ed., *Studies on Asia* (Lincoln: University of Nebraska Press, 1962): 22.

35. Ritsumeikan daigaku, *Saionji Kinmochi den*, 3: 123–124; and *Hara Kei nikki*, 29 Aug. 1911: 3: 160–161.

36. *Hara Kei nikki*, 29 Aug. 1911: 3: 161.

37. *Takarabe Takeshi nikki*, 2 Nov. 1911: 1: 280; and *Hara Kei nikki*, 2 Nov. 1911: 3: 182–183.

38. Cabinet discussion are to be found in *Hara Kei nikki*, 2 Nov. 1911: 3: 182–183.

39. *Takarabe Takeshi nikki*, 21 Nov. 1911: 1: 287.

40. *Takarabe Takeshi nikki*, 24 Nov. 1911: 1: 288–289.

41. *Takarabe Takeshi nikki*, 24 Nov. 1911: 1: 288–289; and discussed in *Hara Kei nikki*, 24 Nov. 1911: 3: 188–189.

42. *Takarabe Takeshi nikki*, 25 Nov. 1911: 1: 289.

43. *Takarabe Takeshi nikki*, 26 Nov. 1911: 1: 290.

44. *Takarabe Takeshi nikki*, 26 Nov. 1911; 1: 290.

45. *Takarabe Takeshi nikki*, 28 Nov. 1911: 1: 291.

46. *Hara Kei nikki*, 1 Dec. 1911: 3: 190.

47. Ibid.

48. *Takarabe Takeshi niiki*, 29 Oct. 1911: 2: 95–96.

49. *Hara Kei nikki*, 17, 18, 30 Aug. 1912: 3: 246–250.

50. Details of the requested plan are found in Ko Hakushaku Yamamoto kaigun taishō denki hensankai, *Yamamoto Gonnohyōe den*, 2: 1013.

51. Lone, *Katsura Tarō*, 177.

52. *Hara Kei nikki*, 30 Aug. 1912: 3: 250.

53. Takakura Tetsu'ichi, *Tanaka Gi'ichi denki* (Biography of Tanaka Gi'ichi), 2 vols. (Tokyo: Tanaka Gi'ichi denki kankōsha, 1958): 1: 497. Also cited in Najita, *Hara Kei in the Politics of Compromise*, 90.

54. *Takarabe Takeshi nikki*, 29 Oct. 1912: 2: 95–96.

55. *Takarabe Takeshi nikki*, 26 Nov. 1912: 2: 106.

56. *Takarabe Takeshi nikki*, 22 Nov. 1912: 2: 103–104.

57. *Takarabe Takeshi nikki*, 23 and 25 Nov. 1912: 2: 104–106.

58. *Takarabe Takeshi nikki*, 26 Nov. 1912: 2: 106.

59. *Takarabe Takeshi nikki*, 27 Nov. 1912: 2: 107.

60. *Hara Kei nikki*, 9 Nov. 1912: 3: 260–261.

61. *Hara Kei nikki*, 11 Nov. 1912: 3: 261.

62. Ibid. Tanaka records the expression as "To increase only the navy is clearly unjust. I feel this is an extremely serious affair that can lead to grave consequences." See, Takakura, *Tanaka Gi'ichi denki*, 1: 497

63. *Hara Kei nikki*, 16 Nov. 1912: 3: 262–263.

64. *Hara Kei nikki*, 23, 24, 25 Nov. 1912: 3: 264–266. Yamagata's maneuvers are discussed in Hacket, "Yamagata and the Taishō Crisis, 1912–1913," 23.

65. *Hara Kei nikki*, 28 Nov. 1912: 3: 267–268.

66. Quoted in Najita, *Hara Kei in the Politics of Compromise*, 100.

67. *Takarabe Takeshi nikki*, 4 Dec. 1912: 2: 111. Matsukata Kōjirō informed Takarabe that on 12 December his father, Msayoshi, had strongly lobbied Yamamoto to accept the post of prime minister. Yamamoto forcefully declined. *Takarabe Takeshi nikki*, 12 Dec. 1912: 2: 115–116.

68. *Takarabe Takeshi nikki*, 9 Dec. 1912: 2: 114.

69. Tokutomi Ichirō, *Yamagata Aritomo den* (Biography of Yamagata Aritomo), 3 vols. (Tokyo: 1934): 3: 817–818. Quoted in Hackett, "Yamagata and the Taishō Crisis," 25.

70. *Takarabe Takeshi nikki*, 14 Dec. 1912: 2: 117.

71. Saitō shishaku kinenkai, *Saitō Makoto den*, 2: 216–218; and *Takarabe Takeshi nikki*, 17 Dec. 1912: 2: 118–119.

72. Details of the budgetary discussion are found in Saitō shishaku kinenkai, *Saitō Makoto den*, 2: 216–225. Newspapers such as the *Tokyo Asahi shinbun* also ran daily columns on the discussion.

73. *Takarabe Takeshi nikki*, 19 Dec. 1912: 2: 121–122.

74. The National Defense Council is discussed in *Takarabe Takeshi nikki*, 18 Dec. 1912: 2: 119–120.

75. *Hara Kei nikki*, 1 Dec. 1912: 3: 190.

76. *Takarabe Takeshi nikki*, 18 Dec. 1912: 2: 120.

77. Saitō shishaku kinenkai, *Saitō Makoto den*, 2: 216.

78. *Takarabe Takeshi nikki*, 18 Dec. 1912: 2: 120–121.

79. *Takarabe Takeshi nikki*, 18 Dec. 1912: 2: 121.

80. As relayed by Saitō to Takarabe. *Takarabe Takeshi nikki*, 19 Dec. 1912; 2: 122.

81. Ibid.

82. *Tokyo Asahi shinbun*, 20 Dec. 1912. It read: "The scheme for expanding the navy was settled long ago and should not be considered a quid pro quo for yet to be considered army expansion. . . . The navy program had its origins in the second Katsura cabinet, and therefore there is no reason for abandoning it now." Also reproduced in *Japan Weekly Mail*, 21 Dec. 1912, 725.

83. *Takarabe Takeshi nikki*, 20 Dec. 1912: 2: 123–124.

84. Saitō's official biography claims that the navy minister decided to resign because Katsura deleted the ¥3 million 1913 component of the proposed budget on 20 December. This is highly unlikely given Katsura's desire to reach a compromise with the navy on the terms that he had spelled out the day before. See Saitō shishaku kinenkai, *Saitō Makoto den*, 2: 217–18.

85. Tokutomi, *Kōshaku Katsura Tarō den*, 2: 613–619.

86. *Takarabe Takeshi nikki*, 21 Dec. 1912: 2: 124.

87. *Takarabe Takeshi nikki*, 22 Dec. 1912: 2: 126.

88. Published in the official news journal of the Seiyūkai, *Seiyū* 48 (Dec. 1912): 45–54. For a wider discussion of the popular protest movement, see Najita, *Hara Kei in the Politics of Compromise*, 101–106.

89. See Najita, *Hara Kei in the Politics of Compromise*, 107–119.

90. *Japan Weekly Mail*, 28 Dec. 1912: 760.

91. See *Jiji shinpō* and *Chūō shinbun*, 21 Dec. 1912.

92. Quoted in Najita, *Hara Kei in the Politics of Compromise*, 99.

93. For in-depth discussion, see Najita, *Hara Kei in the Politics of Compromise*, 125–129.
94. *Hara Kei nikki*, 17 Dec. 1912: 3: 273–274.
95. *Hara Kei nikki*, 10 Feb. 1913: 3: 287–289.
96. For a general discussion, see Hackett, "Yamagata and the Taishō Political Crisis," 31; Najita, *Hara Kei in the Politics of Compromise*, 148–152; and Stephen S. Large, *Emperors of the Rising Sun* (London: Kodansha International, 1997): 90–92.
97. *Hara Kei nikki*, 16 Jan. 1913: 3: 277–278.
98. Quoted in *Japan Weekly Mail*, 15 Feb. 1913: 197.
99. Ōtsu Junichirō, *Dai Nihon kensei shi*, 6: 788–794.
100. *Takarabe Takeshi nikki*, 5 Feb. 1912: 2: 146.
101. Quotes taken from *Takarabe Takeshi nikki*, 28 Jan. 1913: 2: 144.
102. *Hara Kei nikki*, 9 Feb. 1913: 3: 286–287.
103. *Takarabe Takeshi nikki*, 10 Feb. 1913: 2: 148–149.
104. *Takarabe Takeshi nikki*, 10 Feb. 1913: 2: 141.
105. *Hara Kei nikki*, 11 Feb. 1913: 3: 289.

Chapter 7

1. Kobayashi, *Rikken Seiyūkai shi*, 3: 680.
2. House of Peers member Murata Tsuneyoshi (a retired general) made this remark in the upper house on 13 March 1914. See Saitō shishaku kinenkai, *Saitō Makoto den*, 2: 330. Speech reproduced in *Japan Weekly Mail*, 21 Mar. 1914: 338.
3. *Hara Kei nikki*, 14 Mar. 1914: 3: 401–402.
4. Kobayashi, *Rikken Seiyūkai shi*, 3: 680–681.
5. The popular journal *Taiyō* devoted its February 1914 issue to the Siemens scandal and the Seiyūkai's backing of the Yamamoto cabinet.
6. *Takarabe Takeshi nikki*, 11 Feb. 1913: 2: 149.
7. Yamamoto Shirō, *Yamamoto naikaku no kisōteki kenkyū* (Study of the formation of the Yamamoto cabinet) (Kyoto: Kyoto Joshi Daigaku, 1982): 55–56. Hereafter cited as *YNKK*.
8. *Hara Kei nikki*, 12 Feb. 1913: 3: 289–290.
9. *YNKK*, 60.
10. *Takarabe Takeshi nikki*, 12 Feb. 1913: 2: 148.
11. *YNKK*, 63.
12. *YNKK*, 55–56.
13. *YNKK*, 56–57.
14. This group of young hard-liners included Kikuchi Takenori, Matsuda Genji, Nakamura Junkurō, Yamamoto Teijirō, and Fukuzawa Momosuke.
15. *YNKK*, 60.
16. *Hara Kei nikki*, 12 and 13 Feb. 1913: 3: 289–290.
17. Matsuda's actions are discussed in *YNKK*, 62–64; and in much less detail in Najita, *Hara Kei in the Politics of Compromise*, 170–171.
18. *YNKK*, 64–68.
19. *YNKK*, 68.
20. *Hara Kei nikki*, 13–19 Feb. 1913: 3: 290–293; and *YNKK*, 70–73.

21. *Takarabe Takeshi nikki*, 17 Feb. 1913: 2: 151.

22. Kobayashi, *Rikken Seiyūkai shi*, 3: 673–674; *YNKK*, 76–77; *Hara Kei nikki*, and 13–19 Feb. 1913: 3: 290–293.

23. *Takarabe Takeshi nikki*, 17 Feb. 1913: 2: 151.

24. *YNKK*, 84–85.

25. The Seiyūkai majority thus decreased from 207 to 181 seats out of 381 total.

26. *Takarabe Takeshi nikki*, 22 Feb. 1913: 2: 153; and *Hara Kei nikki*, 22 Feb. 1913: 3: 294.

27. "Speedy grab of power" was the term Ozaki used in a reflective interview with the *Jiji shinpō* in 1914. *Jiji shinpō*, 3 Jan. 1914. Also quoted in Najita, *Hara Kei in the Politics of Compromise*, 172.

28. Saitō shishaku kinenkai, *Saitō Makoto den*, 3: 230–232. The following parliamentary exchanges are reproduced in this volume.

29. *Takarabe Takeshi nikki*, 4 Mar. 1913: 2: 156.

30. Saitō shishaku kinenkai, *Saitō Makoto den*, 3: 233–234.

31. *Takarabe Takeshi nikki*, 13 and 14 Mar. 1913: 2: 158–159.

32. *Hara Kei nikki*, 15 Mar. 1913: 3: 299; and *Takarabe Takeshi nikki*, 15 Mar. 1913: 2: 159.

33. Ko Hakushaku Yamamoto kaigun taishō denki hensankai, *Yamamoto Gonnohyōe den*, 2: 1013–1014.

34. *Hara Kei nikki*, 16 Mar. 1913: 3: 299; and *Takarabe Takeshi nikki*, 16 Mar. 1913: 2: 159.

35. *Hara Kei nikki*, 6 Mar. 1913: 3: 297.

36. *Hara Kei nikki*, 8 Mar. 1913: 3: 297.

37. *Hara Kei nikki*, 10 Mar. 1913: 3: 298.

38. Najita, *Hara Kei in the Politics of Compromise*, 179–180.

39. *Takarabe Takeshi nikki*, 18 Apr. 1913: 2: 169.

40. *Takarabe Takeshi nikki*, 11 Apr. 1913: 2: 167.

41. *Takarabe Takeshi nikki*, 26 Apr. 1913: 2: 171.

42. *Hara Kei nikki*, 8 May 1913: 3: 309.

43. This is discussed in more detail in Najita, *Hara Kei in the Politics of Compromise*, 176–177.

44. *Tokyo Asashi shinbun*, 27 and 28 Feb. 1913. See also, Hayashi Shigeru and Tsuji Kiyochi, eds., *Nihon naikaku shiroku*, 2: 174–183.

45. Each of the newspapers listed ran laudatory stories of Yamamoto's retrenchment between 13 and 20 June 1913. Only the *Niroku shinbun*, the mouthpiece of the opposition Dōshikai party, criticized Yamamoto's retrenchment program.

46. Discussed in Najita, *Hara Kei in the Politics of Compromise*, 278 n. 37.

47. In Kagoshima-ken, the Seiyūkai held every national parliamentary seat (9 total) between the 1904 and 1924 elections. In Nagasaki-ken, the Seiyūkai held a majority of the seats (8 total) until the 1915 election. Nagasaki was home to Mitsubishi, one of the two largest private shipbuilding firms in the country. The other, Kawasaki, of Kobe, was owned and managed by the navy-Seiyūkai go-between Matsukata Kōjirō.

48. Zōsen kyōkai (Shipbuilders association), *Nihon kinsei zōsen shi* (A history of the modern Japanese shipbuilding industry) (Tokyo: Hara shobō, 1973): 44–59.

49. *Hara Kei nikki*, 7 Feb. 1914: 3: 387–388.

50. Kawasaki jūkōgyō (Kawasaki heavy industries), *Kawasaki jūkōgyō kabushiki kaisha shi* (A history of the Kawasaki heavy-industry company) (Kobe: Kawasaki jūkōgyō, 1959): 70; and Mitsubishi jūkōgyō (Mitsubishi heavy industries), *Mitsubishi zōsen sōgyō hyakunen no Nagasaki zōsenjo tlkushū* (A centenary of the Nagasaki ship works) (Tokyo: Mitsubishi zōsen, 1957): 48–55.

51. Kawasaki jūkōgyō, *Kawasaki jūkōgyō kabushiki kaisha shi*, 200–205.

52. *Tokyo Asahi shinbun*, 4 Feb. 1910; also reproduced in *Japan Weekly Mail*, 12 Feb. 1910: 208.

53. Comments printed in *Japan Weekly Mail*, 15 Mar. 1913: 328.

54. Yamamoto Shirō, "Dai ichiji sekai taisen ni okeru Amerika no sansen to Nihon: Terauchi naikaku no keizai to seiji" (America's entry into World War I and Japan: Politics and economics of the Terauchi cabinet), *Hisutoria* 43 (March 1966): 37.

55. For a discussion of German industrialists and their role in lobbying political parties to support naval expansion, see Kehr, *Battleship Building and Party Politics in Germany, 1894–1901*, 200–212, 306–359.

56. *Japan Weekly Mail*, 6 Dec. 1913: 715; and ibid., 20 Dec. 1913: 782. Japanese papers that ran stories on each launch include the *Tokyo Asahi* and the *Jiji shinpō*.

57. For technical specifics concerning the *Kongō*, which was designed by the distinguished British naval architect Sir George Thurston, see Evans and Peattie, *Kaigun*, 160–163.

58. A complete list of those cabinet ministers who accompanied emperor Taishō is as follows: Prime Minister Yamamoto Gonnohyōe, Navy Minister Saitō Makoto, Foreign Minister Makino Nobuaki, Army Minister Kusunose Yukihiko, Home Minister Hara Kei, and Vice Navy Minister Takarabe Takeshi.

59. *Tokyo Asahi shinbun*, 10 Nov. 1913. Also discussed in *Japan Times*, 11 Nov. 1913: 8.

60. Saitō shishaku kinenkai, *Saitō Makoto den*, 2: 244–247.

61. *Takarabe Takeshi nikki*, 4 Nov. 1913: 2: 227; and *Hara Kei nikki*, 4 Nov. 1913: 3: 357.

62. *Hara Kei nikki*, 9 Nov. 1913: 3: 358–359.

63. Saitō shishaku kinenkai, *Saitō Makoto den*, 2: 247, 21, 25; *Takarabe Takeshi nikki*, 27 Nov. 1913: 2: 231–234; and *Hara Kei nikki*, 27 Nov. 1913: 3: 367.

64. Saitō's position paper is reproduced in Saitō shishaku kinenkai, *Saitō Makoto den*, 2: 247–253.

65. *Hara Kei nikki*, 27 Nov. 1913: 3: 367.

66. Ko Hakushaku Yamamoto kaigun taishō denki hensankai, *Yamamoto Gonnohyōe den*, 2: 1015.

67. Ōshima Tarō, "Shiimensu-Vikkaasu jiken" (The Siemens-Vickers incident), in Wagatsuma Sakai et al., eds., *Nihon seiji saiban shiroku: Taishō*, 5 vols. (Historical records of the political trials in Japan: Taishō) (Tokyo: Dai ichi hōki shuppan, 1981): 1: 56–57.

68. The following narrative is drawn from newspaper coverage of the Siemens scandal as well as from the testimony of individuals associated with the affair. Transcript of Victor Herrmann's testimony can be found in Mori Zenkichi, ed., *Shiimensu jiken: Kiroku to shiryō* (The Siemens incident: Documents and materials)

(Tokyo: Tokuma shoten, 1976): 219–260. In English, Richard Mitchell gives a very brief overview of the Siemens scandal. See Richard Mitchell, *Political Bribery in Japan* (Honolulu: University of Hawaii Press, 1996): 28–30.

69. The following narrative is based upon trial transcripts in Mori, ed., *Shiimensu jiken: Kiroku to shiryō*, 219–260.

70. *Takarabe Takeshi nikki*, 26 and 27 Nov. 1913: 2: 233–234.

71. Mori, ed., *Shiimensu jiken: Kiroku to shiryō*, 58–64.

72. *Tokyo Nichi nichi shinbun*, 25 Jan. 1914.

73. Saitō shishaku kinenkai, *Saitō Makoto den*, 2: 271–280. See also *DNTG*, 9: 252–258.

74. *Takarabe Takeshi nikki*, 23 Jan. 1914: 2: 252.

75. Saitō shishaku kinenkai, *Saitō Makoto den*, 2: 288. See also *DNTG*, 9: 256–266.

76. Saitō shishaku kinenkai, *Saitō Makoto den*, 2: 288–296.

77. *Hara Kei nikki*, 29 Jan. 1914: 3: 385.

78. *Hōchi shinbun*, 6 Feb. 1914.

79. *Hara Kei nikki*, 5 Feb. 1914: 3: 387.

80. *Hara Kei nikki*, 6 Feb. 1914: 3: 387.

81. *Hara Kei nikki*, 7 Feb. 1914: 3: 387–388.

82. *Hara Kei nikki*, 7 Mar. 1914: 3: 387–388.

83. *Hara Kei nikki*, 8 Mar. 1914: 3: 388–389; and *Takarabe Takeshi nikki*, 9 Mar. 1914: 2: 303–304.

84. Saitō shishaku kinenkai, *Saitō Makoto den*, 2: 303–304.

85. Saitō shishaku kinenkai, *Saitō Makoto den*, 2: 303–305. See also, *DNTG*, 9: 316–319.

86. *Takarabe Takeshi nikki*, 14 Feb. 1914: 2: 259–260; and Saitō shishaku kinenkai, *Saitō Makoto den*, 2: 305–309.

87. *Hara Kei nikki*, 18 Feb. 1914: 3: 393–394.

88. *Takarabe Takeshi nikki*, 5 Mar. 1914: 2: 265.

89. *Hara Kei nikki*, 9 Mar. 1914: 3: 359; and Saitō shishaku kinenkai, *Saitō Makoto den*, 2: 327–329.

90. *Takarabe Takeshi nikki*, 19 Mar. 1914: 2: 268.

91. Saitō shishaku kinenkai, *Saitō Makoto den*, 2: 332; and *Takarabe Takeshi nikki*, 23 Mar. 1914: 2: 270.

92. Ko Hakushaku Yamamoto kaigun taishō denki hensankai, *Yamamoto Gonnohyōe den*, 2: 1019. Reflecting on the Yamamoto cabinet after his party suffered disastrous election results in early 1915, Hara concluded that the compromise with Yamamoto had "turned out to be extremely damaging to the Seiyūkai." *Hara Kei nikki*, 28 Mar. 1915: 4: 92–94.

93. *Hara Kei nikki*, 24 Mar. 1914: 3: 408–409.

94. Ōtsu, *Dai Nihon kensei shi*, 7: 283–285.

95. Although invited into the cabinet, Inukai refused to join. Ozaki, however, accepted an appointment as justice minister. While supported by the opposition parties, he was not strongly supported by the Seiyūkai. For details concerning the relationship between Ōkuma and the Seiyūkai, see Najita, *Hara Kei in the Politics of Compromise*, 191.

96. See Mori, ed., *Shiimensu jiken: Kiroku to shiryō*, 157–201.

97. *Japan Times*, 3 May 1914. The *Tokyo Asahi shinbun* of 21 May 1914 reported that Yashiro announced that "anyone guilty would be punished strictly in accordance with the dictates of the law."

98. Ko Hakushaku Yamamoto kaigun taishō denki hensankai, *Yamamoto Gonnohyōe den*, 2: 1027.

99. Ōshima, "Shiimensu-Vikkaasu jiken," 61–62.

100. The following narrative is taken from Admiral Matsumoto Kazushi's court-martial transcripts, found in Mori, ed., *Shiimensu jiken: Kiroku to shiryō*, 175–201.

101. See Ōshima, "Shiimensu-Vikkaasu jiken," 61.

102. *Tokyo Asahi shinbun*, 14 June 1914. For an extract of Ōkuma's speech before the lower house on 23 June in support of naval expansion, see Kaigunshō, Kaigun daijin kanbō (Navy Ministry, Navy Minister's secretariat), *Kaigun gunbi enkaku* (Development of naval armaments) (Tokyo: Hara shobō, 1970): 169–170.

103. Kaigunshō, Kaigun daijin kanbō, *Kaigun gunbi enkaku*, 175–180.

104. *Japan Times*, 1 Aug. 1914.

Chapter 8

1. Order given to South Seas commanders by the Navy General Staff on 15 October 1914. *Taishō senryaku senji shorui*, vol. 16. Cited in Gabe Masaakira, "Nihon Mikuroneshia senryō to nanshin" (Southern Advance and Japan's occupation of Micronesia) *Keio Daigaku hōgaku kenkyū* 55: 7 (July 1982): 83.

2. *Hara Kei nikki*, 15 Jan. 1918: 4: 353.

3. Minutes of the Fourth Subcommittee for Budget, Lower House, 41st session (5 Feb. 1919). Quoted in Asada Sadao, "Japanese Admirals and the Politics of Limitation: Katō Tomosaburō vs Katō Kanji," in Gerald Jordan, ed., *Naval Warfare in the Twentieth Century, 1900–1945* (London: Croom Helm, 1977): 146.

4. In his excellent monograph on Japan and World War I, Frederick Dickinson astutely points out that various individuals and factions used the war for domestic political purposes. The Japanese naval leadership also used this war for their own political, budgetary, and institutional interests. Frederick Dickinson, *War and National Reinvention: Japan and the Great War, 1914–1919* (Cambridge, Mass.: Harvard University Press, 1999).

5. Sōrifu teikoku kyoku (Statistics bureau, prime minister's office), *Nihon teikoku tōkei nenkan* (Statistical yearbook of imperial Japan), 36 (1917): 574–575; and ibid. 40 (1921): 512–513, 516–517.

6. Quote by Inoue Kaoru, cited in Dickinson, *War and National Reinvention*, 35.

7. The ¥761 million secured in 1920 provided funds for four additional battleships, four additional battle cruisers, twelve cruisers, and thirty-two destroyers. This would bring about the attainment of the desired when all construction was complete in 1927. The total cost of the eight-eight-fleet program, if one includes the vessels begun after the 1911 budget agreement, was ¥1.7 billion. For a breakdown in the figures, see Zōsen kyōkai (Shipbuilders association), *Nihon kindai zōsenshi: Taishō jidai* (The history of Japan's modern shipbuilding industry: The Taishō period) (Tokyo: Hara shobō, 1973): 21–24.

8. Grey to Greene, 18 Aug. 1914: London, Public Record Office (P.R.O.), Foreign Office Papers (F.O.), 371/2017.

9. Greene to Grey, 3 Aug. 1914: in G. P. Gooch and Harold Temperley, *British Documents on the Origins of the War, 1898–1914*, 11 vols. (London: His Majesty's Stationery Office, 1926): vol. 11, no. 571. Hereafter cited as *BD*.

10. Greene to Grey, 3 Aug. 1914: *BD*, vol. 11, no. 571.

11. Luigi Albertini, *The Origins of the War of 1914*, transl. Isabella M. Massey, 3 vols. (London: Oxford University Press, 1957): 3: 694.

12. For a more detailed study of Britain's naval position on the eve of war, see Ian H. Nish, "Admiral Jerram and the German Pacific Fleet, 1913–1915," *Mariner's Mirror* 56 (May 1970): 411–420.

13. For Jordan's belief that fighting would not be necessary in China, see Gaimushō (Japanese Foreign Ministry), *Nihon gaikō bunsho* (Japanese diplomatic documents), Taishō sannen (1914), no. 114. (Hereafter cited as *NGB*, T.3/III). For his concern about a loss of prestige and influence in Asia, see Jordan to Grey, 9 Aug. 1914: London (P.R.O.), F.O. 371/2016. For May's remarks, see May to Harcourt, 10 Aug. 1914: London, Colonial Office, 1910–1915, box no. 3. See also Peter Lowe, *Great Britain and Japan, 1911–1915* (London: Macmillan, 1969): 183.

14. Grey to Greene, 6 Aug. 1914: *BD*, X, appendix 2, 823.

15. *NGB*, T.3/III, no. 104.

16. Itō Masanori, *Katō Takaaki den* (Biography of Katō Takaaki), 2 vols. (Tokyo: Katō haku denki nensan iinkai, 1929): 2: 77.

17. Kajima Morinosuke, *Nichi-Ei gaikōshi* (A history of foreign relations between Japan and Great Britain) (Tokyo: Sanshusha, 1957): 364.

18. While endorsing Katō's initiative, the *genrō* were not pleased with the manner in which Katō failed to consult them before securing cabinet approval and meeting with the emperor. For a discussion of this tension, see Itō, *Katō Takaaki den*, 2: 45–50.

19. Words taken from Katō's earlier communiqué. See Greene to Grey, 3 Aug. 1914: *BD*, XI, no. 571.

20. *NGB*, T.3/III, no. 108; and Itō, *Katō Takaaki den*, 2: 86.

21. *NGB*, T.3/III, no. 108.

22. Itō, *Katō Takaaki den*, 2: 133. Katō had previously been foreign minister in 1900–1901, 1905–1906, and February 1913. He was also ambassador in London from 1909 to January 1913.

23. Itō, *Katō Takaaki den*, 2: 148.

24. On 21 August 1914 the newly appointed Japanese minister to Peking, Hioki Eki, wired Katō suggesting that he be allowed to make preparations for eventual negotiations with Chinese officials concerning the extension of Japanese-leased territories, namely Kwantung and the South Manchurian Railway, in exchange for the ultimate return of German possessions that Japan, he argued, was soon to capture. See Gaimushō (Japanese Foreign Ministry), PVM 12-5, Series 12, 2599–2607.

25. Greene to Grey, 7 Aug. 1914: *BD*, X, appendix 2, 823.

26. *NGB*, T.3/III, no. 154.

27. *NGB*, T.3/III, no. 206, pt. 1.

28. Peattie, *Nan'yō*, 41–43; Kaigun rekishi hozonkai, *Nihon kaigun shi*, 2: 313–315; and Gabe, "Nihon Mikuroneshia senryō to nanshin," 81–82.

29. The 12 September orders that called for the destruction of the German fleet

and ground facilities in the Pacific, but not for the occupation of territory, can be found in Kaigun rekishi hozonkai, *Nihon kaigun shi*, 2: 313; and Hatano Masaru, "Tai-Doku kaisen to Nihon Gaikō" (Japanese diplomacy and the outbreak of war with Germany), *Keiō daigaku hōgaku kenkyū* 61: 8 (Aug. 1988): 67. Yashiro's recommendations to Yamaya are quoted in Gō Takashi, *Nan'yō bōeki go-jūnenshi* (Fifty year history of commerce in the South Seas) (Tokyo: Nan'yō bōeki kabushiki kaisha, 1942): 219; and in Gabe, "Nihon Mikuroneshia senryō to nanshin," 82.

30. Kaigun rekishi hozonkai, *Nihon kaigun shi*, 2: 314.

31. Akiyama was also one of the brightest naval strategists in the Japanese navy at that time. For more information concerning him as well as further discussion concerning his role in the development of Japanese naval doctrine, see Peattie and Evans, *Kaigun*, 69–74.

32. Because Yashiro's orders were somewhat unexpected, Matsumura proceeded to the Naval Affairs Division and the Navy General Staff Offices. He wrote what transpired at these meetings in his own diary, which in 1942 was located at Navy General Staff Offices. Unfortunately, the diary itself did not survive World War II, but Gō Takashi has used Matsumura's notes and other staff documents to reconstruct the events that took place in late September and early October 1914 concerning Japan's occupation of Micronesia. See Gō, *Nan'yō bōeki go-jūnenshi*, 219–240. I would like to thank Mark R. Peattie of the Hoover Institute, Stanford University, for bringing this source to my attention.

33. Gō, *Nan'yō bōeki go-jūnenshi*, 220.

34. Gō, *Nan'yō bōeki go-jūnenshi*, 219–220.

35. Hirama Yōichi, "Akiyama Saneyuki: Nan'yō guntō senryō no suishinsha" (Akiyama Saneyuki: Promoter behind the occupation of the South Sea islands), *Taiheiyō shakai zasshi* 50: 14 (Apr. 1991): 190–191.

36. Gō, *Nan'yō bōeki go-jūnenshi*, 221–22; and Gabe, "Nihon Mikuroneshia senryō to nanshin," *Hogaku kenkyū*, 82.

37. A highly detailed account of Admiral Yamaya's orders and movements, as well as those of the Second South Seas task force under Admiral Matsumura Tatsuo, is given in Kaigun Gunreibu (Naval General Staff), *Taishō san-yonnen kaigun senshi* (History of naval operations, 1914–1915) (Tokyo: Kaigun Gunreibu, n.d.): 5: 5, 625–650. Hereafter cited as Kaigun Gunreibu, *Kaigun senshi*.

38. See Hirama Yōichi, "Kaigunshiteki ni mita nanshin no ichi dammen: Nihon kaigun o Mikuronesia senryō ni fumikiraseta haikei" (One aspect of Japan's southern advance from the viewpoint of naval history: Background of the Japanese navy's occupation of Micronesia), *Seiji keizai shigaku* 250 (Feb. 1987): 95.

39. For a detailed discussion of Yashiro's requests at the Military Affairs Council, see Kaigunshō, Kaigun daijin kanbō, *Kaigun gunbi enkaku*, 185–193. See also Hatano, *Tai-Doku kaisen to Nihon Gaikō*, 67; Gabe. *Nihon Mikuroneshia senryō to nanshin*, 82; *NGB*, T.3/III, no. 627; and Dickinson, *War and National Reinvention*, 76.

40. Occupation details are provided in Kaigun Gunreibu, *Kaigun senshi*, 5: 5, 640–797. I would like to thank Hirama Yōichi for providing me with these materials while I was a graduate student at the University of Hawaii.

41. Kaigunshō, Kaigun daijin kanbō, *Kaigun gunbi enkaku*, 183–185.

42. Ibid.

43. The regulations establishing the Military Affairs Council can be found in Kaigunshō, Kaigun daijin kanbō, *Kaigun gunbi enkaku*, 180–183.

44. Saitō Seiji, "Kokubō hoshin Dai ichiji kaitei no haikei: Dainiji Ōkuma naikaku ni okeru rikukai ryōgun kankei" (The background of the first revision of the national defense plan: The relationship between the Japanese army and navy during the second Ōkuma cabinet), *Shigaku zasshi* 95: 6 (1986): 6–7.

45. Saitō, "Kokubō hoshin Dai-ichiji kaitei no haikei," 7–8.

46. Kaigunshō, Kaigun daijin kanbō, *Kaigun gunbi enkaku*, 185–194.

47. Zōsen kyōkai, *Nihon kindai zōsen shi*, 14–17.

48. Saitō, "Kokubō hoshin Dai-ichiji kaitei no haikei," 8.

49. Saitō, "Kokubō hoshin Dai-ichiji kaitei no haikei," 9–10.

50. *Hara Kei nikki*, 22–25 Dec. 1914: 4: 81–83.

51. Duus, *Party Rivalry and Political Change in Taishō Japan*, 90–91.

52. Suzuki Hajime, ed., *Suzuki Kantarō jiden* (The autobiography of Suzuki Kantarō) (Tokyo: Ōgikukai shuppanbu: 1949): 196–197.

53. Kaigunshō, Kaigun daijin kanbō, *Kaigun gunbi enkaku*, 194–198; and Zōsen kyōkai, *Nihon kindai zōsenshi*, 15–16.

54. Kaigunshō, Kaigun daijin kanbō, *Kaigun gunbi enkaku*, 198–209.

55. Zōsen kyōkai, *Nihon kindai zōsenshi*, 16–18.

56. Kaigunshō, Kaigun daijin kanbō, *Kaigun gunbi enkaku*, 203–204.

57. Kaigunshō, Kaigun daijin kanbō, *Kaigun gunbi enkaku*, 206–207.

58. Katō Gensui denki hensan iinkai (Admiral Katō biographical compilation committee), *Gensui Katō Tomosaburō den* (Biography of Fleet Admiral Katō Tomosaburō) (Tokyo: Miyata Mitsuo, 1928), 80–85 (hereafter cited as *Katō Tomosaburō den*); and Zōsen kyōkai, *Nihon kindai zōsenshi*, 18–19.

59. Dingman, *Power in the Pacific*, 54–55.

60. Dingman, *Power in the Pacific*, 38–40

61. *Katō Tomosaburō den*, 79–87; and Kaigunshō, Kaigun daijin kanbō, *Kaigun gunbi enkaku*, 214–226.

62. Zōsen kyōkai, *Nihon kindai zōsenshi*, 19–21; and Kaigunshō, Kaigun daijin kanbō, *Kaigun gunbi enkaku*, 227–229.

63. Zōsen kyōkai, *Nihon kindai zōsenshi*, 19–20; and Kaigunshō, Kaigun daijin kanbō, *Kaigun gunbi enkaku*, 227–239.

64. Zōsen kyōkai, *Nihon kindai zōsenshi*, 20–21.

65. Saitō Seiji, "Kaigun ni okeru Dai ichiji taisen kenkyū to sono hado" (The navy's research on World War I and its influence), *Rekishigaku kenkyū* 530 (July 1984): 19–21.

66. Saitō, "Kaigun ni okeru Dai ichiji taisen kenkyū to sono hado,"20

67. Saitō, "Kaigun ni okeru Dai ichiji taisen kenkyū to sono hado," 22.

68. Roger Hackett, *Yamagata Aritomo in the Rise of Modern Japan* (Cambridge, Mass.: Harvard University Press, 1971): 308–309.

69. *Katō Tomosaburō den*, 81–83; Kaigunshō, Kaigun daijin kanbō, *Kaigun gunbi enkaku*, 238–239; and *Hara Kei nikki*, 15 Jan. 1918: 4: 353.

70. Kaigunshō, Kaigun daijin kanbō, *Kaigun gunbi enkaku*, 244–258.

71. Zōsen kyōkai, *Nihon zōsen shi*, 21–24; Kaigunshō, Kaigun daijin kanbō, *Kaigun gunbi enkaku*, 239–254; Dingman, *Power in the Pacific*, 125–128.

72. *Katō Tomosaburō den*, 85–91.

73. Spoken before the lower house budget subcommittee. Quoted in Saitō, "Kaigun ni okeru Dai ichiji taisen kenkyū to sono hado," 22.

74. Dingman, *Power in the Pacific*, 124.

75. Quoted in Hackett, *Yamagata Aritomo in the Rise of Modern Japan*, 318.

76. Maeda Renzan, *Hara Kei den* (Biography of Hara Kei), 2 vols. (Tokyo: Takayama Shoin, 1943): 2: 368–369; Kaigunshō, Kaigun daijin kanbō, *Kaigun gunbi enkaku*, 232–234. In English, see Duus, *Party Rivalry and Political Change in Taishō Japan*, 136–137; Dickinson, *War and National Reinvention*, 211–217; Dingman, *Power in the Pacific*, 130–131.

77. Duus, *Party Rivalry and Political Change in Taishō Japan*, 85.

78. Duus, *Party Rivalry and Political Change in Taishō Japan*, 152–157.

79. Dingman, *Power in the Pacific*, 130–131.

80. Kaigunshō, Kaigun daijin kanbō, *Yamamoto Gonnohyōe to kaigun*, 409–410.

81. *Katō Tomosaburō den*, 83–87.

82. Duus, *Party Rivalry and Political Change in Taishō Japan*, 154–157.

83. *Katō Tomosaburō den*, 85–91; and Kaigunshō, Kaigun daijin kanbō, *Kaigun gunbi enkaku*, 244–258.

84. Speech by Inukai on 25 Jan. 1917. Quoted in Saitō, "Kaigun ni okeru Dai ichiji taisen kenkyū to sono hado," 22.

85. Saitō, "Kaigun ni okeru Dai ichiji taisen kenkyū to sono hado," 17–19.

86. Dingman, *Power in the Pacific*, 125. Many of Akiyama's reports were serialized in the *Jiji shinpō* in 1917 and published in English in London under the title *A Japanese View of the War* (London: T. Fisher Unwin, 1917).

87. Shiba Takao, "Fukyō ki no nidai zōsen kigyō," *Keiei shigaku* 18: 3 (1983): 13–15.

88. Jeffrey Safford, "Experiment in Containment: The United States Steel Embargo and Japan, 1917," *Pacific Historical Review* 39 (Nov. 1970): 439–452.

89. Kawasaki jūkōgyō, *Kawasaki jūkōgyō kabushiki kaisha shi*, 80–82.

90. Spoken before the lower house budget subcommittee. Quoted in Saitō, "Kaigun ni okeru Dai ichiji taisen kenkyū to sono hado," 22.

91. Bōeichō bōei kenshūjō senshishitsu (Self-Defense Agency, Self-Defense Research Institute, War History Office), *Kaigun gunsenbi, ichi; Shōwa jūrokunen jūichigatsu made* (Naval armaments and war preparations number one, up to November 1941) (Tokyo: Asagumo shinbunsha, 1969): 1: 146.

92. Asada Sadao, "Japanese Admirals and the Politics of Naval Limitation: Katō Tomosaburō vs Katō Kanji," in Gerald Jordan, ed., *Naval Warfare in the Twentieth Century: 1900–1945* (London: Croom Helm, 1977): 146. Asada quotes from Kobayashi Tatsuo, ed., *Suiusō nikki: Itō ke monjo* (Green rain diary: Itō family papers) (Tokyo: Hara shobō, 1966): 298–304.

93. Dingman, *Power in the Pacific*, 187–189. This report is contained within papers held at the National Institute of Defense Studies of the Defense Agency in Tokyo. This report is contained within the Enomoto Juji (Professor of the Naval Staff College) papers. I would like to thank Professor Asada Sadao for bringing these archival holdings to my attention.

94. The most comprehensive discussion of the internal debates over the limita-

tions issue is found in Asada, "Japanese Admirals and the Politics of Naval Limitation," 141–166.

95. Asada Sadao, "The Revolt against the Washington Treaty: The Imperial Japanese Navy and Naval Limitation, 1921–1927," 86; Katō Kanji Taisho denki kankōkai (Admiral Katō biographical publication association), *Katō Kanji taisho den* (Biography of Admiral Katō Kanji) (Tokyo: Katō Kanji taishō denki hensankai, 1941): 756–757.

96. Asada, "Japanese Admirals and the Politics of Naval Limitation," 149.

97. Asada, "The Revolt against the Washington Treaty," 87.

Conclusion

1. Yamamoto gave this description to a *Chūō shinbun* reporter in 1893. See *Chūō shinbun*, 3 June 1893. Reprinted in Ko Hakushaku Yamamoto kaigun taishō denki hensankai, *Yamamoto Gonnohyōe den*, 1: 345.

2. Gordon Berger, *Parties Out of Power, 1931–1941* (Princeton: Princeton University Press, 1977): 354.

3. Pelz, *Race to Pearl Harbor*, 15.

4. See Mark R. Peattie, "*Nanshin*: The Southward Advance, 1931–1941, as a Prelude to Japanese Occupation of Southeast Asia," in Peter Duus, Ramon Myers, and Mark Peattie, eds., *The Japanese Wartime Empire* (Princeton: Princeton University Press, 1996): 218–219.

5. Quoted by Michael Barnhart, *Japan Prepares for Total War: The Search for Economic Security, 1919–1941* (Ithaca: Cornell University Press, 1987): 39.

6. See *DNTG*, 1: 1441–1492, 1: 1999–2011, 2: 360–376, 2: 616–622.

7. Berger, *Parties Out of Power*, 36.

8. Joseph H. Longford, "The Growth of the Japanese Navy," *The Nineteenth Century and After*, 54: 319 (Sept. 1903): 474. Also quoted in Cornwall, "The Meiji Navy," 42.

Bibliography

Newspapers

Chūō shinbun	*Jiji shinpō*	*Tokyo Nichi nichi shinbun*
Hōchi shinbun	*Jiyū shinbun*	*Tokyo Puck*
Japan Mail	*Kokumin shinbun*	*Yamato shinbun*
Japan Times	*Niroku shinbun*	*Yomiuri shinbun*
Japan Weekly Mail	*Tokyo Asahi shinbun*	*Yorozu chōhō*

Primary Sources in Japanese

Banno Junji, ed. *Takarabe Takeshi nikki* (Diary of Takarabe Takeshi). 2 vols. Tokyo: Hara shobō, 1983.

Enomoto Takeaki. *Shibberia nikki* (Siberia diary). 3 vols. Tokyo: Kaigun yūshūkai, 1935.

Gaimushō (Japanese Foreign Ministry). *Inin tōchiryō Nan'yō guntō* (The South Seas archipelago mandated territory). 2 vols. Tokyo: Gaimushō, 1962.

———. *Japanese Foreign Ministry Archives.* P.V.M. 19-(1-5). Documents relating to Anglo-Japanese relations.

———. *Japanese Foreign Ministry Archives.* M.T. 5.2.1.25. *Nichi-Doku kaisen ikken* (Documents relating to the outbreak of the Japanese-German War, August–September 1914). Reel 608.

———. *Japanese Foreign Ministry Archives.* M.T. 5.2.6.28. Miscellaneous documents relating to the investigation of matters in occupied areas during the war between Japan and Germany. Reel 515.

———. *Nihon gaikō bunsho* (Japanese diplomatic documents). Vol. *Taishō rokunen* (1917). Tokyo: Gaimushō, 1966

———. *Nihon gaikō bunsho* (Japanese diplomatic documents). Vol. *Taishō sannen* (1914). Tokyo: Gaimushō, 1966.

Hara Kei'ichirō, ed. *Hara Kei nikki* (Diary of Hara Kei). 6 vols. Tokyo: Fukumura shuppan, 1965–1967.

Itō Masanori. *Katō Takaaki den* (Official biography of Katō Takaaki). 2 vols. Tokyo: Katō haku denki hensan iinkai, 1929.

Japanese army, navy, and other agencies. [Navy]. *Nan'yō guntō gyōsei kankei* (Documents related to the administration of the South Seas islands). Archives catalogued by John Young: T282 (R73 F94313). Catalogued in *Checklist of microfilm reproductions of selected archives of the Japanese army, navy, and other government agencies, 1868–1945.* Washington, D.C.: Georgetown University Press, 1959.

———— [Navy]. *Taishō sen'eki senji shorui* (Wartime documents of Taishō campaigns). Vol. 18. *Kaigun daijin* (Navy Minister). National Archives. 1914–1920.

Kaigun Gunreibu (Navy General Staff). *Eiryō Kita Boruneoshi* (A record of British North Borneo). Tokyo: Kaigun Gunreibu, 1916.

————. *Taishō san-yonnen kaigun senshi* (History of naval operations, 1914–1915). Tokyo: Kaigun Gunreibu, 1915.

Kaigunshō. Kaigun daijin kanbō (Navy Ministry. Navy Minister's secretariat). *Kaigun gunbi enkaku* (Development of naval armaments). Tokyo: Gannadō shoten, 1970. [Reprint of 1934 edition compiled by Kaigun daijin kanbō.]

————. *Kaigun seido enkaku* (History of naval organization). 26 vols. Tokyo: Hara shobō, 1971–1972.

————. *Yamamoto Gonnohyōe to kaigun* (Yamamoto Gonnohyōe and the navy) Tokyo: Hara shobō, 1966.

Kaigunshō. Kaigun kyōiku honbu (Navy Ministry. Chief of naval education). *Teikoku kaigun kyōiku shi* (A history of education in the Imperial Japanese Navy). 7 vols., plus supplement. Tokyo: Kaigun Kyōiku honbu, 1911.

Kaneko Kentarō ed. *Itō Hirobumi den* (Biography of Itō Hirobumi). 3 vols. Tokyo: Shunpō Ko Tsuishōkai, 1940–1943.

Katō Gensui denki hensan iinkai (Fleet Admiral Katō biographical compilation committee). *Gensui Katō Tomosaburō den* (Official biography of Katō Tomosaburō). Tokyo: Miyata Mitsuo, 1928.

Katō Kanji taishō denki kankōkai (Admiral Katō Kanji biographical publication association), *Katō Kanji taisho den* (Biography of Admiral Katō Kanji). Tokyo: Katō Kanji taishō denki hensankai, 1941.

Katsu Kaishū. *Katsu Kaishū zenshū* (The collected works of Kastu Kaishū). 24 vols. Tokyo: Hara shobō, 1967.

Ko Hakushaku Yamamoto kaigun taishō denki hensankai (Count Yamamoto biographical compilation association). *Yamamoto Gonnohyōe den* (Official biography of Count Yamamoto Gonnohyōe). 2 vols. Tokyo: Ko Hakushaku Yamamoto kaigun taishō denki hensankai, 1938.

Kobayashi Tatsuo, ed. *Suiusō nikki: Itō ke monjo* (Green rain dairy: Itō family papers). Tokyo: Hara shobō, 1966.

Kunaichō (Imperial household agency). *Meiji Tennō ki* (Chronicle of the Meiji Emperor). 13 vols. Tokyo: Yoshikawa kobunkan, 1968–1975.

Kure shishi hensan iinkai (Kure city history compilation association). *Kure shishi* (History of Kure city). 6 vols. Kure: Kure shiyakushō, 1964–1995.

Miyake Setsurei. *Daigaku konjaku tan* (University reminiscence). Tokyo: Gakansha, 1946.

Mori Zenkichi, ed. *Shiimensu jiken: Kiroku to shiryō* (The Siemens incident: Documents and materials). Tokyo: Tokuma shoten, 1976.

Nihon teikoku gikai (Japan's imperial parliament). *Dai Nihon teikoku gikaishi* (A parliamentary history of imperial Japan). 18 vols. Tokyo: Dai Nihon teikoku gikaishi kankōkai, 1926–1930.

Ōshima Tarō. "Shiimensu-Vikkasu jiken." (The Siemens-Vickers incident). In Wagatsuma Sakae, ed. *Nihon seiji saiban shiroku, Taishō* (Historical records of political trials of Japan, Taishō era), 1: 52–106. 5 vols. Tokyo: Dai ichi hōki shuppan, 1969.

Ritsumeikan daigaku (Ritsumeikan University). *Saionji Kinmochi den* (Biography of Saionji Kinmochi). 6 vols. Tokyo: Iwanami shoten, 1990–1997.

Saitō shishaku kinenkai (Viscount Saitō commemorative society). *Viscount Saitō Makoto den* (Biography of Viscount Saitō Makoto). 4 vols. Tokyo: Saito shishaku kinenkai, 1941.

Satō Tetsutarō. *Kaibō sakugi* (A proposal for national defense). Tokyo: n.p., 1912.

——. *Kokubō mondai no kenkyū* (A study of the national defense problem). Tokyo: n.p., 1913.

——. *Teikoku kokubō ron* (On imperial defense). Tokyo: Suikōsha, 1902.

——. *Teikoku kokubō shiron* (On the history of imperial defense). 2 vols. Tokyo: Suikōsha, 1907.

Shiga Fujio, ed. *Shiga Shigetaka zenshū* (Collected works of Shiga Shigetaka). 8 vols. Tokyo: Shiga Shigetaka kankōkai, 1929.

Shiga Shigetaka. *Nan'yō jiji* (Current conditions in the South Seas). Tokyo: Maruzen shoten, 1887.

Sōrifu tōkeikyoku (Statistical Bureau, Office of the Prime Minister). *Dai nihon teikoku tōkei nenkan* (Statistical yearbook of Japan). 59 vols. Tokyo: Sōrifu teikoku kyoku. Published yearly from 1882 to 1940.

Suzuki Tsunenori. *Nan'tō junkōki* (Record of a cruise in the southern islands). Tokyo: Yamato shōten, 1942. [Reprint of 1893 edition published by Kezzai zasshisha.]

——. *Nan'yō tanken jikki* (A true story of exploration in the South Seas). 2 vols. Tokyo: Hakubunkan, 1892.

Takakura Tetsu'ichi. *Tanaka Gi'ichi den* (Biography of Tanaka Gi'ichi). 2 vols. Tokyo: Tanaka Gi'ichi denki kankōsha, 1958.

Takekoshi Yosaburō. *Nankokuki* (The southern countries). Tokyo: Niyūsha, 1910.

Tokutomi Ichirō. *Kōshaku Katsura Tarō den* (Official biography of Prince Katsura Tarō). 2 vols. Tokyo: Hara shobō, 1967.

——. *Kōshaku Yamagata Aritomo den* (Official biography of Prince Yamagata Aritomo). 3 vols. Tokyo: Yamagata Aritomo-ko kinen jigyokai, 1933.

Tsurumi Yūsuke. *Gotō Shinpei* (Biography of Gotō Shinpei). 4 vols. Tokyo: Gotō Shinpei haku denki hensankai, 1937–1938.

——. *Nan'yō yūki* (Travel sketches of the South Seas). Tokyo: Dai Nippon yūbenkai kōdansha, 1917.

Yamada Ki'ichi. *Nan'yō angyashi* (A walking tour of the South Seas). Tokyo: Kōdōken, 1910.

Primary Sources in English

Akiyama, Saneyuki. *A Japanese View of the War*. London: T. Fisher Unwin, 1917.

Albertini, Luigi. *The Origins of the War of 1914*. Transl. Isabella M. Massey. 3 vols. London: Oxford University Press, 1957.

Corbett, Julian S. *History of the Great War, Based on Official Documents: Naval Operations*. 3 vols. London: Greene and Company, 1920.

Gooch, G. P., and Harold Temperley. *British Documents on the Origins of the War, 1898–1914*. 11 vols. London: His Majesty's Stationery Office, 1926.

Grey, Sir Edward. *Twenty-Five Years, 1892–1916*. New York: Frederick A. Stokes, 1925.

Jose, Arthur W. *Official History of Australia in the War of 1914–1918: The Royal Australian Navy*. 12 vols. Sydney: Angus and Robertson, 1937.

Lansing, Robert. *War Memoirs of Robert Lansing*. New York: Bobbs-Merrill, 1935.

Lensen, George A. *The d'Anethan Dispatches from Japan, 1894–1910*. Tokyo: Sophia University Press, 1967.

Mutsu, Munemitsu. *Kenkenroku: A Diplomatic Record of the Sino-Japanese War, 1894–1895*. Transl. Gordon Berger. Princeton: Princeton University Press, 1971.

Ozaki, Yukio. *The Autobiography of Ozaki Yukio: The Struggle for Constitutional Government in Japan*. Transl. Hara Fujiko. Princeton: Princeton University Press, 2001.

Statistic Bureau. *Historical Statistics of Japan*. 5 vols. Tokyo: Japan Statistical Association, 1989.

Takeoshi, Yosaburō. *Japanese Rule in Formosa*. Transl. George Braithwaite. London: Longmans, Green, and Company, 1907.

United States Navy, Office of Naval Intelligence. Naval Intelligence Archives. National Archives, Record Group 45, Subject file 1911–1927, WA 5, Box 702, Folder #8. Washington, D.C.

———. Records of the Chief of Naval Operations. "Suikōsha or Naval Club, Japan." National Archives, Record Group 38, Subject file E-7-d, 07-180. Washington, D.C.

Secondary Sources in Japanese

Bōeichō Bōei Kenshūjō Senshishitsu (Self-Defense Agency, Self-Defense Research Institute, War History Office). *Dai Hon'ei kaigunbu, rengō kantai* (Imperial Headquarters, Navy Division and Combined Fleet Headquarters). Tokyo: Asagumo shinbunsha, 1975.

———. *Kaigun gunsenbi, ichi; Shōwa jūrokunen jūichigatsu made* (Naval armaments and war preparations number one, up to November 1941). Tokyo: Asagumo shinbunsha, 1969.

Chihaya Masataka. *Nihon kaigun no senryaku hassō* (Strategic concepts of the Japanese navy). Tokyo: Purejidentosha, 1982.

Gabe Masaakira. "Nihon Mikuroneshia senryō to nanshin" (Southern Advance and Japan's occupation of Micronesia). *Keio daigaku hōgaku kenkyū* 55: 7 (July 1982): 81–89.

Gō Takashi. *Nan'yō bōeki go-jūnenshi* (Fifty-year history of commerce in the South Seas). Tokyo: Nan'yō bōeki kabushiki kaisha, 1942.

Hatano Masaru. "Tai-Doku kaisen to Nihon gaikō" (Japanese diplomacy and the outbreak of war with Germany). *Keiō daigaku hōgaku kenkyū* 61: 8 (Aug. 1988): 45-77.

Hatano Sumio. "Nihon kaigun to nanshin: sono seisaku to riron no shiteki tenkai" (The Japanese navy and southward advance: the historical develoment of its policies and theory). In Shimizu Hajime, ed., *Ryōtaisenkanki Nihon-Tonanjia kankei no shosō* (Various aspects of Japanese-Southeast Asian relations between both world wars): 207-236. Tokyo: Ajia keizai kenkyūjo, 1986.

Hayashi Katsunari. *Nihon gunji gijutsu shi* (A history of Japanese military technology). Tokyo: Haruki shobō, 1972.

Hayahsi Shigeru and Tsugi Kiyoaki, eds. *Nihon naikaku shiroku* (A history of Japanese cabinets). 6 vols. Tokyo: Dai'ichi hoki shuppan, 1981.

Hirama Yōichi. "Akiyama Saneyuki: Nan'yō guntō senryō no suishinsha" (Akiyama Saneyuki: Promoter behind the occupation of the South Sea islands). *Taiheihyō shakai zasshi* 50: 14 (Apr. 1991): 190–191.

————. "Kaigunshiteki ni mita nanshin no ichi dammen: Nihon kaigun o Mikuronesia senryō ni fumikiraseta haikei" (One aspect of Japan's southern advance from the viewpoint of naval history: Background of the Japanese navy's occupation of Micronesia). *Seiji keizai shigaku* 250 (Feb. 1987): 85–100.

Ikeda Kiyoshi. *Nihon no kaigun* (The Japanese navy). 2 vols. Tokyo: Isseidō, 1967.

Imai Sei'ichi. "Taishō ki ni okeru gunbu no seijiteki chii" (The political position of the military in the Taishō period). *Shisō* 339 (Sept. 1957): 3–21; ibid. 402 (Dec. 1957): 106–122.

Inoue Kiyoshi. *Nihon seiji fuhai shi* (A history of political corruption in Japan). Tokyo: San'itsu shobō, 1948.

————. "Taishōki no seiji to gumbu" (The military and politics in the Taishō period). In Inoue Kiyoshi, ed., *Taishōki no seiji to shakai* (Society and politics in the Taishō period): 351–406. Tokyo: Iwanami shoten, 1969.

Ishii Takashi. *Katsu Kaishū* (Biography of Katsu Kaishū). Tokyo: Yoshikawa kōbunkan, 1974.

Itō Masajirō. *Gunbatsu kōbōshi* (The rise and fall of military cliques). 3 vols. Tokyo: Bungei shunjū, 1958.

Iwao Sei'ichi. *Nan'yō nihonmachi no kenkyū* (A study of Japanese settlements in the South Seas). Tokyo: Iwanami shoten, 1966.

Kaigun rekishi hozonkai, eds. (Navy historical preservation association). *Nihon kaigun shi* (A history of the Japanese navy). 10 vols. Tokgo: Hatsubai Dai'ichi hōkishuppan kabushiki kaisha, 1996.

Kaigun Yūshūkai, eds. (Navy personnel association). *Kinsei teikoku kaigun shiryō* (An outline history of the modern Imperial Japanese Navy). Tokyo: Maruzen, 1938.

Kajima Morinosuke. *Nichi-Ei gaikōshi* (Anglo-Japanese diplomatic history). Tokyo: Sanshusha, 1957.

Katsu Kaishū. *Kaigun rekishi* (A history of the navy). Tokyo: Hara shobō, 1967. [Reprint of the 1929 edition.]

Kawasaki jūkōgyō (Kawasaki heavy industries). *Kawasaki jūkōgyō kabushiki kaisha shi* (A history of the Kawasaki heavy-industry company). Kobe: Kawasaki jūkōgyō, 1959.

Kitaoka Shin'ichi. *Nihon rikugun to tairiku seisaku* (The Japanese army and continental policy). Tokyo: Tokyo Daigaku shuppansha, 1978.

Kobayashi Yūgo, ed. *Rikken Seiyūkai shi* (History of the Seiyūkai). 8 vols. Tokyo: Rikken Seiyūkai shuppan kyoku, 1924–1926.

Koike Sei'ichi. "Taishō kōki no kaigun ni tsuite no ichi kōsatsu" (An examination of the Japanese navy in the late Taishō era). *Gunji shigaku* 25: 1 (1989): 35–53.

Kurihara Ryū'ichi. *Bakumatsu Nihon no gunsei* (The military system in Bakumatsu Japan). Tokyo: Jinbutsu ōraisha, 1972.

Kusō Masahikō. "Nanshin oyobi hokushin to gunbi kankei" (The relation between armaments and southern and northern expansion). *Taiyō* (The Sun) 19: 15 (Nov. 1913): 43–51.

Matsushita Yoshio. *Chōhei seiteishi* (A history of the establishment of the conscription system). Tokyo: Gogatsu shobō, 1981. [Reprint of 1943 edition.]

———. *Meiji gunsei shiron* (A historical discussion of the Meiji military establishment). Tokyo: Yūhikaku, 1959.

———. *Nihon gunbatsu no kōbō* (The rise and fall of Japan's military cliques). 3 vols. Tokyo: Jinbutsu ōraisha, 1967.

———. *Nihon gunsei to seiji* (Politics and the Japanese military system). Tokyo: Kuroshio shuppan, 1960.

Mitani Taichirō. *Nihon seitō seiji no keisei* (Formation of Japanese party politics). Tokyo: Tokyo daigaku shuppankai, 1967.

Mitsubishi jūkōgyō (Mitsubishi heavy industries). *Shin Mitsubishi Kobe zōsenjo gojunen shi* (A fifty-year history of the new Mitsubishi Kobe shipyard). Kobe: Mitsubishi jūkōgyō, 1957.

Miyake Setsurei. *Daigaku konjaku tan* (University reminiscence). Tokyo: Gakansha, 1946.

Morita Akatsuki. *Kokubō to kaigun jujitsu* (Naval preparedness and national defense). Tokyo: Teikoku kaigun no kikki hakkōjo, 1914.

———. *Teikoku kaigun no kiki* (Crisis of the Imperial Navy). Tokyo: Teikoku kaigun no kiki hakkōjo, 1912.

Nan'yō kyōkai (South Seas Association). *Nan'yō kyōkai ni-jūnenshi* (Twenty-year history of the South Seas Association). Tokyo: Nan'yō kyōkai, 1935.

Nihon kindai shiryō kenkyūkai (Historical records study association of modern Japan). *Nihon rikukaigun seido, soshiki, jinji* (The personnel, organization, and institutions of the Japanese army and navy). Tokyo: Daigaku shuppankai, 1971.

Nomura Minoru. *Rekishi no naka no Nihon kaigun* (The Japanese navy in history). Tokyo: Hara shobō, 1980.

Ōtsu Jun'ichirō. *Dai Nihon kenseishi* (A constitutional history of Japan). 12 vols. Tokyo: Hobunkan, 1927–1928.

Ōyama Azusa. *Yamagata Aritomo ikensho* (Opinion of Yamagata Aritomo). Tokyo: Hara shobō, 1966.

Saito Seiji. "Amoy jiken saikō" (A reconsideration of the Amoy incident). *Nihonshi kenkyū* 305: 1 (Jan. 1988): 31–46.

———. "Kaigun ni okeru Dai ichiji taisen kenkyū to sono hado" (The navy's research on World War I and its influence). *Rekishigaku kenkyū* 530 (July 1984): 16–32.

———. "Kokubō hoshin Dai ichiji kaitei no haikei: Dainiji Ōkuma naikaku ni okeru rikukai ryōgun kankei" (The background of the first revision of the national defense plan: The relationship between the Japanese army and navy during the second Ōkuma cabinet). *Shigaku zasshi.* 95: 6 (1986): 1–32.

Satō Saburō. "Meiji 33-nen no Amoi jiken ni kansuru kōsatsu" (Observations on the Amoy incident of 1900). *Yamagata daigaku kiyō: Jinbun kagaku* 5: 2 (Mar. 1963): 1–49.

Shinba Eiji. *Itagaki Taisuke: Jiyū minken no yume to haiboku* (The aspirations and setbacks of the democratic-rights movement). Tokyo: Shinchōsha, 1988.

Shinohara Hiroshi. *Kaigun sōsetsu shi* (History of the naval establishment). Tokyo: Riburopōto, 1986.

Taguchi Ukichi. "Nan'yō keiryaku ron" (Discourse on how to expand into the South Seas). *Tokyo kezzai zasshi* (Tokyo economic journal) 515 (22 March 1890). In Taguchi Ukichi, *Teiken Taguchi Ukichi zenshū* (Collected works of Teiken Taguchi Ukichi). 8 vols. Tokyo: Teiken Taguchi Ukichi hakkōkai, 1927–1929.

Takahashi Shigeo. "Meiji 33-nen Amoi jiken no ichi kōsatsu: Yamamoto kaigun daijin no taido o chūshin to shite" (A study of the Amoy incident of 1900, with special reference to Navy Minister Yamamoto Gonnohyōe's position). *Gunji shigaku* 8: 4 (Mar. 1973): 33–44.

Taniguchi Naomi. "Kaigunkyō Hakushaku Kawamura Sumiyoshi no kōgyō" (The achievements of Navy Minister Count Kawamura Sumiyoshi). In Hirose Hikota, ed., *Dai kaigun hatten hishi* (The secret history of the great navy's development): 23–123. Tokyo: Kōdōkan tosho, 1944.

Toyama Saburō. *Nihon kaigun shi* (History of the Japanese navy). Tokyo: Kyōikusha, 1980.

———. *Ni-Shin, Nichi-Ro, Daitōa kaisen shi* (A naval history of the Sino-Japanese, Russo-Japanese, and Greater East Asian wars). Tokyo: Hara shobō, 1980.

Tsunoda Jun. *Manshū mondai to kokubō hoshin* (National defense policy and the Manchurian problem). Tokyo: Hara shobō, 1967.

———. "Nihon kaigun sandai no rekishi" (Three periods of history in the Japanese navy). *Jiyū* 1: 1 (Jan. 1969): 90–125.

Uchida Kenzō, Kanahara Samon, and Furuya Testuo, eds., *Nihon gikai shiroku* (The history of parliamentary government in Japan). 6 vols. Tokyo: Dai'ichi hoki shuppan, 1990.

Uzaki Rojō. *Satsu no kaigun, Chō no rikugun* (The Satsuma navy and the Chōshū army). Tokyo: Seikyōsha, 1911.

Yamamoto Miono. "Nan'yō shinsenryōchi jijō" (Conditions in the newly acquired territories of the South Seas). *Taiyō* 19: 13 (Sept. 1915): 111–117.

Yamamoto Shirō. "Dai ichiji sekai taisen ni okeru Amerika no sansen to Nihon: Terauchi naikaku no keizai to seiji" (America's entry into World War I and Japan: Politics and economics of the Terauchi cabinet). *Hisutoria* 43 (Mar. 1966): 24–41.

———. *Shoki Seiyūkai no kenkyū* (A study of the early history of the Seiyūkai). Osaka: Seibundo, 1975.

———. *Yamamoto naikaku no kisōteki kenkyū* (Research into the formation of the Yamamoto cabinet). Kyoto: Kyoto Joshi Daigaku, 1982.

Yano Tōru. *Nanshin no keifu* (Genealogy of the southward advance). Tokyo: Chūō shinsho, 1975.

———. *Nihon no Nan'yō shikan* (Japan's historical view of the South Seas). Tokyo: Chūō shinsho, 1979.

Yasui Shōtarō. "Nanshin sakutei no ki" (Opportunity for deciding on a plan for southern advance). *Taiyō* 19: 15 (Nov. 1913): 69–75.

Zōsen kyōkai (Shipbuilders association). *Nihon kindai zōsenshi: Taishō jidai* (A history of modern shipbuilding in Japan: The Taishō period). Tokyo: Hara shobō, 1973.

Secondary Sources in English

Akita, George. *Foundations of Constitutional Government in Modern Japan, 1869–1900.* Cambridge, Mass.: Harvard University Press, 1967.

Akiyama, Saneyuki. *A Japanese View of the War.* London: T. Fisher Unwin, 1917.

Allison, Graham T. *Essence of Decision: Explaining the Cuban Missile Crisis.* Boston: Little, Brown, 1971.

Allison, Graham T., and Morton Halperin. "Bureaucratic Politics: A Paradigm and Some Policy Implications." *World Politics* 24, supplement (Spring 1971): 40–80.

Art, Robert J. "Bureaucratic Politics and American Foreign Policy: A Critique." *Policy Sciences* 4: 4 (Dec. 1973): 467–490.

Asada, Kei'ichi. *Expenditures of the Sino-Japanese War.* London: Oxford University Press, 1922.

Asada, Sadao. "Japanese Admirals and the Politics of Limitation: Katō Tomosaburō vs. Katō Kanji." In Gerald Jordan, ed., *Naval Warfare in the Twentieth Century, 1900–1945,* 141–166. London: Croom Helm, 1977.

———. "The Japanese Navy and the United States." In Dorothy Borg, ed., *Pearl Harbor as History,* 225–259. New York: Columbia University Press, 1973.

———. "The Revolt against the Washington Treaty: The Imperial Japanese Navy and Naval Limitation, 1921–1927." *Naval War College Review* 46: 3 (Summer 1993): 82–97.

Bailey, Jackson. "Prince Saionji and the Taishō Political Crisis." In Sidney Brown, ed., *Studies on Asia,* 39–57. Lincoln: University of Nebraska Press, 1962.

Bailey, Thomas A. "Japan's Protest against the Annexation of Hawaii." *Journal of Modern History* 3 (Mar. 1931): 37–49.

———. "The World Cruise of the American Battle Fleet, 1907–1909." *Pacific Historical Review* 1: 3 (Dec. 1932): 389–423.

Banno, Junji. *The Establishment of the Japanese Constitutional System.* Transl. J. A. A. Stockwin. London: Routledge, 1992.

Barnhart, Michael A. *Japan Prepares for Total War: The Search for Economic Security, 1919–1941.* Ithaca: Cornell University Press, 1987.

Beehler, Commodore W. H. "A Review of Japanese Naval Financial Policy." *Proceedings of the United States Naval Institute* 37: 3 (Sept. 1911): 801–822.

Beeler, John F. *British Naval Policy in the Gladstone-Disraeli Era, 1866–1880.* Stanford: Stanford University Press, 1997.

Berger, Gordon. *Parties Out of Power in Japan, 1931–1941.* Princeton: Princeton University Press, 1977.

Brown, Richard G. "The German Acquisition of the Caroline Islands, 1898–99." In John A. Moses and Paul M. Kennedy, eds., *Germany in the Pacific and Far East, 1870–1914,* 137–155. St. Lucia: Queensland University Press, 1977.

Chen, Edward I-Te. "Japan's Decision to Annex Taiwan: A Study of Itō-Mutsu Diplomacy, 1894–95." *Journal of Asian Studies* 35: 1 (Nov. 1977): 61–72.

Clarke, Ignatius Frederick. *Voices Prophesying War, 1763–1984.* London Oxford University Press, 1966.

Clowes, William Laird. *The Royal Navy: A History from the Earliest Times to the Present.* 7 vols. London: Sampson Low, Marston, 1897–1903.

Connors, Lesley. *The Emperor's Adviser: Saionji Kinmochi and Pre-War Japanese Politics.* London: Croom Helm, 1987.

Cornwall, Peter. "Manning and Training the Japanese Navy in the Nineteenth Century." In Robert W. Love, Jr., ed., *Changing Interpretations and New Sources in Naval History*, 216–228. New York: Garland, 1980.

———."The Meiji Navy: Training in an Age of Change." Ph.D. dissertation, University of Michigan, 1970.

Dickinson, Frederick R. *War and National Reinvention: Japan and the Great War, 1914–1919.* Cambridge, Mass.: Harvard University Press, 1999.

Dillon, Emile J. *The Inside Story of the Washington Conference.* New York: Harper and Brothers, 1920.

Dingman, Roger. *Power in the Pacific.* Chicago: University of Chicago Press, 1976.

Dull, Paul S. *A Battle History of the Imperial Japanese Navy.* Annapolis: Naval Institute Press, 1979.

———. "Count Katō Kōmei and the Twenty-One Demands." *Pacific Historical Review* 19: 2 (May 1950): 28–48.

Duus, Peter. *The Abacus and the Sword: The Japanese Penetration of Korea, 1895–1910.* Berkeley and Los Angeles: University of California Press, 1995.

———. *Party Rivalry and Political Change in Taishō Japan.* Cambridge, Mass.: Harvard University Press, 1968.

Evans, David C. "The Recruitment of Japanese Navy Officers in the Meiji Period." In Robert W. Love, Jr., ed., *Changing Interpretations and New Sources in Naval History*, 229–245. New York: Garland, 1980.

———. "The Satsuma Faction and Professionalism in the Japanese Naval Officer Corps of the Meiji Period, 1868–1912." Ph.D. dissertation. Stanford University, 1978.

Evans, David C., and Mark R. Peattie. *Kaigun: Strategy, Tactics, and Technology in the Imperial Japanese Navy.* Annapolis: Naval Institute Press, 1997.

Fraiser, Andrew. "The House of Peers." In Andrew Fraiser, R. H. P. Mason, and Philip Mitchell, eds., *Japan's Early Parliaments*, 8–36. London: Routledge, 1994.

Frei, Henry. "Japan in World Politics and Pacific Expansion." In John A. Moses and Christopher Pugsley, eds., *The German Empire and Britain's Pacific Dominions, 1871–1919*, 173–196. Claremont, Calif.: Regina Books, 2000.

———. *Japan's Southern Advance and Australia.* Honolulu: University of Hawaii Press, 1991.

Fujitani, Takashi. *Splendid Monarchy: Power and Pageantry in Modern Japan.* Berkeley and Los Angeles: University of California Press, 1996.

Fukasaku, Yukio. *Technology and Industrial Development in Pre-war Japan.* London: Routledge, 1992.

Ganz, A. Harding. "The German Navy in the Far East and Pacific: The Seizure of Kautschou and After." In John A. Moses and Paul M. Kennedy, eds., *Germany in the Pacific and Far East, 1870–1914*, 115–136. St. Lucia: Queensland University Press, 1977.

Gavan, Masako. *Shiga Shigetaka, 1863–1927: The Forgotten Enlightener.* Richmond: Curzon Press, 2001.

Goldrick, James. "The Problems of Modern Naval History." In John Hattendorf, ed.,

Doing Naval History: Essays Toward Improvement, 11–24. U.S. Naval War College Historical Monograph Series, 13. Newport, R.I.: Naval War Press, 1995.

Gow, Ian. "The Evolution of a General Staff System in the Imperial Japanese Navy." *Proceedings of the British Association for Japanese Studies* 4: 1 (Dec. 1979): 73–86.

Hackett, Roger F. "The Meiji Leaders and Modernization: The Case of Yamagata Aritomo." In Marius B. Jansen, ed., *Changing Japanese Attitudes toward Modernization*, 328–351. Princeton: Princeton University Press, 1965.

———. "The Military." In Robert E. Ward and Dankwart A. Rustow, eds., *Political Modernization in Japan and Turkey*, 328–351. Princeton: Princeton University Press, 1964.

———. "Yamagata and the Taishō Crisis." In Sidney D. Brown, ed., *Studies on Asia*, 21–37. Lincoln: University of Nebraska Press, 1962.

———. *Yamagata Aritomo in the Rise of Modern Japan*. Cambridge, Mass.: Harvard University Press, 1971.

Hall, Ivan. *Mori Arinori*. Cambridge, Mass.: Harvard University Press, 1973.

Halperin, Morton H. "Why Bureaucrats Play Games." *Foreign Policy* 26: 2 (Spring 1971): 70–90.

Hamilton, W. Mark. *The Nation and the Navy: Methods and Organization of British Navalist Propaganda, 1889–1914*. New York: Garland, 1986.

Hatano, Sumio, and Asada, Sadao. "The Japanese Decision to Move South (1939–1941)." In Robert Boyce and Edmond Robertson, eds., *Paths to War: New Essays on the Origins of the Second World War*, 383–407. New York: St. Martin's Press, 1989.

Herwig, Holger H. *The German Naval Officer Corps: A Social and Political History, 1890–1918*. Oxford: Clarendon Press, 1973.

Hiery, Herman J. *The Neglected War: The German South Pacific and the Influence of World War I*. Honolulu: University of Hawaii Press, 1995.

Hirama, Yōichi. "Japanese Naval Preparations for W.W. II." *Naval War College Review* 94: 2 (Spring 1991): 1–23.

House, E. H. *The Japanese Expedition to Formosa in 1874*. Taipei, Taiwan: SMC Publishing, 1984. [Reprint of 1875 edition.]

Innes, Robert L. "The Door Ajar: Japan's Foreign Trade in the Seventeenth Century." Ph.D. dissertation, University of Michigan, 1980.

Iriye, Akira. *Pacific Estrangement: Japanese and American Expansion, 1897–1911*. Cambridge, Mass.: Harvard University Press, 1972.

Itō, Masanori. *The End of the Imperial Japanese Navy*. Transl. Roger Pineau. London: Weidenfeld and Nicholson, 1962.

Jansen, Marius. "Opportunists in South China during the Boxer Rebellion." *Pacific Historical Review* 20: 3 (Aug. 1951): 241–250.

Katayama, Kunio. "The Expansion of Japanese Shipping into Southeast Asia before World War I: The Case of the O.S.K." *The Great Circle: Journal of the Australian Association for Maritime History* 8: 1 (Apr. 1986): 1–16.

Kawakami, Kiyoshi K. *Japan and World Peace*. New York: Macmillan, 1919.

Keene, Donald. "The Sino-Japanese War of 1894–95 and Its Cultural Effects in Japan." In Donald H. Shively, ed., *Tradition and Modernization in Japanese Culture*, 121–175. Princeton: Princeton University Press, 1971.

Kehr, Eckart. *Battleship Building and Party Politics in Germany*. Transl. Eugene Johnson and Pauline Johnson. Chicago: University of Chicago Press, 1973.

———. "The German Fleet in the Eighteen-Nineties and the Politico-Military Dualism in the Empire." In Gordon A. Craig, ed., *Economic Interest, Militarism, and Foreign Policy: Essays on German History*, 1–21. Berkeley and Los Angeles: University of California Press, 1977.

Kertzer, David. *Ritual, Politics, and Power*. New Haven: Yale University Press, 1988.

Kim, Key-hiuk. *The Last Phase of the East Asian World Order: Korea, Japan, and the Chinese Empire*. Berkeley and Los Angeles: University of California Press, 1980.

Kobayashi, Tatsuo. "The London Naval Treaty, 1930." In James W. Morley, ed., *Japan Erupts: The London Naval Conference and the Manchurian Incident, 1928–1932*, 11–117. New York: Columbia University Press, 1984.

Kobayashi, Ushisaburō. *War and Armaments Loans of Japan*. New York: Oxford University Press, 1922.

Kornicki, Peter F. "Japan at the Australian Exhibitions." *Australian Studies* 8 (July 1994): 15–59.

Kozak, David C. "The Bureaucratic Politics Approach: The Evolution of the Paradigm." In David C. Kozak and James M. Keagle, eds., *Bureaucratic Politics and National Security*, 1–15. Boulder: Lynne Rienner, 1988.

Lambi, Ivo Nikolai. *The Navy and German Power Politics, 1862–1914*. Boston: Allen and Unwin, 1984.

LaFargue, Thomas E. *China and the World War*. Stanford: Stanford University Press, 1937.

Large, Stephen S. *Emperors of the Rising Sun*. London: Kodansha International, 1997.

Lone, Stuart. *Army, Empire, and Politics in Meiji Japan: The Three Careers of General Katsura Tarō*. London: Macmillan, 2000.

———. "General Katsura Tarō and the Japanese Empire in East Asia." Ph.D. dissertation, Australian National University, 1993.

———. *Japan's First Modern War: Army and Society in the Conflict with China, 1894–1895*. London: St. Martin's, 1994.

Longford, Joseph H. "The Growth of the Japanese Navy." *The Nineteenth Century and After* 54: 319 (Sept. 1903): 472–485.

Lowe, Peter C. *Great Britain and Japan, 1911–1915*. London: Macmillan, 1969.

Marder, Arthur. "The Origin of Popular Interest in the Royal Navy." *Royal United Service Institution Journal* 82 (1937): 763–771.

Masuda, Norimoto. *Military Industries of Japan*. New York: Oxford University Press, 1922.

May, Ernest R. "American Policy and Japan's Entrance into World War I." *Mississippi Valley Historical Review* 40: 2 (Sept. 1953): 253–269.

Millard, Thomas F. *Democracy and the Eastern Question*. New York: Century, 1919.

Mitchell, Richard. *Political Bribery in Japan*. Honolulu: University of Hawaii Press, 1996.

Mizuno, Hironori. *The Japanese Navy*. Western influences in modern Japan publication series, 18. Honolulu: Institute of Pacific Relations, 1929.

Morison, Samuel E. *The Rising Sun in the Pacific, 1933–1941*. Boston: Little, Brown, 1950.

Mutsu, Munemitsu. *Kenkenroku: A Diplomatic Record of the Sino-Japanese War, 1894–1895*. Ed. and transl. Gordon M. Berger. Princeton: Princeton University Press, 1982.

Najita, Tetsuo. *Hara Kei in the Politics of Compromise*. Cambridge, Mass.: Harvard University Press, 1967.

Nish, Ian H. "Admiral Jerram and the German Pacific Fleet, 1913–1915." *Mariner's Mirror* 56: 4 (May 1970): 411–421.

———. *Alliance in Decline: A Study in Anglo-Japanese Relations, 1908–1923.* London: Athlone, 1972.

———. "Japan and the Naval Aspects of the Washington Conference." In William G. Beasley, ed., *Modern Japan: Aspects of History, Literature, and Society,* 67–80. London: George Allen and Unwin, 1975.

Ogasawara Nagayo. *The Life of Admiral Tōgō.* Tokyo: Seito shorin, 1934.

Ōgawa, Gotarō. *Conscription System in Japan.* London: Oxford University Press, 1921.

———. *Expenditures of the Russo-Japanese War.* London: Oxford University Press, 1923.

Ōhkawa, Masazō. "The Armaments Expansion Budgets and the Japanese Economy after the Russo-Japanese War." *Hitotsubashi Journal of Economics* 5 (Jan. 1965): 68–83.

Okamoto, Shumpei. *The Japanese Oligarchy and the Russo-Japanese War.* New York: Columbia University Press, 1970.

Ono, Giʾichi. *War and Armaments Expenditures of Japan.* London: Oxford University Press, 1922.

Ozaki, Yukio. *The Autobiography of Ozaki Yukio: The Struggle for Constitutional Government in Japan.* Transl. Hara Fujiko. Princeton: Princeton University Press, 2001.

———. "Japan's Defective Constitutional Government." In Kawakami Kiyoshi, ed., *What Japan Thinks,* 63–78. New York: Macmillan, 1921.

Parillo, Mark. *The Japanese Merchant Marine in World War II.* Annapolis: Naval Institute Press, 1993.

Peattie, Mark R. "Forecasting a Pacific War, 1912–1933: The Idea of a Conditional Japanese Victory." In James White, ed., *The Ambivalence of Nationalism: Modern Japan between East and West,* 115–129. New York: University Press of America, 1983.

———. *"Nanshin*: The Southward Advance, 1931–1941, as a Prelude to the Japanese Occupation of Southeast Asia." In Peter Duus, Ramon H. Myers, and Mark R. Peattie, eds., *The Japanese Wartime Empire, 1931–1945,* 189–242. Princeton: Princeton University Press, 1996.

———. *Nanʾyō: The Rise and Fall of the Japanese in Micronesia, 1885 to 1945.* Honolulu: University of Hawaii Press, 1987.

Pedisich, Paul E. "Congress Provides a Navy: The Emergence of a Modern Navy as a Force in Congressional Politics, 1882–1916." Ph.D. dissertation, State University of New York, Stony Brook, 1998.

Pelz, Stephen. *Race to Pearl Harbor.* Cambridge, Mass.: Harvard University Press, 1974.

Perry, John C. "Great Britain and the Emergence of Japan as a Naval Power." *Monumenta Nipponica,* 21: 3–4 (1966): 305–321.

———. "Great Britain and the Imperial Japanese Navy." Ph.D. dissertation. Harvard University, 1961.

Pierrad, Richard V. "The German Colonial Society, 1882–1914." Ph.D. dissertation, University of Iowa, 1964.

Pomeroy, Earl S. *Pacific Outpost: American Strategy in Guam and Micronesia.* Stanford: Stanford University Press, 1951.

Purcell, David C. "The Economics of Exploitation." *Journal of Pacific History* 11: 4 (1976): 189–211.

———. "Japanese Expansion in the South Pacific, 1890–1935." Ph.D. dissertation. University of Pennsylvania, 1967.

Pyle, Kenneth. *The New Generation in Meiji Japan*. Stanford: Stanford University Press, 1969.

Rappaport, Armin. *The Navy League of the United States*. Detroit: Wayne State University Press, 1962.

Rattan, Sumitra. "The Yap Controversy and Its Significance." *Journal of Pacific History* 7 (1972): 124–136.

Rawlinson, John L. *China's Struggle for Naval Development*. Cambridge, Mass.: Harvard University Press, 1967.

Reinsch, Paul S. *An American Diplomat in China, 1913–1919*. Garden City: Doubleday, 1922.

Rosenburg, David A., and John T. Sumida. "Machines, Men, Manufacturing, Management and Money: The Study of Navies as Complex Organizations and the Transformation of Twentieth-Century Naval History." In John Hattendorf, ed., *Doing Naval History: Essays Toward Improvement*, 25–40. U.S. Naval War College Historical Monograph Series, 13. Newport, R.I.: Naval War College Press, 1995.

Safford, Jeffrey. "Experiment in Containment: The United States Steel Embargo and Japan, 1917." *Pacific Historical Review* 39 (Nov. 1970): 439–452.

Saitō, Makoto. "The Navy." In Alfred Stead, ed., *Japan and the Japanese*, 1: 121–141. 2 vols. Washington, D.C.: University Publications of America, 1979. [Reprint of 1904 edition published by William Heinemann.]

Scalapino, Robert. *Democracy and the Party Movement in Prewar Japan*. Berkeley and Los Angeles: University of California Press, 1962.

Schencking, J. Charles. "Bureaucratic Politics, Military Budgets and Japan's Southern Advance: The Imperial Navy's Seizure of German Micronesia in the First World War." *War in History* 5: 3 (1988): 308–326.

———. "The Imperial Japanese Navy and the Constructed Consciousness of a South Seas Destiny, 1872–1921." *Modern Asian Studies* 33: 4 (1999): 769–796.

———. "Navalism, Naval Expansion, and War: The Anglo-Japanese Alliance and the Japanese Navy." In Phillips O'Brien, ed., *The Anglo-Japanese Alliance*, 122–139. London: RoutledgeCurzon, 2004.

———. "The Politics of Pragmatism and Pageantry: Selling a National Navy at the Elite and Local Level in Japan, 1890–1913." In Sandra Wilson, ed., *Nation and Nationalism in Japan*, 21–37. London: RoutledgeCurzon, 2002.

Schulman, Mark. "Institutionalizing a Political Idea: Navalism and the Emergence of American Seapower." In Peter Trubowitz, Emily Goldman, and Edward Rhodes, eds., *The Politics of Strategic Adjustment: Ideas, Institutions, and Interests*, 79–101. New York: Columbia University Press, 1999.

Seno, Sadao. "A Chess Game with No Checkmate." *Naval War College Review* 26: 4 (Jan.–Feb. 1974): 26–39.

Shimizu, Hajime. "*Nanshinron*: Its Turning Point in World War I." *Developing Economies* 25: 4 (Dec. 1987): 386–402.

Shōichi, Saeki. "Images of the United States as a Hypothetical Enemy." In Akira Iriye, ed., *Mutual Images: Essays in American-Japanese Relations*, 100–114. Cambridge, Mass.: Harvard University Press, 1975.

Silberman, Bernard S. "Bureaucratic Development and Bureaucratization: The Case of Japan." *Social Science History* 1: 2 (Summer 1978): 385–398.

———. "Bureaucratic Development and the Structure of Decision-making in Japan, 1868–1925." *Journal of Asian Studies* 29: 4 (Winter 1970): 347–362.

———. "Bureaucratic Development and the Structure of Decision-making in the Meiji Period: The Case of the *Genrō*." *Journal of Asian Studies* 27: 2 (Spring 1967): 81–94.

———. *Cages of Reason: The Rise of the Rational State in France, Japan, the United States, and Great Britain.* Chicago: University of Chicago Press, 1993.

Smethurst, Richard J. *A Social Basis for Prewar Japanese Militarism: The Army and the Rural Community.* Berkeley and Los Angeles: University of California Press, 1974.

Smith, Steven R. B. "Public Opinion, the Navy and the City of London: The Drive for British Naval Expansion in the Late Nineteenth Century." *War and Society* 9: 1 (May 1991): 29–50.

Smith, Woodruff D. *The German Colonial Empire.* Chapel Hill: University of North Carolina Press, 1977.

Sondhaus, Lawrence. *Preparing for* Weltpolitik: *German Sea Power before the Tirpitz Era.* Annapolis: Naval Institute Press, 1997.

Stephan, John J. *Hawaii under the Rising Sun.* Honolulu: University of Hawaii Press, 1984.

———. "Hijacked by Utopia: American Nikkei in Manchuria." *Amerasia Journal* 23: 3 (1997): 1–42.

Takekoshi, Yosaburō. *Japanese Rule in Formosa.* Transl. George Braithwaite. London: Longmans, Green and Company, 1907.

Tatsuji, Takeuchi. *War and Diplomacy in the Japanese Empire.* Garden City: Doubleday, Doran, 1935.

Totman, Conrad. *The Collapse of the Tokugawa Bakufu, 1862–1868.* Honolulu: University of Hawaii Press, 1980.

Treat, Payson J. *The Far East: A Diplomatic and Political History.* New York: Harper and Brothers, 1935.

———. "Japan, America, and the Great War." *A League of Nations* 1: 8 (Dec. 1918): 417–432.

Trubowitz, Peter. "Geography and Strategy: The Politics of American Naval Expansion." In Peter Trubowitz, Emily Goldman, and Edward Rhodes, eds., *The Politics of Strategic Adjustment: Ideas, Institutions, and Interests*, 105–138. New York: Columbia University Press, 1999.

Tsunoda, Jun. "The Navy's Role in the Southern Strategy." In James W. Morely, ed., *The Fateful Choice*, 241–296. New York: Columbia University Press, 1980.

Wang, Chia-Chien. "Li Hung-chang and the Peiyang Navy." *Chinese Studies in History* 25: 1 (1991): 52–66.

White, John A. *The Diplomacy of the Russo-Japanese War.* Princeton: Princeton University Press, 1964.

Woodward, E. L. *Great Britain and the German Navy.* Oxford: Clarendon Press, 1935.

Yanaga, Chitose. *Japan since Perry.* New York: McGraw-Hill, 1949.

Young, Louise. *Japan's Total Empire: Manchuria and the Culture of Wartime Imperialism.* Berkeley and Los Angeles: University of California Press, 1998.

Index